Minnesota
Land of
10,000 Lakes

Minnesota
Land of
10,000 Lakes

Amy C. Rea

with photographs by the author

The Countryman Press ✳ Woodstock, Vermont

Explorer's Guide Minnesota, Land of 10,000 Lakes
ISBN: 978-0-88150-954-0

Interior photographs by the author unless otherwise specified
Maps by Erin Greb Cartography, © The Countryman Press
Book design by Bodenweber Design
Composition by PerfecType, Nashville, TN

Published by The Countryman Press, P.O. Box 748, Woodstock, VT 05091

Distributed by W. W. Norton & Company, Inc., 500 Fifth Avenue, New York, NY 10110

Printed in the United States of America

10 9 8 7 6 5 4 3 2 1

DEDICATION

To my brother and sister-in-law, Mike and Diane Frickstad, in hopes they'll spend many happy hours exploring our wonderful state.

And my sincere thanks and appreciation to Lisa Sacks and Justine Rathbun of Countryman Press, for their thoughtful and detailed editing and copyediting, and boundless patience.

EXPLORE WITH US!

WHAT'S WHERE

In the beginning of the book, you'll find an alphabetical listing of special highlights, with important information and advice on everything from antiques to weather reports.

LODGING

The prices range from low off-season rates to higher summer and holiday/event weekend rates, double occupancy.

Very Inexpensive	Less than $40 per night
Inexpensive	$40–70
Moderate	$70–100
Expensive	$100–200
Very Expensive	More than $200

DINING

The dining listings are broken into two categories: *Dining Out,* which is more formal (and pricier), and *Eating Out,* which is more casual (and less expensive).

Average prices refer to a dinner consisting of an entrée, appetizer or dessert, and glass of wine or beer (tax and gratuities not included).

Inexpensive	Up to $15
Moderate	$15–30
Expensive	$30–50
Very Expensive	$50 or more

A NOTE ON PRICES

Please don't hold us or the respective innkeepers/restaurant owners responsible for the rates listed as of press time in 2012. Some changes are inevitable.

Minnesota has a general sales tax of 6.875 percent, although local government units are able (with state approval) to levy additional sales taxes for various reasons; in Hennepin County (home to Minneapolis), for example, the sales tax is 7.275 percent, part of which funds the new Minnesota Twins Target Field stadium, and in Minneapolis itself, the sales tax is 7.775 percent.

KEY TO SYMBOLS

✐ The kids-alert symbol appears next to lodgings, restaurants, activities, and shops of special appeal to youngsters.

🎗 The special-value symbol appears next to lodgings and restaurants that combine high quality and moderate prices.

⚭ The wedding rings symbol appears beside facilities that frequently serve as venues for weddings and civil unions.

🐾 The dog paw symbol appears next to lodgings that accept pets (usually with a reservation and deposit) as of press time.

♿ The wheelchair symbol appears next to lodging, restaurants, and attractions that are partially or fully handicapped accessible.

🍸 The martini glass symbol appears next to establishments that have bars and/or nightclubs on the premises.

❄ The snowflake symbol appears next to establishments that are open during the off-season, which in Minnesota is generally October through April.

((ᵠ)) The tower symbol appears next to businesses that have Internet/Wi-Fi access.

🍃 The leaf symbol appears next to businesses that strive to be ecofriendly.

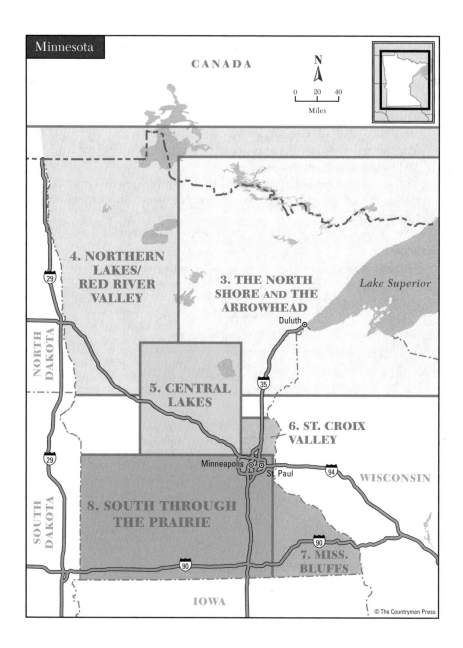

Minnesota

CANADA

N

0   20   40
Miles

4. NORTHERN LAKES/ RED RIVER VALLEY

3. THE NORTH SHORE AND THE ARROWHEAD

Lake Superior

Duluth

NORTH DAKOTA

5. CENTRAL LAKES

6. ST. CROIX VALLEY

Minneapolis

St. Paul

WISCONSIN

SOUTH DAKOTA

8. SOUTH THROUGH THE PRAIRIE

7. MISS. BLUFFS

IOWA

© The Countryman Press

CONTENTS

Maps

INTRODUCTION

Minnesota is a land frequently misunderstood. For those who get their knowledge from popular media, Minnesota appears to be a land inhabited by those wacky gals from the *Mary Tyler Moore Show*, except for the one corner of Minnesota populated by rock stars as glamorized by Prince in *Purple Rain*. The rest of the state? Garrison Keillor's *Prairie Home Companion* and the Coen brothers' classic *Fargo* tell the rest of the story: funny accents, hats with ear flaps, church suppers, fish soaked in lye and served at Christmas dinner, a whole lot of snow, and backyard wood chippers.

As usual, the truth is that the stereotyped images are somewhat true, but not the whole picture. Are there still people in small towns in Minnesota who talk like those people in *Fargo*? Sure. And while Mary Tyler Moore no longer throws her hat on Nicollet Mall, there is a sculpture immortalizing that very action. Prince? Still a Minnesota music icon, but far from the only one.

Personally, I love these images. They do represent certain facets of Minnesota. Perhaps what they best represent is the diversity inherent in the state, where a lively metro area provides excellent access to the arts, pop culture, major league sports, dining, and shopping. For those who want more of an outdoor experience, the state has not 10,000 lakes, but more than 15,000, all with opportunities for swimming, fishing (year-round; ice fishing is nearly as popular as open-water fishing in summer), boating, and water sports. Campgrounds abound throughout the state, as do resorts of all types and prices, from small, rustic mom-and-pops to historic bed & breakfasts to hotels and resorts that represent the height of luxury.

In a region where the seasons are clearly different, Minnesotans have turned each season into a reason for celebration, with each offering its own activities and festivals. If ice fishing isn't your cuppa, perhaps a visit to St. Paul's Winter Carnival would be more enjoyable. Or a getaway to one of Minnesota's thousands of cabin resorts. Once there, it's your choice: Enjoy hearty winter outdoor activities—snowshoeing, anyone?—or curl up with a good book in front of the fireplace or woodstove and listen to the peace and quiet of a snowy day.

As a Minnesotan born and raised, I've lived in both environments, the urban metro and the rural far north. One of the joys of this state is in its ability to offer something for everyone to enjoy. There are visitors to Minnesota who are primarily interested in the Mall of America and base their multiple trips on that. Some visitors come into the Twin Cities from smaller towns, happy to experience the metro life for a few days, while city dwellers set out to find a small town or rural area for a change of scenery. Others use the Twin Cities as a jumping-off point for all kinds of ventures: historical sight-seeing throughout the state (including pioneer sites and villages, literary landmarks memorializing F. Scott Fitzgerald and Sinclair Lewis, a Jesse James reenactment, sobering reminders of the bloody Dakota Conflict, and a comprehensive and fun interactive history of the state at the Minnesota History Center), bike tours around the lakes of Minneapolis or along the Mississippi River to the Headwaters in northern Minnesota, foliage hunting in the fall, and rest and relaxation far from the madding crowd.

In many national livability surveys, Minnesota tends to rank very high, and the factors that contribute to those rankings—high quality of life, diverse leisure time activities, wide variety of cultures and habitats—make Minnesota a leading choice for people of all ages, activity levels, and interests. Throughout the following chapters, I lead you through a wide variety of places to visit, from art museums to giant balls of twine to the deepest recesses of nature to the SPAM Museum. It's all here, and it's yours to pick and choose. This guide will help you learn what the options are and what some of the best choices are in terms of types of attraction, lodging, and dining. There are options of all types: deluxe hotels and resorts, small family-owned cabins, bed & breakfasts; five-star dining, small-town cafés, and quirky little restaurants with just about every cuisine imaginable. Minnesota may be known for its Scandinavian heritage, but the current state residents come from all over the world, with growing Somali, Asian, and Hispanic populations, which have served to greatly improve the state's dining experiences. Shopping? The possibilities are nearly endless, from the massive Mall of America to the chic Galleria, to the antiques stores in Stillwater to the artist's galleries in Grand Marais. It could take months to see and experience everything Minnesota has to offer, but with this guide, you can plan for the time you have available, maximizing whatever experience you want to have—active or relaxed, urban or rural.

As I mentioned, I grew up and have lived in this state most of my life. But while traveling its highways and byways doing research for the second edition of this book, I still found countless things that were new to me and learned that there's more out there to discover. It sounds corny, but I came away from writing this book with a sense that Minnesota is, indeed, a highly worthwhile place to visit, and one of the best things about it is how many different interests can be accommodated in one way or another. Besides that, the pride many Minnesotans take in their hometowns can be very infectious; stop in any of the small regional historic museums listed in this guidebook, and you are likely to meet people who are enthusiastic and well versed in their area's history, and they might very well have some interesting and little-known stories to share with you. Friendliness and helpfulness are in full supply; it's hard to beat the graciousness offered by lakeside resort owners and bed & breakfast proprietors.

In conjunction with this book is my website www.flyover-land.com. For those not familiar with the term *flyover land,* it's a derogatory term implying that only destinations on the East or West Coast are worth visiting. I hope this book will convince you otherwise, and please feel free to stop by the website to take a look. I update the site, along with another site I write called Wander MN (www.wcco.com/wandermn), with practical information about new accommodations, restaurants, activities, and events, plus I offer some potentially wry commentary along the way.

AREA CODE There are seven area codes in Minnesota. In the Twin Cities area, 612 denotes Minneapolis and immediate surroundings; 651 is St. Paul and suburbs, including much of the St. Croix Valley; 763 is the northern Minneapolis suburbs; and 952 is the southern and southwestern Minneapolis suburbs. Northern Minnesota is 218, central Minnesota (outside the Twin Cities metro and suburban area) is 320, and southern Minnesota is 507.

AIRPORTS AND AIRLINES
Minneapolis/St. Paul International Airport (612-726-5555; www.mspairport.com) is the state's largest airport and is served primarily by Delta Air Lines (1-800-221-1212; www.delta.com), but there are several other carriers who serve the area as well. Flights depart to and arrive from all over the United States, as well as various international destinations, including Canada, Europe, the Caribbean, Mexico, and Asia. The following airlines serve the

Lindbergh Terminal 1:
Air Canada (1-888-247-2262; www.aircanada.com), Alaska Airlines (1-800-426-0333; www.airalaska.com), American Airlines (1-800-433-7300; www.aa.com), Continental Airlines (1-800-525-0280; www.continental.com), Frontier Airlines (1-800-432-1359; www.frontierairlines.com), United Airlines (1-800-241-6522; www.united.com), and US Airways (1-800-428-4322; www.usairways.com). At the **Humphrey Terminal 2,** Air Tran Airways (1-800-247-8726; www.airtran.com), Icelandair (1-800-223-5500; www.icelandair.com), Southwest Airlines (1-800-435-9792; www.southwest.com), and Sun Country Airlines (1-800-359-6786; www.suncountry.com) offer a mixture of commercial and charter services.

Bemidji Regional Airport (218-444-2438; www.bemidjiairport.org), **Brainerd Lakes Regional Airport** (218-825-2166), **International Falls International Airport** (218-283-4630 or 1-800-225-2525; www.inter

nationalfallsairport.com), **Range Regional Airport** (218-262-3451; www.rangeregionalairport.com), **St. Cloud Regional Airport** (320-255-7292; www.stcloudair port.com), and **Thief River Falls Regional Airport** (218-681-8506) are all served by Mesaba, linked with Delta Air Lines (1-800-221-1212; www.delta.com). **Duluth International Airport** (218-727-2968; www.duluthairport.com) is also served by Mesaba/Delta as well as United Airlines (1-800-241-6522; www.united.com) and Allegiant Air (702-555-8888; www .allegiantair.com). **Rochester International Airport** (507-282-2328; www.rochesterintlairport .com) is served by Mesaba/Delta (1-800-221-1212; www.delta.com) and American Eagle Airlines (1-800-433-7300; www.aa.com).

AMTRAK There is limited service in Minnesota by rail; **AMTRAK** (1-800-872-7245; www.amtrak .com) runs a train from the northwest corner, near North Dakota, through Minneapolis/St. Paul and onto Wisconsin and Chicago, once daily in each direction. The train is used more to transport people either east to Chicago or west to the Pacific Coast than to travel within Minnesota.

AMUSEMENT PARKS Valley-fair (952-445-6500; www.valley fair.com) in Shakopee is Minnesota's biggest amusement park, with rides for little kids and big ones, too, a water park, mini golf, bumper boats, go-carts, an IMAX

theater, and live music. **Nickel-odeon Universe** (1-888-276-6679; www.nickelodeonuniverse .com), Bloomington, is an indoor theme park at the Mall of America with a more limited selection of rides, but at least it's open year-round.

ANTIQUARIAN BOOKS
The Twin Cities has several good options, including **Magers & Quinn** (612-822-4611; www .magersandquinn.com), **Rulon-Miller Books** (651-290-0700; www.rulon.com), and **James & Mary Laurie Booksellers** (612-338-1114; www.lauriebooks.com), while Stillwater has **Loome Book-sellers** (651-430-1092; www .loomebooks.com), which also has a theological division, and **St. Croix Antiquarian Booksellers** (651-430-0732).

ANTIQUES Antiques shops abound in Minnesota, especially in the Twin Cities and many of the historic towns along the St. Croix, Mississippi, and Minnesota rivers. For detailed listings throughout the state, check with the **Minnesota Antiques Dealers Association** (651-430-0095; www .mnantiquesdealers.com).

AQUARIUMS The **Minnesota Sea Life Aquarium** (952-883-0202; www.visitsealife.com /minnesota) exhibit at the Mall of America in Bloomington has more than 10,000 exotic sea creatures on display in 30 tanks, viewed by a 300-foot "ocean tun-

BALLOONING Hot-air ballooning is particularly popular in Stillwater, where the scenic St. Croix makes for a perfect bird's-eye trip. In the Twin Cities, contact **Minneapolis Hot Air Balloons** (1-800-791-5867; www.1800skyride .com) or **Minnesota Valley Balloons** (952-403-1064). In Stillwater, contact **Aamodt's Hot Air Balloons** (651-351-0101 or 1-888-346-8247; www.aamodtsballoons .com) or **Stillwater Balloons** (651-439-1800; www.stillwater balloons.com).

BEACHES In the land of 10,000 (and more) lakes, it's a given that there's a beach around just about every corner. In many cases, the beaches are attached to resorts that reserve those beaches for paying guests. However, most lake

nel." In Duluth, the **Great Lakes Aquarium** (218-740-3474; www .glaquarium.org) has extensive tanks of fish, but as most of them are freshwater and native to the region, they may not be as interesting as the tropical sea life.

ARTISTS AND ART GALLERIES The Twin Cities has a large, healthy arts community, and the visual arts are no exception. Galleries abound in the Warehouse District and northeast Minneapolis, and in downtown St. Paul. Farther north, the artist community in Grand Marais keeps several galleries busy, and the scenic drives through the southeast portion of the state (Stillwater, Lanesboro) will also yield several art galleries to visit. And don't forget about the outdoor sculpture garden in Franconia.

communities have at least one good-sized public beach, and some have several. The central lakes district, including Brainerd, Willmar, and Mille Lacs, and Alexandria, have hundreds of lakes with beaches public and private. Farther north, the lake areas around Bemidji and Detroit Lakes and up to the Canadian border, along Voyageurs National Park, have beaches, too, although the swimming season may be shorter. In the Twin Cities, Lake Harriet, Lake Nokomis, and Lake Calhoun all have public swimming beaches. Many of the surrounding suburbs have city and county parks that have public beaches.

BED & BREAKFASTS Especially down the eastern side of Minnesota, B&Bs have become tremendously popular as a lodging option, especially given the number of historic homes that exist in those areas. Many are housed in grand 19th-century homes, some of which have prominent local citizens as the original owners. Today's owners take great pride in their properties, lovingly maintaining the historic feel, in many cases with period antiques or original furnishings and decor. The proprietors of these homes are generally well connected with their local community as well, with valuable insights into the history and the best places to go for entertainment and food, and they're more than happy to help. Rates run anywhere from $60 to $250 per night, depending on location and amenities.

BICYCLING All types of biking terrain are present in the state. If you like a relatively flat ride with both lakes and urban vistas, it's hard to beat the **Grand Rounds** in the Twin Cities, which cover 50 miles of trails winding around some of Minneapolis's popular lakes, along the Mississippi River, and near Minnehaha Falls. Outstate, there are literally thousands of miles of trails, ranging from paved or not, hilly or flat railway grade, wooded or riverside, located in the extensive systems of county and state parks, especially in the Brainerd lakes area and the river bluffs along the Mississippi, Minnesota, and St. Croix rivers. The **Minnesota Department of Transportation** (651-296-2216; www.dot.state.mn.us/bike/) has detailed bike maps available on request, broken down by geographic region. **Explore Minnesota** (651-296-5029 or 1-888-868-7476; www.exploreminnesota .com), the state tourism board, also produces bike trail brochures and maps, and many of the larger regional tourist boards have materials related to their area (regional tourist offices are listed at the beginning of each section).

BIRD-WATCHING Given the number of wildlife preserves and state parks, it's no surprise that Minnesota has numerous areas with excellent birding opportunities. The Minnesota chapter of the Audubon Society (http://mn .audubon.org) has detailed lists and maps, showing some of the best places to observe birds, among them the **North Shore** in the northeast, **Big Bog** and **Lake of the Woods** in the north, **Itasca State Park** and **Lac Qui Parle–Big Stone** in the central and central-northwest parts of the state, the **St. Croix and Mississippi rivers** along the eastern border, and the **Minnesota River Valley** in southwest Minnesota.

BOOKS It's intimidating to try and list even a fraction of the literature based in Minnesota or written by Minnesotans, or both. The literary arts community in Minnesota is thriving and has been for decades; Minneapolis's **Open Book** (www.openbookmn.org) is a central stopping place for writing classes and author appearances, and there's a strong network of independent bookstores throughout the state, as well as the ubiquitous **Barnes & Noble.** But if you'd like to get a sense of the literary landscape, consider reading some of the following books.

F. Scott Fitzgerald, of course, produced classics *The Great Gatsby* and *Tender Is the Night,* among other works; he lived in St. Paul with Zelda. Sinclair Lewis, author of *Babbitt* and *Elmer Gantry,* lived in Sauk Center in his youth, and in spite of his skewering the town in the fictional *Main Street,* the community still honors his memory. Charles M. Schulz of *Peanuts* fame was from Minnesota. Ole Rolvaag, author of the classic pioneer tale *Giants in the Earth,* emigrated to the U.S.

from Norway in 1896 and lived the last half of his life in Minnesota. J. F. Powers, National Book Award winner, was a longtime professor and writer in residence at St. John's University and the College of St. Benedict. His books include *Morte d'Urban* and *Wheat That Springeth Green.* Naturalist Sigurd Olson memorably chronicled the beauty of Minnesota wilderness in books like *Reflections from the North Country* and *The Singing Wilderness.* Much-beloved children's authors also have roots in Minnesota, from Laura Ingalls Wilder's Little House series to Maud Hart Lovelace's Betsy-Tacy series and Wanda Gág's *Millions of Cats.*

Contemporary writers who are from or write about Minnesota include Garrison Keillor, who, besides hosting *Prairie Home Companion,* has penned several books, including *Lake Wobegon Days* and *Happy to Be Here.* Tim O'Brien, who won the National Book Award for *Going After Cacciato* and was a finalist for the Pulitzer for *The Things They Carried,* was born in Austin and grew up in Worthington. *Time* named his novel *In the Lake of the Woods* best book of the year in 1994. John Sandford, a pseudonym for John Roswell Camp, is the Minnesota author of the best-selling Rules of Prey series. Robert Treuer had a wide-ranging career path, from teacher to Native American tribal organizer, before settling down as a tree farmer in northern Minnesota. His books,

Voyageur Country: A Park in the Wilderness and *The Tree Farm* are lyrical nonfiction explorations about life and issues in the northern reaches. David Mura, author of *Turning Japanese* and *Song for Uncle Tom, Tonto & Mr. Moto: Poetry & Identity,* is a Minnesota resident, as is memoirist Patricia Hampl, who gracefully writes about growing up in St. Paul in books such as *The Florist's Daughter.* Brian Malloy's novels have detailed life for young gays in the Twin Cities, including *The Year of Ice* and *Brendan Wolf.* Anne Ursu's fictional Minnesota small town facing an emotional crisis in *Spilling Clarence* is for adults, while her trilogy, the Cronus Chronicles (starting with *The Shadow Thieves*), get its start at the Mall of America. Shannon Olson gives us a Minnesotan Bridget Jones with *Welcome to My Planet: Where English Is Sometimes Spoken.* Lorna Landvik congenially covers all manner of small-town foibles and romantic mishaps in her books *The View from Mount Joy, The Tall Pine Polka,* and *Patty Jane's House of Curl.*

BOUNDARY WATERS CANOE AREA WILDERNESS Part of **Superior National Forest** is more than a million acres of pristine wilderness area, including 1,000 lakes, some of which are restricted to nonmotorized boats, known as the **Boundary Waters Canoe Area Wilderness (BWCAW).** The BWCAW is one of the state's top draws. The concept of an untouched, undeveloped, protected wilderness was conceived back in 1919, when the U.S. Forest Service began developing management plans for what would eventually become the BWCAW. Beginning in 1926, roads and development were prohibited in the area, and by the late 1940s the federal government began buying out homeowners and resort owners who still had property in the protected zone. The only exception was Dorothy Molter, a longtime resident known as the Root Beer Lady, who moved into the wilderness in 1934. After locals protested her removal and the Forest Service recognized both the value of her nursing skills and her almost legendary status among the population, she was granted permission to remain in the BWCAW until her death in 1986.

The creation of this quiet, natural preserve was not without controversy. Recreationists who wanted access to the area via airplanes, snowmobiles, and motorboats fought hard in court to preserve the right to bring engines into the area. When the BWCA Wilderness Act was finally passed in 1978, it allowed motorboats on about a quarter of the area's lakes. This remains controversial to this day, as those who want motorboat access continue to push for more access, saying the small amount of water available to them is not enough, while those who have fought for restricting access to motorboats continue their fight, wishing to reclaim that last quarter. It isn't likely that the contentious stances will abate anytime soon, and when visiting the BWCAW, be sure to respect each side's territory.

One thing both sides agree on is the impressive nature of the area. The lakes, tributaries, and forests all combine together to give visitors an unforgettable wilderness experience. There's something for every level of traveler—easy day trips for beginners, and long portages deep into the wilderness for more experienced canoers and campers. Several outfitting companies, particularly in Grand Marais and Ely, can set up permits and equipment rentals, and can also custom design guided trips.

During the most popular season (May 1–September 30), permits are required for day visitors and campers. Also note that although camping reservations are not required, they are definitely recommended, because the area operates under a quota system during that season, and you could find yourself with no place to stay. For permits and reservations, contact **Reserve America** (1-877-444-6777; www.recreation.gov).

One final recommendation: Seriously consider purchasing the **Superior National Forest Visitor Map.** Published by the USDA in conjunction with Superior National Forest, this is an incredibly detailed map of the BWCAW. It wouldn't hurt to buy a magnify-ing glass with which to read it. The BWCAW is full of back roads, often barely more than gravel strips, that don't appear on most state maps. It's easy to get lost unless you're very familiar with the area. The map is available in a sturdy, waterproof plastic version for about $10. Many local gas stations and convenience stores sell it, or contact the **Superior National Forest** headquarters in Duluth (218-626-4300) for information on ordering one.

BUS SERVICE Greyhound Bus Lines (1-800-231-2222; www.grey hound.com) is the primary source of public transit, serving more than 70 communities around the state, including several university locations.

CAMPING It almost seems as if the entire state is one giant campground. From the farthest northern corners of the state right down to the southern borders, state and county parks provide countless opportunities for camping, some with fairly modern campsites with electricity and facilities, others bare-bones in nature. Some require reservations and/or permits, some don't. Many of the major parks and forests, including Voyageurs National Park and the Boundary Waters Canoe Area Wilderness, are covered in this book. Minnesota's **Department of Natural Resources** (www.dnr .state.mn.us) has extensive information about campsites and policies in the state parks and state forests, as well as some online reservations capabilities. The **National Park Service** (www.nps .gov/voya) has camping and reservation information for Voyageurs National Park. **Reserve America** (www.recreation.gov) provides requirements for permits and camping in the Boundary Waters Canoe Area Wilderness, but note that if you're working through an outfitter, they are likely to handle those arrangements for you; be sure to ask.

Wherever you choose to camp, always check with local authorities ahead of time as to fire restrictions. Summer droughts have become increasingly common, and the risk of wildfire is very real; you may find that campfires are prohibited.

Speaking of campfires, it's important to note that when using a state or national campground or park (and many regional parks as well), bringing in nonlocal firewood is not permitted because of the increased spread of forest pests, especially the emerald ash borer. Where there's a park and a campground, there are places to buy wood locally. Just be sure to get a receipt in case you're asked to prove where it came from.

CANOEING AND KAYAKING
Lake Superior; Lake of the Woods; the **Boundary Waters; Lake Kabetogama;** the **Mississippi, Minnesota,** and **St. Croix rivers;** the **Chain of Lakes** in Minneapolis—these are just a few of the options for those who like to explore by water. Rentals and

outfitters abound; where there is water, there is a way to get onto the water. Arrangements can be as elaborate as guided canoeing or kayaking and camping tours, or they can be as simple as an afternoon's rental. Canoeing in the Boundary Waters, where there are entire waterways restricted to nonmotorized boats, needs at least a daily entry permit (or a more formal permit for multiple days and camping).

CHILDREN, ESPECIALLY FOR
Minnesota is generally a childfriendly state, and throughout this guide are numerous activities, museums, festivals, and restaurants that have been marked with the crayon symbol: ✐.

CRAFTS
Conventional wisdom would say it's the result of long winters, but love of crafts is alive and well in the North Star State. In the Twin Cities metro area alone, dozens of craft stores, many

independently owned and operated, sell fabric, yarn, beads, woodworking supplies, and scrapbooking supplies. The diversity of crafts being produced is burgeoning as well, and indie craft shows such as **No Coast Craft-o-Rama** (www .nocoastcraft.com) and **Crafts-travaganza** (http://craftstrava ganza.com/) showcase unusual and funky projects that definitely turn the notion of crafts as fuddy-duddy right on its head.

Which isn't to say traditional craftwork isn't valued. Most notably, the **North House Folk School** (218-387-9762 or 1-888-387-9762; www.northhouse.org) in Grand Marais offers year-round classes in everything from knitting to bread making to canoe building to how to construct your own yurt or outdoor brick oven.

DINING Foodies are sitting up and taking notice at what's happening in Minnesota. No longer a culinary backwater, the state's chefs are generating interest and intrigue for their innovative menus, as well as their increased commitment to using locally grown products for seasonal menus whenever possible. In the Twin Cities, most restaurants are open nightly or, at most, closed Monday. Outstate may find restaurants with more limited weekly or seasonal hours. Recent years have seen numerous chefs and food writers from Minnesota being nominated for—and sometimes winning—the prestigious James Beard Foundation Awards. Res-

taurants with strong reputations with the fine-dining crowd, such as **La Belle Vie** or **Haute Dish,** don't require reservations, but they're strongly recommended. There's also been a rise in the number of ethnic restaurants; immigrants have introduced authentic Asian, African, and Hispanic foods to the state. For diners who prefer their food not to be too Americanized, there are numerous worthwhile options to choose from.

DRESS CODE One thing out-of-towners sometimes comment on is the dress code, or lack thereof, at restaurants and events that would be considered at least semiformal elsewhere. It's not uncommon to see casual khakis and sweaters alongside suits and dresses at fine-dining venues and the theater. Whether or not this is a good thing is up for debate—but don't be surprised when you see it.

EMERGENCIES Call 911 from anywhere in the state. In each section, regional hospitals are listed.

FACTORY OUTLETS Albertville, which is a community north of Minneapolis, has the **Albertville Premium Outlets** (www.premiumoutlets.com), with 100 stores, and is by far the largest outlet center in the state. This is discussed in more detail in the "Minneapolis's Neighboring Communities" chapter.

FALL FOLIAGE September and October can be variable in terms of weather, but when the days are crisp and clear, the fall colors in various parts of the state can be spectacular. Starting up north across the eastern half of the state (along Voyageurs National Park and the Canadian border); through the Boundary Waters, the Iron Range, and the North Shore; and down south through the Twin Cities and the St. Croix, Mississippi, and Minnesota rivers, large areas of forests set on rolling land along water make for prime foliage viewing. Most restaurants, hotels, and bed & breakfasts are open at least weekends during the fall for visitors seeking the turning of the leaves.

FARM STANDS AND FARMER'S MARKETS Whether they're popular as a result of a long agricultural history or because today's foodies are increasingly interested in local, sustainable foods, farmer's markets and farm stands can be found in pretty much every corner of the state. It may be something as simple as a teenager selling corn off the back of a pickup or as elaborate as the revered farmer's markets in Minneapolis and St. Paul, but there's something for everyone. For complete listings, check with the **Minnesota Farmers Market Association** (www.mfma.org). Note: In the Minneapolis and St. Paul sections, information about some of the more prominent city markets is included.

FESTIVALS Minnesota is a state full of festivals. Some are cultural explorations, such as **Kolacky Days** and **Scandinavian Midsommar Tag.** Others celebrate local history or agriculture, such as **Irish Fest** and **Barnesville's Potato Days** (mashed potato wrestling, anyone?) Some sound just plain goofy (**Eelpout Festival, St. Urhu Day**) but are beloved local traditions. Some of the "best of" are listed at the end of each chapter. Additional information and listings can be found by visiting the tourist boards listed in the *Guidance* sections at the beginning of each section, or see my Minnesota blog, *A Closer Look at Flyover Land* (www.flyoverland.com), where I post links to festivals at the beginning of each month.

FIRE Wildfires are always a concern in wilderness areas, and Minnesota is no exception, especially since recent years have seen significant droughts in parts of the state. When planning a camping trip, be sure to find out if there are campfire restrictions. As this can change from one day to the next, it's best to check upon arrival to make sure you're not violating any new restrictions.

FISHING Fishing is a summer and winter sport in Minnesota, with options of open-water fishing

to dropping your line in a hole cut in the ice, usually in an ice house. Many of the lake resorts have become year-round destinations due to the popularity of ice fishing, and it's possible in some areas to rent a sleep-ready ice house, complete with electricity and bathroom facilities. Fishing is a licensed activity, and licenses are generally easy to obtain, usually available from local DNR offices and convenience stores. For information on cost and restrictions, see www.dnr.state.mn.us.

GAMBLING Minnesota has 22 casinos scattered throughout the state, on 11 Indian reservations. All casinos offer slot machines and table games like blackjack and poker, and most offer bingo. Live entertainment is frequently scheduled at the larger casinos, like **Mystic Lake Casino** (www.mysticlake.com) in Prior Lake and **Grand Casino Hinckley** (www.grandcasinomn.com) in Hinckley getting some well-known and current entertainers. In addition, **Canterbury Park** (www.canterburypark.com) in Shakopee offers card games 24/7, live horse racing during the summer, and simulcast horse racing from other tracks year-round.

GOLF Minnesotans are passionate about golf, a fact demonstrated by the extreme weather golfers are willing to cope with in order to get out on the course. The state has nearly 600 courses, public and private, and the terrain varies from lush and meticulously maintained fairways to the northernmost golf course in the U.S., the Northwest Angle Country Club. The **Minnesota Tourism Board** (www .exploreminnesota.com) can provide complimentary golf brochures on request, or check online at www.exploreminnesotagolf.com for a detailed directory.

HANDICAP ACCESS Throughout this book, entries marked with the wheelchair symbol ♿ indicate attractions, lodging, and restaurants that are handicapped accessible.

HIKING Miles and miles of trails, paved and unpaved, flat and rolling, forest and prairie, await visitors statewide. The multitude of state parks offer just about every sort of terrain, wildlife viewing, and flora and fauna imaginable for the region. The **Minnesota Department of Natural Resources** (www.dnr.state.mn.us) has detailed information on each park on its website, and the department also offers two hiking clubs: The Hiking Club offers hikers graduated levels of awards for hiking preset mileage levels, with the ultimate awards coming in the form of free nights of camping. The Passport Club rewards travelers for visiting state parks. The regional tourism offices listed in each section can provide information and maps on that region's hiking opportunities, while the **Minnesota Tourism Board** (www.exploreminnesota .com) can provide complimentary hiking brochures on request.

HISTORY Minnesota's history runs the full gamut from pioneers to fur traders to Native Americans to barons of industry; to famous politicians to contentious or well-beloved authors, actors, and musicians; to devastating natural tragedies to scandalous murders. **Jesse James's** epic arrival in Northfield, **Hubert Humphrey's** presidential campaign, **John Dillinger's** reign in St. Paul, former pro wrestler **Jesse Ventura's** reign as governor, the quintessential pioneer **Laura Ingalls Wilder's** travels through southern Minnesota, **Bob Dylan's** roots on the Iron Range, **Bronko Nagurski's** legendary football career getting its start in International Falls, musical icon **Prince,** and *A Prairie Home Companion's* **Garrison Keillor** are just some of the legends past and present who are associated with Minnesota. And in one way or another, these people (and many more) and events throughout the state's history are commemorated in various displays, exhibits, and festivals.

HUNTING Hunting is a licensed activity in Minnesota. Among the game that's legal to hunt (with the proper license and in season) is bear, deer, pheasant, wild turkey, grouse, and waterfowl. Licenses are generally easy to obtain, usually available from local DNR offices (including some by phone

INTERNET Throughout this book, Internet websites for attractions, recreational sites, lodging, and restaurants have been given whenever they are available. The Internet has been embraced as a wonderful informational tool by smaller businesses, to the advantage of the traveling public, and it's likely that even more companies will have gone online by the time this book goes to press.

Access to high-speed Internet and Wi-Fi, often free, is becoming more prevalent as well. Many hotels, restaurants, coffee shops, libraries, and university campuses can provide online access to visitors. The tower symbol (ᵠ) appears next to businesses that have Internet/Wi-Fi access.

or on the website) and convenience stores. For information on cost and restrictions, see www.dnr.state.mn.us.

INFORMATION ABOUT MINNESOTA, OFFICIAL

Explore Minnesota (651-296-5029 or 1-888-868-7476; www.exploreminnesota) is the central state tourism organization. Visitors are welcome at the headquarters at 121 Seventh Place E. in St. Paul, or at one of the travel information centers located in Albert Lea, Beaver Creek, Dresbach, Bloomington (Mall of America), Fisher's Landing, Grand Portage Bay, Moorhead, St. Cloud, St. Croix, Duluth, and Worthington. Explore Minnesota also partners with various local tourist boards, chambers of commerce, and convention and visitors bureaus all over the state. A thorough listing of local and regional tourism groups is available on the Explore Minnesota website.

LAKES The land of 10,000 lakes is a slight underestimation. There are actually more than 15,000 lakes across the state, nearly 12,000 of which are at least 10

acres in size. The Minnesota DNR says that Minnesota's lakes and rivers have more shoreline than California, Florida, and Hawaii combined. To the delight of visitors, those shorelines provide ample opportunities for enjoyment year-round: boating, fishing (including ice fishing in winter), swimming, waterskiing, and sightseeing. Several state parks have multiple lakes, as does the one national park (**Voyageurs National Park;** www.nps.gov /voya). The **North Shore,** riding along the coast of Lake Superior, provides an almost oceanic viewing experience, while the **Brainerd Lakes District** is among some of the best known in the state for vacationers. Accommodations varying from rustic campsites to deluxe resorts with every possible amenity can be found; the demand is particularly high in summer, so booking in advance is strongly recommended.

LANGUAGE CAMPS The northern region of Minnesota is home to **Concordia Language Villages** (218-299-4544 or 1-800-222-4750; www.concordialanguage villages.org). The program's headquarters are in Moorhead, but most of the year-round villages are just outside Bemidji. The villages are self-contained cultural units, with different camps developed for Spanish, French, German, Russian, Norwegian, and Finnish. Each village is designed to look like a classic village from that country. Additional summer-only villages are offered elsewhere in the state, including camps for Chinese, Italian, Arabic, Korean, and Swedish. There are programs offered for adults and children, most of them on an immersion basis, but it's not just language that's offered; students will learn about customs, culture, and foods of their chosen regions.

Even if you aren't interested in registering for a camp, a visit to the villages is worth the side trip—the attention to detail is impressive, and the villages are nestled in stately forests, giving the visitor an otherworldly feel.

LEFSE AND LUTEFISK Minnesota has a strong Scandinavian heritage, and especially around the holidays or at ethnic festivals, it's inevitable that the classic Scandinavian foods, lefse and lutefisk, will make an appearance. Of the two, lefse is more widely enjoyed; it's a potato pastry, rolled out thin and briefly grilled. Some choose to add butter, sugar, cinnamon, or all three (I recommend the last). Lutefisk is a horse of a different color, falling right into the "love it or hate it" category, and it's the subject of many jokes. Essentially, lutefisk is fish soaked in lye. Although not everyone's first choice, lutefisk is still very popular for holiday church dinners, festivals, and at Christmas time.

LITTER Littering in Minnesota is punishable on the first offense by a misdemeanor charge that goes on the driving record; subsequent offenses are subject to fines of several hundred dollars.

LODGING Minnesota offers a highly diverse group of lodging choices: bed & breakfasts, resorts, cabins deluxe and primitive, motels, private homes, overnight ice fishing houses, upscale hotels, houseboats, even yurts. The rates quoted in this book reflect a per-night rate for two people, and keep in mind that rates are fluid; please don't hold us or the accommodations to the rates quoted, but instead view them as a guideline, not an absolute. In general, most bed & breakfasts don't accept children under 12 (but it's noted if they do), and many cabins or lake resorts have minimum-stay requirements (anywhere from three to seven nights) during peak periods. Pets are not accepted unless the pet symbol 🐾 is shown, and even then it's a good idea to confirm when reserving as to what size or types of pets may be

restricted and if additional fees apply. Nearly all accept credit cards; hotels will accept a credit card as a guarantee for arrival, while bed & breakfasts or lake resorts may require a prepaid deposit, and some smaller resorts prefer checks or cash. Cancellation policies vary, so confirm the policy before committing any money.

MALL OF AMERICA The **Mall of America** (www.mallofamerica .com) is a shopper's paradise, with over 4 million square feet that includes not only more than 500 stores, but 30 fast-food restaurants, 20 sit-down restaurants, an underground aquarium, a convenience store, photo studios, a 14-screen movie theater complex, a wedding chapel, a comedy club, a flight simulator, and an indoor theme park. The retail anchors are Nordstrom, Macy's, Bloomingdale's, and Sears, and the surrounding stores include everything

from clothing to electronics to jewelry to books to cosmetics, to Christmas decorations to crafts to Irish gifts to items made in Minnesota. Across the street from the mall is home furnishings superstore IKEA and a Radisson Hotel with the Waterpark of America, so there's something for everyone to do.

MAPS The **Minnesota Department of Transportation** produces a new Official State Highway Map every other year, and one free copy can be obtained by contacting Explore Minnesota (651-296-5029 or 1-888-868-7476), collecting one in person at one of the state's many travel information centers (see *Information about Minnesota, Official*), or by visiting the DOT's website (www.dot.state .mn.us), where portions of the maps can be downloaded and printed.

For maps detailed with a significant amount of tourist information, **Professor Pathfinder's Supermaps,** published by Hedberg Maps (www.hedbergmaps .com), come in a full-state version as well as regional maps (Twin Cities, northern Minnesota, southern Minnesota, Brainerd lakes) and are clearly marked and easily read.

As noted earlier in *Boundary Waters Canoe Area Wilderness*, a trip to the BWCAW wouldn't be complete without acquiring the **Superior National Forest Visitor Map** (along with a magnifying glass with which to read it). This map, published by the USDA in conjunction with Superior National Forest, is an incredibly detailed map of the BWCAW and is available in a sturdy, waterproof plastic version for about $10. Many local gas stations and convenience stores sell it, or contact the **Superior National Forest** headquarters in Duluth (218-626-4300) for information on ordering one.

If you'd really like to explore off the beaten path, consider buying road maps by county, also offered by the Minnesota Department of Transportation. These maps are highly detailed and include all the minor county roads that don't show up on the full state map. While GPS is useful, it doesn't always keep up with the lesser-used roads; a good map comes in very handy.

MINNESOTA GROWN Among the Minnesota-produced items available for purchase throughout the state are maple syrup, cheese, meats, honey, candles, jams, and, in season, all kinds of fresh vegetables and fruits (some of the latter available from pick-your-own farms). The **Minnesota Department of Agriculture** (651-201-6000 or 1-800-967-2474; www.mda.state.mn.us) has online and print directories for finding locally made items.

MINNESOTA PUBLIC BROADCASTING
Minnesota has both public radio (**Minnesota Public Radio;** www.mpr.org) and public television (**Twin Cities Public Television;** www.tpt.org). Both are headquartered in the Twin Cities, but satellite stations throughout the state carry the public programming. Visit each company's website for specific locations and channels. Also note that MPR has three radio options: MPR itself is a classical radio station, while KNOW is talk and news radio, and the Current plays a widely diverse, eclectic selection of indie, local, and off-the-mainstream music.

MOVIES
Popular movies are easily tracked down in most communities. For those looking for smaller, independent, foreign, or art house movies, good bets in the Twin Cities include the **Uptown Theatre** and **Lagoon Cinema** in Minneapolis and the **Edina Cinema** in Edina (www.landmark theatres.com), as well as the venerable **Oak Street Cinema** (www.mnfilmarts.org/oakstreet/) at the University of Minnesota. The annual **Minneapolis–St. Paul International Film Fest** (www

.mspfilmfest.org) is a big event each year, with nearly 70 films.

MUSEUMS
Minnesota must be given credit for being a state highly supportive of museums big and small. From the world-class **Minneapolis Institute of the Arts** (www.artsmia.org) and the **Walker Art Center** (www.walkerart .org), which together comprise significant collections of classic and contemporary art, to smaller museums like the **Museum of Russian Art** (www.tmora.org) and the **Minnesota Marine Art Museum** (507-474-6626 or 1-866-940-6626; www.minnesotamarine art.org), patrons of the arts have much to choose from. The **Weisman Art Museum** (www.weis man.umn.edu) is a newer member of the arts community, housed in a Frank Gehry building at the University of Minnesota and newly expanded as of late 2011. Duluth has the **Tweed Museum** (www.d .umn.edu/tma/) at the University of Minnesota's Duluth campus, while down south in Winona is the **Minnesota Marine Art Museum** (www.minnesotamarineart.org), devoted to nautical artwork, including works by O'Keeffe, Monet, Picasso, and Van Gogh. Add in options for families, such as the **Minnesota Children's Museum** (www.mcm.org), the **Science Museum of Minnesota** (www.smm.org), and the **Bakken Museum** (www.thebakken.org), as well as historical options including **Mill City Museum** (www.mill citymuseum.org), the **Minnesota**

History Center Museum (www
.mnhs.org), the **Hinckley Fire
Museum** (www.seans.com/sunset
web/hinckley/), the **Bronko
Nagurski Museum** (www.bronko
nagurski.com/museum.htm), and
the nearly countless city and county historical societies that provide
invaluable insights into all aspects
of Minnesota history, and there is
plenty for any museum aficionado
to do.

MUSIC Minnesotans are passionate about their music, whether it's
classical, country, rock, alternative/
indie, jazz, bluegrass, or anything
in between. Live venues of every
size are open in the Twin Cities,
from **Target Center** (www.target
center.com) and **Xcel Energy
Center** (www.xcelenergycenter
.com) to **Orchestra Hall** (www
.minnesotaorchestra.org) and the
Ordway (www.ordway.org) to the
Fine Line (www.finelinemusic
.com), the **Dakota** (www.dakota
cooks.com), and **First Avenue**
(www.first-avenue.com). Those are
just the best-known options, but
there are literally dozens, if not
hundreds, of other clubs, stages,
and bars with live music.

Besides concerts, music festivals are wildly popular in Minnesota, particularly in the summer,
when they can be held outdoors.
Among the big shows are the
annual **WE Fest** (www.wefest
.com), **Moondance Jam** (www
.moondancejam.com), **Sonshine
Festival** (www.sonshinefestival
.com), the **Minnesota Bluegrass
& Old-Time Music Festival**
(www.minnesotabluegrass.org),
and the **Boundary Waters Blues
Festival** (www.elyblues.com).
More festivals and information are
listed in each chapter.

NATURE PRESERVES Min-
nesota has thousands of acres
maintained as nature preserves
(also called Scientific & Natural
Area, or SNA), and as such, they
provide numerous opportunities
for hiking and wildlife viewing,
with the heaviest concentration of
such preserves in the western and
southwestern parts of the state.
The **Minnesota Department of
Natural Resources** (www.dnr
.state.mn.us) and the **Nature
Conservancy** (www.nature.org)
both have comprehensive listings
of locations and what you can
expect to find. Areas like the
**Black Dog Nature Preserve,
Burntside Islands SNA,
Frenchman's Bluff SNA, Glacial Ridge National Wildlife
Refuge,** and **Bluestem Prairie
SNA** are just a few of the more
than 140 preserves across the state
that give glimpses of now hard-to-
find prairies and untouched
forests, not to mention deer,
prairie chickens, eagles, wolves,
falcons, whooping cranes, pheas-
ants, owls, and herons.

**NEWSPAPERS AND
PERIODICALS** In the Twin
Cities, there are two major daily
papers: Minneapolis's *Star Trib-
une* (www.startribune.com) and
St. Paul's *Pioneer Press* (www
.twincities.com). There are also a

by theme or blanketing several topics (dining, shopping, etc.).

Nearly every city of any size has at least a weekly newspaper, and several (Duluth, Bemidji, Brainerd, Rochester, Faribault, International Falls, to name a few) have newspapers published five to seven days a week and available for sale at local stores.

PARKS AND FORESTS, NATIONAL Voyageurs National Park (281-283-9821; www.nps .gov/voya) is the only national park in Minnesota. It borders Canada along the northern edge of Minnesota, nudging up to **Superior National Forest** (218-626-4300; www.fs.fed.us/r9/forests/superior/), which in turn contains the Boundary Waters Canoe Area Wilderness on the U.S. side. Voyageurs National Park and Superior National Forest together comprise some of the most beautiful and remote wilderness areas in the state. Together they account for millions of acres of forests, lakes, and streams; connect the region to Canada; and provide countless opportunities for camping, hiking, canoeing, kayaking, houseboating, fishing, and hunting.

The other national area is **Chippewa National Forest** (218-335-8600; www.fs.usda.gov), a 1.6-million acre preserve south and west of Voyageurs National Park and Superior National Forest. Together with the latter two, Chippewa National Forest provides year-round recreational opportunities. Minnesota's third- and fourth-largest lakes, Leech

number of independent papers that publish weekly or monthly, including **City Pages** (www.city pages.com), which is an excellent resource for local events of every kind and in-depth restaurant reviews.

In terms of periodicals, **Minneapolis–St. Paul Magazine** (www.mspmag.com) is a monthly publication, available at most bookstores, newsstands, and grocery stores, that has information on Twin Cities events and an extensive restaurant guide. **Minnesota Monthly** (www.minnesotamonthly.com), although much of its coverage focuses on the Twin Cities, does provide good resources for restaurants, lodging, and events outside the metro area. A third magazine, **Metro Magazine** (http://metromag.com), focuses specifically on the Twin Cities and picks up some of the edgier, younger events and venues. All magazines publish several "Best Of" issues each year, often

Lake and Lake Winnibigoshish (also known as Lake Winnie), are in the forest, along with another 1,300 lakes. Wildlife is abundant in the three national areas; wolves, bald eagles, deer, moose, bobcats, owls, and cougars are not uncommon.

PARKS AND FORESTS, STATE The **Minnesota Department of Natural Resources** (www.dnr.state.mn.us) is the go-to organization for information about Minnesota's state parks, which rival the national parks and forests for recreation and amenities. There are more than 70 parks spread out across the state, including popular visitor sites such as **Gooseberry Falls** and **Split Rock Lighthouse** on the North Shore and **Itasca** in northern Minnesota (home to the Mississippi River headwaters) to the more remote but equally beautiful **Zippel Bay** in the far north region on Lake of the Woods, and **Mystery Cave** in southern Minnesota.

In addition, Minnesota also has 58 state forests, also managed by the Minnesota State DNR. All but one of these forests is located in the central and northern regions of Minnesota, while the **Richard J. Doner Memorial Hardwood Forest** is in the far southeastern corner of the state. Like the national parks and forests, the state parks and forests offer year-round recreational opportunities, with access to a vast number of lakes and rivers.

PETS Accommodations that accept pets are noted with the 🐾 symbol in each chapter. But be sure to call ahead; most lodgings that take pets have restrictions regarding the types and sizes of pets, and there may be advance reservations and fee requirements.

POPULATION Per the U.S. Census Bureau, the population of Minnesota is 5,266,214 (as of 2009).

RAIL TRAVEL See *AMTRAK.*

SAILING Even though winter puts a damper on the fun, the sheer number of Minnesota lakes makes sailing a popular warm-weather pastime. In the Twin Cities, sailboats can be seen on nearly all of the lakes, especially

Lake Calhoun, Lake Harriet, and Lake Minnetonka. But you can expect to see sailboats on just about any body of water or river throughout the state, and rentals can be arranged in every resort area.

SKIING, CROSS-COUNTRY
State and national parks and forests, combined with county and city parks, provide thousands of miles of groomed and rough trails for cross-country enthusiasts. This is an activity that takes place in virtually every spot in the state, whether it's on flat prairie land with long-range views, through forests and challenging hills, or across lakes and along riverbanks. Rental equipment is available in most resort towns.

SKIING, DOWNHILL Mountains aren't the first things that come to mind when thinking about Minnesota, but the winter season combined with some larger-than-average hills do keep winter visitors busy. Among the biggest and most advanced ski resorts is Lutsen (218-663-7281; www.lutsen.com) on the North Shore, which comes complete with slopeside accommodations and all degree of runs (more information is in the "North Shore/Lutsen" chapter). Book ahead—winter weekends tend to be very popular.

Afton Alps (651-436-5245 or 1-800-328-1328; www.aftonalps.com), just outside of Hastings, is the biggest ski resort within easy range of the Twin Cities. There are no slopeside accommodations here, but there are several options in nearby Hastings.

Among the other downhill ski resorts around the state are Buck Hill (952-435-7174; www.buckhill.com) in Burnsville; Spirit Mountain (218-628-2891 or 1-800-642-6377; www.spiritmt.com) in Duluth; Welch Village (651-258-4567; www.welchvillage.com) in Welch; Buena Vista (218-243-2231; www.bvskiarea.com) in Bemidji; Wild Mountain (651-465-6315 or 1-800-447-4958; www.wildmountain.com) in Taylors Falls; and Mt. Kato (507-625-3363 or 1-800-668-5286; www.mountkato.com) in Mankato. Ski and snowboard lessons and rentals are available on-site, and several resorts have ski lodges and tubing hills as well.

SMOKING As of press time, smoking is banned in restaurants, bars, and other public establishments. Some counties and cities within Minnesota have enacted local legislation for stricter limitations. When in doubt, ask.

SNOWMOBILING Snowmobiling is a popular sport in Minnesota, used for both recreation and as a practical mode of transport, particularly in the western half of the state. However, that doesn't mean snowmobiles can go anywhere; parts of the Boundary Waters Canoe Area Wilderness are off-limits to motorized vehicles,

including snowmobiles. Many state parks and forests have trails for snowmobilers, but be sure to stay on those trails, as wandering off-trail can interfere with the work being done in nature preserves throughout the park systems. The Twin Cities metro area has varying restrictions on snowmobiles, with some cities allowing them and others banning them. To get specific information on annual regulations and requirements, check with the **Minnesota Department of Natural Resources** (www.dnr.state.mn.us /snowmobiling/index.html).

THEATER Minnesota's commitment to the arts community continues into the world of theater. Minneapolis has several world-renowned theatrical companies, including the **Guthrie Theater** (612-377-2224 or 1-877-447-8243; www.guthrietheater.org) and the **Children's Theatre Company** (612-874-0400; www.childrens theatre.org). But theaters of all shapes, sizes, and theatrical genres thrive in communities large and small across the state. The Twin Cities is also home to the **Jungle Theater** (612-822-7063; www .jungletheater.com) and the **Chanhassen Dinner Theatres** (952-934-1525 or 1-800-362-3515; www.chanhassentheatres.com). Outstate, the **Paul Bunyan Playhouse** (218-751-7270; www.paul bunyanplayhouse.com) in Bemidji is one of the state's longest-running summer stock theaters. On the North Shore, the **Grand Marais**

Playhouse (218-387-1284; www.arrowheadcenterfort hearts.org) offers productions year-round. **Commonweal** (507-467-2525 or 1-800-657-7025; www .commonwealtheatre.org) in Lanesboro offers several productions each year—one of them is always by Norwegian playwright Henrik Ibsen—and also sponsors the annual Ibsen Festival. The **Great River Shakespeare Festival** (507-474-7900; www.grsf .org) in Winona takes place annually in the summer with highly professional Shakespearian productions. Other theaters are noted throughout the book.

TRAFFIC Generally speaking, Minnesota roads are reasonably well maintained and well marked. That said, there are always some trouble spots to plan around. The web of intertwining freeways around and through the Twin Cities metro area have routine rush hour slowdowns each weekday, especially during rainy or snowy weather. Friday and Sunday afternoons in the spring and summer find another kind of gridlock—the "going to the cabin" slowdown. Highways leading north from the Twin Cities, particularly I-94, I-494, and I-694, can crawl along at an agonizingly slow pace each weekend, and even worse if it's a holiday weekend. Whenever possible, try to plan driving at other times; you'll get there faster with less aggravation.

Beyond the lakes traffic, be aware that many of the communities around the lakes and rivers have grown in popularity with vacationers faster than their road systems have been expanded. Driving through Brainerd or Stillwater or along MN 61 on the North Shore on a summer's day is almost guaranteed to be slow, with far more vehicles crowding the roads than usual, and bottlenecks occurring every block with stoplights or left-turning cars. Adding to the frustration is the increase in road construction and repair projects that take place in the summer. A good map can give you ideas of side roads to take, but it's not recommended to do that on a whim; a 5-mile paved road detour might turn into a 35-mile gravel road detour if your choice of side road is also undergoing construction. When planning driving routes, always check with the **Minnesota Department of Transportation** (651-296-3000 or 1-800-657-3774; www.dot.state .mn.us), which publishes frequent or real-time updates on road conditions and traffic problems all over the state.

WEATHER Minnesota definitely has a winter season; although it's more pronounced the farther north you go, it's not as wicked as legends would have it. That said, if you're traveling in the winter, be absolutely sure to keep an eye on local weather forecasts (local radio and TV stations carry forecasts from the National Weather Service, or the website www.weather .com provides up-to-the-minute

information), especially if you're headed north. Snow is one concern, but for those heading to the western part of the state, wind and cold can be as big, if not a bigger, concern; the long flat plains and prairies have no way to break the wind, which can push snow into conditions of whiteout, and following a road can be close to impossible. When there is a travel advisory listed for a specific region, pay heed, and consider staying put. The snowflake symbol ❄ appears next to establishments that are open during the off-season, which in Minnesota is generally October through April.

WEBSITES Wherever available, website addresses have been included for accommodations, restaurants, attractions, tourist boards and chambers of commerce, and hospitals. When one isn't listed, that's only because none was offered at time of publication. In addition, feel free to visit www.flyover-land.com, my website, for additional and updated information on all things Minnesota.

WINERIES Several entrepreneurial and hardy souls have attacked the notion that wine cannot be produced in a wintry seasonal climate. Wineries have begun to appear in all regions of Minnesota, some using specially cultivated grapes that are better able to withstand winter, and others using fruits besides grapes (blueberries, rhubarb) to create unusual and fun wines. **Alexis Bailly Vineyard** (651-437-1413; www.abvwines.com) in Hastings was one of the first to work with grapes in Minnesota, producing its first vintage in 1978. Today there's even a **"Wine Trail"** (www.three riverswinetrail.com)—a group of five wineries in the St. Croix, Mississippi, and Cannon river valleys in southeast Minnesota, all pro-

ducing wines that are increasingly enjoying acclaim and success. At this point, most are still in the southern half of the state, where the climate is a bit more temperate, but not far from Bemidji is **Forestedge Winery** (www.forest edgewinery.com), which works with local fruits (chokecherries, raspberries, Honeycrisp apples) to create some flavorful wines.

Minneapolis and Neighboring Communities

1

MINNEAPOLIS

MINNEAPOLIS'S NEIGHBORING
COMMUNITIES

MINNEAPOLIS

I t's called the City of Lakes, and for a reason: The city of Minneapolis is home to seven lakes, five of which (Harriet, Lake of the Isles, Calhoun, Cedar, and Brownie) are connected by trails through the Grand Rounds National Scenic Byway. The lakes serve as a present-day memento from glacier movement centuries ago, and today they are a center of social and recreational activity. But it's not so much the lakes that brought Minneapolis into prominence as its location on the Mississippi River. The Mississippi was a necessary thoroughfare for the development of the logging and milling industries that set Minneapolis on the path from sleepy river town to a thriving economic and cultural force.

The land surrounding Minneapolis was originally settled by Dakota Indians, who turned over that parcel to the U.S. government in 1805. It's thought that the first white man to explore the area was Father Louis Hennepin, a French missionary. Whether or not he was the first, his name was bestowed to the county and one of the major avenues through the city. Originally the area had two towns: St. Anthony (named for the St. Anthony Falls on the Mississippi) and Minneapolis, but in 1872 the two merged. What followed was an economic boom as Minneapolis became the leading lumber and flour milling center in the United States.

Those glory days were done by 1930, as northern forests were becoming deforested and logging mills shut down. Flour milling began to take hold in other parts of the country, reducing Minneapolis's lock on the market.

GRAND ROUNDS NATIONAL SCENIC BYWAY

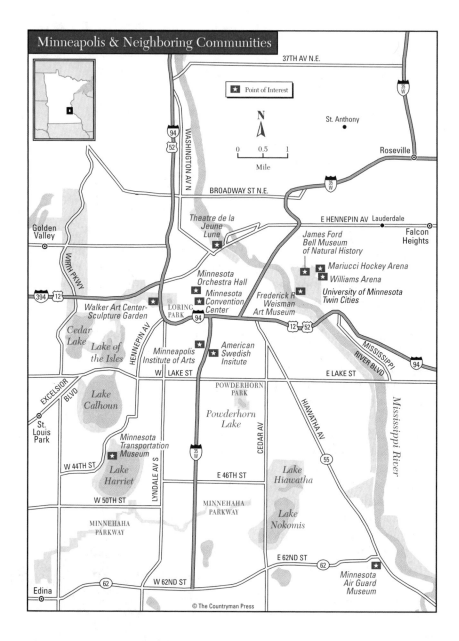

Minneapolis & Neighboring Communities

★ Point of Interest

N

0   0.5   1
Mile

37TH AV N.E.

St. Anthony

Roseville

BROADWAY ST N.E.

WASHINGTON AV N

Theatre de la Jeune Lune

E HENNEPIN AV   Lauderdale

James Ford Bell Museum of Natural History

Falcon Heights

Golden Valley

Mariucci Hockey Arena

Williams Arena

Minnesota Orchestra Hall

Minnesota Convention Center

Frederick R Weisman Art Museum

University of Minnesota Twin Cities

WIRTH PKWY

Walker Art Center-Sculpture Garden

LORING PARK

Cedar Lake

Lake of the Isles

HENNEPIN AV

Minneapolis Institute of Arts

W LAKE ST

American Swedish Insitute

E LAKE ST

MISSISSIPPI RIVER BLVD

EXCELSIOR BLVD

Lake Calhoun

POWDERHORN PARK

Powderhorn Lake

CEDAR AV

Mississippi River

St. Louis Park

Minnesota Transportation Museum

W 44TH ST

Lake Harriet

LYNDALE AV S

HIAWATHA AV

Lake Hiawatha

W 50TH ST

E 46TH ST

MINNEHAHA PARKWAY

Lake Nokomis

MINNEHAHA PARKWAY

E 62ND ST

Edina

W 62ND ST

Minnesota Air Guard Museum

© The Countryman Press

Today flour milling is still an important industry, as General Mills is headquartered here. Other agricultural and industrial companies related to the food industry began here and remain powerful today, including Cargill and Super Valu. Other industry giants that either were or are still headquartered in the City of Lakes include Honeywell, Medtronic, Best Buy, and Target. The University of Minnesota's Minneapolis campus grew exponentially during this time, particularly its medical and research departments, which have been leading innovators in medical procedures, including the first open heart surgery.

With major companies bringing in people and money, Minneapolis began to see growth of cultural institutions. The Guthrie Theater, now a world-renowned company, opened in 1960; the Minneapolis Institute of the Arts began receiving visitors in 1915; and the Walker Art Center began focusing on contemporary art in 1940s. Sports fans were given something to cheer about when the major league Minnesota Twins debuted in 1960 and went on to win the World Series in 1987 and 1991. The Minnesota Vikings brought NFL football to the state and have played in the Super Bowl four times. More recently, professional basketball teams (the men's Timberwolves and women's Lynx) have brought crowds in to Target Center.

A dynamic combination of history, industry, arts, and popular culture has made Minneapolis a vibrant city to visit. Oh, and the lakes are fun, too.

Like any large city, Minneapolis has myriad neighborhoods. For the purposes of this book, lodging, dining and shopping will be broken out by Downtown, North Loop (otherwise known as the Warehouse District on the north edge of downtown), Northeast (across the river from downtown, the nearest area of which is sometimes called Near Northeast/ Riverfront), South (which includes the Uptown area), the Mississippi riverfront area (which has developed into a thriving community with recreation and restaurants), the University of Minnesota's East Bank area (which is full of fun

OLD MILL RUINS AND MILL CITY MUSEUM, MINNEAPOLIS

eateries), and the university's Dinkytown area (a small corner packed full of shops and restaurants).

GUIDANCE Minneapolis Regional Chamber of Commerce (612-370-9100; www.minneapolischamber.org), 81 S. Ninth St., Suite 200, Minneapolis. Open weekdays 8–5. The chamber's website has a thorough overview of the cultural, entertainment, sports, and outdoor activities available in the city, and they offer links and order forms for informational brochures and maps.

Greater Minneapolis Convention and Visitors Association (612-767-8000; www.minneapolis.org), 250 Marquette Ave. S., Suite 1300, Minneapolis. Open weekdays 8:30–5. An extensive listing of tourist info, including online booking for air and hotel reservations.

GETTING THERE *By air:* The primary airport is the Terminal 1–Lindbergh at the **Minneapolis–St. Paul International Airport** (612-726-5555; www.mspairport.com); next door is the **Terminal 2–Humphrey** (612-726-5800), a smaller secondary terminal serving mostly no-frills and charter airlines. Both airports are in Bloomington, a western suburb. Taxis, limos, rental cars, and light rail service is available from the airports into the city.

By bus: **Greyhound** has a terminal downtown (612-371-3325; www.greyhound.com).

By car: I-94, I-394, I-35W, and MN 55 all lead into downtown Minneapolis.

By rail: **AMTRAK** (1-800-872-7245; www.amtrak.com) has a rail station off University Ave. between Minneapolis and St. Paul (730 Transfer Rd.).

MINNESOTA'S "FIFTH SEASON"

Like any northern clime, Minnesota struggles to get as much road construction and repair done during the warm months as possible. Consequently, the old phrase "you can't get there from here" seems to hold an unfortunate truth at various points during the summer construction season. Spring, summer, and fall can present other inconveniences, such as rare but not unheard-of flooding that closes roads. The bottom line is when planning your travel, particularly if you're traveling by car, check out current road conditions by visiting the Minnesota Department of Transportation's road and traffic conditions website (www.511mn.org) or call 511 (or 1-800-657-3774) for updated information.

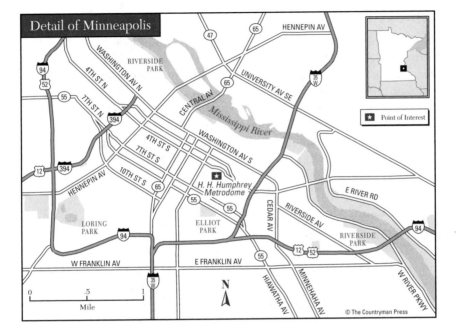

Detail of Minneapolis

★ Point of Interest

Mississippi River

H. H. Humphrey Metrodome

RIVERSIDE PARK

HENNEPIN AV

WASHINGTON AV N

UNIVERSITY AV SE

CENTRAL AV

4TH ST N

7TH ST N

4TH ST S

7TH ST S

WASHINGTON AV S

10TH ST S

HENNEPIN AV

LORING PARK

ELLIOT PARK

CEDAR AV

RIVERSIDE AV

E RIVER RD

RIVERSIDE PARK

W FRANKLIN AV

E FRANKLIN AV

HIAWATHA AV

MINNEHAHA AV

W RIVER PKWY

N

0 .5 1
Mile

© The Countryman Press

GETTING AROUND For travel within the city, **Metro Transit** (612-373-3333; www.metrotransit.org) provides extensive service designed primarily to transport students and employees from outlying homes to work and school within the city. Currently, light rail service runs from downtown Minneapolis to the Metrodome stadium, Historic Ft. Snelling, the Mall of America, and the airport, with a commuter line (the Northstar) that travels north to Big Lake, mostly for commuters; more service has been proposed but hasn't been built. For maximum flexibility, a car is recommended, unless you're staying in the downtown area and can walk or take a brief taxi ride to other downtown destinations.

WHEN TO COME The warmer months of spring, summer, and fall are always popular in the Twin Cities, but even the colder months can be an attractive time to visit. If staying in a downtown hotel, visitors may have access to the city's extensive system of skyways, allowing people to travel across the heart of the city without setting foot outdoors. And while the temperatures may be cold, the city's theater season, nightclub scene, and basketball/football seasons are going strong. But for those who like winter, outdoor events and sports are in full bloom January through March, including cross-country and downhill skiing, ice skating, snowshoeing, and ice fishing.

MEDICAL EMERGENCY Call 911.

In the downtown area, the closest hospital is **Hennepin County Medical Center** (612-873-3000; www.hcmc.org), 701 Park Avenue. Elsewhere in Minneapolis are the following hospitals: **University of Minnesota Medical Center–Fairview,** located at the University of Minnesota (612-273-3000; www.uofmmedicalcenter.org), at either 2312 Sixth Street S. or 500 Harvard Street; **Abbott Northwestern** (612-863-4000; www.abbottnorth western.com), 800 E. 28th Street; and **Children's Hospital,** located next to Abbott Northwestern (612-813-6000; www.childrensmn.org), 2525 Chicago Avenue S.

✳ To See and Do

MUSEUMS 𝄞 ♿ ✳ **Minneapolis Institute of the Arts** (612-870-3100 or 1-800-642-2787; www.artsmia.org), 244 Third Avenue S. Open Tues. through Sat. 10–5 (Thurs. until 9) and Sun. 11–5. General admission is free, but special traveling exhibits may require paid tickets, varying in price. The Art Institute, Minneapolis's so-called traditional museum, has seen significant growth over the past decade, with funding and donations reaching record levels and culminating with the 2006 grand opening of a new addition to the venerable neoclassical building. Exhibits are varied and lively, including an impressionist gallery, an extensive collection of American photography, a gallery showcasing local artists, a display of Frank Lloyd Wright architectural pieces, and a wide array of ancient Asian and African artifacts. The institute has proven itself willing to take risks with its visiting exhibitions, which in recent years have included such

MINNEAPOLIS INSTITUTE OF THE ARTS

diverse offerings as an Egyptian exhibit; a Villa America exhibit, featuring such contemporary American artists as Georgia O'Keeffe, Grant Wood, and Arthur Dove; an exhibit featuring completed and in-progress works from the St. John's Bible Project; and an exhibit of treasures from the Louvre. The institute offers a variety of programs, including Family Sundays, docent-led tours, lecture series, and the annual Art in Bloom fundraiser. The institute has a D'Amico & Sons Café for lunch and an extensive gift shop with a wide variety of art-related gifts. Parking is free in the attached parking ramp, but only if you get there early—there are few spots, and competition is fierce from the Children's Theatre and the Minneapolis College of Art and Design, which are all part of the institute complex. Street parking is available with meters. Bring quarters.

✄ ♿ ⓨ ❊ **Walker Art Center** (612-375-7600; www.walkerart.org), 1750 Hennepin Avenue. Open Tues. through Sun. 11–5 (Thurs. and Fri. until 9). Adults $10, seniors 65 and older $8, students/teens with student IDs $6. Free for Walker Center members, children under 12, for visitors with a same-day event ticket, and on Thurs. nights after 5 and the first Sat. of each month. As the Art Institute is known as the traditional museum, the Walker is solely focused on contemporary artwork in a wider variety of mediums: painting, sculpture, video, performance art, and Internet art. The Walker offers special events tailored for families, gays, singles, and film buffs; traveling exhibitions include the famed Diane Arbus retrospective, an examination of Picasso and his influences, an exhibit curated by John Waters, and a rare Frida Kahlo exhibit. Diners have a choice between two restaurants by the D'Amico family, one casual (Garden Cafe) and one more formal (Gather). The Minneapolis Sculpture Garden (see *Green Space* and Outdoor Activities) is free. Parking is available in a ramp beneath the museum or a pay lot across the street. Some street parking is available, but it can be difficult to get.

✄ ♿ ❊ **Frederick R. Weisman Art Museum** (612-625-9494; www.weis man.umn.edu), 333 E. River Road (on the East Bank of the University of Minnesota). Open Tues. through Fri. 10–5 (Thurs. until 9) and Sat. and Sun. 11–5. Admission is free. Looming over Washington Avenue on the University of Minnesota's East Bank is a large modern structure designed by Frank Gehry. A building both loved and hated, the Weisman Art Museum is visually hard to miss, and inside is a collection of 20th- and 21st-century art masters, including Georgia O'Keeffe and Alfred Maurer, as well as a large collection of Korean furniture and international ceramics. An expansion project completed in late 2011 added five new galleries to showcase even more of the Weisman's permanent collection as well as collaborations with local artists and art students. While the Weisman doesn't have a restaurant on-site, there are several small but good restaurants in the nearby Stadium Village (walking distance). The museum offers a parking ramp for a fee; free parking is pretty much nonexistent on this end of the university.

&. ❄ **The Museum of Russian Art** (612-821-9045; www.tmora.org), 5500 Stevens Avenue S. Open Mon. through Fri. 10–5, Sat. 10–4, and Sun. 1–5. Adults $7, with voluntary donations asked of adults older than 60. Located in a small building reminiscent of Spanish architecture in south Minneapolis, the Museum of Russian Art is the only permanent museum of Russian art and artifacts in North America. The building itself is worth a visit; originally a church, it eventually was used as a funeral home before providing its current occupant with an unexpectedly perfect venue for Russian art. Galleries range in size from small, low rooms in the basement to a two-story chapel-esque gallery on the main floor. Be sure to visit the gift shop on the second floor, behind the main gallery; it's full of Russian treasures, including a fine collection of hand-painted lacquered boxes.

✂ &. ❄ **The American Swedish Institute** (612-871-4907; www.american swedishinst.org), 2600 Park Avenue S. Open Tues. through Sat. noon–4 (Wed. until 8) and Sun. 1–5; Sat. 10–5, Nov. and Dec. Adults $6, seniors 62 and older $5, children 6–18 $4, children under 6 free. Free admission is offered the first Wed. of every month. Housed in the opulent Turnblad mansion (which is on the National Register of Historic Places), the institute houses an extensive collection of artwork and craft pieces from Swe-

THE AMERICAN SWEDISH INSTITUTE

den, as well as a permanent exhibition examining the relationship between Sweden and Swedish immigrants to Minnesota. This may sound subdued, but make no mistake, the institute is entirely child friendly. The first Sat. of every month, a special story hour is held in the story attic, a third-floor space where new and classic Swedish tales are told. Folk-song fests, mid-summer celebrations, a packed holiday season, and quarterly Swedish smorgasbords are just a few of the events on the museum's busy calendar.

✍ ♿ ✳ **The Bell Museum of Natural History** (612-624-7083; www.bell museum.org), 10 Church Street SE (on the East Bank of the University of Minnesota). Open Tues. through Fri. 9–5, Sat. 10–5, and Sun. noon–5. Adults $5; seniors 62 and older, non–University of Minnesota students, and children 3–16 $3; children under 3 free. Admission is free for museum members; University of Minnesota staff, faculty, and students; and for all on Sun. The Bell Museum is located at the University of Minnesota–Minneapolis campus, an apt location as it's both a working scientific facil_ ity and a center of nature in the heart of the city. The diorama halls introduce the natural world of Minnesota, while other galleries delve into nature and wildlife from around the world. The Touch & See room is ideal for kids, or anyone just curious as to what a live snake or the skull of a long-dead mammal looks and feels like. Once a month, the museum hosts an artist's sketch night, inviting people to bring their art materials in to draw selected items from the museum's collection.

✍ ♿ ✳ **The Mill City Museum** (612-341-7555; www.millcitymuseum .org), 704 S. Second Street. Open Tues. through Sat. 10–5 and Sun. noon–5. Holiday hours may apply. Adults $10, senior citizens and college students $8, children 6–17 $5, children 5 and under free. Admission is free for Minnesota Historical Society members. Mill City, built along the Mississippi River in downtown Minneapolis, gives visitors a vivid glimpse of Minneapolis's role in the history of grain production and milling. The museum has several interactive exhibits; groups that book ahead can participate in a baking session in the kitchen. A partially demolished remnant of the original mill exists and can be explored, or enjoyed as the venue for occasional outdoor concerts sponsored by the museum.

✍ ♿ ✳ **The Bakken Museum** (612-926-3878; www.thebakken.org), 3537 Zenith Avenue S. Open Tues. through Sat. 10–5 (Thurs. until 8). Adults $7, senior citizens and students $5, children 4 and under free. Admission is free for Bakken Museum members. The Bakken is a family-friendly museum that offers kids a chance to do some hands-on experiments involving electricity and magnetism. Not as dry as it sounds, the Bakken keeps things lively, although their science research is scholarly and impressive. The surroundings are worth a visit, too; the museum is in a Tudor mansion near Lake Calhoun.

✳ **The Carl W. Kroening Interpretive Center** (763-694-7693), 4900 Mississippi Court. Open Mon. through Sat. 9–5 and Sun. noon–5. Admission is free. This center is a small but informative resource on anything you ever wanted to know about the heritage of the proud Mississippi. Call ahead to find out which organized programs are being offered; events vary seasonally.

✳ Green Space and Outdoor Activities

BICYCLING Minneapolis isn't called the City of Lakes for nothing, and one of the best aspects of the city's chain of lakes is the 50-mile bike trail that connects the **Four Lakes Loop** (Lake Harriet, Lake Calhoun, Lake of the Isles, and Lake Nokomis). Well maintained and clearly marked, the trails around the lakes offer vistas of the best the city has to offer: blue waters, wildlife, houses of the rich and famous, and excellent people watching. Trails are available in other parts of the city as well, including along the Mississippi River, a route that takes riders into Minnehaha Park. **Calhoun Cycle,** located near the lake of the same name, rents bikes and in-line skates.

Nice Ride MN (1-877-551-6423; www.niceridemn.org), 2834 10th Avenue S. A feature new to the City of Lakes in 2010 was the installation of 65 Nice Ride locations. Nice Ride is a bike rental system, where riders can rent a bike (during the nonsnow months) for anywhere from an hour to days. Bikes can be returned to the location where they were originally rented or to any Nice Ride location. The first year saw high demand and interest in Nice Ride, and plans are in progress to nearly double the number of locations and add several hundred more bikes.

BOATING Those who would rather be on the lake than biking by it can bring their own water craft or stop by Lake Calhoun's boat rental station to rent canoes, kayaks, or paddleboats. Motorboats are not allowed. Depending on weather, rentals are available seasonally 11–7 daily. Sailboats and windsurfers are also allowed on the chain of lakes, and the **Lake Calhoun Sailing School** offers classes for adults and children (612-927-8552; www.lakecalhoun.org).

PARKS AND OUTDOOR SPACES Minneapolis might be known as the City of Lakes, but it could also be known as the City of Green Spaces. Nearly every community and neighborhood has some kind of park, with facilities varying from playground equipment to basketball courts to tennis courts to swimming pools. For full details about the range of park offerings in the city, check with the **Minneapolis Park & Recreation Board** (www.minneapolisparks.org) for full details. What follows is a selected list of outdoor spaces to enjoy.

Minneapolis Sculpture Garden (612-370-4929; http://garden.walker art.org/), 726 Vineland Place. The garden is open daily 6–midnight; the Cowles Conservatory is open Tues. through Sat. 10–8 and Sun. 10–5. Admission is free. The sculpture garden is a joint exhibit created and managed by the Minneapolis Park & Recreation Board and the Walker Art Center. There are 11 beautifully manicured acres, with both an indoor and outdoor floral garden and more than 40 sculptures, including the iconic *Spoonbridge and Cherry* fountain. Although most of the exhibits are permanent, some temporary sculptures have also appeared, including a mini golf course in which each hole was designed by a different contemporary artist. Parking is easiest in an adjoining pay lot. Some free or metered street parking is available, but it goes quickly.

Loring Park (612-370-4929; www.minneapolisparks.org), 1382 Willow Street. Across Hennepin Avenue from the Minneapolis Sculpture Garden, Loring Park is an oasis in the city. The small but charming park offers a community pool, a basketball court, and a boat dock for the small lake at its heart. Bike and walking trails through the park are connected to trails leading to other parts of the city. Annual festivals, such as the Pride Festival (see *Special Events*) and the Loring Park Art Festival, are held here each year. And if you're hungry after enjoying nature, Café Lurcat (see *Where to Eat*) and Joe's Garage are right across the street.

Minnehaha Park (612-230-6400; www.minneapolisparks.org), 4801 Minnehaha Avenue S. Perhaps one of the most beautiful spaces in Minneapolis, Minnehaha (which means "laughing waters") is a 193-acre park that encompasses Minnehaha Falls, limestone bluffs, and views of the river. A small rail museum pays homage to the park's history as a railway station, two historical homes are open for visitors, and Longfellow Gardens and Pergola Garden showcase both formal gardens and wildflower displays. Hiking trails wind through the park, including near the waterfall. Picnic tables and a bandstand combine for relaxed weekend outings. Wheel Fun Rentals (www.wheelfunrentals.com) rents bicycles, and Sea Salt Eatery (see *Where to Eat*), open Apr. through Oct., serves fresh seafood, wine, and beer for your dining pleasure.

Lake Harriet (612-230-6475; www.minneapolisparks.org), 43rd Street W. and E. Lake Harriet Parkway. Located near the charming Linden Hills neighborhood, Lake Harriet has a public beach, a boat launch (it's a popular sailboating lake), a beautiful rose garden, and a bandshell that features live music during the summer. New to the park is Bread and Pickle (www .breadandpickle.com), a walk-up eatery. The walking and biking trails around the lake give you the chance to enjoy the view, both of the lake and of the historic mansions that surround it.

Lake Calhoun (3000 Calhoun Parkway) and **Lake of the Isles** (2500 Lake Isles Parkway). These neighboring lakes give you the best of both lake worlds; Calhoun is another boater's favorite, not to mention sunbathers and people watchers. Tin Fish (see *Where to Eat*) gives you a quick and tasty meal before you strap on your blades and go for a ride. When you cross over to Lake of the Isles, you'll find a quieter, more scenic lake, with elegant historic homes lining the way. For more information, get in touch with Minneapolis Park & Recreation Board (612-230-6400; www.minneapolisparks.org).

Theodore Wirth Parkway (612-230-6400), 1339 Theodore Wirth Parkway. Theodore Wirth, at 759 acres, is the largest regional park in the Minneapolis park system. It's technically in adjacent Golden Valley, but Minneapolis is proud to claim this park, which has something for everyone: a lake, fishing pond, sledding hill, golf, hiking/biking trails, tennis courts, soccer fields, prairie, forest, children's garden, bird sanctuary, and a winding parkway to explore it all.

✴ Lodging

HOTELS

Downtown

 & ♈ ❄ (((•))) **The Nicollet Island Inn** (612-331-1800; www.nicollet islandinn.com), 95 Merriam Street. Visitors looking for historic charm and ambience will be most successful at this small (24 rooms) but upscale hotel on Nicollet Island. Built in 1893, this limestone building with its timber-and-beam interior was originally a door manufacturer, then a men's shelter run by the Salvation Army, before the Minneapolis Park & Recreation Board bought it and turned it into an inn. All rooms have views of the Mississippi River and the Minneapolis skyline. Rooms include plasma TVs, plush robes, and 400-thread-count Egyptian cotton bedding. The inn has its own highly regarded dining room, but many other Minneapolis dining and entertainment spots are within walking distance or a few minutes'

drive. Rates start at $139, with the higher rates on corner rooms, which are larger and have more views; the Deluxe Corner Room has a four-poster bed. Packages and specials available.

 & ♈ ❄ (((•))) **The Grand Hotel** (612-288-8888 or 1-866-843-4726; www .grandhotelminneapolis.com), 615 Second Avenue S. Housed in the former Minneapolis Athletic Club is a hotel that matches its predecessor in quiet elegance. This boutique hotel, represented by Preferred Hotels, has 140 rooms, many of which offer four-poster beds and marble soaking tubs in the bath. Ideally located for visitors staying downtown, the Grand Hotel also offers a 58,000-square-foot athletic area (a well-preserved remnant from its days as an upscale athletic club) and the Zahtar restaurant. Rates start at

$145, with some specials and packages offered.

  Y ❄ ((ρ)) **Graves 601** (612-677-1100 or 1-866-523-1100; www.graves601hotel.com), 601 First Avenue N. This high-fashion, high-tech hotel with tasteful, comfortable rooms and suites is by far the best thing to come to the Block E entertainment complex, with its stylish and spacious public spaces and the well-regarded Cosmos restaurant (see *Where to Eat*). For a price, visitors can book the Skybox Suite, a luxury penthouse overlooking the Minnesota Twins' Target Field. Room rates start at $224, with special packages available.

🐾 & Y ❄ ((ρ)) **Le Meridien Chambers Hotel** (612-767-6900 or 1-800-543-4300; www.chambersminneapolis.com), 901 Hennepin Avenue. This is a hotel with its own brand of trendy charm. Billing itself as a "fine art hotel," Chambers is housed in a restored building near the Orpheum and State theaters. The hotel offers only 60 rooms and suites, but they are designed for luxury and comfort. An extensive collection of art pieces runs through the hotel, including the guest rooms; paintings, sculptures, and even video art are available for viewing 24 hours a day. Chambers is also the home of the D'Amico Kitchen (see *Where to Eat*), a restaurant run by the D'Amico organization. Rates start at $139. Packages are available.

🐾 & Y ❄ ((ρ)) **W Minneapolis at the Foshay** (612-215-3700; www.starwoodhotels.com), 821 Marquette Avenue. Located within the historic Foshay Tower is this luxury hotel, which plays off its art deco beginnings and cheekily names its room categories things like Wonderful, Fantastic, and Spectacular (with the highest level reserved for the Extreme WOW Suite). Try dinner at the popular Manny's steakhouse (see the "Steakhouses" sidebar), and follow that with a trip to the Prohibition Bar. Spa services can be arranged. Surprisingly, pets are welcome. Rates start at $239, with packages and weekend discounts offered.

🐾 & Y ❄ ((ρ)) **The Radisson Plaza** (612-339-4900; www.radisson.com), 35 S. Seventh Street. The Radisson is attached to Macy's in the heart of downtown and across the street from the Marriott. Small but comfortable rooms, each furnished with a Sleep Number bed, and a well-regarded restaurant (the FireLake Grill; see *Where to Eat*), make this a good choice both for businesspeople and tourists in for a weekend of major league sports or theater and shopping. Rates start at $209, with weekend discounts and packages available.

🐾 & Y ❄ ((ρ)) **Marriott Minneapolis City Center** (612-349-4000; www.marriott.com), 30 S. Seventh Street. The Marriott was recently renovated and has, besides its standard hotel rooms, bi-level suites and a private concierge level. The hotel also has the Northern Shores Grille, which serves standard American fare, but for guests with more adventurous tastes, a trip into City Center itself to Fogo de Chao (see *Where to Eat*) would be recommended. Rates start at $199, with packages and weekend discounts offered.

✤ 🐾 ♿ ⅄ ❄ (((ŋ))) **The Westin Minneapolis Hotel** (612-333-4006; www.starwoodhotels.com), 88 S. Sixth Street. The Westin should be a case study in how to renovate a historic building. The company took Farmers & Mechanics Bank Building and created a luxury hotel with a highly touted bar and restaurant (appropriately named BANK; see *Where to Eat*), but they kept the bank's vintage accoutrements while providing guest rooms with ergonomic work chairs and iPods. Rates start at $259, with packages and weekend discounts offered.

♿ ⅄ ❄ (((ŋ))) **The Hyatt** (612-370-1234; www.hyatt.com), 1300 Nicollet Mall. On Nicollet Avenue, where downtown Minneapolis begins to segue into neighborhoods, resides this active conference hotel. The Hyatt is close enough to walk to several downtown attractions. But with one of the city's most popular restaurants (Oceanaire Seafood Room; see *Where to Eat*) on-site, you may not need to go far. Rates start at $199, with packages and weekend discounts offered.

♿ ⅄ ❄ (((ŋ))) **The Millennium Hotel** (612-332-6000; www.millennium hotels.com), 1313 Nicollet Mall. Across the street from the Hyatt, the Millennium is a comfortable hotel that caters to the business crowd and is connected by skyway through to the convention center. Rates start at $169, with packages and weekend discounts offered.

🐾 ♿ ⅄ ❄ (((ŋ))) **The Hilton Minneapolis** (612-376-1000; www .hilton.com), 1001 Marquette Avenue. The Hilton is in a prime location for convention visitors, as it's connected by skyway to the convention center. The Hilton offers standard hotel rooms and suites, and a set of executive rooms, which feature upscale furnishings and amenities. The hotel restaurant, Skywater, is open three meals a day, but for variety's sake, many options are within blocks of the hotel. Rates start at $209, with packages and weekend discounts offered.

Near the River
✤ 🐾 ♿ ⅄ ❄ (((ŋ))) **The Depot Minneapolis** (www.thedepot minneapolis.com), 225 S. Third Avenue. There are two lodging options at the old Milwaukee Road railway depot that's been converted into an entertainment complex, complete with a 15,000-square-foot indoor water park and a seasonal ice rink. The first, the **Depot Renaissance** (612-375-1700 or 1-866-211-4611), while still historic in nature, is geared more toward businesspeople, with

smaller rooms and extensive technological amenities. The deluxe historic suites section of the Renaissance lives up to its name with generous suites decorated in early-20th-century style, with large windows overlooking the city. Rates begin at $219, with packages and weekend discounts offered. The second, the **Residence Inn** (612-340-1300 or 1-800-331-3131) is an extended-stay format, with each unit containing a full kitchen. Rates begin at $219, with packages and weekend discounts offered.

♪ ♥ ⚹ ☿ ❄ ((ŋ)) **Aloft: A W Hotel** (612-455-8400 or 1-877-462-5638; www.starwoodhotels.com), 900 Washington Avenue S. Cheerful rooms and suites with high ceilings and high-tech amenities combined with family-friendly kids' accommodations and a willingness to accept pets makes this a good choice for family travelers who like a touch of contemporary upscale. No sit-down dining available on-site, but there are restaurants within walking or short cab distance. Rates start from $119; packages and weekend discounts available.

University of Minnesota— East Bank

⚹ ☿ ❄ ((ŋ)) **The Radisson University** (612-379-8888; www.radisson.com), 615 Washington Avenue SE. This hotel is an attractive option on the East Bank of the university, close to restaurants and easy walking distance to Northrop

Auditorium and the Weisman Museum. The only restaurant on-site is an Applebee's, but the hotel's Stadium Village location puts it in easy walking distance to several cafés and restaurants. Rates start at $103.

♥ ⚹ **The Days Inn University of Minnesota** (612-623-3999; www.daysinn.com), 2407 University Avenue SE. The Days Inn is on the edge of the East Bank but still within walking distance to many university locations. Rates start at $63, with packages and weekend discounts offered.

❄ Where to Eat

The Minneapolis restaurant scene continues to expand, both in quality and in types of foods offered. Visitors who think of Minnesota as the land of white food—Swedish meatballs, mashed potatoes, lutefisk, and lefse—will be in for a tasty surprise. Some of the upper-end restaurants have gained national attention (La Belle Vie, Restaurant Alma, 112 Eatery) and several James Beard Award nominations (with La Belle Vie's Tim McKee and 112 Eatery's Alex Roberts taking home awards), while numerous small ethnic cafés have begun to change the city's culinary landscape to reflect the growing ethnic diversity. A caveat: The restaurant industry is always a volatile one, and the Twin Cities are not immune to the rapid turnover that can occur. Use the contact info to check the current status before arrival.

DINING OUT Minneapolis has gone from being a culinary backwater to a foodie destination. But one thing that might surprise visitors to the area is the general casual approach to dining out. For better or for worse, Minnesota diners tend to be more on the informal side when it comes to dressing up for dinner. That's not to say that you won't see suits and ties, but it's not uncommon to see people in business casual—or even completely informal—at some of the leading restaurants.

Downtown

&. Y ※ **Café Lurcat** (612-486-5500; www.cafelurcat.com), 1624 Harmon Place. Open daily for dinner at 5. Café Lurcat overlooks Loring Park and delights patrons with an inventive and tasty à la carte menu. Chef Adam King is well known for his miso-marinated Chilean sea bass, and the warm sugar-cinnamon doughnuts are a perfect touch for dessert. The adjoining Bar Lurcat offers live music as well as an extensive wine list, including 40 wines served by the glass. Summer brings the opening of the patio. Expensive.

&. Y ※ **Masa** (612-338-6272; www.masa-restaurant.com), 1070 Nicollet Mall. Open Mon. through Fri. 11:30–2:30 for lunch, Mon. through Sat. at 5 for dinner. While the authentic Hispanic food scene has thankfully grown in the Twin Cities, providing numerous small outlets for great food, Masa is one of the few upscale, "night out"

restaurants serving authentic Mexican. Expensive.

&. Y ※ **BANK** (612-656-3255; www.bankmpls.com), 88 S. Sixth Street. Open daily for all three meals. Located at the Westin Minneapolis Hotel (see *Lodging*) in the old Farmers & Merchant's Bank, BANK's developers wisely took the banking theme and ran with it, creating an unusual but lovely tribute to the olden days of banking. The food plays up the opulent setting. Very expensive.

&. Y ※ **Cosmos** (612-312-1168; www.cosmosrestaurant.com), 601 First Avenue S., in the Graves 601 Hotel (see *Lodging*). Open daily for all three meals. Quite possibly one of the most beautiful restaurants in the Twin Cities, Cosmos offers world-class cuisine that rises above standard hotel-restaurant food, a stellar wine list, and desserts by the master, pastry chef Khan Tranh. Expensive.

&. Y ※ **D'Amico Kitchen** (612-767-6960; www.damico-kitchen.com), 901 Hennepin Avenue. Open daily for all three meals. This buzz-worthy restaurant is run by the D'Amico empire, located in one of the area's best hotels, Chambers (see *Lodging*). This is upscale Italian with creative twists, such as lobster gnocchi and pizza with butternut squash, guanciale, pear, and blue cheese. The wine list is extensive, with a wide variance of prices. Expensive.

&. Y ※ **Sanctuary** (612-339-5058; www.sanctuaryminneapolis.com), 903 Washington Avenue S. Open

Mon. through Sat. for dinner. This quiet gem, an easy walk to the Guthrie Theater, has at its helm Chef Patrick, who has a creative way with seasonal ingredients. Depending on what's in season, you might enjoy strawberry margarita soup; grilled kebab of tomato, sweet onion, and lamb; or a macaroni and chipotle goat cheese gratin. A small but beautifully appointed patio is perfect for warm evenings. Expensive.

✇ ✆ ⛾ ❊ **FireLake Grill** (612-216-3473; www.firelakerestaurant.com), 31 S. Sixth Street, in the Radisson Plaza Hotel (see *Lodging*). Open daily for all three meals. The restaurant has won considerable acclaim for its attention to local produce, cheese, and meat producers, and artisanal-quality fare. A seasonal menu offers the chef the ability to tailor dishes to what's in season, such as locally fished walleye during the summer, prepared over a real fire and seasoned to perfection. Expensive.

✆ ⛾ ❊ **Oceanaire Seafood Room** (612-333-2277; www.theoceanaire.com), 1300 Nicollet Mall (in the Hyatt Hotel—see *Lodging*—but at press time had announced plans to move; check before visiting). Open daily at 5 for dinner. This eatery fast became a local favorite both for its vintage interior harking back to the 1940s and its extensive fresh seafood menu. Very expensive.

✇ ✆ ⛾ ❊ **Crave** (612-332-1133; www.craveamerica.com), 825 Hennepin Avenue. Open Mon. through Sat. for lunch, daily for dinner. Located across the street from the Orpheum and down the street from the State Theatre, Crave has rapidly become a popular Twin Cities dining spot. Its casual American fare is well executed, and it's a good choice for those looking for convenient pretheater dining. It has additional locations, including in Edina (see the "Minneapolis's Neighboring Communities" chapter). Expensive.

✆ ⛾ ❊ **Vincent: A Restaurant** (612-630-1189; www.vincentrestaurant.com), 1100 Nicollet Mall. Open Mon. through Fri. for lunch, Mon. through Sat. for dinner. Closed Sun. The eponymous restaurant of Vincent Francoual was a success from the moment it opened. Vincent has earned national acclaim for its southern French food, served at lower-than-expected prices, as well as its casually elegant interior. Stop by for the happy hour, or bring a group in for the tasting menu. Expensive.

✇ ✆ ⛾ ❊ **La Belle Vie** (612-874-6440; www.labellevie.us), 510 Groveland Avenue. Open daily at 5 for dinner. Located near Loring Park and the Walker Art Center, La Belle Vie has at its helm chef and proprietor Tim McKee, widely considered one of the best chefs in the state, and his commitment to high quality and using local ingredients has made him a local darling. The style is French Mediterranean, and diners might seasonally see items like quail sautéed with ramps, asparagus, and dill, or sautéed sea scallops with morcilla, chorizo, radish, and potato. Tasting menus are available. Very expensive.

&. Ÿ ❄ **Sea Change** (612-225-6499; http://seachangempls.com), 818 S. Second Street. Open Tues. through Sun. for lunch, daily for dinner. This is the place for dining at the Guthrie Theater (see *Entertainment*), not just because it's located in the same building, but because both its culinary offerings and dramatic interior satisfy all senses. Tim McKee of La Belle Vie designed the thoughtful, seafood-based menu that empha-

sizes sustainability as much as it does flavor. The raw bar is open for dinner, or you can sample sardine on toast or tuna spaghetti and meatballs. Expensive.

Northeast
&. Ÿ **Rosa Mexicano** (612-656-7144; www.rosamexicano.com), 609 Hennepin Avenue. Open daily for lunch and dinner. The latest arrival in downtown dining is the New York City darling of Mexican food. The vividly colorful interior is both chic and playful, and the menu is sophisticated and authentic (and has a number of gluten-free and vegetarian items). Service is friendly and professional, and

---

STEAKHOUSES

Minnesotans love their fish and seafood, and vegetarians and vegans are finding an ever-growing selection of dining options, but there are still many Minnesotans who wouldn't dream of turning their back on a prime piece of beef. Downtown Minneapolis is home to several outstanding steakhouses, which all seem to coexist peacefully; apparently there are plenty of steak lovers to keep them busy.

&. Ÿ ❄ **Murray's** (612-339-0909; www.murraysrestaurant.com), 24 S. Sixth Street. Open Mon. through Fri. for lunch, daily for dinner. This is the original Minneapolis steakhouse, famous for its "silver butter knife" tender steaks. Its reputation as a hometown favorite, as well as its tremendous steaks, keep it a serious contender. Groups of two or three can order strip sirloin to be carved tableside. Diners willing to arrive early can take advantage of early dinner specials, and Twins fans can get their burgers and beer on before games. Very expensive.

&. Ÿ ❄ **Ruth's Chris** (612-672-9000; www.ruthschris.com), 920 Second Avenue S. Open daily for dinner. This is one of the more economical offerings in the often-expensive steakhouse category, but the restaurant doesn't spare quality for price. Very expensive.

the bar has a number of intriguing cocktails, including a mezcal martini. Expensive.

✄ & ⅄ ❋ **Red Stag Supperclub** (612-767-7766; www.redstag supperclub.com), 509 First Avenue NE. Open daily for lunch and dinner, Sat. and Sun. for breakfast. Red Stag made a name for itself by being the first LEED-CI certified restaurant to open in Minnesota, but it's the food that made it a success. Chef Jason Blair gave the menu a contemporary supper club feel, using local and organic ingredients to create twists on supper club standards, such as the popular smelt fries and grilled pork belly. Expensive.

& ⅄ ❋ **Masu Sushi & Robata** (612-332-6278; www.masusushi androbata.com), 330 E. Hennepin Avenue. Open Mon. through Fri. for lunch, daily for dinner. Another Tim McKee success story, Masu brought a new generation of Japanese dining to the Twin Cities with not only top-notch sushi, but with ramen dishes that have no resemblance to the little grocery-store packets, and robata, the ancient Japanese technique of charcoal cooking. Expensive.

& ⅄ ❋ **Restaurant Alma** (612-379-4909; www.restaurantalma .com), 528 University Avenue SE. Open daily for dinner. Local, seasonal, organic—that's been

& ⅄ ❋ **Manny's** (612-339-9900; www.mannyssteakhouse.com), 821 Marquette Avenue (in the W Minneapolis at the Foshay; see *Lodging*). Open daily for all three meals. Manny's reinvigorated itself with a move into the heart of downtown, in the historic Foshay Tower. This is the steakhouse that provides a predinner show in the form of a meat cart and well-trained servers. Very expensive.

& ⅄ ❋ **Capital Grille** (612-692-9000; www.thecapitalgrille.com), 801 Hennepin Avenue. Open Mon. through Fri. for lunch, daily for dinner. This is where local people of prominence go for steaks, as well as to store their personal wine selections in the cellar. Very expensive.

✄ & ⅄ ❋ **Fogo de Chao** (612-338-1344; www.fogodechao.com), 645 Hennepin Avenue. Open Mon. through Friday 11–2 for lunch; Mon. through Fri. at 5 for dinner, Sat. at 4:30, Sun. at 4. This is a carnivore's fantasy swathed in Brazilian traditions. Rather than ordering from a menu, diners are served by gauchos who sidle through the restaurant, cutting meat to order off sizzling skewers. Sides are served family style, and all of this is presented as a fixed-price option. The sumptuously decorated interior, lined with murals of Brazilian ranch life, dark woods, and endless bottles of wine, inspires a true feeling of decadence. Very expensive.

Restaurant Alma's mantra since opening, and consequently the menu changes frequently, but always to great acclaim. Expensive.

♿ ₧ ✺ **Erte** (612-623-4211; www .ertedining.com), 323 13th Avenue NE. Open Mon. through Sat. for dinner. This gorgeous restaurant and adjacent Peacock Lounge serves contemporary supper club food (think steaks and seafood), lushly prepared in generous portions. Expensive.

♿ ₧ ✺ **Nye's Polonaise Room** (612-379-2021; www.nyespolonaise .com), 112 E. Hennepin Avenue. Open daily for dinner. Restaurants come and go, but Nye's is forever. A Polish supper club with hearty portions and a well-stocked bar, Nye's also has a popular piano bar. Expensive.

North Loop
In the Warehouse District, a number of small restaurants and bistros have built niches as destination dining for fine-cuisine aficionados.

♿ ₧ ✺ **112 Eatery** (612-343-7696; www.112eatery.com), 112 N. Third Street. Open daily for dinner. 112 Eatery's chef and owner, Isaac Becker, was the 2011 winner of the James Beard Best Chef–Midwest Award. He's been dazzling diners since opening this restaurant in 2005. It's small (only 48 seats), so reserve ahead and be willing to be flexible with your dining time. You'll be rewarded with choices of entrées like tagli-

atelle with foie gras meatballs; a bacon, egg, and harissa sandwich; or braised pork belly with shell peas. Expensive.

♿ ₧ ✺ **Bar La Grassa** (612-333-3837; www.barlagrassa.com), 800 N. Washington Avenue. Open daily for dinner. Isaac Becker may have won the James Beard Award for his work with 112 Eatery, but he's equally admired for his work at this nearby restaurant. Bar La Grassa has an extensive and innovative Italian menu, with choices like soft eggs and lobster bruschetta, pachheri with milk-braised chicken, and farfalle with braised tripe and sweetbreads. Some dishes are made with dry pastas, others with fresh; the pasta dishes are all available in half portions. Expensive.

♿ ₧ ✺ **Origami** (612-333-8430; www.origamirestaurant.com), 30 N. First Street; also in Minnetonka. Open Mon. through Fri. for lunch, daily for dinner. Origami's location in a historic, narrow stone building in the Warehouse District gives it a perpetual cool factor, but it's the extraordinary sushi and other Japanese entrées, as well as a well-stocked bar, that keep people coming back. All the sushi is made to order, which means it's tremendously fresh, but it also means service can be slow when the restaurant is busy. It's worth the wait, as long as you're prepared. Expensive.

♿ ₧ ✺ **Sapor** (612-375-1971; www.facebook.com/saporcafe), 428 Washington Avenue N. Open

Mon. through Fri. for lunch, Mon. through Sat. for dinner. Sapor has a quiet, comfortably upscale feel, and the chefs provide some truly inspired melding of cuisines (crêpe with caramelized catfish, anyone?). Expensive.

  ♿ ♀ ❋ **HauteDish** (612-338-8484; www.haute-dish.com), 119 Washington Avenue N. Open daily for dinner. Chef Landon Schoenfeld made quite a splash when he opened this upscale, yet tongue-in-cheek restaurant next door to Sex World. The name plays on the Minnesota staple "hot dish," and the menu plays with it, too, serving up unexpected variations on basic comfort foods. The mac 'n' cheese here comes with lobster and truffle; the Tater Tot Haute Dish features short ribs in a porcini béchamel. HauteDish earned raves from the moment it opened and continues stretching the boundaries. Very expensive.

South

♿ ♀ ❋ **Heidi's** (612-354-3512; http://heidismpls.com), 2903 Lyndale Avenue S. Open Tues. through Sun. for dinner. Stewart Woodman and wife Heidi have made quite a splash with this restaurant, creating unique versions of old standbys (an eggless eggs Benedict, for example). Expensive.

♿ ♀ ❋ **Chino Latino** (612-824-7878; www.chinolatino.com), 2916 S. Hennepin Avenue. Open daily for dinner. Chino Latino pulls off a melding of Asian and Hispanic cuisine while maintaining its cutting-edge social reputation. Expect crowds and a noisy atmosphere, but also expect to have an exciting culinary experience. Expensive.

♿ ♀ ❋ **Lucia's** (612-825-1572; www.lucias.com), 1432 W. 31st Street. Open Tues. through Sun. for lunch and dinner. A small, intimate bistro quietly tucked away from the bustle of the Lake-Hennepin intersection, Lucia's is a romantic eatery directed by the inestimable Lucia Watson, a local culinary legend. Menu changes daily; local foods are used whenever possible. Expensive.

✐ ♿ ♀ ❋ **Fuji-Ya** (612-871-4055; www.fujiyasushi.com), 600 W. Lake Street (with another location in St. Paul). Open daily for dinner. Fuji-Ya made a welcome transition from its previous smaller quarters on Lyndale Avenue to larger facilities on W. Lake Street. Part of the expansion was in adding Japanese tearooms (reservations are a must), in which diners can enjoy their dinner quietly in a small, enclosed room, sitting on the floor in the traditional Japanese way. But tearoom or no tearoom, Fuji-Ya serves some of the best Japanese food in the state. Their sushi is top quality, freshly made to order, and beautifully presented. But beyond sushi, Fuji-Ya also shines, with a wide variety of Japanese salads, noodle bowls, bulgogi, and meat and seafood entrées. Possibly because so much care is taken with preparation, service is slow;

OUTDOOR EATING

Whether it's because Minnesota is a state rich in the bounty of the natural world or because the winter months make everyone long to be outside, Minnesotans are very fond of eating outdoors. The good news is
that many restaurants have options for doing just that; the bad news is
often the outdoor venues are as dismal as seating on a sidewalk adjacent to a busy road with heavy bus traffic or overlooking vast asphalt
parking lots. Here's a quick list of places where excellent food—and
excellent outdoor views—have come together perfectly.

& Y ❄ **Solera** (612-338-0062; www.solera-restaurant.com), 900 Hennepin Avenue. Open daily for dinner. Solera serves a huge variety of
tapas, and in the summer, their rooftop patio is the perfect place to
enjoy tasty morsels while enjoying views of the city. For those prefer-
ring a more traditional dinner, regular plated entrées are offered, too.
Expensive.

✐ & Y ❄ **Brit's Pub** (612-332-3908; www.britspub.com), 1110 Nicollet
Mall. Open daily for lunch and dinner. A casual British pub with exemplary British dishes (fish-and-chips, ploughman's lunch), Brit's also has
a rooftop bowling green surrounded by tables and umbrellas. The bowling green isn't just for looks—there are leagues that play throughout
the summer. It's a bit of British refinement above the city. Moderate.

✐ & Y ❄ **It's Greek to Me** (612-825-9922; www.itsgreektomemn.com),
626 W. Lake Street. Open Tues. through Fri. for dinner, Tues. through
Sun. for lunch and dinner. A long-term fixture at the corner of Lake and
Lyndale, It's Greek to Me has food that's tasty and reasonably priced,
and a lovely, secluded private patio. Moderate.

✐ & Y ❄ **The Black Forest** (612-872-0812; www.blackforestinnmpls
.com), One E. 26th Street. Open daily for all three meals. This neighborhood standby, serving up great German food since 1965, has an unexpectedly charming garden hidden behind the main restaurant.
Moderate.

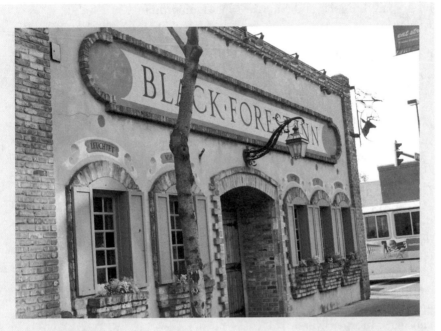

THE BLACK FOREST

🗝 ♿ 🍸 ❄ **Psycho Suzi's Motor Lounge and Tiki Garden** (612-788-9069; www.psychosuzis.com), 1900 Marshall Street NE. Open daily for lunch and dinner. Psycho Suzi's moved to a new location in 2011 and never forgot the popularity of its previous location's patio. The new restaurant boasts an even larger, even more tiki-themed outdoor space that's just perfect for an exotic drink. Moderate.

🗝 ♿ **Tin Fish** (612-823-5840; www.thetinfish.net), 3000 Calhoun Parkway E. Open daily for lunch and dinner, May through mid-Oct., weather permitting. It's hard to beat the scenery of Tin Fish, located right on the shores of one of the city's most popular lakes, Lake Calhoun. Moderate.

🗝 ♿ 🍸 **Sea Salt Eatery** (612-721-8990; www.seasalteatery.com), 4801 Minnehaha Avenue S. Open daily for lunch and dinner, Apr. through Oct. This one gives Tin Fish a run for its scenic money, placed as it is in the lovely Minnehaha Park overlooking Minnehaha Falls. Try a po'boy sandwich, large enough for two, but go early—the lines start forming before it opens on sunny days. Moderate.

be prepared to relax and enjoy. Expensive.

EATING OUT There are almost countless options for more casual, less expensive quality dining throughout Minneapolis. What follows should be viewed as great suggestions rather than a fully comprehensive list.

Dinkytown

⌀ & ❄ **Al's Breakfast** (612-331-9991), 413 14th Avenue SE. Open daily for breakfast. A miniscule venue with just 14 seats, Al's nearly always has a wait, but the fare is worth it. However, service can be less than friendly. Don't miss the pancakes. Inexpensive.

⌀ & ⛾ ❄ **Loring Pasta Bar** (612-378-4849; www.loringpastabar .com), 327 14th Avenue S. Open daily for lunch and dinner. Tucked into the Dinkytown/University of Minnesota area, the Loring serves global food in a sumptuous interior. Sun. nights feature a live tango band. Moderate. U of M students get a 30 percent discount with valid student ID.

⌀ ❄ **Annie's Parlour** (612-379-0744), 313 14th Avenue SE. Open daily for lunch and dinner. This friendly café has been a Dinkytown/University of Minnesota fixture for decades, and for good reason; the burgers and fries are close to perfect, but save room for the hot fudge sundaes— the hot fudge is so delicious, you won't need the ice cream. Inexpensive.

Downtown

⌀ & ⛾ ❄ **Hell's Kitchen** (612-332-4700; www.hellskitcheninc .com), 89 S. 10th Street. Open daily for all three meals. Hell's Kitchen is a Gothic haunt in downtown Minneapolis. The signature "damn good" breakfast foods can't be beat, and weekend servers might show up for work in their PJs. Live music is frequently offered in the spacious bar. If you can only go once, go for breakfast and try the lemon-ricotta hotcakes or the huevos rancheros; in either case, get a side of toasted sausage bread with house-made peanut butter. Moderate.

& ⛾ ❄ **Barrio Tequila Bar** (612-333-9953; www.barriotequila .com), 925 Nicollet Avenue (with locations in St. Paul and Edina). Open daily for lunch and dinner. An enormous tequila list (and well-versed servers who can explain the different kinds) is well matched to its small plates menu of reasonably priced tacos and enchiladas. Moderate.

⌀ & ⛾ ❄ **Pizza Lucé** (612-333-7359, 119 N. Fourth Street; 612-827-5978, 3200 Lyndale Avenue S.; 612-332-2525, 2200 Franklin Avenue E.; with other locations in Hopkins, St. Paul, and Duluth; www.pizzaluce.com). Open daily for lunch and dinner. From lunch to late night, Pizza Lucé serves some of the best pizza the Twin Cities offers, along with substantive hoagies and pastas. Whether you prefer traditional pizzas or feel adventurous, Pizza Lucé has something for you. This is also a good spot for vegans, with several non-animal-product offerings. Inexpensive.

Northeast

♦ ᇈ ᛎ ✳ **The Sample Room** (612-789-0333; www.the-sample -room.com), 2124 NE Marshall Street. Open daily for lunch and dinner. A casual noshing spot located in a historic building in the Northeast area. The eclectic menu includes one of the best meat loaf dinners ever. Inexpensive.

♦ ᇈ ᛎ ✳ **Gorkha Palace** (612-886-3451; www.gorkhapalace .com), 23 Fourth Street NE. Open Mon. through Sat. for lunch, daily for dinner. Nepali, Indian, and Tibetan foods, cooked with no MSG and full of lively combinations. Don't miss the momos, a Nepali version of a pot sticker. Inexpensive.

♦ ᇈ ✳ **Kramarczuk Sausage Company** (612-379-3018; www .kramarczuk.com), 215 E. Hennepin Avenue. Open daily for lunch and dinner. This cafeteria-style restaurant specializes in eastern European foods, often made with the adjoining food store's top-notch sausages and meats. Inexpensive.

♦ ᇈ ✳ **Brasa Rotisserie** (612-379-3030; www.brasa.us), 600 E. Hennepin Avenue (with another location in St. Paul). Open daily for lunch and dinner. Meat eaters can't go wrong here with the succulent, Caribbean-flavored rotisserie offerings. But vegetarians will find plenty to eat from the hearty sides, including yams, yucca, and plantains. Moderate.

♦ ᛎ ✳ **The Anchor Fish and Chips** (612-676-1300; www.the anchorfishandchips.com), 302 13th Avenue NE. Open daily for dinner, Sat. and Sun. for lunch. Fish-and-chips, perfectly done, are the draw here, but other pub items—curry or gravy chips, pasties, shepherd's pie—are also well worth trying. This popular restaurant usually involves a wait to be seated. Moderate.

♦ ᇈ ᛎ ✳ **The Bulldog NE** (612-378-2855; www.thebulldognorth east.com), 401 E. Hennepin Avenue. Open daily for lunch and dinner. A bar and grill that rises above the category with killer burgers and hot dogs. Moderate.

♦ ᇈ ᛎ ✳ **Gardens of Salonica** (612-378-0611; www.gardensof salonica.com), 19 Fifth Street NE. Open Tues. through Sat. for lunch and dinner. Traditional Greek food, with standard favorites like gyros and more unusual offerings like bougatsa. Moderate.

North Loop

♦ ᇈ ᛎ ✳ **Be'Wiched Deli** (612-338-2108; http://bewicheddeli .com), 800 Washington Avenue N. Open daily for lunch, Sat. and Sun. for brunch. The folks at Be'Wiched take their sandwiches seriously, and it shows. House-cured meats, including a succulent pastrami, and inventive ingredient lists make this the go-to place for a sandwich that's completely different than what's served by any other sandwich place in town. Inexpensive.

ETHNIC FOOD

Going deeper into Northeast, away from downtown, you'll come across a strip of ethnic restaurants that draw visitors from all over the metro, for good reason.

✍ & ❊ **Holy Land Deli** (612-781-2627; www.holylandbrand.com), 2513 Central Avenue NE (with another outlet at the Midtown Global Market). Open daily for all three meals. Half restaurant, half grocery store, and wholly worth the drive, Holy Land Deli doesn't look like much from the outside, but drop by for the hearty and flavorful lunch and dinner buffets (or order à la carte), then pop into the grocery side for Middle Eastern staples not found elsewhere. Inexpensive.

✍ & ❊ **Sen Yai Sen Lek** (612-781-3046; www.senyai-senlek.com), 2422 Central Avenue NE. Open Mon. through Sat. for lunch and dinner. The restaurant's name means "big noodle, little noodle," which is apt:

SEN YAI SEN LEK

✍ & ♈ ❊ **Black Sheep Coal-Fired Pizza** (612-342-2625; www.blacksheeppizza.com), 600 Washington Avenue N. (with another location in St. Paul). Open daily. If Be'Wiched is the grown-up palate's spot for sandwiches, then just down the street is that palate's

On the menu are Thai noodles and sticky rice dishes, flavorful and authentic, served at reasonable prices. There are plenty of vegetarian options. Moderate.

✆ ♿ ❋ **El Taco Riendo** (612-781-3000), 2416 Central Avenue NE. Open Mon. through Sat. for lunch and dinner. An extensive and inexpensively priced menu will please diners who want their Mexican food to be authentic as well as those who prefer it Americanized. Portions are enormous. Inexpensive.

EL TACO RIENDO

✆ ♈ ❋ **Chimborazo** (612-788-1328; www.chimborazorestaurant.com), 2851 Central Avenue NE. Open daily for lunch and dinner. Ecuadorean foods, served in hearty portions, from a menu created by the Ecuadorean owner. Inexpensive.

✆ ♿ ❋ **Marrakech Café & Grill** (612-788-0405), 1839 Central Avenue NE. Open Mon. through Sat. for lunch and dinner. Tagines are the star here, and the kebabs are worth trying, too. Inexpensive.

choice for pizza. Black Sheep's delightful coal-fired pizzas come with creative topping choices, such as fennel sausage, hot salami, onion, and cracked green olive. Moderate.

South

🍴 ♿ 🍸 **Pizza Lucé** (612-827-5978; www.pizzaluce.com), 3200 Lyndale Avenue S. Open daily for lunch and dinner. See the listing in *Downtown* for details.

🍴 ♿ 🍸 ❄ **Pizzeria Lola** (612-424-8338; www.pizzerialola.com), 5557 Xerxes Avenue S. Open Tues. through Sun. for lunch and dinner. Quirky, delicious pizzas, including a Korean pizza with house-made kimchi and the Sunnyside—served with soft eggs. Moderate.

🍴 ♿ 🍸 ❄ **Tilia** (612-354-2806; www.tiliampls.com), 2726 W. 43rd Street. Open daily for lunch and dinner, Sat. and Sun. for breakfast. This little neighborhood spot in the Linden Hills area opened to long lines and great acclaim. Its sophisticated menu with thoughtful preparation goes hand in hand with a kids' menu that allows for family meals without choosing the lowest common denominator. Moderate.

🍴 ♿ 🍸 ❄ **Broder's Pasta Bar and Deli** (612-925-9202; www.broders.com), 5000 Penn Avenue S. Open daily for dinner. Broder's is a reasonably priced neighborhood pasta bistro with far-above-average offerings. Each pasta dish is cooked to order with freshly made pasta and imaginative sauces. Across the street is Broder's Deli, open for lunch and take-out daily. Stop by for some lunch to take to Lake Harriet for a perfect afternoon picnic. Moderate.

🍴 ♿ ❄ **Café Zumbro** (612-920-3606; www.thezumbro.com) 2803 W. 43rd Street. Open Tues. through Sun. for breakfast and lunch. This small café in the Linden Hills neighborhood near Lake Harriet is something of a local tradition. The specialty is breakfast (the huevos and eggs Benedict are both popular), and a limited breakfast menu is available over the lunch hour as well, but you'd miss out on the gourmet sandwiches, soups, and salads. Moderate.

🍴 ♿ 🍸 ❄ **El Meson** (612-822-8062; www.elmesonbistro.net), 3450 Lyndale Avenue S. Open Mon. through Sat. for lunch and dinner, Sun. for dinner. El Meson bills itself as a Spanish-Caribbean bistro, and this longtime neighborhood favorite knows what it's doing. Allow extra time for the paella; it's worth the wait. If you're in a hurry for lunch, check out their buffet, full of vegetable- and meat-based Caribbean dishes of varying spiciness. On Sat., a flamenco dancer performs. Moderate.

🍴 ♿ ❄ **The Egg and I** (612-872-7282; www.eggandimn.com), 2828 Lyndale Avenue S. (with another location in St. Paul). Open daily for breakfast and lunch. The Egg and I knows a thing or two about breakfasts. Their pancakes are huge and fluffy; their egg dishes are perfectly cooked in generous portions. Lunch is served, but breakfast is what you'll want. Inexpensive.

MIDTOWN GLOBAL MARKET

🌿 ♿ 🍷 ❋ **Midtown Global Market** (www.midtownglobalmarket.org), Lake Street and Chicago Avenue. Open daily for all three meals (restaurants open for meals vary). The Midtown Global Market represents a major effort on the part of the city to not only revitalize a faltering neighborhood and restore a long-vacant Sears tower, but also to pay tribute to the ever-growing ethnic and culinary diversity in the area. Most of the food outlets here are quick-service, but they have surprisingly good quality and reasonable prices. This is an excellent place to wander on a weekend afternoon, trying different cuisines while taking in the live music or dancing in the central plaza. Places to try include **Holy Land Deli, A La Salsa, Jakeeno's Trattoria,** and **Manny's Tortas,** all of which have restaurants in other parts of the Twin Cities; also worthy of a stop are **La Loma Tamales, Safari Express, Taqueria Los Ocampo,** and **Andy's Garage.** Whatever you choose, finish it off with dessert from the **Salty Tart.**

HOLY LAND DELI

EAT STREET

None of these restaurants clustered together over several blocks on Nicollet Avenue just outside of downtown are formal. But they do make up a broad ethnic swath, mostly at reasonable prices and of excellent quality. You could spend days exploring the world in just a few blocks.

✏ ♿ ❄ **Bad Waitress** (612-872-7575; www.thebadwaitress.com), 2 E. 26th Street. Open daily for all three meals. The name might seem like a warning, but actually it's a tease: Diners fill out their own order sheets at their tables and turn them in to the cashier to get their choice of delectable pancakes and sandwiches. Inexpensive.

✏ ♿ ❄ **Peninsula Malaysian Cuisine** (612-871-8282; www.peninsula malaysiancuisine.com), 2608 Nicollet Avenue. Open daily for lunch and dinner. Offers a broad and fascinating overview of Malaysian food. Prices are surprisingly low, given the range of food options. Moderate.

✏ ♿ ❖ ❄ **Christos** (612-871-2111; www.christos.com), 2632 Nicollet Ave S. (with other locations in St. Paul and Minnetonka). Open daily for lunch and dinner. Serves a solid Greek menu, from the traditional gyros and hummus to lamb, chicken, and pork dishes as well as a lengthy vegetarian menu. Moderate.

✏ ♿ ❄ **Quang** (612-870-4739; www.quangrestaurant.com), 2719 Nicollet Avenue S. Open Wed. through Mon. for lunch and dinner. Provides jumbo

EAT STREET

PENINSULA MALAYSIAN CUISINE

Vietnamese noodle bowls, delicious and inexpensive, although the service is not always friendly. Fri. is a popular day, as it's the only day the sea bass soup is offered. Inexpensive.

🍴 ♿ ♈ ❄ **Rainbow Chinese** (612-870-7084; www.rainbowrestaurant.com), 2739 Nicollet Avenue. Open daily for lunch and dinner. The prices are quite reasonable for top-notch food at this casual but nice Chinese restaurant, a longtime Eat Street staple. Inexpensive.

🍴 ♿ ❄ **Pho 79** (612-871-4602), 2529 Nicollet Avenue (with another location in St. Paul). Open daily for lunch and dinner. Serves heaping bowls of Vietnamese pho, perfectly seasoned. Wear easy-wash clothing, as slurping your soup can get messy, but it's worth it. Inexpensive.

🍴 ♿ ♈ ❄ **Salsa a la Salsa** (612-813-1970; www.salsaalasalsa.com), 1420 Nicollet Avenue (with another location at Midtown Global Market). Open daily for lunch and dinner. Salsa a la Salsa has a menu encompassing both authentic and Americanized Mexican food. While some restaurants interpret *spicy* as slightly more than mild, Salsa a la Salsa takes the word seriously, especially in the Chicken Chiltepin. Be sure to have one of their homemade margaritas. Moderate.

✳ **Entertainment**

LIVE PERFORMANCES

Minneapolis is a theater- and music-lover's town. From large, internationally renowned companies like the Guthrie Theater and the Children's Theatre Company, arena rock at the Target Center, and the theaters that host Broadway tours to smaller inventive and experimental groups like the Jungle Theater and the intimate jazz space of the Dakota Jazz Club, there's something for every taste.

✵ � ♈ ✳ **The Guthrie Theater** (612-377-2224 or 1-877-447-8243; www.guthrietheater.org), 818 S. Second Street. This internationally renowned theater company completed an ambitious move in 2006 when it left its original location adjacent to the Walker Art Center (see *To See and Do*) for the growing arts and restaurant area near the Mississippi River. Besides developing three separate stage areas, the Guthrie also included what is considered to be some of the city's top-end dining with Sea Change (see *Where to Eat*). The Wurtele Thrust Stage hosts large-scale productions, such as classics and musicals, while the McGuire Proscenium Stage hosts more contemporary works, as well as productions from touring companies. The Dowling Studio acts as a training ground for University of Minnesota and Guthrie Theater acting students. Even if you don't want to see a particular play, a visit to the building itself is worth the time; the dramatic Endless Bridge, a cantilevered lobby with spectacular views of the Mississippi River falls, is a perfect place to start, followed by a stop at one of the building's restaurants or bars. Most of the public spaces are open to the public every day except Mon., even when no play is in production.

✵ ♿ ✳ **The Children's Theatre Company** (612-874-0400; www.childrenstheatre.org), 2400 Third Avenue S. The CTC has an international reputation for its outstanding and innovative productions. The theater itself is adjacent to the Minneapolis Institute of the Arts (see *To See and Do*). Appropriately family friendly, the stage area has comfortable stadium seating with extra spacing between rows—helpful when transporting young children to the bathrooms during productions with minimal discomfort to other theatergoers. Snacks and coffee are sold in the lobby during intermission and after the show. Each season includes a variety of productions geared toward different age groups. Some of the classics that appear periodically include *The 500 Hats of Bartholomew Cubbins* (which leaves both kids and adults wondering, "How did they do that?"), *How the Grinch Stole Christmas*, and *A Year With Frog and Toad*. Free parking is available in a ramp next to the theater, but arrive early; the spaces are limited, and on busy museum days, the competition for those spots is heavy. Street park-

THE CHILDREN'S THEATRE COMPANY

ing (metered on weekdays) is also available.

🛈 ♿ ❋ **The Cowles Center for Dance** (612-206-3600; http://the cowlescenter.org), 528 Hennepin Avenue. The newest performing arts venue in town is the realization of a decades-long effort to rehabilitate two run-down historic buildings in downtown Minneapolis and join them with a third building as an education center. The Cowles opened in the fall of 2011 and is home to the Minnesota Dance Theater and the Hennepin Center for the Arts. Besides showcasing the works of those groups, the Cowles Center also hosts touring dance troupes and other performing arts groups.

🛈 ♿ ♈ ❋ **The Hennepin Theatre District** (612-339-7007; www.hennepintheatredistrict.org). The district is made up of a series renovated theaters in downtown Minneapolis: the State, the Orpheum, Hennepin Stages, and the Pantages, all located between Seventh and 10th streets on Hennepin Avenue. The Orpheum and the State are Minneapolis's home base for Broadway touring productions as well as headlining music, magic, and comedy acts. Hennepin Stages presents smaller-scale musical productions and concerts. Pantages is home to an intimate concert venue for touring musicians.

♿ ❋ **The Jungle Theater** (612-822-7063; www.jungletheater

.com), 2951 Lyndale Avenue S. A small (150 seats) theater focused on intimate productions, mainly of a contemporary nature, and occasional musical performances.

Northrop Auditorium

(612-624-2345; http://northrop.umn.edu), 84 Church Street SE. Situated at the top of Northrop Mall on the University of Minnesota's East Bank, Northrop's stately architecture gives access to a wide variety of performances: musicians of nearly every genre, comedians, and the annual Northrop Dance Series, which features a diverse selection of touring and local dance troupes. Note: At press time, Northrop was closed for renovation and scheduled to reopen in 2013.

Target Center (612-673-0900; www.targetcenter.com), 600 First Avenue N. Home to the Minnesota Timberwolves (see *Sporting Events*) as well as many touring musical acts. There are two large parking ramps connected by skyway, and Target Center also offers a "parent's room" for adults who bring their offspring to concerts that the parent doesn't necessarily want to attend. Some of the music industry's most popular performers stop here, but it's not because of the great acoustics; St. Paul's xCel Centre is a much better musical setting. But when that certain band comes to town, Target Center may be where they end up playing, even if the acoustics aren't ideal.

Brave New Workshop

(612-332-6620; www.bravenewworkshop.com), 2605 Hennepin Avenue S. The long-standing home of improvisational and sketch comedy on Hennepin Avenue near Uptown. The company develops and produces original shows made up of several short pieces built around one theme, usually societal or political. Weekend shows often have improv after the official performances. Beer, wine, and snacks available for purchase at the theater.

Fine Line Music Café

(612-338-8100; www.finelinemusic.com), 318 First Avenue N. Located in the Consortium Building, a historic site in the Warehouse District, the Fine Line quickly established itself as a first-rate music club, showcasing both local and national performers. This is not so much a dance club as an actual music club; Lady Gaga, the Pixies, the Cowboy Junkies, the Avett Brothers, and the Neville Brothers have all performed here. Acoustics are great, and the ambience is calmer than at nearby First Avenue (listing follows).

Dakota Jazz Club & Restaurant (612-332-1010; www.dakotacooks.com), 1010 Nicollet Avenue. Located right in the heart of downtown Minneapolis. Truly a jazz and blues lover's haven, the Dakota has a packed schedule of musicians in its intimate performance space, and it offers excellent food as well.

♿ Y ❇ **First Avenue** (612-332-1775; www.first-avenue.com), 701 First Avenue N. The granddaddy of rock venues. Still operating at its original location, the nationally acclaimed First Avenue continues to serve the rock and alternative scene with both major players and up-and-coming musicians, including a wide range of local groups. This bar is truly about the music—the environment does not lend itself well to comfort, and the smell of stale beer permeates the air (replacing the cigarette odors that dominated until the city banned smoking in all indoor public places). If ambience is what you want, this isn't the place. But for a true rock music experience, it can't be beat.

♿ ❇ **The Varsity Theater** (612-604-0222; www.varsitytheater.org), 1308 Fourth Street SE. Located in the University of Minnesota's Dinkytown neighborhood, the Varsity is rapidly becoming another popular destination for local and smaller touring bands. Although heavily frequented by U of MN students, the Varsity is by no means college only; the theater has been lauded for its sound and light systems and for its comfortable interior, as well as its willingness to book a wide variety of acts.

♿ Y ❇ **The Nomad World Pub** (612-338-6424; www.nomadpub.com), 501 Cedar Avenue. If you'd like to experience the Twin Cities jazz scene at its finest—and most diverse—check out the Nomad, which features established jazz

performers early in the evening, up-and-comers later at night.

♿ Y ❇ **The Cedar Cultural Center** (612-338-2674; www.thecedar.org), 416 Cedar Avenue S. The Cedar has had a lasting impact on the Twin Cities live-music scene, presenting musicians from all over the world.

♿ Y ❇ **El Nuevo Rodeo** (612-728-0101; www.elnuevorodeo.com), 3003 27th Avenue S. An example of the growing Hispanic influence on the Twin Cities, restaurant and nightclub El Nuevo Rodeo provides live music and a lively Mexican menu.

SPORTING EVENTS

✎ ♿ **Target Field** (612-659-3400), 1 Twins Way. In 2010, the Minnesota Twins baseball team moved out of the Metrodome (listing follows) and into their brand-new outdoor stadium, a beauty on the north edge of downtown and within easy reach of light rail and buses. Target Field is not only an attractive venue, it's popular—plan ahead to get tickets for specific games. Once inside, you'll be well fed; several local food purveyors were tapped to come up with better-than-average stadium-food offerings.

✎ ♿ Y ❇ **Target Center** (612-673-1600; www.targetcenter.com), 600 First Avenue N. Home to the Minnesota Timberwolves men's basketball team and the Minnesota Lynx women's basketball team. The Wolves and Lynx both have loyal fan bases; call ahead for tickets. Target Center also hosts touring sports exhibitions, such as figure skating and the timeless Harlem Globetrotters.

✐ ♿ ﻌ ✳ **The Metrodome** (612-332-0386; www.msfc.com), 900 S. Fifth Street. The Metrodome is—for now—the home of the Minnesota Vikings football team. The Twins recently built a new stadium outside of Minneapolis, and the Vikings are considering doing the same. But for the time being, their regular seasons are played at the Metrodome.

✐ ♿ ✳ **The Minnesota Gophers** (www.gophersports.com). The official sports teams of the University of Minnesota are spread out across several athletic facilities, including the Metrodome and the university-sited Mariucci Arena, Williams Arena, and the new TCF Bank Stadium.

OTHER ENTERTAINMENT
✐ ♿ ﻌ **Elsie's** (612-378-9701; www.elsies.com), 729 Marshall Street NE. If bowling is what you want, venture northeast to this neighborhood favorite for a bite to eat and some rounds of glow-in-the-dark bowling.

♿ ﻌ ✳ **Bryant-Lake Bowl** (612-825-3737; www.bryantlakebowl .com), 810 W. Lake Street. As its name implies, Bryant-Lake Bowl offers bowling, but it also doubles as a live theater venue.

✳ **Selective Shopping**

Downtown
The downtown area of Minneapolis is home to many large chain stores like **Neiman Marcus,** the **Saks Fifth Avenue outlet store, Barnes & Noble,** and **Target** (which has its corporate headquarters downtown as well). The city's extensive network of second-floor skyways that connect many of the buildings in the center of town (very handy for inclement weather) are home to numerous small retailers, usually gift shops or small clothing boutiques. To find more of the unique little shops, heading out of downtown is the best bet.

Northeast
✐ ✳ **I Like You!** (612-208-0249; www.ilikeyouonline.com), 501 First Avenue NE. Open daily. The tagline is "Small things for a prettier life," and the shop is full of them, from jewelry to gifts to small pieces of art. The store offers a wide variety of classes, from book binding to copper enameling to knitting and sewing simple projects.

✐ ✳ **Crafty Planet** (612-788-1180; www.craftyplanet.com), 2833 Johnson Street NE. Open daily. Sewing and yarn supplies, with a definite twist of the unexpected. This is not your mother's supply shop.

✳ **Spinario Design** (612-396-1860; www.spinariodesign.com), 1300 Second Street NE. Open Fri. through Sun., other days by appointment. All things midcentury modern.

❊ **Shuga Records** (612-455-6285; www.shugarecords.com), 165 13th Avenue NE. Open Tues. through Sun. Used vinyls, CDs, and music memorabilia.

❊ **Architectural Antiques** (612-332-8344; www.archantiques .com), 1330 Quincy Street NE. Open Mon. through Sat. Exactly what it says—antique fireplace surrounds and mantels, doors, entryways, and ecclesiastical artifacts.

❊ **Key North** (612-455-6666; www.keynorthusa.com), 515 First Avenue NE. Open daily. Women's

THE NORTHEAST MINNEAPOLIS ARTS DISTRICT

Arts are alive and well across the Twin Cities (and the rest of the state), but one area where they're really flourishing is in northeast Minneapolis, where a number of artist's studios have sprung up in historic buildings, many of which were built 100-plus years ago. Each of the following has multiple artists actively working. Hours of exhibit depend on the artist; see the websites or call for specific open information.

The Northrup King Building (612-363-5612; www.northrupkingbuilding .com), 1500 Jackson Street NE. This large complex originally belonged to the Northrup King seed company and is home to nearly 200 artists as well as several nonprofits and entrepreneurs. Artists set their own hours; see the website for info.

The California Building (www.californiabuilding.com), 2205 California Street NE. Housed in a former grain mill, the California is home to up to 80 artists and offers monthly open studios and other events.

Casket Arts Building (www.casketarts.com), 681 17th Avenue NE. Former home of the Northwestern Casket Company, Casket Arts provides studios for 100 artists and offers several public events.

Van Buren Building (www.vanburenbuilding.com), 1400 Van Buren Street NE. Van Buren has a smaller number of artists coexisting with several companies, but the lovingly restored building itself is worth a visit.

Grain Belt Studios (no phone), 77 13th Avenue NE. It used to be the Grain Belt bottling house and warehouse; now it's home to 30 artists who exhibit periodically.

clothing and accessories, with an emphasis on fair trade, organic materials, and responsible manufacturing.

North Loop

Right on the edge of downtown are several interesting and sometimes-quirky independent retailers.

❊ **Lightworks** (612-724-8311; www.lightworkslighting.com), 404 Washington Avenue N. Open Mon. through Sat. Even if you don't think you're in the market for lighting, give this place a visit—it's a huge collection of restored vintage and historically accurate redesigned lighting.

❊ **Mitrebox Framing Studio** (612-676-0696; www.mitrebox framing.com), 213 Washington Avenue N. Open Tues. through Sat. Ostensibly a framing shop, Mitrebox is much more than that, with all kinds of quirky gifts, one-of-a-kind pieces of costume jewelry, and cards.

❊ **Indigo** (612-333-2151; www .indigompls.com), 530 N. Third Street. Open Tues. through Sat. A treasure trove of Asian and Native arts.

INDEPENDENT BOOKSTORES

Barnes & Noble has several locations across the Twin Cities metro area, but there is a group of sturdy independent stores that are holding steady in the competitive retail book field.

✐ ❊ **Magers & Quinn** (612-822-4611; www.magersandquinn.com), 3038 Hennepin Avenue S. Open daily. One of the premier independents in the Twin Cities, and also one of the largest, Magers & Quinn, located in the Uptown area, sells new and used books, including collectible items.

✐ ❊ **Birchbark Books** (612-374-4023; www.birchbarkbooks.com), 2115 W. 21st Street. Open daily. A small, cozy, family-friendly bookstore owned by novelist Louise Erdrich. The store specializes in Native American items but also carries a good selection of fiction and has a children's area with a "tree house."

❊ **Uncle Edgar's Mystery** (612-824-9984; www.unclehugo.com) and **Uncle Hugo's Science Fiction** (612-824-6347; www.unclehugo.com), 2864 Chicago Avenue S. Open daily. Next door to each other down the road from Abbott Northwestern Hospital, Uncle Edgar's and Uncle

❊ **Circa Gallery** (612-332-2386; www.circagallery.org), 210 N. First Street. Open Tues. through Sat. Contemporary artworks, with a new exhibit opening nearly every six weeks.

❊ **Form + Content Gallery** (612-436-1151; www.formand content.org), 210 Second Street N. Open Thurs. through Sat. Eclectic contemporary art.

❊ **Antiques Riverwalk** (612-339-9352; www.antiquesriverwalk.net), 210 Third Avenue N. Open Tues. through Sun. A multidealer antiques shop.

❊ **Kilroys** (612-339-5848; www .kilroysusa.com), 219 N. Second Street, Suite B-100. Open Mon. through Sat. Antiques with a specialization in the kitschy items found in soda fountains, diners, juke joints, and gas stations.

South
✐ ❊ **Kitchen Window** (612-824-4417; www.kitchenwindow.com), 3001 Hennepin Avenue. Open daily. A longtime stalwart in Uptown's Calhoun Square, Kitchen Window has just about every possible kitchen gadget you

Hugo's have developed strong followings with their extensive selections of mystery and sci-fi books.

❊ **Once Upon a Crime** (612-870-3785; www.onceuponacrimebooks.com), 604 W. 26th Street. Open daily. All mysteries, all the time, and a knowledgeable staff earned this store a 2011 Raven Award from the Mystery Writers of America.

✐ ❊ **True Colors Bookstore** (612-821-9630; www.truecolorsbookstore.com), 4766 Chicago Avenue S. Open daily. True Colors specializes in women's and lesbian studies, and also has a sizeable children's area.

✐ ❊ **Dreamhaven Books** (612-823-6161; www.dreamhavenbooks.com), 2801 E. 38th Street. Open Tues. through Sat. A sci-fi/fantasy/comic book shop with a busy schedule of readings and author visits from prominent writers, and they also publish a line of books.

Wild Rumpus. See the "Linden Hills Shopping" sidebar.

✐ ❊ **Big Brain Comics** (612-338-4390), 1027 Washington Avenue S. Open daily. As its name implies, Big Brain specializes in comics of all sizes and genres for all ages.

need, and a full roster of classes and events to boot.

✄ ❋ **Patina** (612-872-0880; www.patinastores.com), 1009 W. Franklin Avenue (with another location at 5001 Bryant Avenue S.). Open daily. Loads of fun and quirky gifts, jewelry, and home accessories.

❋ **My Sister's Closet** (612-222-2819; www.mysistersclosetmn .com), 2741 Hennepin Avenue S. (with another location in St. Paul). Open daily. Contemporary and vintage consignment clothing.

❋ **The Smitten Kitten** (612-721-6088); 3010 Lyndale Avenue S. Open daily. Yes, it's a sex-toy shop, but its philosophy is that its wares are like any other life-enhancing products—not something to be ashamed of. Unlike other shops selling such items, this one isn't seedy, it's in a reasonably good neighborhood, and it's owned and run by women.

✄ ❋ **Electric Fetus** (612-870-9300; www.electricfetus.com), 2000 Fourth Avenue S. (with other locations in Duluth and St. Cloud). Open daily. This longtime

LINDEN HILLS SHOPPING

This small neighborhood in south Minneapolis, near Lake Harriet, has several fun shops all in one place. Some of these shops have additional locations, which are noted in the description.

✄ ❋ **Bibelot** (612-925-3175, 4315 Upton Avenue; 300 E. Hennepin Avenue, 612-379-9300; also in St. Paul; www.bibelotshops.com). Open daily. Featuring gifts and novelties, Bibelot is not just another tacky souvenir shop; it carries all kinds of guilty pleasures, from locally made jewelry to unique women's clothing to off-the-wall kitchen and bath items. Their greeting card selection is good for more than a few giggles, and there is a well-chosen line of toys for the kids.

✄ ❋ **Great Harvest Bread Co.** (612-929-2899; www.greatharvest.com), 4314 Upton Avenue (with other locations in St. Paul, Minnetonka, Burnsville, and Woodbury). Open daily. Healthy and delicious are combined to the best effects of both here. (Be sure to try the whole wheat chocolate chip cookies.)

✄ ❋ **Creative Kidstuff** (612-927-0653; www.creativekidstuff.com), 4313 Upton Avenue (with other locations in St. Paul, Edina, St. Louis Park, Wayzata, Woodbury, and Maple Grove). Open daily. A mecca for young

Minneapolis music retailer is much loved by locals, and it carries a wide variety of music on vinyl and CD, new and used. Check the store's website for frequent in-store performances.

✳ Special Events

April: ♿ **Minneapolis/St. Paul International Film Festival** (612-331-7563; www.mspfilmfest .org), various locations. More than 75 films, from local filmmakers and worldwide documentarians, are presented across several venues in late Apr. Several events and galas are also scheduled, and discussions with film directors are offered.

April to November:
✐ ♿ **Minneapolis Farmer's Markets** (612-333-1718; www.mplsfarmersmarket.com), 312 E. Lyndale Avenue N. Open daily 6–1, mid-Apr. to mid-Nov. While there are several offshoots (once-weekly offerings on Nicollet Mall and at the Mill City Museum), this is the granddaddy of the Minneapolis farmer's market scene. It can take some patience to get there—the signature red

children, the store, housed in three sections of an old office building, is chock-full of toys, educational and otherwise, and perhaps even better, is well staffed by knowledgeable and helpful clerks who aren't against the idea of kids trying out toys before buying them.

✳ **Coffee & Tea Ltd.** (612-920-6344; www.coffeeandtealtd.com), 2730 W. 43rd Street (with another location at the Mall of America in Bloomington). Open daily. Don't be deceived by its hole-in-the-wall size and ambience; this little shop has an excellent variety of coffee and tea products, and the staff is passionate on the topic.

✐ ✳ **Wild Rumpus** (612-920-5005; www.wildrumpusbooks.com), 2720 W. 43rd Street. Open daily. One of the best children's bookstores ever, it comes complete with its own pets, including a tail-less cat and a chicken; the front door has a small-fry door as well. Whatever you need to know, just ask; the staff seems to know everything worth knowing about children's literature.

✳ **Linden Hills Yarns** (612-929-1255; www.lindenhillsyarn.com), 2720 W. 43rd Street. Open Mon. through Sat. Down the street from Wild Rumpus (just past Café Twenty-Eight and Rice Paper) is this haven for yarn enthusiasts. The upscale hand-painted yarns are every knitter's and crocheter's dream, but be aware—service can vary depending on the mood of the proprietor.

shed roofs that are visible from the freeway don't necessarily mean it's easy to find. But a huge selection of local produce and crafts that vary throughout the season make it a worthwhile visit, if nothing else than to munch on samples for bread, nuts, cheese, and syrup, as well as seasonal fruits and vegetables.

May: ♿ 🍸 **Art-a-Whirl** (612-788-1679; www.nemaa.org). This annual event, which takes place the third weekend of May, serves to highlight the growing and active Northeast Minneapolis arts community. Local and national artists exhibit their work, while visitors get to see a rich variety of art while enjoying the artistic ambience of this corner of Northeast.

June: ♿ 🍸 **Pride Festival and Parade** (612-305-6900; www.tcpride.org). This is one of the nation's largest GLBT pride events, occurring every year in June. The raucous parade is a centerpiece of the festival, which also includes an art show, boat cruise, picnics, and Grand Marshall's Ball. An outdoor component of the festival is held at Loring Park, with booths and tents set up with informational, retail, and food vendors.

July: ♿ 🍸 **Basilica Block Party** (612-317-3511; www.basilicablockparty.org), Hennepin Avenue and 17th Street. Who says Minnesotans can't be tolerant? This annual event, a two-day rock concert sponsored in part by local radio station Cities 97, takes place on the grounds of the Basilica of St. Mary. Besides nationally prominent acts, the block party also features a fiercely competitive battle of the bands for local acts. As it takes place each year in early July, the weather is often ideal, but if not, its location on the edge of downtown is convenient to other venues if being outside becomes too much.

🖍 ♿ 🍸 **Aquatennial** (612-338-0634; www.aquatennial.com). Billed as the "best 10 days of summer," the Aquatennial is spread across various venues in Minneapolis. Events include sailing regattas, tennis tournaments, classic car shows, triathlons, sandcastle competitions, milk-carton boat races (yes—full-sized boats built out of milk cartons), historic exhibits, a block party, and a torchlight parade. Held annually for more than 65 years, the Aquatennial is a well-organized and fun batch of events.

August: 🖍 ♿ 🍸 **The Metris Uptown Art Fair** (612-823-4581; www.uptownartfair.com). The Twin Cities are home to several annual art fairs, but this is the biggest, busiest, and perhaps best located—within easy walking distance to Lake Calhoun. Taking place each year in Aug., the three-day juried art event allows 450 artists to take their highly coveted spot near the Uptown area. Besides artists of all sorts, food and beverage vendors also set up shop. This event attracts upward of 350,000 visitors each year, so parking can be a problem; either

BASILICA OF ST. MARY

plan to arrive early and park locally, or consult bus maps for routes
from downtown. In a nice twist,
recent years have seen the
Uptown Art Fair join forces with
two other local art fairs, the Powderhorn Park Art Fair and the
Loring Park Art Fair, and complimentary city bus service is available to transport visitors among
the three.

&. Ÿ **Minnesota Fringe Festival**
(612-872-1212; www.fringefestival
.org). A growing and popular
event, the Fringe Festival takes
place over roughly 11 days in early
Aug. During that time, more than
20 venues present 160-plus shows,
some live, some recorded, nearly
all an hour or less in length. Quality

and themes vary wildly, but enthu-
siasm is universal.

August through September:
✐ 🐾 &. Ÿ **Minnesota Renaissance Festival** (952-445-7361 or
1-800-966-8215; www.renaissance
fest.com), US 169 S., Shakopee.
Open weekends and Labor Day
9–7, mid-Aug. through Sept.
Adults $18.95, seniors $16.95,
children 6–12 $9.95, children
under 6 free. Discount tickets
available on the website. Dogs (on
leashes) and cats welcome at $10
per pet, per day, through the Pet
Gate (proof of immunizations
required). At this rowdy, sometimes bawdy re-creation of the
Renaissance era, live music, jugglers, comedians, craft demonstra-

tions and sales, and endless amounts of food (the turkey legs and sweet corn are not to be missed) are featured. Most weekends have a theme, such as Irish Heritage or Highland Fling. Note: A good time to go is the weekend before and the weekend of Labor Day, when crowds are less than normal due to the Minnesota State Fair (see the "Minnesota State Fair" sidebar in the "St. Paul" chapter).

October: ♂ & **Medtronic Twin Cities Marathon** (763-287-3888; www.mtcmarathon.org). Taking place the first weekend in Oct., the Twin Cities Marathon begins near the Metrodome in Minneapolis and finishes 26.2 miles later at the State Capitol in St. Paul. For those not willing to go the distance, the event also offers a 10-mile, 5K run/walk, and family events including a Diaper Dash and a Toddler Trot. Note: All events require preregistration; see the website for details. Some of the events end up in a lottery situation, so register early.

November to December: ♂ & **Holidazzle** (www.holidazzle.com). A cherished holiday event, the Holidazzle Parade takes place several nights a week from Thanksgiving to Christmas Eve. Fairy-tale characters come to life, dressed in extravagantly lit (with real lights) costumes. Plan ahead if you'd like to eat downtown—Holidazzle brings in hundreds of viewers who want dinner before or after the parade.

MINNEAPOLIS'S NEIGHBORING COMMUNITIES

T here are several tiers of communities surrounding Minneapolis. The dreaded *s* word—*suburb*—technically defines them, but many started out as small towns in their own right before the sprawl of the city reached out and made them part of the metro area. Nevertheless, many of these communities have attractions, dining, and shopping that make them worth stepping out of the Minneapolis city limits.

EDINA

Edina is in an older suburb, but it's lost none of its cachet as a well-heeled destination with upscale shops and some far-better-than-average suburban dining spots.

✄ ᵫ ❄ **Southdale** (952-925-7874; www.simon.com), 66th Street and France Avenue. Open daily. Edina is the city that gave the rest of the United States enclosed shopping malls. Southdale, which opened in 1956, was the first to offer the indoor shopping mall experience, and as decades have passed, the mall has renovated and remodeled in order to keep up with changing tastes and clientele. It's still a bustling, busy mall, anchored by primary tenants Macy's and JCPenney department stores and AMC Theatres. A robust mix of smaller stores includes the Apple Store, Gap, Ann Taylor, Abercrombie & Fitch, and Aeropostale. Food options include a few fast-food outlets in the food court, or sit-down dining at P.F. Chang's, California Pizza Kitchen, or the Cheesecake Factory. While parking is ample on all sides of the mall, this is a very popular shopping destination—plan ahead and arrive early to avoid parking in the outfield.

✄ ᵫ ❄ **The Galleria** (952-925-4321; www.galleriaedina.com), 69th Street and France Avenue. Open daily. Right across the street from Southdale is this smaller, more upscale shopping center. The Galleria offers more boutiques than large-scale stores. While the center is anchored by Barnes &

Noble and Gabberts Design Studio and Fine Furnishings, other shops include brand boutiques Cole Haan, Coach, Bang & Olufsen, Brighton Collectibles, and L'Occitane. Other shops include local kids' toy store Creative Kidstuff; clothiers Blue Willi's, Epitome, Len Druskin, and Fawbush's; and home accessories stores Crate and Barrel, Pottery Barn, and Ampersand. There is no food court, but there are five restaurants to visit, all popular and busy at main meal times: the Good Earth, serving healthy, hearty meals; Big Bowl, a fast-paced Asian restaurant with a "pick your own" stir-fry bar; Pittsburgh Blue, a steakhouse; People's Organic Coffee and Wine Café, a casual eatery; and Crave, an American cuisine restaurant with a sushi bar.

✐ ♿ ❄ **50th and France** (952-922-1524; www.50thandfrance.com), 50th Street and France Avenue. Open daily. A small neighborhood collection of upscale shops and restaurants, this is not an enclosed shopping mall, but it's in a small enough area to make it easy to walk. Women's clothing stores include Hot Mama, Monique Lhuillier, and Bluebird Boutique; gourmet kitchen items can be found at Cooks of Crocus Hill and Sur La Table. Hand-painted tiles and plates can be found at Gather. In the midst of the retail is the Landmark Edina Cinema, which has four screens showing a mix of popular and art-house movies.

50th and France is not short of places to eat, and a variety of cuisines are represented. Rice Paper has tasty Asian fusion food, while Cocina del Barrio offers new takes on Mexican food (and a considerable tequila menu). Salut Bar Americaine offers a friendly and occasionally cheeky casual French ambience ("Le Basic Burger," anyone?). Beaujo's is a wine bar with a limited but thoughtful menu of salads, small plates, and entrées. The Edina Grill bills itself as an urban diner, and that's exactly what you

DOWNTOWN EXCELSIOR

THE EDINA CINEMA, 50TH AND FRANCE

can expect, but with a larger selection (beer-battered green beans, eggplant Parmesan) and better quality than you might expect. The casual Italian restaurant Arezzo Ristorante can seem pricey, but the food redeems the cost. If you're looking for a "quick but quality" option, check out D'Amico & Sons, which is the casual quick food outlet of the D'Amico group (see *Where to Eat* in "Minneapolis"). Finally, don't pass up the chance to enjoy some locally made ice cream at the Edina Creamery.

Complimentary parking ramps are available on each side of 50th, but watch the signs—some parking areas are reserved for local grocer Lunds Foods. Also pay attention to the maximum parking times allowed on the lower levels of the ramps—the parking police do closely monitor these ramps, and tickets will be issued if you overstay the time allotted.

SALUT BAR AMERICAINE, 50TH AND FRANCE

SHAKOPEE

This small town, southwest of Minneapolis along the Minnesota River, is home to four popular attractions, all very different in nature.

♂ ⅏ **Valleyfair** (952-445-6500; www.valleyfair.com), One Valleyfair Drive. Open daily Memorial Day to Labor Day, weekends only in early May and late Sept. Visitors 48 inches tall and up pay $41.99; kids three years old and under 48 inches tall, as well as senior citizens, pay $9.99. Kids under two are free. There is no discount admission for nonriding chaperones.

BLOOMINGTON

It may be located near Edina and its chic shopping areas, but Bloomington has a claim to fame that no other suburb can match: the nation's largest shopping mall.

♂ ♂ ⅏ ⅄ ❋ (ⵯ) **The Mall of America** (952-883-8800; www.mallof america.com), 60 E. Broadway. This behemoth of retail and entertainment options opened in 1992 and encompasses more than 4 million square feet, which includes not only more than 500 stores, but 30 fast-food restaurants, 18 sit-down restaurants, an underground aquarium, a 14-screen movie theater complex, a wedding chapel, and an indoor theme park. During its planning, local residents wondered why the area needed so much retail; in general, the Twin Cities are not short of malls and other retail venues. But since its opening, the Mall of America has proven to be a major draw, both for locals and for visitors outside the Cities (and even outside the U.S.).

So what can you do at the mall? For starters, you can walk; there are more than 4,000 registered participants in the mall's mall-walking club (walking around one level is slightly over 0.5 mile). You can visit the retail anchors, Nordstrom, Macy's, Bloomingdale's, and Sears, or the adjacent IKEA. You can browse through any of the more than 500 stores in just about every conceivable category; there are clothing stores for men, women, and kids; video game, electronics, and computer stores; jewelry, art, book, gift, athletic wear, Christmas decoration, bathing suit, and craft stores; cosmetics and body products stores; shops selling toys, Irish gifts, and made in Minnesota items; photo studios; and even a convenience store.

Parking is $10, or $12 if you're using an oversize vehicle such as an RV that requires more than one space. A permanent outdoor amusement park, Valleyfair has something for almost everyone, including a wide variety of gentle rides, including a miniature roller coaster, for younger park adventurers, and more intense rides and coasters for thrill seekers, including the 2007 addition of a new wooden roller coaster, the Renegade, bringing the park's total to eight coasters. The Whitewater Country Waterpark, included in admission, offers respite from hot summer days (swimsuits are available for sale, and a changing area is provided). The six-story

MALL OF AMERICA, BLOOMINGTON

✔ ♿ ❋ **The Water Park of America** (952-698-8888; www.waterparkofamerica .com), I-494 and Cedar Avenue. For the members of your traveling party who are not as inclined to spend hours at the Mall of America, book a stay at the Radisson Hotel at the park. The hotel has more than 400 rooms, and the water park comes complete with slides, a mile-long family raft ride, a wave pool, and a Flow Rider. Not interested in water activities? There's also a huge arcade and a spa. The water park is available without a hotel stay for a fee, but plan ahead—hotel guests get first priority, and public admission closes if the park becomes too full.

IMAX theater runs giant-sized movies, and live performances take place around the park throughout the season. Challenge Park, which requires both park admission and additional fees, offers a mountainous mini golf course, bumper boats, go-carts, and RipCord, a bungee-jumping assimilation.

🐾 ♿ ❄ **The Landing** (763-694-7784; www.threeriversparkdistrict.org), 2187 E. County Route 101. Open daily mid-Mar. to Dec.; Mon. through Fri. Jan. to mid-Mar. Year-round special events and private tours available. Park admission is free; fees apply for events. Right down the road from Valleyfair is this historical site, a pioneer village comprising 40 buildings set up to demonstrate life for Minnesota pioneers in the late 1800s. Visiting on the weekends during summer will find the addition of a living-history component, with guides dressed in clothing specific to that period, explaining how life was lived in those days. The Pioneer Kids Play House is exactly what it says—a house set up to be hands-on for kids, who can try on pioneer costumes, do laundry in a washtub, use printing blocks to make a newspaper, and simulate cooking.

♿ 🍸 ❄ **Canterbury Park** (952-445-7223; www.canterburypark.com), 1100 Canterbury Road. Live horse racing is offered from early May until Labor

THE MINNESOTA RIVER, SEEN FROM THE LANDING IN SHAKOPEE

Day; simulcast racing is available year-round. The Card Club allows you to indulge your whims for blackjack and poker.

MINNEAPOLIS'S NEIGHBORING COMMUNITIES

✈ **Sever's Corn Maze** (952-974-5000; www.severscornmaze.com), next to Canterbury Park. Open Sat. and Sun. 11–6, late Sept. to late Oct.; also open the Thurs. and Fri. of MEA (Minnesota Education Association) weekend, usually the third weekend in Oct. Admission is $11 for ages four and up; children under four free. Local farm stand company Sever's opens this cornfield annually, but every year the field is laid out in a different design (past years have included the *Titanic*, the U.S., and an Egyptian sphinx). Participants are given a map with clues to find their way through. A smaller hay bale maze is set up for younger kids, along with a petting zoo and camel rides. The Corn Pit acts like a ball pit, only with kernels of corn (an oddly soothing place to play, even for adults), and if you need to get some aggression out, try the Pumpkin Slinger. Concessions available. Be sure to wear sturdy shoes or boots, and be sure you don't mind if they get dirty—if there's been rain, the field will be muddy.

PRIOR LAKE

A western suburb, Prior Lake is home to the Shakopee Mdewakanton Sioux Community, which is the largest employer in the city.

⚐ ☗ ❋ **Mystic Lake Casino** (952-445-9000 or 1-800-262-7799; www.mysticlake.com), 2400 Mystic Lake Boulevard. Open 24 hours. Casinos are popular attractions throughout the state, but the sheer size of Mystic Lake is astonishing. Slots are big business here, with more than 4,000 machines, and sprawling displays of table games and bingo as well. The sheer mass of Mystic Lake can be intimidating, but inside the casino is kept in sparkling condition, with ample nonsmoking areas. Food is available at several cafés and restaurants nearly 24/7. An attached theater is a fine venue for one of the many live performances the complex books, which in the past have included such venerable performers as Tony Bennett and Carrie Underwood. The Mystic Lake Casino Hotel and Spa has 600 rooms and suites, but if you're staying elsewhere, the casino offers complimentary bus service around the Twin Cities.

CHANHASSEN

North of Bloomington is the small town of Chanhassen. It's a busy and rapidly growing community, and for visitors there is a notable place to visit.

✈ ⚐ ☗ ❋ **The Chanhassen Dinner Theatres** (952-934-1525 or 1-800-362-3515; www.chanhassentheatres.com), 501 W. 78th Street. This long-standing Chanhassen venue serves full dinner and drinks with each

CHANHASSEN DINNER THEATRE

production in its three theaters. Primarily musical in nature, the Chanhassen Dinner Theatres companies are definitely of professional stature, and while the food may not be on par with many of the Twin Cities top restaurants, it's reasonably good and completes the experience.

CHASKA

Bordering Chanhassen, Chaska offers one of the loveliest green spaces in the suburbs.

✄ ♿ ❄ **Minnesota Landscape Arboretum** (952-443-1400; www .arboretum.umn.edu), 3675 Arboretum Drive. Open daily 8–8 (or sunset, whichever comes first), year-round; closed Thanksgiving and Christmas. Adults $9, arboretum members and children 15 and under free. The University of Minnesota is the proprietor of these 1,000-plus acres of gardens, landscaping, woodlands, wetlands, and trails. The arboretum has a 3-mile paved road that is used by motorists and people on foot, and there are several off-road trails, including cross-country ski and snowshoe trails, that wind throughout the grounds. The Oswald Visitor Center has a large gift shop and cafeteria; picnic lunches are available with preorder. Seasonal programs and events include annual and perennial exhibits, demonstrations about making maple syrup, an annual holiday decoration sale and Christmas tea, and fall foliage walks.

EXCELSIOR

Just down the road from Chanhassen, the small town on the southern shores of Lake Minnetonka is a visitor's dream, especially in the summer. Small shops, intimate restaurants, and parks and trails make for an inviting place to relax and unwind—once you've found a place to park.

✳ To See and Do

✒ ⅋ **The Excelsior Streetcar** (www.trolleyride.org). Available early May through early Sept. Adults $2, children under three free. Reservations are not necessary; just arrive early at the Water Street Station, at the intersection of Water and George streets. The Minnesota Streetcar Museum offers a ride through Excelsior's past with a summer service of vintage streetcar riding.

✒ ⅋ **The Steamboat *Minnehaha*** (952-474-2115; www.steamboatminne haha.org), Water Street. Open Sat., Sun., and holidays, Memorial Day weekend through Labor Day. Basic lake cruises are $10 for adults, $5 for children 12 and under. If you'd like your history on water, take a ride on the little yellow steamboat with the colorful history. Part of a fleet of steamboats that were workhorses in the early 1900s, the *Minnehaha* was scuttled and sank to the bottom of Lake Minnetonka, where it remained until rediscovered 50 years later. Brought up to the surface and refurbished, the *Minnehaha* now provides visitors with a scenic tour of the lake.

✳ Where to Eat

DINING OUT ⅋ ⑂ ✳ **Bielle Ristorante** (952-474-8881; www.biella -restaurant.com), 227 Water Street. Open daily for dinner. This sumptuous restaurant provides top-notch cuisine with an admirable wine list. Expensive.

✒ ⅋ ⑂ ✳ **Jake O'Connor's** (952-908-9650; www.jakeoconnors.com), 200 Water Street. Open daily for

SPRING AT THE MINNESOTA LANDSCAPE ARBORETUM

lunch and dinner. Hearty pub food, both Irish and American. Expensive.

EATING OUT ✷ **Adele's Frozen Custard** (952-470-0035; www .adelescustard.com), 800 Excelsior Boulevard. Open daily Feb. through Christmas Eve. A tiny café near MN 7 coming into Excelsior, Adele's doesn't look like much on the outside—just a run-down little house with a deck. But inside, along with a limited sand-wich menu, is homemade frozen custard, available in cones, sun-daes, and malts. Flavors vary daily. Forget about counting calories and indulge. Inexpensive.

✳ **Antiquity Rose** (952-474-2661; www.antiquityrose.com), 429 Second Street. Open Mon. through Sat. for lunch. A small lunch-only restaurant within an antiques shop, Antiquity Rose brings back the best of yester-year's entrées: salmon loaf with creamed peas and new potatoes, and tortilla casserole. Be sure to try the bran muffins (the sugar content must outweigh any nutri-tional benefit) and pick up a copy of the café's cookbook on the way out. Inexpensive.

✷ ♿ ♒ ✳ **318 Café** (952-401-7902; www.three-eighteen.com), 318 Water Street. Open daily for all three meals. Located in the his-toric Excelsior Mill (see *Selective Shopping*), 318 is a small, cozy establishment with a fireplace, rough-hewn wood floors, an out-door patio, and delectable soups,

salads, sandwiches, and baked goods. Wine bar by night, 318 also offers live music on a regular basis. Moderate.

✳ Selective Shopping

The Excelsior Mill (952-474-7428; www.excelsiormill.com), 310–340 Water Street. Open daily. This former lumber mill is now a miniature shopping mall with a handful of specialty shops, all worth a visit. Of note are **DB & Company, TaDah!** (952-474-7428), filled with whimsical home accessories, especially on quality tea and the items with which to serve it; **Provisions** (952-474-6953; www.provisionsmn.com), a kitchen and home gifts store; and **Farrington's** (952-473-3106), offering fair trade home accessories.

Coldwater Collaborative (952-401-7501; www.coldwateryarn .com), 347 Water Street. A cozy yarn shop across from the Excel-sior Mill with a wide variety of materials and tools for fiber enthusiasts.

Bay Tree (952-470-8975), 261 Water Street. Home accessories and gift baskets, as well as Min-nesota-themed clothing.

Capers (952-474-1715), 207 Water Street. A gift shop with a solid line of humor-filled gifts, as well as inexpensive jewelry and kids' items.

Heritage II (952-474-1231; www.heritageii.com), 50 Water Street. Also in White Bear Lake (see "St. Paul's Neighboring Communities"). The source for Scandinavian and British Isles merchandise, including clothing, tableware and accessories, and gifts.

✐ **Excelsior Bay Books** (952-401-0932; www.excelsiorbaybooks.net), 36 Water Street. Small bookstore with a good variety of reading materials for kids and adults alike.

WAYZATA

Like Excelsior, Wayzata (pronounced why-ZET-ta) has the good fortune to be situated on Lake Minnetonka, and it counts as its residents and visitors many well-heeled lake lovers. The city is busy during the summer months, but don't discount a visit during the winter, when the shops and restaurants are not quite as busy.

✳ To See and Do

✐ ♿ ✳ **Minnetonka Center for the Arts** (952-473-7361; www.minnetonkaarts.org), 2240 N. Shore Drive. Open Mon. through Sat. Just outside the town, the Minnetonka Center for the Arts has become a thriving school and gallery for local artists, budding and professional. The center is open year-round and offers a variety of events (check the website or call for specifics).

✳ Where to Eat

DINING OUT ♿ ♟ ✳ **Blue Point Restaurant** (952-475-3636; www.bluepointrestaurantandbar.com), 739 E. Lake Street (with another location in Bloomington). Open daily at 4 for dinner. Blue Point is a sleek seafood restaurant right across the street from Lake Minnetonka. The seafood choices vary greatly beyond what's found in Minnesota lakes, with mussels, shrimp, and salmon among the many options. Expensive.

✐ ♿ ♟ ✳ **Gianni's Steakhouse** (952-404-1100; www.giannis-steakhouse.com), 635 E. Lake Street. Open Mon. through Sat. for lunch, daily for dinner. Gianni's is a con-genial steakhouse with a traditional menu full of steaks, ribs, and fish. Very expensive.

EATING OUT ✐ ♿ ♟ ✳ **Sunsets** (952-473-5253; www.sunsetsrestaurant.com), 700 E. Lake Street (with another location in Woodbury). Open daily for lunch and dinner. Sunsets is a very popular casual restaurant, due in no small part to its location right on the lake. During the summer months, patio dining is available, but be prepared to wait. The menu is a broad assortment of pastas, sandwiches, and various grilled specialties. Moderate.

✳ Selective Shopping

✐ ✳ **The Bookcase** (952-473-8341; www.bookcaseofwayzata .com), 607 E. Lake Street. Open daily. An independent and busy bookstore that hosts many author events each year; check the website for current information.

✳ **Blanc de Blanc** (952-473-8275; www.blancdeblancltd.com), 691 Lake Street. Open Mon. through Sat. True to its name, Blanc de Blanc is themed in white, and the store carries a wide variety of upscale products: home

and kitchen, bed and bath, holiday, even pet items.

✳ **Polly Berg** (952-920-0183; www.pollyberg.com), 18285 E. Minnetonka Boulevard, Deephaven (near Wayzata). Open Mon. through Sat. Polly Berg specializes in luxurious bed linens and lingerie.

✳ **Five Swans** (952-473-4685; http://fiveswans.com), 309 E. Lake Street. Open Mon. through Sat. Housed in a century-old building, Five Swans offers upscale gifts and home accessories.

MAPLE GROVE

From small town to one of the most rapidly growing suburbs, Maple Grove saw intense growth during the 1990s. Where there were once empty fields, there are now acres of retail and restaurants. Maple Grove implemented the idea of a "walkable downtown," something other communities are looking at and considering emulating. But be warned—the main shopping area in Maple Grove can be slow going for motorists. There are countless stoplights, and lines can form.

✐ ❧ ♈ ✳ **The Shoppes at Arbor Lakes** (763-424-0504; www.shoppes atarborlakes.com), I-94/I-694 and Hemlock Lane. Despite the rather prissy name, Arbor Lakes has made progress in reducing the concept of "soulless suburb" by providing a mix of retail and dining in actual city blocks with sidewalks to give it a small-town-center feel. While many of the usual chain-store suspects are present (Gymboree, Abercrombie & Fitch, J.Crew and J.Jill, Pottery Barn), the strolling-friendly layout over four city blocks makes the shopping experience feel less suburban mall and more charming village. Dining options are pretty much casual, with a mix of fast food (Qdoba Mexican, Potbelly Sandwiches) and sit-down dining (Biaggi's Ristorante Italiano, P.F. Chang's, Pittsburgh Blue, Granite City Food & Brewery).

ALBERTVILLE

On the far north end of the Minneapolis area is the town of Albertville, which is home to a massive outlet mall.

✂ & ❋ **Albertville Premium Outlets** (763-497-1911; www.premium outlets.com), 6415 Labeaux Avenue NE. A sprawling collection of 100 outlet stores, including Polo Ralph Lauren, Tommy Hilfiger, Banana Republic, Nike, Coach, Claire's Accessories, Le Creuset, Harry & David, and Bath and Body Works. The outlet center offers occasional live concerts outdoors during the summer months, and the website lists events and promotions offered by the individual retailers.

St. Paul and Neighboring Communities

2

ST. PAUL

ST. PAUL'S NEIGHBORING
COMMUNITIES

ST. PAUL

St. Paul serves as the capital for the state; it also at times suffers from being neglected in favor of its twin across the river. Take in a concert at the Xcel Energy Center and see what happens if the performer onstage makes the mistake of thanking the Minneapolis audience; it's a frequent and unfortunate occurrence.

While not as cutting-edge as Minneapolis in terms of trendy dining and shopping, St. Paul holds its own for sheer beauty in its neighborhoods and downtown area. The ornate buildings downtown and grand mansions along many of the city's prominent streets (Summit Avenue being the most noticeable) reflect the city's historical roots. Named by a French priest who felt that the city's original name, Pig's Eye Landing, was not grand enough, St. Paul became the state's capital in 1849, an event that caused a population explosion of sorts, doubling in size in just three weeks. But the expansion didn't come without criticism; in the late 1800s, a New York newspaper cast aspersion on the local climate, saying it wasn't fit for human habitation. City officials disagreed, and thus was born one of the city's most cherished annual events, the St. Paul Winter Carnival (see *Special Events*).

The 20th century brought highs and lows to the city on the river. The 1920s saw increased crime and the presence of gangsters, due to the tolerance of the local police department. But when the U.S. government determined that the favored hiding spot of John Dillinger needed attention, police began to crack down on crime and make St. Paul a safer place to be.

Regardless of safety, St. Paul lagged behind Minneapolis in terms of cultural growth, at least until the 1990s. As St. Paul became more aggressive toward drawing visitors, development funds were given to projects like the Ordway Center for the Performing Arts, a popular and beautiful live performance venue (see Entertainment), and RiverCentre, a convention center that is also home to the Xcel Energy Center, the acoustically superior counterpart to Minneapolis's Target Center. The

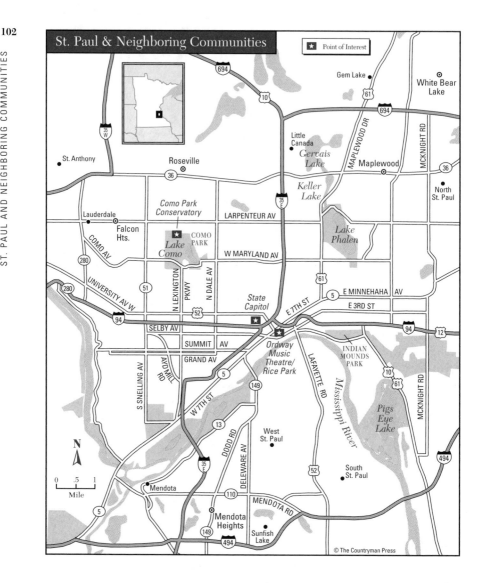

St. Paul & Neighboring Communities

★ Point of Interest

694

Gem Lake

White Bear Lake

61

694

10

Little Canada

Maplewood Dr

Maplewood

Mcknight Rd

St. Anthony

Roseville

Gervais Lake

36

35 W

36

Keller Lake

35 E

North St. Paul

Como Park Conservatory

LARPENTEUR AV

Lauderdale

Falcon Hts.

COMO PARK

Lake Phalen

Como Av

★

Lake Como

W MARYLAND AV

280

61

University Av W

280

51

N Lexington Pkwy

N Dale Av

State Capitol

E MINNEHAHA AV

5

E 3RD ST

94

52

E 7TH ST

94

12

SELBY AV

★

SUMMIT AV

Ordway Music Theatre/ Rice Park

INDIAN MOUNDS PARK

10

S Snelling Av

A'd Mill Rd

GRAND AV

Lafayette Rd

61

Mcknight Rd

5

149

Mississippi River

W 7TH ST

13

Pigs Eye Lake

N

Dodd Rd

West St. Paul

Deleware Av

494

0 .5 1
Mile

35 E

South St. Paul

5

Mendota

110

MENDOTA RD

52

5

Mendota Heights

149

494

Sunfish Lake

© The Countryman Press

Science Museum of Minnesota (see *To See and Do*) benefited from a move down the street to a larger home and has become one of the premier science museums in the country.

Today St. Paul continues to grow, adding new entertainment and dining options to the city. One note for visitors: Former governor and pro wrestler Jesse Ventura once commented, to the consternation of loyal St. Paulites, that the city's streets had apparently been designed by a "drunken Irishman." Whoever designed them, Ventura had a point; the winding one-ways and dead-ends can be confusing, especially during rush hour. A good downtown city map is crucial for finding your way, and don't hesitate to ask for help.

GUIDANCE St. Paul Convention and Visitors Authority (651-265-4900 or 1-800-627-6101; www.visitstpaul.com), 175 W. Kellogg Blvd., Suite 502, St. Paul. Offers extensive lodging and activity information for St. Paul.

GETTING THERE *By air:* The primary airport is the Terminal 1–Lindbergh Terminal at the **Minneapolis–St. Paul International Airport** (612-726-5555; www.mspairport.com); next door is **Terminal 2–Hubert** (612-726-5800), a smaller secondary airport serving mostly no-frills and charter airlines. Both airports are in Bloomington, a western suburb. Taxis, limos, rental cars, and light rail service are available from the airports into the city.

By bus: **Greyhound** has a terminal (612-371-3325; www.greyhound.com) a few blocks from the capitol.

By car: I-94, I-35E, US 12, US 61, and US 10 all lead into downtown St. Paul.

By rail: **AMTRAK** (1-800-872-7245; www.amtrak.com) has a rail station off University Ave. between Minneapolis and St. Paul (730 Transfer Rd.).

GETTING AROUND Having a vehicle is a necessity when traveling around the northern Lakes region. For travel within the city, **Metro Transit** (612-373-3333; www.metrotransit.org) provides extensive service

THE ORDWAY, RICE PARK

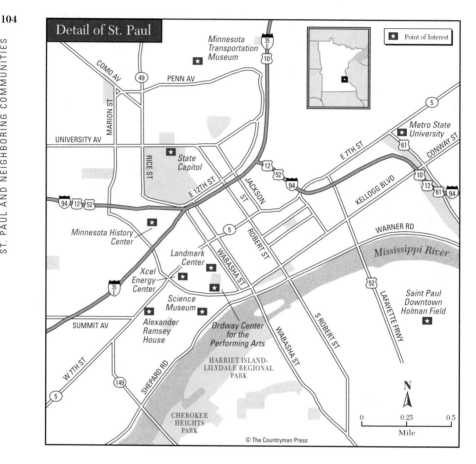

Detail of St. Paul

designed primarily to transport students and employees from outlying homes to work and school within the city. For maximum flexibility, a car is recommended, unless you're staying in the downtown area and can walk or take a brief taxi ride to other downtown destinations.

WHEN TO COME The summer months see an influx of tourists who come to enjoy the multitude of lakes and parks, but St. Paulites keep active in the winter, too, especially with the annual St. Paul Winter Carnival (see *Special Events*), which has myriad activities for visitors and residents alike.

MEDICAL EMERGENCY Call 911.

Regions Hospital (651-254-3456; www.regionshospital.com), 640 Jackson St.

Children's Hospital St. Paul (651-220-6000; www.childrensmn.org), 345 N. Smith Ave.

United Hospital (651-241-8000; www.unitedhospital.com), 333 N. Smith Ave.

St. Joseph's Hospital (651-232-3000; www.stjosephs-stpaul.org), 69 W. Exchange St.

✳ To See and Do

MUSEUMS AND HISTORIC SITES ⌀ ♿ ✳ **Minnesota History Center** (651-259-3000; www.minnesotahistorycenter.org), 345 Kellogg Boulevard W. Open Tues. 10–8, Wed. through Sat. 10–5, Sun. noon–5. Adults $10, senior citizens and college students $8, children 6–17 $5, children 5 and under and Minnesota Historical Society members free. Despite its rather dull name, the history center takes a lively, hands-on approach to history that makes it interesting and fun, even (and especially) for kids. Serious history buffs can find specialized research help; kids can crawl through a grain silo and explore the world of Minnesota music in a recording booth. An ongoing exhibit about Minnesota's weather extremes includes a torna-do simulator that's scarily realistic. The gift shop is fun, and even the cafe-teria is far above average.

⌀ ♿ ✳ **State Capitol** (651-296-2881; www.mnhs.org/statecapitol), Univer-sity Avenue between Dr. Rev. Martin Luther King Jr. Boulevard and Cedar Street. Open Mon. through Fri. 8:30–5, Sat. 10–3, Sun. 1–4. Gen-eral tours are free; special events may have varying admission fees. Groups of 10 or more should reserve tours two weeks in advance. Just down the street from the Minnesota History Center is another piece of Minnesota's past and present. Guided and self-guided tours are available through the venerable white marble building. Weather permitting, group tours explore the rooftop to visit the golden horses sculpture.

⌀ ♿ ✳ **Capitol Mall** (www.mnhs.org). Stretched out below the State Capitol is the Capitol Mall, which has been developed into a large-scale memorial and park. A walking tour will take visitors past memorials repre-senting Minnesota politicians and veterans of wars. The artwork is diverse and thoughtful, and it's well worth an afternoon's exploration.

⌀ ♿ ✳ **The James J. Hill House** (651-297-2555; www.mnhs.org/places /sites/jjhh), 240 Summit Avenue. Open Wed. through Sat. 10–3:30, Sun. 1–4. Adults $8, senior citizens $6, children 6–17 $5, and children under 6 and Minnesota Historical Society members free. This was the residence of railroad impresario James J. Hill, and his prominence shows in the rich mansion. Inside, besides a piece of history, is a two-story art gallery with several pieces from Hill's own collection, focused primarily on French landscapes. Under the Minnesota Historical Society's innovative management, the Hill House has numerous events each year that are above and beyond the usual house tours, including Victorian Poetry Slams at Valentine's and a Nooks and Crannies tour in the summer that takes visitors into parts of the property not usually explored during regular tours.

✄ ❄ **The Wabasha Street Caves** (651-292-1220; www.wabashastreet caves.com), 215 S. Wabasha Street. Hours and admission fees vary depending on season and type of tour. The caves have a legendary history involving moonshiners and mobsters, and besides, they're caves. Tours are offered year-round, both with the caves as the primary attraction and as part of other tours (Gangster Tours in the summer, Ghosts and Caves in Oct.).

✄ ♿ ❄ **The Science Museum of Minnesota** (651-221-9444; www.smm .org), 120 Kellogg Boulevard W. Open Tues. and Wed. 9:30–5, Thurs. through Sat. 9:30–9. Hours are sometimes extended in the summer and during special events. Admission for exhibits only is $11 for adults, $8.50 for children and senior citizens, free for museum members. Admission to the 3D Cinema, the Omnitheater, and special exhibitions cost extra. The Science Museum has utilized its executive and marketing staffs to become one of the premier science museums in the United States. A flexible management gives this staff the ability to make decisions more quickly than larger bureaucracies, enabling them to pounce on prime traveling exhibits. A large permanent collection covers all aspect of science, mostly from a hands-on perspective; visiting exhibits tend to be major events, with past visits including the Body Worlds exhibit, the Dead Sea Scrolls, remnants from the *Titanic,* and treasures of King Tut. The Omnitheater has a giant surrounding movie screen with specially made movies (many by the Sci-

THE SCIENCE MUSEUM OF MINNESOTA

ence Museum's staff) on view. When the weather's nice, stop by the mini golf course behind the museum to learn some geology lessons while having fun with a golf club.

✍ ♿ ❋ **Minnesota Children's Museum** (651-225-6000; www.mcm.org), 10 W. Seventh Street. Open Mon. through Thurs. 9–4, Fri. and Sat. 9–8, Sun. 9–5. Adults $9, children under the age of one and museum members free. A large, rollicking space for kids and adventurous parents. Displays are highly active and interactive; educational is an important part, but fun always rules. When weather permits, be sure to visit the Rooftop ArtPark, an installation combining nature exploration with art play.

✍ ♿ **Historic Fort Snelling** (612-726-1171; www.mnhs.org/places /sites/hfs), MN 5 and MN 55, near the Minneapolis–St. Paul Airport. Open Tues. through Sat. 10–5 and Sun. noon–5, Memorial Day through Labor Day; open Sat. 10–5, Sept. through Oct. Adults $10, senior citizens and college students $8, children 6–17 $5, and children under 6 and Minnesota Historical Society members free. This fort, built in the early 1800s at the junction of the Minnesota and Mississippi rivers, was an army outpost to establish control of river traffic, but it quickly became a regional center for trade and social activities as well. The fort was used through World War II, when it was a processing and training camp, but it closed after the war's end. Today it's a living-history museum with costumed guides and hands-on activities during the summer, and home to several events each year, often focused on some aspect of fort life, whether it's cooking, the blacksmith's shop, or aspects of World War II military intelligence.

❋ Green Space and Outdoor Activities

Rice Park, 109 W. Fourth Street. It's tiny, only one city block, but it has the Ordway Center on one side, the St. Paul Hotel across the way, and the St. Paul Public Library alongside, all of which are beautiful and, with the exception of the Ordway, decades-old buildings. The park itself has a walking path and a fountain; it's a prominent gathering place for visitors to the Ordway, and many of the city's festivals utilize the space for events and displays. Of special note is the annual St. Paul Winter Carnival (see *Special Events*), in which Rice Park is host to an ice sculpture competition that always has stunning pieces for visitors to see.

✍ ♻ **Como Park, Zoo, and Conservatory** (651-487-8200; www.como zooconservatory.org), 1225 Estabrook Drive. Open daily 10–4. Admission is free, but a donation of $2 per adult and $1 per child is requested for the park's maintenance. It's like a city within a city; Como Park and Zoo comprise several acres with a lake, pool, mini golf, and golf course (the last three open summers only); walking trails; and even a mini amusement

HARRIET ISLAND

An island on the Mississippi across from downtown St. Paul, Harriet Island's public park has gained prominence in recent years. Amenities include a bandshell, stage, public boat launch, playground, river walk, and jumping-on points for a number of trails. The wide, flat space at the river's edge is ideal for setting up large-scale events, and the view of the St. Paul skyline makes a perfect backdrop.

But that's not all. Harriet Island is also home to the Minnesota Centennial Showboat (see *Entertainment*), the Covington Inn Bed and Breakfast (see *Lodging*), the St. Paul Yacht Club, and the Padelford Packet Boat Company, which offers public river cruises.

Harriet Island has also become a venue for concerts and a central location for many of St. Paul's festivals, at least those of which can be held outdoors. Besides being easier logistically and in terms of security for the city, they've also made it pretty easy for visitors—many of the festivals offer patrons the option of parking in downtown St. Paul, then catching a free shuttle bus for the quick ride across the bridge to the island. There is some parking near the island, but it's limited. See *Special Events* for information about the St. Paul Winter Carnival and the Irish Fair, just two of the regular events held on Harriet Island.

GREEN SPACE AT HARRIET ISLAND

park. The Marjorie McNeely Conservatory has an extensive, lush indoor garden, a favorite for weddings and parties. For a slightly different kind of tour, sign up for the Como Pedicab Tour (651-646-3648), which will give you a rickshaw ride through the park.

Indian Mounds Park (651-632-5111), Earl Street at Mounds Boulevard. Open daily. Across the river from downtown St. Paul is this park, which serves both as a public park and a historical site with six Indian burial mounds. Some of the mounds date back 2,000 years and hold remains of the Hopewell tradition and the Dakota tribe. The park offers beautiful views of downtown St. Paul as well.

Crosby Regional Park (651-632-5111), Shepard Road at Homer Street. Open daily. A nature area with several miles of paved trails for hiking and biking, lakes for fishing, and a boat launch.

Fort Snelling State Park (612-725-2389; www.dnr.state.mn.us/state _parks/fort_snelling), 101 Snelling Lake Road. Open daily 8 AM–10 PM. Admission is $10 per car; free with a Minnesota State Park permit. Not far from the international airport is this state park, where the Mississippi and Minnesota rivers converge. The park offers 18 miles of hiking trails and 10 miles of mountain bike trails, as well as cross-country ski and snowshoe trails. Pike Island, located where the rivers meet, has 3 miles of hiking trails, too. The Thomas C. Savage Visitor Center has exhibits explaining the history and geographical significance of the area.

✳ Lodging

BED & BREAKFASTS

Downtown

✳ **Covington Inn Bed and Breakfast** (651-292-1411; www .covingtoninn.com), 100 Harriet Island Road. Four suites are available aboard the permanently moored towboat the *Covington,* which spent its first 30 years as a river towboat, moving cargo ships into place. Now it's a luxury guesthouse; all rooms have a private bath, fireplace, and air-conditioning. The decor reflects the glorious past days of river travel, and there are several salvaged fixtures and antiques. Expensive. Packages are available.

HOTELS

Downtown

🚹 ♈ ✳ ((•)) **The St. Paul Hotel** (651-292-9292 or 1-800-292-9292; www.saintpaulhotel.com), 350 Market Street. This elegant old-world hotel, just over a century old, is situated on Rice Park, right across from the Ordway Center and just steps from Xcel Energy Center (see *Entertainment*), the Science Museum (see *To See and Do*), and several excellent restaurants (as well as having two top-notch restaurants in the hotel; see *Where to Eat*). Its 250-plus sumptuously appointed rooms are among the loveliest in the city, and if you're feeling posh, the Penthouse Suite has a dining room that seats 12, a fireplace, surround sound in the living room, a full kitchen, and two bedrooms and baths. The St. Paul Hotel has been host to numerous high-profile guests, including actors, politicians, and gangsters. Very expensive. Packages are available.

&. ❄ (ᵧ) **Hotel 340** (651-280-4120; www.hotel340.com), 340 Cedar Street. An upscale extended-stay hotel with suites and rooms in a 1907 building in the heart of downtown St. Paul. Cherrywood floors, high-quality furnishings, and TVs. Moderate.

✎ &. ⵑ ❄ (ᵧ) **Crowne Plaza St. Paul Riverfront** (651-292-1900 or 1-800-593-5708; www.ichotels

THE ST. PAUL HOTEL

group.com), 11 E. Kellogg Boulevard. This popular conference hotel overlooks the river and is just blocks away from the Ordway Center and Xcel Energy Center. There's an indoor pool and whirlpool, and the Restaurant 11 offers better-than-expected hotel dining. Expensive.

✎ &. ⵑ ❄ (ᵧ) **Holiday Inn** (651-225-1515 or 1-888-465-4329; www.ichotelsgroup.com), 175 W. Seventh Street. Right across from Xcel Energy Center and an easy walk to the Ordway and Rice Park, the Holiday Inn offers the usual amenities and a reasonable price for a downtown location. The cheerful Irish pub the Liffey (see *Where to Eat*) is on-site. Moderate.

✎ &. ⵑ ❄ (ᵧ) **Embassy Suites** (651-224-5400 or 1-800-362-2779; http://embassysuites1.hilton.com), 175 E. 10th Street. This all-suite hotel is within easy walking distance or very short drives to downtown St. Paul attractions, dining, and entertainment options. There's an indoor pool, and daily cooked-to-order breakfast is included in the rates. The casual Cork's Pub is open daily for lunch and dinner. Expensive. Weekend discounts and packages are available.

✎ 🐾 &. ⵑ ❄ (ᵧ) **Best Western Kelly Inn** (651-227-8711; www.bestwesternstpaul.com), 161 St. Anthony Avenue. Located near the State Capitol, this Best Western offers less-expensive accommodations. The hotel has an indoor pool and restaurant. Moderate. Packages are available.

✳ Where to Eat

DINING OUT

Cathedral Hill

ᴕ ⴲ ✳ **W.A. Frost** (651-224-5715; www.wafrost.com), 374 Selby Avenue. Open daily for lunch and dinner. One of the most romantic restaurants in the area, W.A. Frost has excellent food. The interior, dark but not gloomy, with high copper ceilings, speaks to intimacy, while the outdoor patio garden is a gem for nature lovers. There's a traditional menu, an early seating fixed-price menu, and a sizeable bar menu. Expensive.

ᴕ ⴲ ✳ **Moscow on the Hill** (651-291-1236; www.moscowonthehill.com), 371 Selby Avenue. Open Tues. through Sat. for lunch, daily for dinner. Hearty Russian food served the Russian way—don't plan on eating in a hurry, but not in a bad way. This upscale bistro also has an excellent array of vodka (available in tasting flights). Expensive.

Downtown

ⴲ ✳ **Forepaugh's** (651-224-5606; www.forepaughs.com), 276 S. Exchange Street. Open daily for dinner, Sun. for brunch. This fine restaurant, in an old historic mansion on the edge of downtown St. Paul, offers a layout that results in several small, intimate dining rooms with Victorian decor fitting the house. The excellent food—classics such as beef Wellington—

is served on china from the period and accompanied by a fine wine list. If you're going to the Minnesota Opera (or selected special events) at the Ordway afterward, make arrangements for the shuttle bus—you can park for free at Forepaugh's if you eat there beforehand. Expensive.

✎ ᴕ ⴲ ✳ **St. Paul Grill** (651-224-7455; www.stpaulgrill.com), 350 Market Street. Open daily for lunch and dinner. Located in the St. Paul Hotel (see *Lodging*), the St. Paul Grill is right across Rice Park from the Ordway Theater. It's definitely a special-occasion restaurant, with an upscale American menu including steaks, lobster, and lamb chops. The bar is a great stop for a before-dinner or after-theater visit, with extensive wine and Scotch lists. Expensive.

ᴕ ⴲ ✳ **Meritage** (651-222-5670; www.meritage-stpaul.com), 410 St. Peter Street. Open Tues. through

MOSCOW ON THE HILL

THE ENTRANCE TO FOREPAUGH'S

Sun. for lunch and dinner. Chef Russell Klein built his menu from traditional French foods, then played off that by drawing on seasonally available ingredients. The result is a highly regarded restaurant that also offers an oyster bar, patio (in season), and crêpe stand on special occasions. Expensive.

& Y ❋ **Pazzaluna** (651-223-7000; www.pazzaluna.com), 360 St. Peter Street. Open daily for dinner. Chef's table available; reserve in advance. This informal but upscale Italian restaurant offers a menu that changes seasonally but is always tasteful. Service can vary in terms of friendliness, but fortunately the food is consistent in quality. It's a popular spot, but if you don't have a reservation and there's a long wait, consider eating in the bar, which is quick and attractive. Expensive.

& Y ❋ **Kincaid's Fish, Chop, and Steak House** (651-602-9000; www.kincaids.com), 380 St. Peter Street (with another location in Bloomington). Open Mon. through Fri. for lunch, daily for dinner. Kincaid's offers all the usual steakhouse suspects, beautifully prepared, and with the occasional fun twist; try the bacon-wrapped Kobe meat loaf with horseradish mashed potatoes. Expensive.

🍸 & Y ❋ **Fuji-Ya** (651-310-0111; www.fujiyasushi.com), 465 Wabasha Street (with another location in Minneapolis). Open Mon. through Fri. for lunch, Sat. for dinner. Fuji-Ya serves some of the best Japanese food in the state. Their sushi is top quality, freshly made to order, and beautifully presented. But beyond sushi, Fuji-Ya also shines, with a wide variety of Japanese salads, noodle bowls, bulgogi, and meat and seafood entrées. Possibly because so much care is taken with preparation, service is slow; be prepared to relax and enjoy. Expensive.

✍ ☙ 👗 ✳ **Mancini's Char House & Lounge** (651-224-7345; www.mancinis.com), 531 W. Seventh Street. Open daily for dinner. This venerable family-run steakhouse has been serving char-broiled steaks and lobster, along with generous martinis, for more than 40 years. Live music is offered in the lounge several times a month. Expensive.

✍ ☙ 👗 ✳ **Sakura Restaurant and Sushi Bar** (651-224-0185; www.sakurastpaul.com), 350 St. Peter Street. Open daily for lunch and dinner. Sakura has come a long way from its humble, tiny beginnings. Now the restaurant is two stories, has a sushi bar, and has private tearooms. Best of all is the sushi, splendidly fresh and beautifully prepared. Expensive.

☙ 👗 ✳ **Heartland** (651-699-3536; www.heartlandrestaurant.com), 289 E. Fifth Street. Open Tues. through Sun. for dinner. Heartland prides itself—and justifiably so—on its creative use of local and regional produce. The adjacent wine bar is considered a worthy destination on its own. Very expensive.

✍ ☙ 👗 ✳ **FACES Mears Park** (651-209-7776; www.facesmearspark.com), 380 Jackson Street. Open Mon. through Fri. for lunch and dinner, Sat. and Sun. for dinner and happy hour. The name plays off the restaurant's location, facing Mears Park. The menu is filled with gourmet pizza, pasta, and meat dishes, including a set of lovely tagines. Expensive.

Other Areas of St. Paul
☙ 👗 ✳ **Ristorante Luci** (651-699-8258; www.ristoranteluci.com), 470 Cleveland Avenue. Open Tues. through Sat. for dinner. This tiny, very romantic bistro serves lovingly made Italian food, including not just pasta but sharp takes on meat dishes as well. Expensive. Tues. and Thurs. are "2 for $40" night, when a four-course taster's dinner is offered at $20 per person for at least two people.

✍ ☙ 👗 ✳ **The Strip Club** (651-793-6247; www.domeats.com), 378 Maria Avenue. Open Tues. through Sun. for dinner, Sat. and Sun. for brunch. No, it's not *that* kind of strip club—we're talking meat here, and heavy on the beef, with some duck, pork, and fish. One of the top restaurants for a decadent dinner. Very expensive.

✍ ☙ 👗 ✳ **Muffuletta** (651-644-9116; www.muffuletta.com), 2260 Como Avenue. Open daily for lunch and dinner. This cozy restaurant with its changing daily menu is tucked into a little neighborhood just blocks from the St. Paul campus of the University of

Minnesota. Using local and seasonal foods when possible, Muffuletta provides inventive and delicious food, such as Argentine pot roast with sweet potatoes and black beans. Expensive.

EATING OUT

Cathedral Hill

✍ ₤ ⚏ ❈ **The Happy Gnome** (651-287-2018; www.thehappy gnome.com), 498 Selby Avenue. Open daily for lunch and dinner. A neighborhood bar and grill with a more sophisticated menu. Try the lamb scallopini or the venison burger, and admire the lengthy and well-chosen beer list. Moderate.

✍ ₤ ⚏ ❈ **The Muddy Pig** (651-254-1030; www.muddypig.com), 162 Dale Street. Open daily for lunch and dinner. Offers a more traditional bar and grill menu, including burgers and sandwiches, but also heartier fare like chicken cordon bleu. Moderate.

✍ ₤ ❈ **Cheeky Monkey Deli** (651-224-6066; www.cheeky monkeydeli.com), 525 Selby Avenue. Open daily for lunch and dinner. Creative deli foods, includ-

---

ASIAN FOOD

While Minneapolis has Eat Street and the Midtown Global Market, St. Paul has its own ethnic neighborhoods filled with immigrants and authentic and delicious home cooking. University Avenue is home to dozens of small, casual Asian restaurants that don't always rely on Americanization to sell their foods.

✍ ₤ ❈ **Hoa Bien** (651-647-1011), 1105 University Avenue. Open daily for lunch and dinner. Excellent Vietnamese food, especially the seafood dishes. Inexpensive.

✍ ₤ ❈ **Que Nha Vietnamese** (651-290-8552), 849 University Avenue. Open daily for lunch and dinner. Authentic, flavorful Vietnamese cuisine, including several noodle bowls and variations on pho. Inexpensive.

✍ ₤ ⚏ ❈ **Ngon Vietnamese Bistro** (651-222-3301; www.ngonbistro.com), 799 University Avenue. Open daily for lunch and dinner. An unexpectedly elegant entry into the city's Asian restaurants, Ngon has extensive wine and beer lists and fusion food—and some of the best pho around. Moderate.

ing a mac 'n' cheese made with rosemary and goat cheese, and a mushroom and Brie sandwich. Moderate.

✿ ও ❋ **Nina's Coffee Cafe** (651-292-9816), 165 Western Avenue N. Open daily for all three meals. With a limited but quality menu of pastries, sandwiches, and soups, Nina's is a neighborhood hangout enhanced by its location upstairs from Common Good Books (see *Selective Shopping*). Free Wi-Fi is available to patrons, and Nov. finds Nina's acting as the unofficial gathering spot for the locally active NaNoWriMo group (National Novel Writing Month; www.nanowrimo.org). Inexpensive.

Downtown

✿ ও ❣ ❋ **Black Sheep Coal-Fired Pizza** (651-227-4337; www.blacksheeppizza.com), 502 N. Robert Street (with another location in Minneapolis). Open daily for lunch and dinner. Black Sheep's delightful coal-fired pizzas come with creative topping choices, such as fennel sausage, hot salami, onion, and cracked green olive. Moderate.

✿ ও ❋ **Saigon Restaurant and Bakery** (651-225-8751), 601 University Avenue. Open daily for lunch and dinner. Extensive Asian menu, backed up by excellent cooking and low prices. Hot selling items are the banh mi and the pho. If you're particularly hungry, you can take the pho challenge—eat 10 pounds of pho in less than 45 minutes to earn free pho, a T-shirt, and your picture on the wall. Inexpensive.

✿ ও ❋ **Cheng Heng** (651-222-5577), 448 University Avenue. Open daily for lunch and dinner. Cambodian food, varied and tasty. Try the Asian crêpes. Moderate.

✿ ও ❋ **Krua Thailand** (651-224-4053), 432 University Avenue. Open Mon. through Sat. for lunch and dinner. Thai food for serious Thai food foodies. The chefs don't buy into the "Minnesotans can't handle spice" urban legend; when they say something is spicy, beware. The interior could use some refurbishing, but that shouldn't stop you from trying it. Moderate.

✿ ও ❣ ❋ **Little Szechuan** (651-222-1333; www.littleszechuan.com), 422 University Avenue. Open daily for lunch and dinner. With a casual but attractive interior and a menu with more than 200 items, this Asian cookery focuses on its specific cuisine with educated and inspired results. Moderate.

✂ ও Ⴤ ❋ **M Street Café** (651-228-3855; www.mstreetcafe.com), 350 Market Street. Open daily for breakfast and lunch. Located in the lower level of the St. Paul Hotel (see *Lodging*), the M Street Café offers breakfast classics and soups, salads, and sandwiches. Moderate.

✂ ও ❋ (( )) **Q Kindness Café** (651-224-6440; www.qkindness .com), 350 St. Peter Street. Open Mon. through Sat. for breakfast and lunch. Kindness is in the name, and the food shows it, with simply prepared but tasty sandwiches and breakfast plates. Inexpensive.

✂ ও Ⴤ ❋ **Nook** (651-698-4347), 492 Hamline Avenue S. Open daily for lunch and dinner. Sure, it's a dive bar—but a dive bar with one of the best burgers in the state. People line up when it opens, so plan accordingly. Inexpensive.

✂ ও ❋ **Cossetta's** (651-222-3476), 211 W. Seventh Street. Open daily for lunch and dinner. Cossetta's has been in this location for almost a century, and there's a reason for that. The casual Italian restaurant cooks up seriously delicious pastas and pizzas, and the adjacent Italian market has fresh ingredients to take home. Inexpensive.

✂ ❋ **Mickey's Diner** (651-222-5633; www.mickeysdiningcar .com), 36 W. Seventh Street. Open daily, 24 hours. This is truly a St. Paul institution, listed on the National Register of Historic Places. A rehabbed dining car with a tasty breakfast and burger grill menu, Mickey's is the classic quick-and-cheap eating spot. The waitresses are trained to deliver food, not make friends—and make sure you follow the posted rules regarding minimum dollars spent and maximum time allowed. Inexpensive.

✂ ও ❋ **Keys Café** (651-731-5397; www.keyscafe.com), 767 Raymond Avenue. Open daily for breakfast and lunch. Breakfast is served all day at this location, and you really don't need to look at the lunch menu (although it's good, too). Enormous cinnamon rolls and giant omelets (including a Loon omelet with wild rice and mushroom sauce) will take care of your appetite. Inexpensive.

✂ ও Ⴤ ❋ **The Liffey** (651-556-1420; www.theliffey.com), 175 W. Seventh Street. Open daily for all three meals. An Irish pub with an American and Irish menu, so you can have corned beef and cabbage or a burger. Moderate.

ও Ⴤ ❋ **Barrio Tequila Bar** (651-222-3250; www.barriotequila .com), 235 Sixth Street E. Open Mon. through Sat. for lunch and dinner, Sun. for dinner. Upscale, authentic Mexican food at reasonable prices—and an extensive tequila list. Moderate.

✂ ও Ⴤ ❋ **Tanpopo Noodle Shop** (651-209-6527; http://tanpopo restaurant.com), 308 Prince Street. Open Mon. through Sat.

for dinner. This cozy little spot in St. Paul's Lowertown has heaping bowls of noodles and rice dishes, and a considerable sushi list. Moderate.

✍ ♿ ⍦ ❊ **The Bulldog Lowertown** (651-221-0750; www.the bulldoglowertown.com), 237 Sixth Street E. Open daily for lunch and dinner. An offshoot of the Bulldog NE (see *Where to Eat* in the "Minneapolis" chapter), St. Paul's Bulldog also has a robust menu of sandwiches, burgers, and hot dogs. Moderate.

Grand Avenue

Parking on or near Grand Avenue can be difficult. There is a ramp at Grand and Victoria, but given that the retail and dining area stretches more than 30 blocks, the ramp may not be near where you're going, and the restaurants often don't have their own parking lots. When looking for side-street parking, pay close attention to road signs; many side streets are for residents with permits only, and violating that can lead to tickets and towing.

✍ ♿ ⍦ ❊ **Saji-Ya** (651-292-0444; www.sajiya.com), 695 Grand Avenue. Open Mon. through Sat. for lunch and dinner, Sun. for dinner. Japanese cuisine, including extensive sushi options and teppanyaki tables. Moderate.

✍ ⍦ ❊ **Barbary Fig** (651-290-2085; www.thebarbaryfig.com), 720 Grand Avenue. Open Mon. through Sat. for lunch and dinner,

Sun. for dinner. Moroccan and North African cuisine is served in this rehabbed two-story house. Try the garlic sausage. Moderate.

✍ ♿ ❊ **Grand Ole Creamery** (651-293-1655), 750 Grand Avenue. Open daily at 10 AM. Homemade ice cream. Need I say more? Inexpensive.

✍ ♿ ⍦ ❊ **Wild Onion** (651-291-2525; www.wild-onion.net), 788 Grand Avenue. Open daily for lunch and dinner. This neighborhood bar and grill's menu is heavy on sandwiches, burgers, and pizza. Prime rib is offered on Fri. and Sat. Moderate.

✍ ♿ ❊ **Café Latte** (651-224-5687; www.cafelatte.com), 850 Grand Avenue. Open daily for lunch and dinner. It may be a cafeteria, but forget tasteless casseroles and limp iceberg salads. Latte serves up fresh, lively food, often taking advantage of seasonal produce for a changing daily menu of soups and salads. Whatever you choose, leave room for dessert—Café Latte has one of the most decadent bakeries in the Twin Cities. Inexpensive.

✍ ♿ ⍦ ❊ **Brasa Rotisserie** (651-224-1302; www.brasa.us), 777 Grand Avenue (with another location in Minneapolis). Open Mon. through Sat. for lunch and dinner. Their lively menu features Creole- and Caribbean-flavored meats and sides. Moderate.

✍ ♿ ❊ **Uptowner Café** (651-224-0406), 1100 Grand Avenue. Open

DISTRICT DEL SOL DINING

Across the Mississippi from St. Paul, the District del Sol (www.district delsol.com) is a large Hispanic settlement with tempting food options. If you're in town for Cinco de Mayo, stop by for the festivities (see *Special Events*).

✐ ♿ 🍸 ❄ **El Burrito Mercado** (651-227-2192; www.elburritomercado.com), 175 Cesar Chavez. Open daily for all three meals. This longtime Mexican grocer has served the District del Sol for more than 25 years, offering Hispanic foods at low prices. Summer often finds a corn feed of sorts on the sidewalk outside, with ears of corn served with chile powder and sour cream. El Café Restaurant, in the back of the mercado, has both cafeteria and table service, but more importantly, excellent food at low prices. You can go for the Americanized versions or stick to the more authentic foods, such as steamed mussels or carnitas platters. Mexican beer and wine are offered. It is also open daily. Inexpensive.

✐ ♿ ❄ **El Amanecer Restaurant** (651-291-0758), 194 Cesar Chavez. Open daily for all three meals. A small restaurant focused on tasty, authentic

EL BURRITO MERCADO

BOCA CHICA

Mexican food, El Amanecer's brightly colored exterior is a hint to what awaits inside, namely the lush murals decorating the walls. Inexpensive.

🌶 ❄ **Don Panchos Bakery** (651-225-8744), 140 Cesar Chavez. Open daily. In an unassuming white house is this little bakery. It may not look like much outside or in, but the aroma of fresh bakery goods wafting out the door will make you not care what the ambience is. Look for the guava-cheese turnovers. Inexpensive.

🌶 ♿ ❄ **Blue Cat Coffee & Tea** (651-291-7676), 151 Cesar Chavez. Open Mon. through Sat. 7–4. Across from the El Burrito Mercado is this neighborhood caffeine provider, a cozy bistro. Inexpensive.

🌶 ♿ 🍸 ❄ **Boca Chica** (651-222-8499; www.bocachicarestaurant.com), 11 Cesar Chavez. Open daily for lunch and dinner. Mexican foods made from scratch on-site. Minnesota's favorite fish, walleye, is given an exemplary Mexican take. Live mariachi music offered monthly; call for schedule. Moderate.

daily for breakfast and lunch, Fri. and Sat. for late-night munching. This small but delicious café serves impeccable breakfast foods, including late on weekends for the after-bar crowds. Moderate.

✐ ⚐ ⍦ ❈ **Everest on Grand** (651-696-1666; www.evereston grand.com), 1278 Grand Avenue (with another location at the Midtown Global Market in Minneapolis). Open daily for lunch and dinner. Nepali food served in a friendly atmosphere. The kothe (deep-fried meat) is delicious, as are the many curries. Vegetarians have lots of choices. Moderate.

CARIBE BISTRO

Other Areas in St. Paul

✐ ⚐ ⍦ ❈ **Luci Ancora** (651-698-6889; www.ristoranteluci.com), 2060 Randolph Avenue. Open Tues. through Fri. for lunch, daily for dinner. The sister restaurant to Ristorante Luci (see *Dining Out*) is more casual and relaxed restaurant than the dinner-only bistro. It's also slightly larger, but reservations are still recommended. Moderate.

✐ ⚑ ⚐ ⍦ ❈ **Rusty Taco** (651-699-1833; www.rustytacomn.com), 508 Lexington Parkway. Open daily for all three meals. Breakfast tacos, lunch tacos, and dinner tacos. Inexpensive.

✐ ⚐ ❈ **Caribe Bistro** (651-641-1446; http://caribemn.com), 791 Raymond Avenue. Open Tues. through Sun. for lunch and dinner, Sat. and Sun. for brunch. This small, brightly hued Caribbean restaurant is an especially welcome oasis in the winter, but it is great anytime. Try the doubles, a Trinidadian sandwich of curried chickpeas, or the conch fritters; you can't go wrong with the Jamaican Rundown, a stew of coconut, crab, carrots, onions, peppers, and sweet potatoes. Moderate.

✐ ⚐ ⍦ ❈ **Korean and Sushi World Restaurant** (651-645-2000), 694 N. Snelling Avenue. Open daily for lunch and dinner. A Korean restaurant with servers in traditional Korean dress, appropriate for the authentic menu. Specialties are the Korean grilled meats, served (as all entrées are) with panchan, six or seven small side dishes. The Korean sushi is quite good, too. Moderate.

✪ ♿ ✳ **Pho 79** (651-644-2327), 2233 Energy Park Drive (with another location in Minneapolis). Open daily for lunch and dinner. If you need a heaping, hearty bowl of flavorful soup, look no further. Inexpensive.

✪ ♿ ♉ ✳ **Blue Door Pub** (651-493-1865; http://thebdp.com), 1811 Selby Avenue. Open daily for lunch and dinner. Blue Door gives the Nook (see *Eating Out—Downtown*) a run for its money in the burger department. Its most famous burger is the Juicy Blucy (featured on *Diners, Drive-Ins and Dives*), a half pound of beef stuffed with blue cheese and garlic. Moderate.

✳ Entertainment

LIVE PERFORMANCES

✪ ♿ ✳ **The Fitzgerald Theater** (651-290-1200; http://fitzgerald theater.publicradio.org), 10 E. Exchange Street. This downtown St. Paul venue is the home of Garrison Keillor's radio program, *A Prairie Home Companion.* Call ahead for tickets, as this is a local favorite when in production. When it's not, the Fitzgerald hosts other performances, often in conjunction with Minnesota Public Radio (www.mpr.org) across the street.

✪ ♿ ✳ **Ordway Center for the Performing Arts** (651-224-4222; www.ordway.org), 345 Washington Street. The Ordway is a spectacular theater set on the edge of downtown St. Paul, on Rice Park and within easy walking distance to several prime St. Paul

THE ORDWAY

restaurants (Pazzaluna, Sakura, Meritage, St. Paul Grill; see *Where to Eat*). Home of the renowned Minnesota Opera, the Ordway also hosts touring musicians, dancers, and Broadway musicals, as well as presents several locally developed theatrical shows each year. Place your bar order ahead of time to have it ready and waiting during intermission.

✏ ♿ ❋ **Landmark Center** (651-292-3233; www.landmarkcenter .org), 75 W. Fifth Street. Across the street from the Ordway is this impressive building, originally built in 1902 to serve as a federal courthouse and post office. Today it's a cultural center, with a variety of events—music, dance, theater—taking place throughout the year. The building also houses several art galleries.

♿ **Minnesota Opera** (612-333-2700; www.mnopera.org), Ordway Center, 345 Washington Street. The Minnesota Opera formed in the 1970s, and in the mid-1980s it became one of the original tenants of the new Ordway Center. Today the company produces four or five full operas each year, using both local and international opera performers in innovative stagings. The primary focus is bel canto, and each season includes at least one bel canto masterpiece. The company has also premiered several new works and brought back Bernard Herrmann's *Wuthering Heights*, a rarely performed piece.

♿ **Penumbra Theatre** (651-224-3180; www.penumbratheatre.org),

270 N. Kent Street. Penumbra is one of only three African American theaters in the country to produce a full season each year. Creative director Lou Bellamy has lead the company to national prominence with quality productions and high-profile theatrical premiers, including several August Wilson works. The company's *Black Nativity* is one of the Twin Cities's popular holiday events each year.

✏ ♿ **St. Paul Chamber Orchestra** (651-291-1144; www.thespco .org), 408 St. Peter Street, fourth floor. The SPCO is a full-time professional chamber orchestra, and they are a busy group; besides performing in their own music hall on St. Peter Street, they also headline the Ordway Center and offer suburban venues, including in Wayzata and Eden Prairie. The company gives more than 150 performances each year, including a set of children's concerts and occasional international tours.

✏ ♿ **Minnesota Centennial Showboat** (651-227-1100; www .showboat.umn.edu), Harriet Island. A theater on a boat, docked at Harriet Island across the river from downtown St. Paul. The theater showcases acting talent from the University of Minnesota's theater department, with emphasis on comedies and mysteries.

✏ ♿ ❋ **Xcel Energy Center** (651-265-4800; www.xcelenergy center.com), 175 W. Kellogg Boulevard. Part of the larger

MINNESOTA CENTENNIAL SHOWBOAT

RiverCentre entertainment and convention complex, the Xcel Energy Center is home to the Minnesota Wild NHL team (see *Sporting Events*) and plays host to a wide variety of touring performers. Like its counterpart across the river, the Target Center, Xcel brings in top-level entertainers and bands; unlike Target Center, Xcel was built with concert acoustics in mind. Locals rejoice when their favorites play here, because the sound is much better.

♪ ♿ **History Theatre** (651-292-4323; www.historytheatre.com), 30 E. 10th Street. A theater company devoted to original plays focused on the American experience, primarily Minnesotan, both historical and current.

♿ ✳ **Artists' Quarter** (651-292-1359; www.artistsquarter.com),

408 St. Peter Street. Open daily. Live jazz every evening, from local gems to national acts. The Quarter does not accept reservations, so plan on arriving early, especially for weekend performances. Food is not served, but two nearby restaurants can deliver.

♪ ♿ **Circus Juventas** (651-699-8229; www.circusjuventas.org), 1270 Montreal Avenue. Circus Juventas is a performing-arts circus school for people ages 3 to 21. Besides offering workshops and camps, the Juventas troupes put on two shows annually. Call or check the website for a schedule.

SPORTING EVENTS ♪ ♿ **St. Paul Saints** (651-644-6659; www.saintsbaseball.com), 1771 Energy Park Drive. The Saints is the Twin Cities's minor league baseball team, owned in part by actor Bill Murray. Until the Twins' new stadium is complete, the Saints are the only professional baseball team offering outdoor play; Midway Stadium is wide open for beautiful sunsets and views of the lights from the state fair at the end of August. They may not have the name power of the Minnesota Twins, but the Saints do have goofy activities and displays between innings, including a live pig as mascot.

✐ ♿ **Minnesota Wild** (651-602-6000; http://wild.nhl.com), 175 W. Kellogg Boulevard. Minnesota's NHL hockey team plays its home games at the Xcel Energy Center.

✐ ♿ **Minnesota Swarm** (1-888-667-9276; www.mnswarm.com), Xcel Energy Center. While professional lacrosse hasn't quite achieved the popularity of baseball, football, and hockey in the Twin Cities, interest is growing. It's worth a visit—watching professional lacrosse is a goofy mix of serious athleticism combined with raucous humor.

✳ Selective Shopping

Stores are open year-round unless otherwise noted.

BOOKS ✐ ♿ ✳ **Common Good Books** (651-225-8989; www.commongoodbooks.com), 165 Western Avenue N. Open daily. This bookstore is Garrison Keillor's contribution to the world of independent bookstores. Small, but with a diverse selection of

books, Common Goods also resides in the same building as Nina's Café and across the street from W.A. Frost and Moscow on the Hill (see *Where to Eat*).

✐ ✳ **Micawbers** (651-646-5506; www.micawbers.com), 2238 Carter Avenue. Open daily. This small but well-stocked bookstore is a local favorite, with frequent book events and a knowledgeable, friendly staff. Located around the corner from Muffuletta (see *Where to Eat*).

✐ ♿ ✳ **Red Balloon Bookshop** (651-224-8320; www.redballoon bookshop.com), 891 Grand Avenue. Open Mon. through Fri. 10–8, Sat. 10–6, Sun. noon–5. This bookstore in a refurbished house focuses solely on children's books, and their expertise is considerable. The shop carries a wide range of books, and they host several

THE RED BALLOON

events every month. The staff is knowledgeable and friendly.

Sixth Chamber Used Books (651-690-9463; www.sixthchamber.com), 1332 Grand Avenue. Open daily. Books bought and sold daily, and the inventory is attractively displayed in a comfy, cheerful shop.

YARN Possibly because of the climate in the winter, or just because arts and creativity are prized in this community, the Twin Cities metro area has an unusually large selection of yarn shops. *Selective Shopping* in the "Minneapolis" chapter details yarn shops on that side of the river. The following shops are in St. Paul unless otherwise noted.

Borealis Yarns (651-646-2488; www.borealisyarn.com), 1340 Thomas Avenue. Open daily. A large, rambling yarn store with a wide selection of yarns and supplies, plus a room at the back with sale items.

The Yarnery (651-222-5793; www.yarnery.com), 840 Grand Avenue. Open daily. A tiny cottage of a shop, but with a good selection and a small sales annex.

Three Kittens Needle Arts (651-457-4969; www.threekittensyarnshoppe.com), 750 Main Street, Mendota Heights. Open daily. A sizable yarn shop with a wide variety of products.

Sheepy Yarn Shoppe (651-426-5463 or 1-800-480-5462; www.sheepyyarnmn.com), 2185

Third Street, White Bear Lake. Open Mon. through Sat. A cozy shop, complete with fireplace, for yarn lovers to relax, shop, or pursue their favorite yarn activity.

Knit'n From the Heart (651-702-0880; www.heartknits.com), 1785 Radio Drive, Woodbury. Open daily. Carries a wide and changing variety of yarns, including new and unusual brands.

Yarn Garage (651-423-2590; www.yarngarage.com), 2980 W. 145th Street, Rosemount. Open daily. Run by the self-proclaimed "Glitter Knitter," Steven Berg, the Yarn Garage is housed in an old retail building on a vintage small-town street, but inside is pretty much anything a yarn enthusiast needs. The store is floor-to-ceiling yarns and supplies, as well as vintage buttons and handles, numerous samples, cheeky gift ideas, and plentiful help.

✳ Special Events

Spring and fall: **St. Paul Art Crawl** (651-292-4373; www.stpaulartcrawl.org), downtown. Held twice each year, in the spring and fall, and allows more than 200 local artists and galleries to open their studios to visitors and potential buyers.

Year-round: **Minnesota Historical Society** (http://events.mnhs.org/calendar/). The historical society, which maintains sites all over the state, has numerous events, some annual, some one time only.

GRAND AVENUE SHOPPING

Just outside of downtown St. Paul is Grand Avenue, which runs parallel to Summit Avenue, home to many sumptuous St. Paul mansions (including the governor's mansion). Grand Avenue itself is a walker's paradise of restaurants and shops, many in rehabbed homes. The heart of the area is Victoria Crossings, the intersection of Grand Avenue and Victoria, where a public parking ramp and several restaurants are situated. An annual festival, Grand Old Day, showcases the neighborhood (see *Special Events*). Following is an overview of some of the shops to visit (see www .grandave.com for details).

🖉 ♿ ❋ **Bibelot** (651-222-0321, 1082 Grand Avenue; 2276 Como Avenue, 651-646-5651; with another location in Minneapolis; www.bibelotshops.com). Open daily; hours vary by location. Bibelot stores carry all kinds of guilty pleasures, from locally made jewelry to unique women's clothing to off-the-wall kitchen and bath items, greeting cards, and toys for kids.

🖉 ♿ ❋ **Creative Kidstuff** (651-222-2472; www.creativekidstuff.com), 1074 Grand Avenue (with another location in Woodbury). Open daily. This store is chock-full of toys, educational and otherwise, and perhaps even better, is well staffed by knowledgeable and helpful clerks who aren't against the idea of kids trying out toys before buying them.

🖉 ❋ **Cooks of Crocus Hill** (651-228-1333; www.cooksofcrocushill.com), 877 Grand Avenue (with another location in Edina). Open daily. All the fine cooking supplies you ever thought, or never knew, you needed. Cooks also offers an extensive class list.

♿ ❋ **Garden of Eden** (651-293-1300; www.gardenofedenstores.com), 867 Grand Avenue. Open daily. A luxurious assortment of bath and body goods, many of which are natural products. Customers can create their own fragrances.

♿ ❋ **Northern Brewer** (651-223-6114; www.northernbrewer.com), 1150 Grand Avenue. Open daily. Supplies for home-brew or winemaking beginners and aficionados.

🖉 ♿ ❋ **Treadle Yard Goods** (651-698-9690; www.treadleyardgoods.com), 1338 Grand Avenue. Open daily. Fabric and supplies for those interested in sewing, including some unusual and high-end items.

COOKS OF CROCUS HILL

  ♿ ❄ **My Sister's Closet** (651-222-2819; http://mysisters closetmn.com), 1136 Grand Avenue. Open Mon. through Sat. Vintage and upscale women's consignment shop.

  ✂ ♿ ❄ **Quince** (651-225-9900; www.quincegifts.com), 850 Grand Avenue. Open daily. Tucked behind Café Latte is this gift and women's clothing shop, carrying fun and funky items.

  ❄ **Susan Metzger for C'est Fou** (651-602-9133; www.susan metzgerfd.com), 1128 Grand Avenue. Open daily. Local designer carries her own one-of-a-kind outfits for women. Accessories are usually made by local artists.

  ✂ ♿ ❄ **Golden Fig** (651-602-0144; www.goldenfig.com), 790 Grand Avenue. Open daily. It may not look like much from the outside, but this is a small gem. Gourmet foods, treats, spices, local artisanal cheese, and heavenly chocolates. The proprietors care enough about their local products (including award-winning chocolatiers B.T. McElrath and Sweet Goddess Chocolates) that during the warm summer months, they personally pick up the products directly from the chocolatier to make sure the chocolates aren't allowed to languish in a hot delivery truck.

GOLDEN FIG SPECIALIZES IN LOCAL FOODS.

Red Balloon Bookshop and **Sixth Chamber Used Books.** See *Selective Shopping.*

Check their website for information on upcoming festivities at their St. Paul headquarters, as well as around St. Paul and the state, including Historic Fort Snelling (see *To See and Do*). Special events around various holidays, including haunted State Capitol tours for Halloween and multitudes of historical Christmas celebrations, are of special interest.

January: **Winter Carnival** (651-223-4700; www.winter-carnival.com), various sites. Legend has it that this festival began in response to comments about St. Paul made by a New York reporter who said winters were "unfit for human habitation." Hence, a carnival to prove that not only is the winter not uninhabitable, but it can be quite hospitable and even fun. For 10 days starting in late Jan., St. Paul hosts a wide variety of events, including a coronation of winter royalty, a torchlight parade, snow sculpting and ice carving contests, a medallion treasure hunt, numerous kids' activities, and a "Frozen" 5K and half marathon. Check the website for details of each year's events; some years have included the building of an ice palace.

May: **Festival of Nations** (651-647-0191; www.festivalofnations.com), RiverCentre, 175 W. Kellogg Boulevard. Held annually in early May, this festival celebrates the melting-pot diversity of America and, increasingly, Minnesota. Nearly 100 different ethnic groups are represented, with shops, cafés, musical and dance performances, craft demonstrations, and displays of cultural traditions.

Cinco de Mayo (651-222-6347; www.districtdelsol.com), District del Sol. St. Paul's vibrant West

ICE SCULPTURES AT THE ST. PAUL WINTER CARNIVAL

Minnesota State Fair (651-288-4400; www.mnstatefair.org), 1265 N. Snelling Avenue. Open for 10 days through Labor Day. Adults $11, senior citizens $9, children 5–12 $8, children under 5 free. Various discounts are offered; check the website for details. Billed as the "Great Minnesota Get-Together," the fair is the classic rite of passage from summer to fall. Attended by well over 1 million people each year, the state fair is held on permanent fair-

BUTTER SCULPTING AT THE MINNESOTA STATE FAIR

grounds in St. Paul. Parking can be tricky and expensive; most public transit companies around the Twin Cities offer state fair buses that bypass the parking issue. The fair has something for everyone: animals (farm and pets); farm machinery; rides small and large; live entertainment all day (some included in the admission, some incurring extra costs, especially the grandstand shows that tend to have the "name" performers); exhibits with crafts and fine arts; games; a Miracle of Birth Center, where animals are on display during their birth process; parades; haunted house; hands-on exhibits from vendors; and food. The fair is well-known for its food, much of which lacks a healthy quality but makes up for it in taste. Most of it is on a stick: pizza on a stick, pickle on a stick, you-name-it on a stick. And where else could you get SPAM curds? Go early, go often.

Side, already the home to many Hispanic restaurants and shops (see *Where to Eat*), hosts this annual event. Two days of food, fun, live entertainment, a low-rider car show, parade, 5K and 1-mile races, salsa-tasting contests, and children's activities are all part of the celebration. Proceeds are reinvested into the neighborhood.

June: **Grand Old Day** (651-699-0029, http://grandave.com/grand oldday/), Grand Avenue. Held the first Sun. in June. It's only one day, but what a day. Grand Old Day kicks off with races of varying lengths (8K, 5K, 0.5 mile, 0.25 mile), followed by food, parades, an art fair, kids' activities, live music, and a teen battle of the bands.

August: ✆ **Irish Fair** (952-474-7411; www.irishfair.com), Harriet Island. Just as summer is starting to wind down, Harriet Island hosts three days of everything Irish: music, food, dance, drink, rugby matches, sheepherding, Gaelic

football games, kids' activities, and a Best Legs in a Kilt contest.

September: **St. Paul Bike Classic Bike Tour** (952-882-3180; www .bikeclassic.org), University of St. Thomas. Not a race, but an actual tour; there are two routes, 15 and 30 miles, for bikers to choose from, which cycle along the Mississippi River and then on to either Summit Avenue or up to Indian Mounds Park and around Lake Phalen. Routes can change; check the website for details. The bike tour is a fund-raiser for the Neighborhood Energy Connection (www.firstgiving.com/nec).

November: **Hmong New Year** (651-265-4800; www.rivercentre .org), RiverCentre, 175 W. Kellogg Boulevard. This annual holiday celebrates and educates visitors about the Hmong New Year with traditional foods, clothing, music, dance, and shopping. The Hmong population in the Twin Cities is one of the largest in the U.S., and this celebration has taken place for more than 35 years.

ST. PAUL'S NEIGHBORING COMMUNITIES

Many of the suburbs around St. Paul began life as small towns, becoming suburbs as the city spread out to meet them. Some of the older communities, like White Bear Lake, have grown while still retaining the small-town charm associated with tiny stores in old brick buildings along narrow streets, making for a most pleasant way to spend an afternoon.

APPLE VALLEY

Apple Valley in its present form has only existed since the mid-20th century, but for decades before that it was farmland—not surprising given its proximity to the rolling, fertile land along the Minnesota River.

♂ ♿ ❄ **Minnesota Zoo** (952-431-9200 or 1-800-366-7811; www.minnesota zoo.org), 13000 Zoo Boulevard. Open daily; hours vary by season. Adults $18, senior citizens and children 3–12 $12, children under 3 and zoo members free. Parking is additional, as is admission to the IMAX theater. This is one of the two major zoos in the Twin Cities area. The other is Como Park, Zoo, and Conservatory in St. Paul (see *Green Space and Outdoor Activities* in the "St. Paul" chapter), in the heart of the city; the Minnesota Zoo is out in the country, and the two zoos are different enough to justify visiting both. The emphasis at the Minnesota Zoo is on natural habitat, so instead of regular cages, many of the larger animals have large parcels of land to call their own. Some of the traditional zoo animals, such as elephants and giraffes, aren't seen here, unless in a visiting exhibition. But there is plenty to see, including a wide variety of monkeys and large cats, and a new dolphin area has regular shows. The adjacent IMAX theater offers a variety of nature programs interspersed with popular culture movies on the giant screen. The zoo offers numerous special events each year, including an indoor sandbox and beach day in Feb. Check the website for details.

MENDOTA

The name Mendota comes from the Dakota word for "where the waters meet." It's a tiny town—the population is less than 200—but is known for its prominent historic site, the Sibley House.

✍ **Sibley House Historic Site** (651-452-1596; www.historicfortsnelling .org/sibley-house-historic-site), 1357 Sibley Memorial Highway. Open Sat. 10–4 and Sun. 12:30–4, Memorial Day through Labor Day. Adults $6, senior citizens $5, children 6–17 $4, children under 6 and Minnesota Historical Society members free. Some of the state's oldest remaining buildings are at this site, the former home of Henry Hastings Sibley, who worked at the trade center for the American Fur Company in the mid-1800s and eventually became governor. Guides are available to lead visitors through three buildings, including the residence and the fur company cold store.

DOWNTOWN WHITE BEAR LAKE

WHITE BEAR LAKE

This small town on a lake has risen above its suburban roots to become a destination for the dining and shopping crowd.

✸ Where to Eat

DINING OUT & ♈ ❄ **Ursula's Wine Bar and Café** (651-429-9600; www.ursulaswb.com), 2125 Fourth Street. Open daily for dinner. This cozy bistro has a limited but tasteful menu of appetizers, pasta, and meat to go with the more extensive wine menu. Expensive.

✍ & ♈ ❄ **Ingredients Café** (651-426-6611; www.ingredientscafe .com), 4725 US 61 N. Open daily for lunch and dinner. A menu that changes monthly, focusing on fresh, locally available foods, and good wine and martini lists make this place worth a visit. Expensive.

NAPPING COLOBUS MONKEY,
MINNESOTA ZOO

✄ ♿ 🍸 ❋ **Rudy's Redeye Grill**
(651-653-6718; www.rudysredeye
.com), 4940 US 61 N. Open daily
for lunch and dinner. Upscale
steakhouse with a wide variety of
steaks, seafood, and pasta, plus a
full bar. Expensive.

EATING OUT ✄ ♿ 🍸 ❋ **Washington Square Bar & Grill**
(651-407-7162; http://washington
squareonline.net), 4736 Washington Square. Open daily for all
three meals. Neighborhood bar
and grill with outstanding burgers.
The outdoor patio is used three
seasons and is a lovely spot.
Moderate.

✄ ♿ **Ban Thai Restaurant** (651-
407-8424), 2186 Third Street.
Open daily for lunch and dinner.
This little restaurant is often said
to be one of the best, if not the
best, Thai restaurant in the Twin
Cities. Moderate.

❋ **Selective Shopping**

♿ ❋ **Truly** (651-426-8414; www
.trulyonline.com), 2175 Fourth
Street. Open Tues. through Sat.
Shop specializing in handmade
gifts by independent artists and
artisans.

✄ ♿ ❋ **Backdoor Candy Store**
(651-762-8200; www.backdoor
candystore.com), 4746 Washington Square. Open Mon. through
Sat. Treats for the young and the
young-at-heart, including a wide
selection of nostalgia candy.

✄ ♿ ❋ **Heritage II** (651-429-
4541; www.heritageii.com), 2183
Third Street (with another location in Excelsior; see "Minneapolis's Neighboring Communities").
Open daily. The source for Scandinavian and British Isles merchandise, including clothing,
tableware and accessories, and
gifts.

✄ ♿ ❋ **The Farmer's Daughter**
(651-653-6768; http://thefarmers
daughterwbl.com), 4905 Long
Avenue. Open Tues. through Sun.
Features handmade gift items
from local artists and artisans.

THE SIBLEY HOUSE, MENDOTA

WOODBURY

Woodbury was first settled in the mid-19th century, primarily as a farming community for Scandanavian, Irish, and Scottish settlers. Today it's a growing suburb with an emphasis on shopping.

✄ ♿ ❄ **Woodbury Lakes** (651-251-9500; www.woodburylakes.com), 9000 Hudson Road. Open daily. Opened by the same company that handled the Shoppes at Arbor Lakes (see "Maple Grove" in the "Minneapolis's Neighboring Communities" chapter), Woodbury Lakes is designed to feel more like a small-town shopping center rather than a giant mall by providing a mix of retail and dining in actual city blocks with sidewalks. While many of the usual chain-store suspects are present (Gap, Banana Republic, Victoria's Secret, and J.Jill), the strolling-friendly layout over four city blocks makes the shopping experience feel less suburban mall and more charming village. Dining options are much more limited than in Maple Grove, with only two sit-down restaurants and an ice cream shop.

North Shore and the Arrowhead

3

NORTH SHORE
AND THE ARROWHEAD

In a state that has stately forests, lakes small and large, prairies, and rolling countryside, it's hard to pick one area as the most scenic. But the North Shore and the Arrowhead region (named after its shape) have arguably some of the loveliest vistas in the state, and the region is one of the state's most popular for visitors.

The eastern edge of the Arrowhead runs along the shores of Lake Superior, while the northern border runs along Canada, areas rich in geological and historical interest. Much of the Lake Superior area was inhabited by the Ojibwe before the arrival of the Europeans, who came searching for trade routes and posts. The French were prominent explorers and settlers in this area, looking for furs and other goods for trade, and their influence is seen in community names like Grand Marais and Grand Portage. Fur trading was a central activity until about 1840, when most of the traders and trappers moved elsewhere, including the Mississippi Headwaters area. However, the arrival of railroads in 1869, combined with increased ship traffic on Lake Superior, lead to a population boom. The growth of commercial fishing as well as the development of the iron ore industry, combined with more sophisticated infrastructure and shipping methods, lead not only to established communities but to the beginning of the tourism industry.

While fishing and mining enjoyed their heydays, the lumber and agricultural industries were booming as well, at least until the Depression years, when competition in other parts of the country reduced their prominence.

Today's North Shore and Arrowhead still sees considerable commercial fishing and mining activity, but tourism has come to play an ever-increasing role in the local economy. The establishment of the million-plus-acre Boundary Waters Canoe Area Wilderness within Superior National Forest, which keeps this wilderness preserved nearly as it was in the days of the

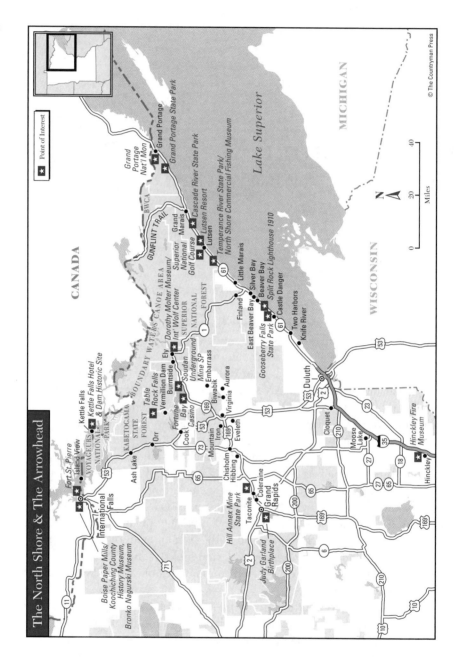

The North Shore & The Arrowhead

★ Point of Interest

CANADA

MICHIGAN

WISCONSIN

Lake Superior

© The Countryman Press

N

0   20   40

Miles

voyageurs, brings thousands of visitors each summer for camping, hiking, and boating. But whereas visitors used to come only in the summer for fishing and hiking, now they come year-round, taking advantage of the area's winter landscape for activities like skiing, snowmobiling, snowshoeing, and even dogsledding.

GUIDANCE Hinckley Convention and Visitors Bureau (320-384-0126 or 1-800-952-4282; www.hinckleymn.com), P.O. Box 197, Hinckley, MN 55037. Contact them via their website or phone number to order a visitors guide to the area.

Cloquet Area Tourism Office (218-879-1551 or 1-800-554-4350; www.visitcloquet.com), 225 Sunnyside Dr., Cloquet.

Duluth Convention and Visitors Bureau (218-722-4011 or 1-800-438-5884; www.visitduluth.com), 21 W. Superior St., Suite 100, Duluth. The Duluth CVB has extensive information about the city on the lake, but be aware that the website is packed full of text and images, and can be overwhelming.

Lutsen-Tofte Tourism Association (218-663-7804 or 1-888-616-6784; www.americasnorthcoast.org), 7136 W. MN 61, Tofte. Provides information for visitors to this popular ski resort.

Grand Marais Area Tourism (218-387-2524, ext. 1 or 1-888-922-5000; www.grandmarais.com), 13 N. Broadway Ave., Grand Marais. Local resource for all things Grand Marais.

Gunflint Trail (1-800-338-6932; www.gunflint-trail.com). An online and phone service providing information for tourists of the Gunflint Trail area.

Boundary Waters (www.bwca.com). A website full of practical information and resources on visiting the Boundary Waters area.

Reserve America (1-877-444-6777; www.recreation.gov). A major national site where visitors to the Boundary Waters area can reserve sites and permits.

Ely Chamber of Commerce (218-365-6123 or 1-800-777-7281; www.ely.org), 1600 E. Sheridan St., Ely. The Ely Chamber can provide help and information not just on Ely itself, but also on the Boundary Waters.

International Falls and Rainy Lake Convention and Visitors Bureau (1-800-325-5766; www.rainylake.org), 301 Second Ave., International Falls. A well-organized CVB devoted to tourism along the Canadian border and into the Voyageurs National Park area.

Voyageurs National Park Association (612-333-5424; www.voyageurs.org), 126 N. Third St., Suite 400, Minneapolis. Provides information and resources for visitors to the state's only national park.

Kabetogama Lake Tourism Bureau (1-800-524-9085; www.kabetogama .com), 10124 Timber Wolf Tr., Lake Kabetogama. Tourist information for the Lake Kabetogama region.

Iron Range Tourism Bureau (218-749-8161 or 1-800-777-8497; www.ironrange.org), 403 N. First St., Virginia. The Iron Range Tourism Bureau offers a free print guide to the Iron Range as well as online information.

GETTING THERE *By air:* The primary commercial airport in the region is the **Duluth International Airport** (218-727-2968; www.duluthairport .com), served by Delta, with flights to Minneapolis/St. Paul and Detroit; United Airlines, with flights to Chicago; and Allegiant Air, with flights to Las Vegas. International Falls also has an airport served by Mesaba Airlines (a subsidiary of Delta) with a feeder route from Minneapolis–St. Paul. Many of the smaller cities have municipal airports that can handle smaller jets or prop planes. Taxis, limos, rental cars, and light rail service is available from the airports into Duluth and surrounding areas.

By car: From the Twin Cities, I-35W N. will take you up to Duluth and scenic MN 61, which leads all the way up to the Canadian border. If you're heading to the eastern half of the Boundary Waters or the Gunflint Trail, this is the best route to take. If you're looking for the western parts of the Boundary Waters, you can take I-35W toward Duluth, then take MN 61 north of Silver Bay to MN 1, which takes you directly to Ely and parts west. An additional option between the Twin Cities and Duluth is the **Skyline Shuttle** (www.skylineshuttle.com), which operates out of the Minneapolis–St. Louis International Airport with daily round-trip bus service.

If you're driving toward Voyageurs National Park, you can take US 169 north out of the Twin Cities through the Iron Range to Chisholm, where you could pick up MN 73, which merges farther north with US 53, which continues to International Falls. An alternate route would be I-94 W. to St. Cloud, crossing over to US 10 to MN 371 through Brainerd and merging with US 71 south of Bemidji. US 71 then continues north to International Falls.

GETTING AROUND Duluth has a public bus system that covers the metro area, with reduced service on weekends and holidays. The service is designed primarily to transport students and employees from outlying homes to work and school within the city. Contact **Duluth Transit Authority** (218-722-7283; www.duluthtransit.com) for more information. For maximum flexibility, a car is recommended and is a necessity if you're traveling outside of Duluth. If you're staying in the downtown Duluth area and can walk or take a brief taxi ride to other downtown destinations, you could survive without a car.

The remaining regions of northeastern Minnesota require a vehicle.

WHEN TO COME The summer months are a particularly popular time in the Duluth, greater North Shore, and Voyageurs National Park areas, where the cooler temperatures generated by Lake Superior keep the heat from rising to intolerable levels. The scenery is beautiful, and countless events and festivals up and down the shore take advantage of that. Autumn months draw foliage visitors to all parts of the North Shore and Arrowhead region, while winter draws sports enthusiasts, particularly skiers to Lutsen and snowmobilers, snowshoers, and ice fishers to the more remote areas. Be aware that the winter months can produce some bitterly cold temperatures, particularly in the far northern reaches, but local stores are well prepared to provide the necessary outerwear. And if you're not fond of cold weather, bundle up in one of the many bed & breakfasts or lodges with cozy fireplaces and enjoy the snowy scenery from the warmth of indoors.

MEDICAL EMERGENCY Call 911.

St. Luke's Hospital (218-249-5555 or 1-800-321-3790; www.slhduluth .com), 915 E. First St., Duluth.

Lake View Memorial Hospital (218-834-7300; www.lvmhospital.com), 325 11th Ave., Two Harbors.

Cook County North Shore Hospital (218-387-3040; www.nshore hospital.com/), 515 Fifth Ave. W., Grand Marais.

Fairview University Medical Center–Mesabi (218-262-4881 or 1-888-870-8626; www.range.fairview.org), 750 E. 34th St., Hibbing.

Ely Bloomenson Community Hospital (218-365-3271; www.ebch.org), 328 W. Conant St., Ely.

Grand Itasca Clinic & Hospital (218-326-3401; www.granditasca.org), 1601 Golf Course Rd., Grand Rapids.

Rainy Lake Medical Center (218-283-4481; www.rainylakemedical .com/), 1400 US 71, International Falls.

HINCKLEY

About halfway between the Twin Cities and Duluth on I-35W is the small community of Hinckley.

✳ To See and Do

GAMING ♿ 🍸 ✳ **Grand Casino Hinckley** (1-800-472-6321; www.grand casinomn.com), 777 Lady Luck Drive. Open 24/7. Grand Casino offers extensive gaming opportunities for slots, blackjack, and bingo. Five restaurants are available for dining, and the on-site Kids Quest provides child care for kids too young to be on the casino floor.

MUSEUMS ✐ ♿ **Hinckley Fire Museum** (320-384-7338; www.seans .com/sunsetweb/hinckley), 106 First Street. Open Tues. through Sat. 10–5 and Sun. noon–5, May through mid-Oct. On Sept. 1, 1894, a historic event occurred in the quiet logging town of Hinckley, just south of Duluth. A fire started, and while any fire that burns out of control in the wilderness can be considered a wildfire and therefore devastating, the fire that consumed Hinckley was worse. Its technical name is "firestorm"; flames shot up 4 miles into the air, and 20 square miles of land were destroyed in less than four hours. The firestorm evolved much like a natural disaster, with cyclones of fire advancing and wreaking havoc. The only other comparable firestorms in the 20th century were related to the launching of atomic bombs in Hiroshima.

HINCKLEY FIRE MUSEUM

The Hinckley Fire Museum is housed in a small building that previously served as the town's railroad depot (the one built to replace the one destroyed by the firestorm). Though small, it has a sizable collection of fire artifacts, as well as a brief documentary movie and Native American items. The friendly staff knows the history of the firestorm well and is happy to answer questions or provide information on the individual artifacts.

✳ Lodging

BED & BREAKFASTS

✍ ♿ ✻ (ꉞ) **Dakota Lodge** (320-384-6052; www.dakotalodge.com), 40497 MN 48. The Dakota offers a wide variety of accommodations: four bed & breakfast lodge rooms, all with private bath and fireplaces; cabins; and a two-bedroom guest-house. The bed & breakfast rooms come with a full breakfast daily. The property is a naturalist's haven, with easy access to nearby St. Croix State Park. Expensive.

✻ **Woodland Trails Bed & Breakfast** (320-655-3901; www.woodlandtrails.net), 40361 Grace Lake Road. Built in 2003, this country charmer is situated on 500 acres of woodland. The property includes 4 miles of trails for hiking as well as access to Grace Lake for bird-watching, paddleboating, or catch-and-release fishing. The five guest rooms all have private baths and electric fireplaces; full breakfast is included. Expensive.

HOTELS ✍ ♿ ¥ ✻ (ꉞ) **Grand Casino Hinckley Hotel** (1-800-468-3517; www.grandcasinomn .com), 777 Lady Luck Drive. This is the larger of the Grand Casino Hinckley hotels, with 281 rooms and suites. Moderate.

✍ ♿ ¥ ✻ (ꉞ) **Grand Hinckley Inn** (1-800-468-3517; www.grandcasino mn.com), 111 Lady Luck Drive. The inn, operated by the Grand Casino Hinckley, has 154 rooms and suites, as well as an indoor pool. Inexpensive.

DULUTH

Duluth is a wonderfully historic community right on the shores of Lake Superior. Originally settled by Sioux and Chippewa, its position on the lake made it a boomtown during the logging, shipping, and mining years, and at one point it was home to more residents per capita than anywhere else in the United States. Today it's home to a lively waterfront area with an extensive walkway and a host of historic lodgings.

✳ To See and Do

FOR FAMILIES ✍ ⟡ & ✳ **Great Lakes Aquarium** (218-740-FISH; www.glaquarium.org), 353 Harbor Drive. Open daily 10–6; closed Christmas Day. Adults $12.95, senior citizens $9.95, children 3–11 $6.95, children under 3 free. Located along the shore near Canal Park, the Great Lakes Aquarium specializes in freshwater fish and aquatic life. Given that most regional fish are fairly monochromatic in color, the exhibits may be of more interest to people with a strong interest in marine biology than for families with kids who want to see colorful tropical fish. Recent exhibitions have included more fanciful creatures, such as sea horses, in an effort to broaden the appeal.

MUSEUMS AND HISTORIC SITES ✍ & ✳ **The Tweed Museum of Art** (218-726-7823; www.d.umn.edu/tma), 1201 Ordean Court, University of Minnesota–Duluth. Open Tues. 9–8, Wed. through Fri. 9–4:30, Sat. and Sun. 1–5. Closed Mon. Admission free, with a requested donation of $2 for individuals, $5 for families, or $1 for senior citizens or students. UMD students with ID and children under six are free. Named after art collectors George and Alice Tweed, the Tweed Museum focuses on early-20th-century American and European artwork as well as brings in exhibits from regional artists past and present.

✍ & ✳ **The Lake Superior Railroad Museum** (218-727-8025; www.lsrm.org), 506 W. Michigan Street. Open daily; hours vary by season.

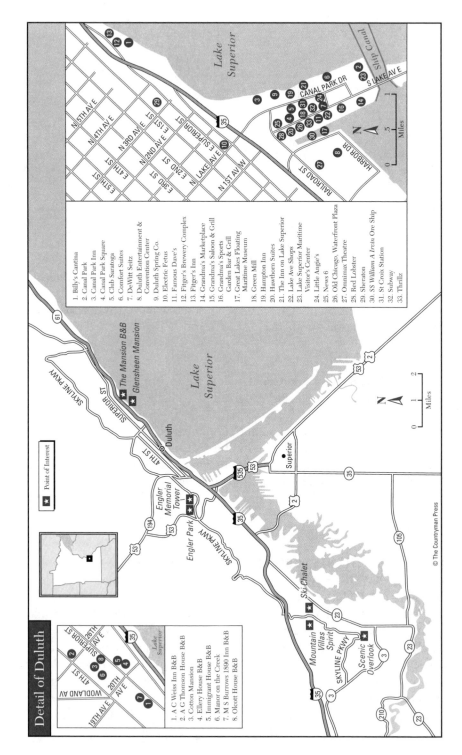

Adults 14 and older $10, children 3–13 $5.50, children under 3 and museum members free. Admission includes entrance to Depot Square. This small museum is devoted to Duluth's locomotive history, including vintage wood-burning steam engines (including the largest one ever built), railroad snowplows, and an operating model train exhibit. Between Memorial Day and Labor Day, visitors can ride a vintage electric trolley around the museum or sign up to take a ride on the North Shore Scenic Railroad, which has a number of options. (Visitors who purchase a ride on the North Shore Scenic Railroad are eligible for discounts on museum admission.)

✇ ⚅ ❄ **Depot Square** (218-727-8025; www.lsrm.org), 506 W. Michigan Street. Open daily; hours vary by season. Adults 14 and older $10, children 3–13 $5.50, children under 3 and museum members free. Admission includes entrance to the Lake Superior Railroad Museum. This historical complex is a re-creation of two Duluth streets set in 1910. Also on-site is the Duluth Children's Museum (218-733-7543) and the Duluth Art Institute (218-733-7560).

✇ ♂ ⚅ ❄ **Glensheen** (218-454-4536; www.d.umn.edu/glen/), 3300 London Road. Open daily 9–5:30, Memorial Day weekend through late Oct.; Sat. and Sun. 9:30–3:30, late Oct. through late May. Tours vary in price from $5 to $24. Just north of downtown Duluth, on a stretch of Lake Superior shoreline, is the 39-room mansion Glensheen. Built in the early 1900s by the prosperous Congdon family, Glensheen is now open as a historical site (maintained by the University of Minnesota). There are three

GLENSHEEN

THE GLENSHEEN CARRIAGE HOUSE AND GARDENS

levels of tours available: the home's exterior and grounds; the home's exterior, grounds, and first and second floors; or all of these plus the third floor, attic, and basement. The last tour takes the longest (and can be toasty in warmer weather—central air was not an available amenity when the mansion was built), but if you can, it's worth the extra time. The docents are well trained and full of interesting tidbits about the history and construction of the 39-room mansion, filled with mostly original furniture, decorations, and artwork. Ahead of their time, the Congdons incorporated electricity throughout (but maintained gaslights as well, as Chester Congdon was not convinced that electricity wasn't just a fad), as well an early version of a central vacuum system. The grounds, set on a wide expanse of shoreline, include a rocky beach, a boathouse, a carriage house, and a gardener's home, as well as extensive, lavish gardens.

One thing that is not mentioned on the tour, but you can now ask about it at the end (in earlier years, docents were not allowed to talk about it), is the murder of Elisabeth Congdon and her nurse at Glensheen in 1977. For some, this is reason enough to visit, but even if you have no interest in the real-life murder and subsequent trials, visiting Glensheen provides an unusually detailed and carefully preserved view into a lost way of life.

✒ **S.S. *William A. Irvin*** (218-722-7876, ext. 234; www.williamairvin .com), Duluth Entertainment Convention Center, 301 Harbor Drive. Open daily Memorial Day through mid-Oct.; hours vary by season. Adults $9, children $6. Run by the Great Lakes Floating Maritime Museum, the

S.S. *William A. Irvin* spent more than 40 years delivering coal and iron ore as well as transporting dignitaries around the Great Lakes region. During Oct., special Ship of Ghouls tours are available.

✳ Green Space and Outdoor Activities

PARKS AND PARKWAYS Skyline Parkway. A narrow road that winds through residential and rural areas, Skyline Parkway can be maddening to follow (it's not terribly well marked, especially on the northern end), but it's worth the effort if you want to catch some spectacular views of Lake Superior, the city of Duluth, and western Wisconsin. Take a detailed Duluth map with you, and be aware that parts of the road are closed during the winter months. And don't forget your camera.

Enger Park. Located along Skyline Parkway, Enger Park is a small but lush picnic area complete with its own stone tower. During the summer months, the floral display is breathtaking, and shaded picnic tables are spread generously throughout the grounds. Climb the tower for a wide-open view of Duluth and Lake Superior.

Leif Ericson Park. A large park set along Lake Superior, Leif Ericson Park has an open-air amphitheater that hosts live performances during the

A HARBOR VIEW FROM THE SKYLINE PARKWAY

THE LEIF ERICSON PARK ROSE GARDEN

summer months, and a lovely and (in season) fragrant rose garden. It's a great place for strolls along the lakeside.

RAFTING Superior Whitewater Rafting (218-384-4637; www .minnesotawhitewater.com), 950 Chestnut Avenue, Carlton. Open daily May through Sept. Must be 12 years of age and older. Fifteen miles south of Duluth, Superior Whitewater Rafting offers rafting and sea kayaking on the St. Louis River. Kayaking can be done as a guided tour or as a rental only. Reserve early for Sat. excursions.

SKIING Spirit Mountain (218-628-2891 or 1-800-642-6377; www.spirit mt.com), 9500 Spirit Mountain Place. While the word *mountain* might be overstating things a bit, the Spirit Mountain area is a popular stop for winter visitors to Duluth. Skiing is available daily, and while there aren't nearly as many runs or levels of difficulty as northern neighbor Lutsen-Tofte, for those who want to get a little skiing in without venturing farther north, Spirit Mountain works fine. During the summer, campsites with panoramic views of Lake Superior and the city are available for rental. Book lodging at the Mountain Villas Resort, a collection of 14 octagonal tree houses that make up the only lodging on the mountain.

ENGER PARK

TOURS 𝄢 ⚙ ♿ 🍸 **Vista Fleet Sightseeing and Dining Cruises** (218-722-6218 or 1-877-883-4002; www.vistafleet.com), 323 Harbor Drive. Rates vary. Vista offers several daily cruises during the season, some of which board in

Duluth and some of which board across the lake in Superior. Sightseeing, natural history, brunch, lunch, and dinner cruises are offered.

✳ Lodging

HOTELS

Canal Park

There are several hotels in the compact Canal Park area, all offering convenient access to shops, dining, and strolling along the Lake Walk. Given the popularity of summer in Duluth, plan ahead—many of these hotels fill to capacity in advance, especially on weekends.

✐ ⴲ ✳ (ᵞ) **Canal Park Lodge** (218-279-6000 or 1-800-777-8560; www.canalparklodge.com), 250 Canal Park Drive. One of the newer properties in Canal Park, the lodge has 116 rooms with a pool, hot tub, and high-speed Internet and Wi-Fi access. Full breakfast included with accommodations. Expensive. Weekend discounts and packages available.

✐ ⴲ ✳ (ᵞ) **Comfort Suites Canal Park** (218-727-1378 or 1-800-424-6423; www.stayinduluth.com), 408 Canal Park Drive. One of the smaller Canal Park properties, this all-suite hotel has a pool and whirlpool, some in-room whirlpools, and high-speed Internet and Wi-Fi access. All rooms come with refrigerator, microwave, and coffeemaker. Continental breakfast included with accommodations. Expensive. Weekend discounts and packages available.

✐ ⴲ ✳ (ᵞ) **Hampton Inn–Duluth** (218-720-3000 or 1-800-426-7866; www.hamptoninn.com/hi/duluth), 310 Canal Park Drive. This Canal Park lodging has mostly hotel rooms, with a handful of Jacuzzi suites, and offers high-speed Internet and Wi-Fi access. The property has a pool and whirlpool, and daily continental breakfast for guests. Moderate. Weekend discounts and packages available.

✐ 🐾 ⴲ ✳ (ᵞ) **The Inn on Lake Superior** (218-726-1111 or 1-888-668-4352; www.theinnonlakesuperior.com), 350 Canal Park Drive. The inn is one of the larger properties in Canal Park, offering both hotel rooms and suites. All rooms have refrigerator, microwave, and coffeemaker. Some rooms have fireplaces and whirlpools. The property has two pools, one indoor and one outdoor, and in an unusual twist for this climate, the outdoor pool is open year-round; it's situated on the roof with a sheltering wall, and the water is kept luxuriously warm. Also offered year-round is the evening s'mores tradition, where kids of all ages can come out by the shoreline and toast marshmallows. Expensive. Weekend discounts and packages available.

✐ ⴲ ✳ (ᵞ) **The Suites Hotel** (218-727-4663 or 1-800-794-1716; www.thesuitesduluth.com), 325 Lake Avenue S. This all-suite hotel has an indoor pool, full kitchens in each suite, continental breakfast daily, and charging privileges at several local restau-

BED & BREAKFASTS

Just north of the center of Duluth is a stretch of historical homes open for tours (including the Congdon mansion, Glensheen; see *To See and Do*). Within this area, not on Lake Superior itself but nearby, is a cluster of bed & breakfasts.

❄ ⌖ **The Firelight Inn on Oregon Creek** (218-724-0272 or 1-888-724-0273; www.firelightinn.com), 2211 E. Third Street. A luxurious entry in the bed & breakfast category, the Firelight offers rooms with private baths, all with fireplaces and Jacuzzis. A full breakfast is served in the room. Expensive.

❄ ((ⁱ)) **The Mathew S. Burrows 1890 Inn** (218-724-4991 or 1-800-789-1890; www.1890inn.com), 1632 E. First Street. This late-19th-century home has seen many changes since its days as a "bachelor pad," complete with third-floor ballroom, but it now offers five rooms, all with private bath. Expensive.

❄ ((ⁱ)) **The Olcott House** (218-728-1339 or 1-800-715-1339; www.olcott house.com), 2316 E. First Street. This 1904 mansion includes luxurious accommodations within the home—five suites with private baths—as well as a separate carriage house suite. Several of the suites have fireplaces and whirlpool tubs; all have air-conditioning, LCD TVs, and either four-poster or canopy beds. Expensive. Some packages are available.

rants, including Bellisio's, Grandma's, and Little Angie's Cantina. Expensive. Weekend discounts and packages available.

City of Duluth

♪ 🐾 ♿ ⅄ ❄ ((ⁱ)) **Radisson** (218-727-8981 or 1-800-395-7046; www.radisson.com/duluthmn), 505 W. Superior Street. The Radisson is the distinctly circular building in downtown Duluth, with views of Lake Superior from many of its rooms. The Radisson is a local landmark both because of its shape and because it was one of the first upscale hotels in the area. The property has a pool, sauna, hot tub, and whirlpool, and high-speed Internet and Wi-Fi access.

❄ ⟨ᵗᵖ⟩ **The Ellery House** (218-724-7639 or 1-800-355-3794; www.elleryhouse .com), 28 S. 21st Avenue. Ellery House's four elegant suites all have private baths, robes, and feather beds; one suite has a private sunporch, while another has a separate sitting area. Wi-Fi is available throughout the property. Breakfast can be served in the rooms if requested. Expensive. Some packages are available.

❄ ⟨ᵗᵖ⟩ **A.G. Thomson House** (218-724-3464 or 1-877-807-8077; www.thomson house.biz), 2617 E. Third Street. Built in 1909 by architect Edwin H. Hewitt, the A.G. Thomson House has four rooms with private bath in the main house as well as three rooms with private bath in the adjacent carriage house. Full breakfast is available in the dining room, or a continental breakfast can be served to the room. Expensive. Some packages are available.

❄ **Cotton Mansion** (218-724-6405 or 1-800-228-1997; www.cottonmansion .com), 2309 E. First Street. This 16,000-square-foot 1908 Italianate mansion offers seven rooms and suites, all sumptuously appointed. A full breakfast is served each morning by candlelight, and an afternoon wine and cheese service is provided daily. Expensive. Some packages are available.

❄ ⟨ᵗᵖ⟩ ⤳ **Solglimt** (218-727-0596 or 1-877-727-0596; www.solglimt.com), 828 S. Lake Avenue. This inn, not grouped with the others on or near Superior Street, is located across the Aerial Lift Bridge from Canal Park. Rather than a mansion, Solglimt is more of a seaside cottage, with three suites with private baths. Amenities include full breakfast daily, robes, beach towels, and binoculars. Expensive. Some packages are available.

The hotel's signature restaurant, Top of the Harbor (see *Where to Eat*), is open daily for breakfast, lunch, and dinner, in a revolving restaurant at the top of the hotel. Moderate. Weekend discounts and packages available.

♂ ♿ ▼ ❄ ⟨ᵗᵖ⟩ **Sheraton Duluth** (218-733-5660 or 1-800-325-3535; www.starwoodhotels.com), 301 E. Superior Street. Opened in 2007, the Sheraton is just a few blocks from the Canal Park area in downtown Duluth. The hotel has an indoor pool, and rooms have flat-screen TVs and high-speed Internet access. The Sheraton Club level offers larger rooms with sitting areas, as well as daily breakfast and afternoon appetizers.

DULUTH'S RADISSON HOTEL

Expensive. Weekend discounts and packages available.

🐾 ⚐ ♀ ❄ ((ợ)) **Fitger's Inn** (218-722-8826 or 1-888-348-4377; www.fitgers.com), 600 E. Superior Street. Fitger's started life as a beer brewery in 1881, and today the large complex (listed on the National Register of Historic Places) is a mix of hotel, retail, and restaurants. The inn is a small boutique hotel with views of both downtown Duluth and Lake Superior. A variety of room types is available, from a comfortable standard room to sumptuous whirlpool penthouse suites, which also include fireplaces, balconies, skylights, and large living areas. Expensive to very expensive.

✳ Where to Eat

DINING OUT ⚐ ⚐ ♀ ✳ **Bellisio's** (218-727-4921; www.grandmas restaurants.com), 405 Lake Avenue S. Open daily for lunch and dinner. This upscale offshoot from the Grandma's Restaurant group offers excellent Italian cuisine and a sizable wine list. Expensive.

⚐ ⚐ ♀ ✳ **Top of the Harbor** (218-727-8981), 505 W. Superior Street (in the Radisson Hotel). Open daily for breakfast, lunch, and dinner. Top of the Harbor's major claim to fame is that it is a circular revolving restaurant providing generous views of Duluth and Lake Superior. The food is basic American cuisine. Expensive.

⚐ ✳ **New Scenic Café** (218-525-6274; www.newsceniccafe.com), 5461 N. Shore Drive. Open daily for lunch and dinner. Just north of Duluth is this destination dining spot, a favorite of locals and visitors alike. New Scenic Café serves sophisticated, seasonal contemporary American cuisine, sourced locally whenever possible. In the summer, allow time to enjoy the surrounding gardens. Expensive.

EATING OUT ⚐ ⚐ ♀ ✳ ((ợ)) **At Sara's Table** (218-723-8569; www.astccc.net), 1902 E. Eighth Street. Open Mon. through Sun. for all three meals. Located near the University of Minnesota campus, At Sara's Table goes by two other names as well: Chester Creek Café and Taran's Market Place. Don't let the abundance of

AT SARA'S TABLE

names intimidate you; this restaurant, casual and friendly, serves delicious meals, often using local food sources in season. Breakfasts are hearty and plentiful; lunch and dinner can be simple or elaborate, depending on your mood. A library in the back is available for lounging, or even purchasing the books. Free Wi-Fi is offered to customers. Moderate.

✍ ♿ ❄ **New London Café** (218-525-0777; www.newlondoncafe .com), 4721 E. Superior Street. Open daily for breakfast and lunch. This is where the locals gather. A tiny café on Duluth's busy E. Superior Street, it's not fancy, but it does prove that simple food prepared well can be outstanding. Be sure to have the New London Potatoes. Inexpensive.

✍ ♿ ❄ **Uncle Louie's Café** (218-727-4518), 520 E. Fourth Street. Open daily for breakfast and lunch. Diner food, the way it's supposed to be. Hearty pancakes

and Greek-influenced lunches. Inexpensive.

✍ ♿ 🍸 ❄ **Fitger's Brewhouse and Grill** (218-279-2739; www .brewhouse.net), 600 E. Superior Street. Open daily for lunch and dinner. Located in the historic Fitger's complex, Fitger's Brewhouse is a cheerful take on the "burger and beer" concept. Hearty sandwiches, burgers, and quesadillas all available with your choice of brew. Moderate.

✍ ♿ 🍸 ❄ **Lake Avenue Cafe** (218-722-2355; http://lakeavenue cafe.com), 394 S. Lake Avenue. Open daily for lunch and dinner. This quiet and tasteful restaurant in the Dewitt-Seitz Marketplace (see *Selective Shopping*) focuses on local and seasonal when possible, getting creative with "deconstructed" fish-and-chips and oxtail lasagna. Moderate.

✍ ♿ 🍸 ❄ **Baja Billy's Cantina & Grill** (218-740-2300), 600 E. Superior Street. Open daily for lunch and dinner. The menu may not be unique, but the cheerfully Americanized Mexican entrées are skillfully prepared in hearty portions and are especially tasty when combined with the house margarita. Moderate.

✍ ♿ 🍸 ❄ **Grandma's Saloon & Grill** (218-727-4192; www .grandmasrestaurants.com), 522 Lake Avenue S. Open daily for lunch and dinner. This hometown favorite has a cheerfully American menu packed with steaks, sandwiches, and pasta. Summer is especially popular at Grandma's, as it has deck seating overlooking the Aerial Lift Bridge. Moderate.

✿ ⅙ ⅄ ✳ **Little Angie's Cantina** (218-727-6117; www.grandmas restaurants.com), 11 E. Buchanan Street. Open daily for lunch and dinner. Southwest and American foods served in jumbo portions, with an agreeable assortment of margaritas and cocktails. Try the black bean tacos. In summer, enjoy Little Angie's outdoor deck while having a drink and watching the crowds on Canal Park. Moderate.

SHOPPING IN CANAL PARK

✳ Entertainment

✳ **Duluth Entertainment Convention Center** (218-722-5573; www.decc.org), 350 Harbor Drive. The DECC is home to touring concerts and productions that come through Duluth, as well as host to the Duluth-Superior Symphony Orchestra and the Minnesota Ballet. Besides the theater and convention center, the DECC is also home to the Duluth OMNIMAX and the S.S. *William A. Irvin* (see *To See and Do*).

✳ Selective Shopping

The Canal Park area, geared as it is for tourists, has several enticing shops.

✿ ⅙ ✳ **The Dewitt-Seitz Marketplace** (218-722-0816; www.dewittseitz.com), 394 Lake Avenue S. Located in the heart of Canal Park, the marketplace is housed in a century-old manufacturing and warehouse site that's now on the National Register of Historic Places. Tourist shops worth a stop include **Minnesota Gifts by Sandra Dee,** full of north-woods-themed apparel and souvenirs; **J. Skylark,** an engaging toy and game shop for kids; **Blue Heron Trading,** which has cooking items and gifts; and the **Art Dock,** which sells regional art and crafts. **Hepzibah's Sweet Shoppe** can easily take care of that chocolate craving, but if you'd rather have a quick bite to eat, stop by either the **Amazing Grace Bakery & Café,** which offers heavenly baked goods, or **Lake Avenue Café,** a small but surprisingly creative deli. Looking for tasty goodies to take home? **Northern Waters Smokehaus** has the finest smoked fish and meats and a diverse selection of cheeses.

✧ ♿ ✳ **Fitger's Brewery** (218-722-8826; www.fitgers.com), 600 E. Superior Street. Besides a hotel (see *Lodging*) and restaurants (including Fitger's Brewhouse and Grill; see *Where to Eat*), Fitger's also has a variety of retail to explore through its ambling hallways. Not immune to the downturned economy, some of Fitger's is sadly empty, but there are still enough retailers where you can spend some shopping time while waiting for your dinner reservation. Shops include **Benetton,** with its trademark "world of Benetton" colors; **Fitger's Wine Cellars,** a small but carefully stocked wine and spirits shop; **Jake's Lake Place,** full of the Life is Good clothes and products; **Wintergreen Clothing,** a retail outlet for the Ely outdoor-clothing manufacturer; **Snow Goose,** which carries locally made crafts and gifts; and the **Bookstore at Fitger's,** a charming store with a mix of popular and literary books and gift items.

✳ **The Electric Fetus** (218-722-9970; www.electricfetus.com), 12 E. Superior Street. Just steps away from the waterfront, the Electric Fetus has one of the largest music inventories in the state (along with its sister locations in the Twin Cities and St. Cloud), as well as gifts and jewelry.

✳ **Blue Iris Gallery** (218-720-3300; www.blueirisgalleryduluth mn.com), 723 Lake Avenue S. Carries a range of regional artists, particularly of photography, prints, jewelry, and fine crafts.

✳ **Blue Lake Gallery** (218-725-0034; www.bluelakegallery.com), 395 Lake Avenue S. Regional artists are represented with their pottery, jewelry, and sculpture (some of which is located in an outdoor sculpture garden).

✳ Special Events

January: **John Beargrease Sled Dog Marathon** (218-722-7631; www.beargrease.com). One of the most beloved events in this region, the Beargrease (as it's known), held annually since 1983, is the longest sled dog event in the Lower 48. The event draws dogsled teams and visitors from across the country.

June: **Grandma's Marathon** (218-727-0947; www.grandmas marathon.com), Duluth. Grandma's Marathon is one of the premier marathon events in Minnesota. Taking place over the third weekend of June, the marathon has a variety of activities besides the marathon itself—a health and wellness expo, kids' races and a 5K run, live evening entertainment, and a spaghetti dinner. Plus, of course, the actual marathon.

August: **Bayfront Blues Festival** (www.bayfrontblues.com), Bayfront Festival Park. This annual three-day celebration of the blues in early Aug. is a popular and long-running event; ordering tickets early and making hotel or camping reservations well in advance is recommended.

Glensheen's Festival of Fine Art and Craft (218-726-8910 or 1-888-454-4536; www.d.umn.edu /glen/visit/calendar.html), Glensheen Mansion, 3300 London Road. Glensheen is itself worthy of a visit (see *To See and Do*), and in mid-Aug. it hosts a fine-art festival on its grounds that attracts thousands of people annually. It's hard to imagine a better setting than this opulent 19th-century mansion and its sumptuous gardens.

NORTH SHORE/LUTSEN

Once you leave Duluth, you will want a car, if for no other reason than to be able to stop on a whim and visit scenic overlooks, trails, shops, and cafés. Make sure you take Scenic Highway 61 (MN 61) out of Duluth; you'll miss the lake views if you take Superior Street instead.

✳ To See and Do

✿ 🐾 ♿ ❄ **Gooseberry Falls** (218-834-3855; www.dnr.state.mn.us), 3206 MN 61 E., Two Harbors. Open daily 9–5. Admission is free. This waterfall area is by no means the largest waterfall in the United States, but it's visitor friendly, with a sizable visitors center and extensive trails and walkways. Pets are allowed, and there are "doggie bags" strategically placed to encourage owners to clean up after their pets. The park twists and turns around the base of the falls, allowing access to both sides. Be sure to wear sturdy shoes; crossing wet rocks is a tricky proposition in the best of footgear, and flip-flops could be downright dangerous.

✿ ♿ **Split Rock Lighthouse** (218-226-6372; www.mnhs.org), 3713 Split Rock Lighthouse Road, Two Harbors. Open daily 10–6, May 15 through Oct. 15. Adults

GOOSEBERRY FALLS

TWO HARBORS

North of Duluth is the iron ore and fishing port of Two Harbors. Turn off Scenic Highway 61 (MN 61) onto Waterfront Drive to visit the historic shore area, and to tour the *Edna G.*, the last coal-fired, steam-powered tugboat. Towering over the *Edna G.* is an enormous ore dock, still in use today. Nearby is the Duluth and Iron Range Depot, formerly the headquarters for that company and home to the Depot Museum. A short distance from the museum is the Two Harbors Light Station. First lit in 1892, the light station is still operational, although automation has replaced the lighthouse keeper. The site is a historic museum open seasonally, and part of the lighthouse serves as the Lighthouse Bed and Breakfast, for guests who enjoy a historic stay. The grounds have short but scenic hiking trails, including a breakwater out into Lake Superior that affords great views of the dock and the town.

THE *EDNA G.* TUGBOAT AND IRON ORE DOCKS AT TWO HARBORS

$8, senior citizens and college students with ID $6, children 6–17 $4, children under 6 free. North of Duluth on MN 61 is Split Rock Lighthouse. This small beacon for passing ships is not large in stature, but placed as it is on a dramatic, steep cliff, it has proved its worth for decades. Now it's open for tourists to visit, along with a large visitors center with gift shop and video presentation. If you're feeling fit, take the trail that leads down the side of the cliff to the beach below (171 steps each way) for amazing views of the lighthouse and the surrounding shorelines. The lighthouse grounds are connected to the Gitchi-Gami State Trail (see *Green Space and Outdoor Activities*), which can be used by bikers or inline skaters. Split Rock is open seasonally, with a special opening each Nov. 10 (call for hours) to commemorate the sinking of the *Edmund Fitzgerald.*

✤ ♿ ❀ **North Shore Commercial Fishing Museum** (218-663-7804; www.commercialfishingmuseum.org), 7136 MN 61, Tofte. Open daily 9–5, Apr. 1 through Dec. 1. Adults $3, children 6–16 $1, children under 6 free. This museum is dedicated to preserving and giving insight into the long history of commercial fishing on Lake Superior.

✳ Green Space and Outdoor Activities

The North Shore is all about the outdoors, whether it's summer or winter.

DOGSLED RIDING Stoney Creek Kennels (218-663-0143; www.stoneycreeksleddogs.com), 142 Sawbill Trail, Tofte. Open seasonally depending on snowfall, usually Dec. through Mar. Experience firsthand the thrill of riding behind a team of well-trained sled dogs. Excursions can run anywhere from 15 minutes to a full day.

HIKING Superior Hiking Trail (218-834-2700; www.shta.org). Run by the Superior Hiking Trail Association (SHTA), this collection of hiking byways and trails covers 277 miles along the Lake Superior shoreline from Jay Cooke State Park south of Duluth to the Canadian border west of Grand Portage. It's a work in progress; one of its special features is that it has been constructed mostly by volunteers over the past 20 years, with a tentative completion date of

SPLIT ROCK LIGHTHOUSE

2012. Frequent campsites and parking lots allow visitors to choose between backpacking and taking short day hikes. Contact the SHTA for information on their lodge-to-lodge hiking programs.

Gitchi-Gami State Trail (www.ggta.org). Long-term plans show an ambitious 86 miles of nonmotorized trails extending from Two Harbors to Grand Marais. By the end of 2011, about 29 miles have been completed and are open for visitors. A large section is open beginning at Gooseberry Falls through to Tofte.

Palisade Head, 4 miles northeast of Silver Bay. The road to Palisade Head is a short, narrow, gravel road that brings you to a parking lot and a scenic overlook off a 200-foot rock cliff formed by lava more than a billion years ago. It's a popular spot for rock climbers, but even if you don't climb, you'll be rewarded with the panoramic views of Lake Superior and the shoreline for miles on a clear day—all the way to Split Rock Lighthouse to the south, the Sawtooth Mountains to the northeast, and Wisconsin's Apostle Islands directly east. Hang on to small children—there are no safety fences.

PALISADE HEAD

PARKS Tettegouche State Park (218-226-6365; www.dnr.state .mn.us/state_parks/tettegouche /index.html), 5702 MN 61, Silver Bay. Tettegouche has nearly every kind of natural feature—Lake Superior shoreline, waterfalls and rivers (including the 60-foot-tall High Falls), mountainous hiking terrain, six inland lakes, and dense forests. There are 23 miles of hiking trails; in winter, cross-country skiers have 15 miles of trails. Snowmobilers and ATV users have limited trail access as well.

❉ **Temperance River State Park** (218-663-7476; www.dnr.state.mn .us/state_parks/temperance_river /index.html), MN 61, Schroeder. A heavily wooded state park with waterfalls, rivers, hiking trails, camping, snowmobiling, cross-country skiing, and rock climbing. Hikers should be sure to take the

HISTORY AND SCENERY COMBINED

Near Schroeder, you'll see a sign pointing the way to Father Baraga's Cross. Father Baraga was a Slovenian priest who took on the arduous task of ministering to a number of Ojibwa settlements in Minnesota, Wisconsin, and Michigan, often traveling by snowshoe or canoe. After surviving a devastating storm in his canoe when it was tossed by the wind into the mouth of the Cross River, Father Baraga erected a wooden cross in thanks, which was later replaced with the granite cross that stands there today. A visit to the site in inclement weather gives you some idea what Father Baraga faced and why he was so thankful to have survived.

FATHER BARAGA'S CROSS

HIKING TRAIL AT TETTEGOUCHE STATE PARK

trail that winds upstream from the parking lot until you reach the Temperance River gorge, incredibly narrow and leading to spectacular waterfalls.

SKIING Lutsen Mountains (218-663-7281; www.lutsen.com), Ski Hill
Road (County Route 5), Lutsen. Lutsen is Minnesota's largest ski area,
with 90 runs of varying difficulty across four mountains. Downhill skiers,
snowboarders, and cross-country skiers have 1,000 acres of land at their
disposal, along with an alpine slide and a mountain tram for prime sight-
seeing. Horse-drawn sleigh rides are available during the winter. Lutsen is
not just popular in the winter, although that's its prime season; hiking,
horseback riding, mountain biking, rock climbing, and kayaking and
canoeing are all offered in the summer, when the lush greenery attracts
skiers and nonskiers alike.

TOURS North Shore Charters and Tours (218-663-7384; www.north
shorevisitor.com/charterfishing), 6921 W. MN 61, Tofte. North Shore
Charters offers Lake Superior sight-seeing tours as well as sportfishing
packages, available in half- or full-day segments.

✳ Lodging

There is a seemingly endless supply of lodging along the North
Shore from Duluth to Lutsen,
from small mom-and-pop motels
to bed & breakfasts to large,
deluxe resorts. But in spite of the
number of accommodations you
see, they do book up during prime
seasons (winter for the Lutsen
area, summer along the North
Shore in general), so plan ahead.

BED & BREAKFASTS
✐ ✳ ((ɣ)) **Northern Rail Traincar
Bed and Breakfast** (218-834-
0955 or 1-877-834-0955; www
.northernrail.net), 1730 County
Route 3, Two Harbors. It's not
false advertising—this is a bed &
breakfast built out of actual train
cars. The cars have been developed into surprisingly tasteful and
comfortable suites. Guests check

in at the "depot" before arriving at
one of the 18 suites (all are
themed, including north woods,
Victorian, and safari themes). The
property provides guests with private baths, continental breakfast,
trail access, snowshoe rental, and
summer bonfires, all tucked into a
quiet wooded area. Moderate.
Packages are available.

✐ ✳ **Lighthouse Bed & Breakfast** (218-834-4898 or 1-888-832-
5606; www.lighthousebb.org), 1
Lighthouse Point, Two Harbors.
Built in 1892, the Lighthouse is on
the National Register of Historic
Places; proceeds from guests contribute to the Lighthouse's ongoing
restoration. There are four rooms
with shared bath, all with views
of Lake Superior. A full Scandinavian breakfast is served daily by

LIGHTHOUSE BED AND BREAKFAST, TWO HARBORS

candlelight. Children accepted with prior arrangements. Expensive.

❄ (ᵠ) **Baptism River Inn** (218-353-0707 or 1-877-353-0707; www.baptismriverinn.com), 6125 MN 1, Silver Bay. *Cozy* doesn't do justice to this charming three-bedroom bed & breakfast. Each room has a private bath; all have the rustic qualities of a log cabin. As it's situated on the Baptism River, guests have easy access to hiking and skiing. Children ages 11 and older accepted. Expensive.

CABINS ✎ ❄ **Temperance Landing** (1-877-723-6426; www.temperancelanding.com), Temperance Trail, Schroeder. Comprised of 3,000-square-foot log cabins, Temperance Landing is a Lake Superior luxury option. Each cabin has at least three bedrooms and baths; all come with fireplaces (some gas, some wood burning), fully equipped kitchens, access to hiking trails and canoe/kayak launch areas, and a fully restored classic Finnish sauna. Very expensive.

RESORTS AND LODGES

✎ 🐾 ♿ ❣ ❄ (ᵠ) **Superior Shores Resort & Conference Center** (218-834-5671 or 1-800-242-1988; www.superiorshores.com), 1521 Superior Shores Drive, Two Harbors. This large resort complex has all the bells and whistles: pebbled beach on Lake Superior; lodge rooms or lake homes; indoor and outdoor pools; easy access to hiking, cross-country skiing, and snowmobiling trails; and close proximity to an 18-hole golf course. Moderate. Weekend discounts and packages are available.

✎ 🐾 ♿ ❣ ❄ **Cascade Lodge** (218-387-1112 or 1-800-322-9543; www.cascadelodgemn.com), 3719 W. MN 61, Lutsen. The best of both worlds, Cascade Lodge is nestled into Cascade River State Park, with access to several trails and stellar views of Lake Superior. Accommodations vary from motel rooms and lodge rooms to cabins and two private homes. Stop at the restaurant for dinner (see *Where to Eat*). Moderate. Packages are available.

✎ 🐾 **Solbakken Resort** (218-663-7566 or 1-800-435-3950; www.solbakkenresort.com), 4874 W.

MN 61, Lutsen. Open mid-Apr. through Nov. A combination resort with motel rooms, lodge rooms, and lakeshore cabins and homes, Solbakken offers direct access to cross-country ski trails. Moderate.

⚓ 🐾 ♿ ☂ ❄ (ᵞ) **Bluefin Bay on Lake Superior** (1-800-258-3346; www.bluefinbay.com), 7192 W. MN 61, Tofte. Studios and condominium units are available for rental at this resort right on Lake Superior. The property boasts year-round indoor and outdoor pools, dining at the Bluefin Grille (see *Where to Eat*), and massage therapy (available by appointment). Expensive. Packages are available.

⚓ 🐾 ☂ ❄ (ᵞ) **Caribou Highlands Lodge** (218-663-7241 or 1-800-642-6036; www.caribouhighlands .com), 371 Ski Hill Road, Lutsen. A year-round resort nestled into Sawtooth Mountain in Lutsen, Caribou Highlands offers lodge rooms, town homes and condos, and Poplar Ridge homes, log cabins with multiple bedrooms and fireplaces. During the winter, the property offers ski-in, ski-out access to Lutsen Mountains. There is a restaurant and coffee shop at the lodge, as well as indoor and outdoor pools, saunas, and tennis courts. Other amenities include evening bonfires, massage, and Wi-Fi. During the summer, the Mountain Kids Camp offers half- or full-day themed camp programs for kids ages 4–10. Expensive. Packages are available.

✳ **Where to Eat**

DINING OUT ⚓ ♿ ☂ ❄ **Bluefin Grille** (218-663-6200; www.blue finbay.com), 7192 W. MN 61, Tofte. Open daily for all three meals. Located at the Bluefin Bay resort (see *Lodging*), Bluefin Grille serves American food with an emphasis on local, particularly Lake Superior seafood when available. Expensive.

⚓ ♿ **Cascade Lodge** (218-387-1112 or 1-800-322-9543; www .cascadelodgemn.com), 3719 W. MN 61, Lutsen. Open daily for all three meals. The restaurant at Cascade Lodge (see *Lodging*) provides hearty American fare in a casual, North Shore–themed setting. Expensive.

EATING OUT ⚓ ♿ ❄ **Betty's Pies** (218-834-3367 or 1-877-269-7494; www.bettyspies.com), 1633 MN 61, Two Harbors. Open daily for all three meals. Local legend Betty's Pies has everything, from attitude ("Pies just like Mom used to make, before she took up bingo, cigarettes & beer") to truly delectable pies. A limited short-order menu includes broasted chicken, burgers, sandwiches, salads, and "pie shakes." But it's the pies that will bring you back again and again. Inexpensive.

⚓ ♿ ❄ **Rustic Inn Café** (218-834-2488; www.rusticinncafe .com), 2773 MN 61, Two Harbors. Open daily for all three meals. Breakfast is served all day, but there are separate lunch and dinner menus, which include burgers, sandwiches, and slow-roasted pork and beef. Moderate.

✳ Selective Shopping

MN 61 has about as many small shops along the drive as it does small restaurants and cafés. As winter sports have picked up traffic farther north, many of these shops stay open year-round.

❋ **Playing with Yarn** (1-877-693-2221; www.playingwithyarn.com), 276 MN 61, Knife River. Open Wed. through Mon. This small but packed yarn shop, located right on the shores of Lake Superior, offers everything needed for the fiber enthusiast. Even better if you're a dog lover—the owner's dogs reside in the house next door and can be introduced upon request.

❋ **Russ Kendall's Smoke House** (218-834-5995), MN 61, Knife River. Open Mon. through Sat. As the name suggests, this is a great spot for smoked items, especially the fish—lake trout, herring, salmon. Gifts are also available.

❋ **Northwoods Pioneer Gallery & Gifts** (218-834-4175; www.pioneercrafts.com), 2821 MN 61, Two Harbors. Open daily Memorial Day through mid-Oct., Fri. through Sun. mid-Oct. through Dec., Sat. and Sun. Jan. through Memorial Day. Art and crafts items made by local artisans.

✳ Special Events

March: **St. Urho's Day** (218-353-7337; www.finlandmnus.com), 7344 MN 1, Finland. Possibly one of the oddest historical festivals in Minnesota. Located in Finland, a tiny town just north of Silver Bay, St. Urho is celebrated each year in mid-Mar. with a four-day festival. What's odd is that there is no St. Urho; the people of Finland (the city in Minnesota, not the country) created him to have something to celebrate. Ostensibly he drove the grasshoppers out of Finland (the country) in an act similar to St. Patrick driving the snakes out of Ireland. Regardless of veracity, the festival goes on; even in the country of Finland, St. Urho has a pub named after him.

August: **Two Harbors Kayak Festival** (www.kayakfestival.org). This annual event, usually held the first weekend in Aug., is about all things kayak: kayak races, beginning and advanced lessons, equipment demonstrations, and a gear swap.

September: **North Shore Inline Marathon/Half-Marathon** (218-723-1503; www.northshoreinline.com). Held on a Sat. in mid-Sept., the inline marathon begins in Two Harbors and flies 26.2 miles along Scenic Highway 61 (MN 61), ending at the Duluth Entertainment Convention Center. The half marathon begins at the 13.1-mile point, ending at the same destination. Participants must be 13 and older; there is a kids' sprint on Fri. night.

November: **Annual *Edmund Fitzgerald* Memorial Beacon Lighting** (651-259-3000 or 1-800-657-3773; www.mnhs.org/places

TWO HARBORS

/sites/srl/index.htm), Split Rock Lighthouse, 3713 Split Rock Lighthouse Road, Two Harbors. On Nov. 10, 1975, the freighter *Edmund Fitzgerald* sank in raging gales in Lake Superior; all 29 men onboard were lost. The somber anniversary, commemorated in the Gordon Lightfoot song "The Wreck of the *Edmund Fitzgerald*," is marked each year with a ceremony at Split Rock Lighthouse. If you plan to visit, please dress appropriately, as the weather can be cold and windy; the Minnesota Historical Society recommends bringing a flashlight.

Master's Bluegrass Festival (218-387-1284, ext. 4; www.boreal .org/music), Lutsen Resort. This annual festival takes place the first weekend in Nov., a perfect time to cozy up to the fireplace and listen to the masters of bluegrass.

GRAND MARAIS/GRAND PORTAGE/GUNFLINT TRAIL

The farthest northeast corner of the state, running along the Canadian border through the Boundary Waters, is a nature lover's paradise. The opportunities for kayaking, canoeing, fishing, hunting, bird-watching, hiking, biking, and observing wildlife are countless. Which is not to say there are not other things to do in the area—but they act as accompaniments to the natural centerpiece.

A car is pretty much a necessity, and if you're planning on venturing into the Boundary Waters, it's strongly recommended to purchase the Superior National Forest Visitor Map. Published by the USDA in conjunction with Superior National Forest, this is an incredibly detailed map of the Boundary Waters Canoe Area Wilderness (BWCAW). It wouldn't hurt to buy a magnifying glass with which to read it. The BWCAW is full of trails that don't appear on most state maps, and it's easy to get lost unless you're very familiar with the area. The map is available in a sturdy, waterproof plastic version for about $10. Many local gas stations and convenience stores sell it, or contact the **Superior National Forest** headquarters in Duluth (218-626-4300) for information on

SUNSET AT GRAND MARAIS HARBOR

ordering one. Also be sure to check out *Green Space and Outdoor Activities* for some suggested outfitters.

✴ To See and Do

ARTS AND CRAFTS ✎ ✳ **North House Folk School** (218-387-9762 or 1-888-387-9762; www.northhouse.org), MN 61, Grand Marais. North House is a nonprofit organization committed to rekindling interest in and developing abilities of old-style crafts and survival techniques. More than 200 courses are offered each year, some as short as a day, some taking several days. Courses include not only how to cook and bake in an outdoor brick oven, but how to build the oven; constructing kayaks and canoes; building yurts and a facsimile of Thoreau's cabin; knitting, papermaking, and jewelry making; and ancient Native American techniques for basket weaving.

✎ ✳ **Grand Marais Art Colony** (218-387-2737; www.grandmaraisart colony.org), Grand Marais. The city itself is known as an art colony, a quiet seasidelike community with diverse seasons that attracts resident and visiting artists. It's no wonder then that the official Grand Marais Art Colony is a popular and active organization. The colony sponsors year-round art classes, art events and competitions, and an annual arts festival (see *Special Events*).

VINTAGE STOVE AT CHIK-WAUK MUSEUM AND NATURE CENTER

GAMING ✳ **Grand Portage Casino** (1-800-543-1384; www .grandportage.com), MN 61, Grand Portage. Open 24/7. This casino takes the north woods theme and runs with it, including a northern lights display in the carefully designed ceiling. The casino has a hotel (see *Lodging*) and offers a shuttle to Thunder Bay, Ontario (U.S. citizens will need passports to cross the border).

MUSEUMS ✎ ♿ **Chik-Wauk Museum and Nature Center** (218-388-9915; www.chikwauk .com), 28 Moose Pond Drive, Grand Marais. Open daily 10–5, May through mid-Oct. Admission is $2 per person, $5 per family, or

GRAND MARAIS SHORELINE

free for Gunflint Trail Historical Society members. The Chik-Wauk is a new addition to the Gunflint Trail, located on the farthest end from Grand Marais, and well worth a visit. A small but packed nature center details the history and geography of the Trail, while five hiking trails crisscross through the site's 50 acres with varying levels of difficulty, including one ADA trail.

✳ Green Space and Outdoor Activities

BOUNDARY WATERS CANOE AREA WILDERNESS ADVENTURES
Be aware that visitors to the BWCAW, except for day-only visitors, need to reserve a permit ahead of time. Your outfitter can do this for you, or you can contact Reserve America (1-877-444-6777; www.recreation.gov).

Boundary Country Trekking (218-388-4487 or 1-800-322-8327; www .boundarycountry.com), 11 Poplar Creek Drive, Gunflint Trail. Ted and Barbara Young, proprietors of the Poplar Creek Guest House (see *Lodging*), offer a variety of adventure arrangements in the Gunflint Trail/ Boundary Waters area. They can organize lodge-to-lodge hiking and biking trips, canoe/biking trips, mountain biking trips, and canoeing trips.

Clearwater Canoe Outfitters & Lodge (218-388-2254 or 1-800-527-0554; www.canoebwca.com), 774 Clearwater Road, Gunflint Trail. Residing along Clearwater Lake in the Boundary Waters area, Clearwater offers

⌗ ♿ **Grand Portage National Monument and Heritage Center** (218-475-0123; www.nps.gov/grpo), 170 Mile Creek Road, Grand Portage. The historic site itself is open daily 9–5, late May through mid-Oct., while the heritage center is open year-round. Admission is free. This monument is really a don't-miss for visitors to the area. An extensive re-creation of the life of traders and Native Americans before there was a United States and Canada, the national monument has a traditional Ojibwe village, a reconstruction of the Northwest Company's stockade (including a great hall and kitchen), a fur trade canoe under construction, and historic gardens that

THE HERITAGE GARDENS AT GRAND PORTAGE NATIONAL MONUMENT

both a lodge (see *Lodging*) and an outfitting company. The proprietors can assist you with canoeing, hiking, fishing, birding, and even wildlife photograph trips.

Sawbill Canoe Outfitters (218-663-7150; www.sawbill.com), 4620 Sawbill Trail, Tofte. Sawbill has been arranging BWCAW trips for more than 50 years, and they've got keen insight into navigating the wilderness. Saw-

GRAND PORTAGE NATIONAL MONUMENT AS SEEN FROM THE TOP OF THE MOUNT ROSE TRAIL

represent what the original trading villages grew. Kids' programs are offered in the summer, and costumed historical guides are available to answer questions. Trails outside the stockade take visitors deep into the northern wilderness, and there are snowshoe trails available during the winter. The national monument also serves as the departure point for the ferry to Isle Royale, which is the largest island in Lake Superior (and technically is part of Michigan). After visiting the monument, if you feel ambitious, cross the street and hike the Mount Rose Trail, a 0.5-mile, very steep trail that will reward you with panoramic views of the monument, Lake Superior, and the Sawtooth Mountains.

bill offers full and partial outfitting, canoe touring, and even food-only arrangements.

PARKS AND PARKWAYS From Grand Marais north is an abundance of state parks and wildlife areas. Be sure to check local conditions before visiting—nearly annual droughts have brought severe fire restrictions in

DEVIL'S KETTLE

parks and campsites in recent years, and some park access is limited during wildfires. Check with individual parks for up-to-the-minute information.

Judge C.R. Magney State Park (218-387-3039; www.dnr.state.mn.us /state_parks/judge_cr_magney/index.html), 4051 E. MN 61, Grand Marais. Open daily Apr. 1 through Oct. 31. This park, located between Grand Marais and Grand Portage, is home to the Brule River. The Brule leads to Devil's Kettle, a unique 50-foot waterfall that is rumored to have a bottomless cauldron. Nine miles of hiking trails, including an ascent to Devil's Kettle, are open during the season, as well as several fishing sites. Campsites are available; advance reservations are recommended.

❄ **Grand Portage State Park** (218-475-2360; www.dnr.state.mn.us/state _parks/grand_portage/index.html), 9393 E. MN 61, Grand Portage. Open daily. This park, the only Minnesota state park operated jointly with an Indian tribe, has naturalists on hand during the summer months who are tribe members that can speak about local Ojibwa history. The park also boasts Minnesota's highest waterfall, the 120-foot-tall High Falls. Camping is not available, but the falls are easily accessible for day visitors via a 0.5-mile trail and boardwalk.

Gunflint Trail (1-800-338-6932; www.gunflint-trail.com). A 57-mile paved road leading from Grand Marais to Saganaga Lake near the Canadian border, the Gunflint Trail is hands down one of the most beautiful drives in the region. Acres of forest uninterrupted by more than the occasional café or shop, the trail also has an extensive collection of lodging options (see *Lodging*) nestled within the trees, as well as a new historical center and hiking spot at Chik-Wauk Museum (see *To See and Do*). Watch your speed as you drive; it's not unusual to have a deer, wolf, or even a moose appear on the road, and all of these animals can do as much harm to you and your vehicle as you can do to them. The area has enjoyed a growth in year-round tourism, thanks to the increased popularity of winter sports joining the ranks of other favored pastimes, such as birding, mountain biking, fall foliage viewing, canoeing and kayaking, camping, fishing, and even mushroom and berry picking.

WILDLIFE ABOUNDS ON THE GUNFLINT TRAIL.

GRAND MARAIS AS SEEN FROM THE GUNFLINT TRAIL

In extreme weather the road may be closed, but since there are year-round residents, it is plowed whenever feasible.

✳ Lodging

BED & BREAKFASTS

Grand Marais

Superior Overlook Bed and Breakfast (218-387-9339 or 1-877-387-9339), 1620 E. MN 61. Two well-appointed rooms, each with private bath, overlooking Lake Superior. A sauna is available for guests. Expensive.

✳ **Skara Brae** (218-387-2861 or 1-866-467-5272; www.skarabraebb .com), 1708 E. MN 61. This small but charming Scottish-themed bed & breakfast offers, for adults and children ages 12 and up, lovely accommodations in two rooms and a cottage, all with private bath.

Breakfast and afternoon tea are available daily, and discounts for North House Folk School students are offered. Inexpensive.

Gunflint Trail

✐ ✳ **Poplar Creek Guest House** (1-800-322-8327; www.littleollie lodging.com), 11 Poplar Creek Drive. Tucked into a peaceful wooded area off the Gunflint Trail, the Poplar Creek Guest House has two guest rooms, each with private bath, and a suite. The rooms are graciously appointed, and they share a common room with kitchenette, fireplace, and private deck. The suite has a private kitchen area as well as deck. Hosts Barbara and Ted have run a bed & breakfast in the north woods for many years, and they know exactly how to do it right, especially when it comes to the full breakfast served in the cheerful, welcoming breakfast room. Poplar Creek can also arrange a variety of lodge-to-lodge arrangements (see *Green Space and Outdoor Activities*). Also available are two cabins and a year-round yurt (see *Lodging* in the "Boundary Waters/Ely" chapter). Expensive. Packages are available.

✳ **Pincushion Bed & Breakfast** (218-387-2969; www.pincushion bb.com), 968 Gunflint Trail. Pincushion is on 43 acres just 3 miles from Grand Marais and, sitting on the Sawtooth Mountain ridgeline, has impressive views and on-site access to hiking trails. This peaceful inn has four rooms, all with

private bath, and a common living area with fireplace. Full breakfast served daily. Expensive.

CABINS, VILLAS, AND TOWN HOUSES

Grand Marais
✐ ♿ ✳ (((•))) **Cobblestone Cove Villas** (218-387-2633 or 1-800-247-6020; www.cobblestone covevillas.com), 17 S. Broadway. Located on the harbor, Cobblestone Cove Villas is a newer townhouse property with upscale accommodations within easy walking distance to shops and restaurants. Expensive.

✐ **Opel's Lakeside Cabins** (1-800-950-4361; www.opelslake sidecabins.com), Croftville Road. Open mid-May through mid-Oct. Opel's has five cabins available, all directly on the Lake Superior shoreline. The cabins are rustic but charming, and the views

GRAND MARAIS HARBOR

and location are hard to beat. Moderate.

Gunflint Trail

🌲 🐾 **Cross River Lodge** (218-388-2233 or 1-866-203-8991; www.crossriverlodge.com), 196 N. Gunflint Lake Road. Open May through Oct. and Jan. through Mar. Cross River Lodge, the former Moosehorn Lodge, is situated on Gunflint Lake. The property offers two lovely bed & breakfast rooms, each with private bath, and four cabins near or on the lake, with fireplaces, complete kitchens, and decks with barbecues. Expensive.

🌲 ❄ **Bearskin Lodge** (218-388-2292 or 1-800-338-4170; www .bearskin.com), 124 E. Bearskin Road. Located almost 30 miles from Grand Marais on the Gunflint Trail, Bearskin Lodge is a model of peace and retreat. The resort has 11 cabins and two lodges with townhouse accommodations. There's a hot tub and sauna on-site, and massage can be arranged. During the summer, boats, canoes, and pontoons are available, as well as bikes; children's naturalist programs can be arranged. Expensive.

🌲 🐾 **Clearwater Canoe Outfitters & Lodge** (218-388-2254 or 1-800-527-0554; www.canoebwca .com), 774 Clearwater Road. Open May through Oct. This lodge has seven cabins, plus a suite and two bed & breakfast rooms in the lodge (breakfast served daily for lodge guests only). The resort also offers full outfitting and tour services (see *Green Space and Outdoor Activities*). Moderate.

🌲 🐾 ☿ ❄ **Gunflint Lodge** (218-388-2294 or 1-800-328-3325; www.gunflint.com), 143 S. Gunflint Lake. Gunflint Lodge has 23 cabins of varying amenities, from the more rustic Canoers Cabins (bunk beds, shared bath in a nearby building) to the Romantic Cottages (lakeview cabins with fireplace, hot tub, and full kitchen) to the Gunflint Lake Home (with two to fourbedrooms, fireplace, hot tub, and sauna). A restaurant on-site offers an alternative to cooking in the cabin (see *Where to Eat*), and an extensive list of year-round activities includes winter and summer sports as well as massage. Moderate to expensive.

HOTELS

Grand Marais

🌲 🐾 ♿ ❄ (ᵂ) **Best Western Superior Inn & Suites** (218-387-2240 or 1-800-780-7234; www .bestwestern.com/superiorinn), MN 61. A solid choice for midprice travelers, the Best Western offers high-speed Internet, microwaves, and refrigerators, and upgraded rooms have fireplaces. There are winter vehicle plug-ins, plus parking for trailers and snowmobiles. Moderate.

🌲 🐾 ♿ ❄ (ᵂ) **East Bay Suites** (218-387-2800 or 1-800-414-2807; www.eastbaysuites.com), 21 Wisconsin Street. Located right on Lake Superior, close to restaurants

THE PATIO AT THE GUNFLINT LODGE

and shops, Easy Bay Suites all have decks or patios overlooking the lake, as well as full kitchens, fireplaces, washers and dryers, and Wi-Fi. Accommodations vary in size from studio to three-bedroom, with some suites offering bunk beds. Moderate.

Grand Portage

🌿 ♿ **Naniboujou Lodge** (218-387-2688; www.naniboujou.com), 20 Naniboujou Trail. Open daily from mid-May to late Oct. and specific weekends from Christmas through Mar. Call for specific dates. Naniboujou is listed on the National Register of Historic Places, and its colorful history matches its bright interior. Built in the 1920s as a private club for founding members that included

Babe Ruth and Jack Dempsey, it never reached its potential as the country reached the Depression

THE FAMOUS DINING ROOM AT NANIBOUJOU LODGE

years. Eventually reborn as a hotel and lodge, Naniboujou has a beautifully decorated great hall, painted in designs reflective of the Cree Indians, that serves as the dining room (see *Where to Eat*). The rooms are tastefully and comfortably set up, and there are no TVs or telephones in order to preserve the sense of getting away from it all. Moderate.

✧ ♿ ♈ ❄ ((ŋ)) **Grand Portage Lodge & Casino** (1-800-543-1384; www.grandportage.com), MN 61. Located just south of the Canadian border, the Grand Portage Lodge has spacious rooms and a friendly staff ready to help with anything you need. The hotel offers an indoor pool and sauna, a full-service restaurant overlooking Lake Superior, and a seasonal (mid-May to mid-Oct.) RV Park. Inexpensive.

✷ Where to Eat

DINING OUT

Grand Marais

❄ **The Crooked Spoon** (218-387-2779; www.crookedspoon cafe.com), 17 W. Wisconsin Street. Open daily for lunch and dinner. Contemporary American cuisine, presented as dress-up food in a casual atmosphere. Expensive.

Chez Jude (218-387-9113; www.chezjude.com), 411 W. MN 61. Open Tues. through Sun. for lunch, dinner, and afternoon tea, May through Oct., Thurs. through Sat. Nov. and Dec. (groups can reserve special catered events

other nights during Nov. and Dec.). Chez Jude is small in size but big in flavor, with proprietor Judi Barsness bringing an international flair to her locally inspired menu. Afternoon tea provides the option of a traditional British tea or a North Shore tea complete with smoked trout and lingonberry jam. A well-chosen wine list and good selection of microbrews completes the experience. Expensive.

✧ **Naniboujou Lodge** (218-387-2688; www.naniboujou.com), 20 Naniboujou Trail. Open daily for all three meals, early May to late Oct. Naniboujou's major claim to fame—and it alone is worth the visit—is the resplendent public dining room, with its 20-foot domed ceiling, massive stone fireplace, and the vividly painted Cree-themed walls and ceilings. The menu is contemporary American cuisine, with plenty of local ingredients. Expensive.

Gunflint Trail

✧ ❄ **Old Northwoods Lodge** (218-388-9464; www.oldnorth woods.com), 7969 Old Northwoods Loop. Open daily for breakfast and lunch, Thurs. through Sun. for dinner. If you're looking for something beyond a café, check out the Old Northwoods Lodge. Seating is at large wooden tables, under massive wooden beams and beside a large stone fireplace. Options vary from pancakes and bacon to mango walleye and rib-eye steaks. Wine list is offered. Expensive.

♪ ❢ ✳ **Gunflint Lodge** (218-388-2294; www.gunflintlodge.com), 143 S. Gunflint Lake. Open daily year-round for all three meals except for a week in Nov. and Apr. The Gunflint Lodge has a beautiful restaurant and bar open to the public, with a stone terrace overlooking the beach outdoors and a massive stone fireplace inside. The food is contemporary American cuisine, often with locally sourced, native ingredients. Expensive.

EATING OUT

Grand Marais

♪ ✳ **The Pie Place** (218-387-1513; www.northshorepieplace .com), 2017 W. MN 61. Open daily for all three meals. This pie shop gives Betty's Pies in Two Harbors (see *Where to Eat* in "North Shore/Lutsen") serious competition. Flaky crusts and traditional and innovative fillings will leave you wanting more. Inexpensive.

♪ ✳ **My Sister's Place** (218-387-1915; http://mysistersplace restaurant.com/), 401 E. MN 61. Open daily for lunch and dinner in the summer, Mon. through Sat. in the off-season. Not much to look at on the outside, My Sister's Place has friendly service and solid soups and sandwiches that will satisfy any taste and hunger (including some vegetarian options, such as The Fungi mushroom sandwich). Moderate.

♪ ✳ **South of the Border** (218-387-1505), 4 W. MN 61. Open daily for breakfast and lunch. Don't be confused by the name—the "border" referred to is the Canadian border, not the U.S.-Mexico border. Instead of Mexican food, you'll find hearty home cooking. Inexpensive.

♪ **Dockside Fish Market & Deli** (218-387-2906; www.dock sidefishmarket.com), 418 W. MN 61. Open daily for lunch and dinner, Apr. through Dec. This retail market also has a deli with a limited but delicious menu, including several varieties of fish caught locally. Moderate.

♪ **World's Best Donuts** (218-387-1345; www.worldsbestdonuts mn.com), 10 E. Wisconsin Street. Open daily at 7 AM (the walk-up window opens at 4:30 AM), mid-May through mid-Oct. No matter that the name doesn't seem modest; the doughnuts are truly wonderful. Inexpensive.

♪ ✳ **Sven and Ole's** (218-387-1713; www.svenandoles.com), 9 W. Wisconsin Street. Open daily for lunch and dinner. You can't have a northern Minnesota experience without the quintessential Sven and Ole's. Contrary to the name, this is no bland Scandinavian fare, but a local pizza haunt with hearty, flavorful pizzas. The menu does include an option for a lutefisk pizza, but unless you have the $1 million in cash that the pizza is priced at, it's better to order one of the other offerings. Inexpensive.

Angry Trout Café (218-387-1265; www.angrytroutcafe.com), 416 W. MN 61. Open daily for lunch and dinner, May to mid-Oct. The Angry Trout has indoor or outdoor dining, with a strong focus on local ingredients and sustainability. And be sure to check out the artsy bathrooms. Moderate.

✍ ❊ **Gunflint Tavern** (218-387-1563; www.gunflinttavern.com), 111 Wisconsin Street. Open daily for lunch and dinner. This cheerful tavern serves up tasty food in enormous portions, a more-than-decent menu of microbrews on tap. Many menu items are made with organic and/or local ingredients. Moderate.

Gunflint Trail
✍ **Trail's End Café** (218-388-2212 or 1-800-346-6625; www.wayofthewilderness.com/cafe.htm), 12582 Gunflint Trail. Open daily for all three meals, mid-May through mid-Oct. Trail's End serves basic but hearty meals, including burgers, sandwiches, and pizzas. The knotty pine interior fits well with the wooded wonderland outside. Inexpensive.

❊ **Entertainment**

Grand Marais Playhouse (218-387-1284; www.arrowheadcenterforthearts.org), 51 W. Fifth Street, Grand Marais. The playhouse runs local theatrical productions periodically during the year, primarily in the summer and during the pre-Christmas season.

❊ **Selective Shopping**

✍ ❊ **Drury Lane Books** (218-387-3370 or 1-888-887-3370; www.drurylanebooks.com), 12 E. Wisconsin Street, Grand Marais. Open Mon. through Sat. This shop is small, but it has an excellent selection of books for all your North Shore needs, whether escapist fiction or local information. Authors frequently make appearances, and writing workshops are occasionally offered.

✍ ❊ **Beth's Fudge & Gifts** (218-387-2081), 11 S. Broadway, Grand Marais. Open Mon. through Sat. If the doughnuts and pie in Grand Marais haven't satisfied your sweets craving, Beth's Fudge will. Creamy, smooth, and very much a treat.

✍ ❊ **Lake Superior Trading Post** (218-387-2020; www.lstp.com), 10 S. First Avenue W., Grand Marais. Open daily. Part souvenir shop, part outfitter for rural experiences, the trading post is staffed with friendly people who know their stock. The log cabin construction gives it a north woods feel, and Lake Superior is right outside the door.

✍ ❊ **Gunflint Mercantile** (218-387-9228; www.gunflintmercantile.com), 12 First Avenue W. Open daily. A food store for backpackers and general visitors alike. Come in for the free fudge sample, view the extensive supply of lightweight foods for the trail, and then stay for the coffee and soup.

❄ **Wilderness Waters** (218-387-2525; www.wilderness-waters.com), MN 61, Grand Marais. Open daily. Wilderness Waters is one-stop shopping for outdoor survival gear, from books and maps to clothing and gear. Wilderness Waters also provides canoe outfitting services.

✳ Special Events

March: **Winter Tracks** (218-387-3191 or 1-800-338-6932; www.donorth.mn/wintertracks/index.php), Gunflint Trail. This annual event, taking place in early Mar., is the result of a collaboration by resort and inn owners on the Gunflint Trail. For three days there are various activities, including scavenger hunts, making snow sculptures, dogsled rides, skiing, snowshoeing, sledding, and geocaching.

July: **Grand Marais Arts Festival** (218-387-2737; www.grandmaraisartcolony.org), Grand Marais. An annual juried art show held annually in mid-July.

North Shore Dragon Boat Festival (218-387-9076; www.northshoredragonboat.com/), Grand Marais. This newer festival is a great excuse to hang out along Grand Marais's harbor and enjoy the sight of vividly painted dragon boats being rowed by ambitious oarsmen (and women) in a series of races.

September: **Crossing Borders Studio Tour** (www.crossingbordersstudiotour.com). A tour of artist studios along Lake Superior's northern end, including stops in Lutsen, Grand Marais, Grand Portage, and Thunder Bay, Ontario. (Note: If you venture into Canada, you'll need to present your passport for reentry into the U.S.)

October: **Moose Madness** (1-888-922-5000; www.grandmarais.com), Grand Marais. Always held the third weekend in Oct., the same time as when schools are closed for the annual statewide teachers convention, this festival has contests, moose tours, a treasure hunt, and moose essay- and poetry-writing contests.

BOUNDARY WATERS/ELY

South of Grand Marais, MN 61 connects with MN 1, a brief stretch of highway that moves inland from Lake Superior to Ely, a gateway city into the Boundary Waters. Ely is a tourist town, and one well prepared for the outdoors enthusiasts who flock through the area each year.

A car is pretty much a necessity, and if you're planning on venturing into the Boundary Waters, it's strongly recommended to purchase the Superior National Forest Visitor Map. Published by the USDA in conjunction with Superior National Forest, this is an incredibly detailed map of the Boundary Waters Canoe Area Wilderness (BWCAW). It wouldn't hurt to buy a magnifying glass with which to read it. The BWCAW is full of trails that don't appear on most state maps, and it's easy to get lost unless you're very familiar with the area. The map is available in a sturdy, waterproof plastic version for about $10. Many local gas stations and convenience stores sell it, or contact the **Superior National Forest** headquarters in Duluth (218-626-4300) for information on ordering one.

✴ To See and Do

✐ **Dorothy Molter Museum** (218-365-4451; www.rootbeerlady.com), MN 169, Ely. Open Mon. through Sat. 10–5:30 and Sun. noon–5:30, Memorial Day to Labor Day; weekends in Sept. and the first three Sat. in Oct. (call for hours). Adults $6, seniors $5, children 6–17 $4, children under 6 free. This is a loving tribute to the last living person in the Boundary Waters. Dorothy Molter lived a great deal of her adult life in a cabin in the BWCAW, and even when the U.S. government evicted other tenants when declaring the area a wilderness, she was granted lifetime tenancy. During her many years in her rustic cabin, she brewed homemade root beer for boaters and anglers coming through her area, earning the nickname "the root beer lady." After her death, her log cabin was painstakingly disassembled and reassembled on the east edge of Ely and turned into a museum. The cabin is crammed full of Dorothy's things, and

DOROTHY MOLTER'S CABIN

the adjacent gift shop sells books about her as well as cases of root beer (worth the purchase). The only downside is the noise of traffic from nearby MN 169, which can make visitors (this one, at least) wonder why they couldn't have sited the museum just a bit farther down the road in an effort to recapture something more similar to the peace of nature enjoyed by Molter.

✦ ⚅ ❄ **The International Wolf Center** (218-365-4695; www.wolf.org), 1396 MN 169, Ely. Open daily 10–5, May 15 through June 14; daily 10–7, June 15 through Aug. 14; Wed. through Sun. 10–5, Aug. 15 through Oct. 14; Sat. and Sun. 10–5, Oct. 15 through May 14. Open additional hours during the Education Minnesota Professional Conference in Oct. and the Ely Winter Festival in Feb.; check website for specific dates. Adults $8.50, senior citizens $7.50, children 3–12 $4.50, children under 3 free. Internationally renowned for wolf education and information, the center tries to address public fears and concerns about wolf behaviors through press relations and public visits. The center has hands-on exhibits and Wolf Cams allowing visitors to watch wolves from a great distance; they also coordinate learning vacations that bring visitors into the wilderness to meet "ambassador" wolves.

✦ ⚅ ❄ **North American Bear Center** (218-365-7879; www.bear.org), 1926 MN 169, Ely. Open daily 9–7, May through Labor Day; daily 10–5, Labor Day through Education Minnesota Professional Conference in Oct.; Fri. and Sat. 10–5, late Oct. through late Nov.; daily 10–4, Dec. 26

TED THE BEAR, AT THE NORTH
AMERICAN BEAR CENTER

through Jan. 1. Adults and teens $8.50, senior citizens $7.50, children 3–12 $4.50, children under 3 and members free. One mile west of Ely is this center, similar in intent to the International Wolf Center. Visitors can learn more about bears through videos and exhibits, then watch the bears in their 2-acre habitat from a viewing deck.

✧ **Soudan Underground Mine** (218-753-2245; www.dnr.state .mn.us/state_parks/soudan_under ground_mine/index.html), MN 169, Soudan. Open daily 10–4, Memorial Day through Labor Day. Admission to the grounds is free; guided tours are $10 for adults, $6 for children 6–12, and free for children under 6. The Soudan Mine gives visitors insight into the daily life of miners in this once-operational mine. Adventurous tourists can take the tour, which carries them 27 stories beneath the ground. (Note that extensive walking is required, including through confined areas.) Those who don't wish to go below can wander the grounds for free. The scenery from the hillside mine is breathtaking, particularly during fall foliage season. (Note: At press time, the underground tours have been disrupted by a fire that took place in spring 2011. Call ahead to see when tours will resume.)

✳ Green Space and Outdoor Activities

BOUNDARY WATERS The Boundary Waters is an amazing natural preserve within Superior National Forest, encompassing more than a million acres of woods and at least 2,500 of Minnesota's famed lakes, teeming with wildlife. It is largely meant to be explored as explorers of old traveled: by canoe, with backpack and tent. While a few areas have opened up to motorized vehicles, the beauty of this area is the peacefulness caused by the lack of motors, allowing visitors to hear the myriad bird calls, wolf howls, and the sound of water and wind.

It is possible to day trip in the Boundary Waters, or least along the edges, by starting from Ely or the Gunflint Trail (see the "Grand Marais/Grand Portage/Gunflint Trail" chapter). More ambitious travelers may want to portage in with canoes and set up camp. Experienced canoers and campers can plot their routes, but if you're fairly new to this type of adventure, you might consider working with an outfitter. There are several in the Ely area, including Piragis Northwoods Company (see *Selective Shopping*).

Be aware that visitors to the Boundary Waters, except for day-only visitors, need to reserve a permit ahead of time. Your outfitter can do this for you, or you can contact Reserve America (1-877-444-6777; www.recreation .gov). Permits for camping visitors are required in order to limit the number of entrances each day into the BWCAW, an effort made to keep the wilderness, well, wild.

Lake Vermilion State Park (www.dnr.state.mn.us/state_parks/lake _vermilion/index.html), Soudan. This is Minnesota's newest state park, and at press time it was not fully open to the public. However, the beginnings of recreation are in place, with some day-use areas and hiking available. The potential for this park, which will eventually be combined with the adjacent Soudan Underground Mine (see *To See and Do*), is high: the 3,000-acre tract has 10 miles of shoreline along Lake Vermilion, along with areas of massive rocky areas that are billions of years old. Hiking trails to the highest point in the park will afford views for miles in every direction on a clear day.

LAKE VERMILION STATE PARK

DOGSLED RIDING ✒ **Winter-green Dogsled Lodge** (218-365-6022 or 1-877-753-3386; www.dog sledding.com), 1101 Ring Rock Road, Ely. With more than 30 years of dogsled adventures under their belt, the proprietors of the Wintergreen Dogsled Lodge know a thing or two about taking visitors on a dogsled trip, whether it's first-timers or seasoned sledders. Trips can be arranged with stays at the lodge itself, just east of Ely, as lodge-to-lodge treks or as camping excursions. Multiple-night or one-day-only trips available. Special opportunities include parent-daughter trips and photography workshops.

✳ Lodging

Not surprisingly, the Boundary Waters area is surrounded by countless places to stay, everything from rustic mom-and-pop resorts to more elaborate, deluxe accommodations. What follows is a sample of recommended places, which also represents the diverse offerings available.

BED & BREAKFASTS

✎ ✳ (ᵛᵖ) **A Stay Inn Ely** (218-365-6010; www.stayinnely.com), 112 W. Sheridan Street, Ely. This charming three-story bed & breakfast has newly remodeled rooms, all with private bath, and a large common area with full kitchen. Kids (and adults!) who like hideaways will particularly enjoy staying in the Indigo Room, an attic room tucked under a slanted roof. Moderate.

✳ (ᵛᵖ) ↝ **Blue Heron Bed & Breakfast** (218-365-4720; www .blueheronbnb.com), 827 Kawishiwi Trail, Ely. Five beautifully decorated rooms, some with exposed log walls, make up this charming bed & breakfast. Rooms come with private baths, lake views, full breakfast, use of canoes or snowshoes, and use of the sauna. Expensive.

CABINS ✎ 🐾 ✳ (ᵛᵖ) **Timber Trail Lodge** (218-365-4879 or 1-800-777-7348; www.timbertrail .com), 629 Kawishiwi Trail, Ely. Timber Trail has 15 cabins ranging from one to six bedrooms as well as four motel units with kitch-

enettes. The resort can arrange boat rentals and guides, massage is offered on-site, and once-weekly float plane rides are offered to guests. Moderate.

✎ 🐾 ✳ **Tall Pines Yurt** (1-800-322-8327; www.littleollielodging .com), 11 Poplar Creek Drive, Boundary Waters. For a true wilderness experience, the Tall Pines Yurt is open year-round for summer or winter adventures. Four people can sleep on bunk beds or a futon, although additional bedding can be provided for more guests. A fully equipped kitchen is included; an outhouse is steps away, as is a traditional Finnish sauna. Moderate.

✎ ✳ **Log Cabin Hideaways** (218-365-6045; www.logcabinhide

A STAY INN ELY

A BOAT AT BURNTSIDE LAKE

aways.com), 1321 N. County Route 21, Ely. For those truly wanting the wilderness experience, Log Cabin Hideaways provides hand-hewn log cabins on the

BURNTSIDE LAKE

edge of the BWCAW. Each cabin comes with a canoe, but no electricity or indoor plumbing. Propane is provided for cooking; most units have a Finnish sauna. Some of the cabins are accessible by water only. None of the cabins have "neighbors"; each cabin is on its own secluded site. Expensive.

🖊 🍸 ((ɣ)) **Burntside Lodge** (218-365-3894; www.burntside.com), 2755 Burntside Lodge Road, Ely. Open mid-May to late Sept. West of Ely, on Burntside Lake, Burntside Lodge has been offering gracious hospitality to guests for nearly a century, and it's arguably one of Minnesota's most famous accommodations. The resort offers several cabins in varying sizes, all tucked into the woods or near the lake; the peaceful ambience is assisted by the lack of

TVs and telephones. The lodge itself is on the National Register of Historic Places, and its dining room (see *Where to Eat*) serves delicious food in a large, open room. The adjoining gift shop has several items of local interest. Expensive.

HOTELS *🖊 🐾 ♿ ⌐ ❄* **Grand Ely Lodge** (218-365-6565 or 1-800-365-5070; www.grandelylodge .com), 400 N. Pioneer Road, Ely. Just outside of the city of Ely is this resort, the largest in Ely, with 61 rooms and suites (and ice-fishing houses for day occupancy in the winter). The resort is very family friendly, with kids under 10 staying and eating free with paid adults. There's an indoor pool and sauna, and lake activities are provided at the marina on Shagawa Lake. The Evergreen Restaurant is open all day; there's also a lounge. Mountain bikes are avail-

able to guests who want to use the Trezona Trail across the street, which connects to the International Wolf Center (*see To See and Do*). Expensive.

🖊 🐾 ❄ ⌐ **Adventure Inn** (218-365-3140; www.adventureinn-ely .com), 1145 E. Sheridan Street, Ely. Right in the heart of downtown Ely, the Adventure Inn is a small but charming motel with economy and standard/deluxe rooms, which are clean and comfortable; several of the rooms boast handmade quilts. The hotel is a member of Green America and the Green Hotels Association. Expensive.

🖊 ♿ ⌐ ❄ (()) **Fortune Bay Resort Casino** (1-800-555-1714; www .fortunebay.com), 1430 Bois Forte Road, Tower. Seemingly in the middle of nowhere, this newer resort and casino is on Lake Vermilion and offers attractive rooms

BURNTSIDE LODGE

and suites, an indoor pool, dining room, 24-hour casino, and golf course. An on-site marina has fishing boats, pontoons, canoes, and paddleboats available for rent, or you can bring your own boat and dock it at the marina. Moderate. Packages are available.

✳ Where to Eat

DINING OUT ❄ **Ely Steak House** (218-365-7412; www.ely steakhouse.com), 216 E. Sheridan Street, Ely. Open daily for dinner. Steakhouse and bar with fresh fish specials, prime rib on weekends, and steak whenever you like. Expensive.

🛶 ⅄ **Burntside Lodge** (218-365-3894; www.burntside.com), 2755 Burntside Lodge Road, Ely. Open

daily for dinner, Sat. and Sun for breakfast, mid-Apr. to late Sept. One of the nicest restaurants in the Ely area is in this historic lodge (see *Lodging*), just west of Ely. The dining room serves ambitious fare focused on seasonal specialties, while the adjacent bar has a more casual atmosphere and menu. Expensive.

EATING OUT 🛶 ❄ **Sir G's** (218-365-2699), 520 E. Sheridan Street, Ely. Open daily for lunch and dinner. Italian food, including pasta made on-site. Inexpensive.

🛶 **The Chocolate Moose** (218-365-6343), 101 N. Central Avenue, Ely. Open daily for all three meals, summer only. A popular cabinlike restaurant serving casual meals, the Chocolate Moose has a

THE CHOCOLATE MOOSE, ELY

LIVE MUSIC AT THE FRONT PORCH, ELY

patio for outdoor dining during good weather. Vegetarians will find plenty of hearty options; look for the sourdough cornmeal pancakes. Moderate.

✐ ❄ ((ᵞ)) **Front Porch Coffee and Tea** (218-365-2326; www.front porchcoffeeandtea.com), 343 E. Sheridan Street, Ely. Open daily for breakfast and lunch. A cozy, inviting coffeehouse with a limited but tasty menu of soups and pastries. Free Wi-Fi with purchase. Inexpensive.

✐ ♈ ❄ **Boathouse Brewpub and Restaurant** (218-365-4301; www .boathousebrewpub.com), 47 E. Sheridan Street, Ely. Open daily for all three meals. A cheerful pub with typical bar food—burgers and sandwiches—and walleye, the Minnesota staple. Moderate.

❋ **Selective Shopping**

Ely has several blocks of shops with a good variety of merchandise, from regular tourist things like shirts and mugs to specialty items and artwork.

❋ **Brandenburg Gallery** (218-365-6563 or 1-877-493-8017; www.jimbrandenburg.com), 11 E. Sheridan Street. Open daily. The gallery showcases the award-winning nature photography of Jim Brandenburg, who has traveled the world for *National Geographic* and who has a special love for the Boundary Waters area (he makes it his home part of the year).

❋ **Wintergreen Designs** (218-365-6602 or 1-800-584-9425; www .wintergreennorthernwear.com), 205 E. Sheridan Street. Open daily. Specialists in high-quality and attractive outdoor apparel, Wintergreen produces its work in Ely and sells it at this local retail store (another store is open in Duluth).

❄ **Piragis Northwoods Company** (218-365-6745 or 1-800-223-6565; www.piragis .com), 105 N. Central Avenue. Open daily. This large outfitting shop sells and/or rents all manner of outdoor gear, including canoes and camping gear. Piragis also offers guided canoeing and camping trips in the BWCAW.

❄ **Second-Floor Bookstore** (218-365-6745), 105 N. Central Avenue. Open daily. On the second floor of Piragis is this bookstore, a small but congenial gathering space for book lovers with a solid selection of both fiction and local resource books. The shop is accessible only by going through Piragis.

✎ ❄ **Steger Mukluks & Moccasins** (1-800-685-5857; www .mukluks.com), 100 Miners Drive. Open daily. Inspired by Native American designs, these mukluks and moccasins are made in Ely from moose hide and are highly regarded for their comfort and winter protection.

✳ **Special Events**

February: **Ely Winter Festival** (218-365-7669; www.elywinter festival.com), Ely. It's never too cold for a festival, as this annual midwinter event shows. Snowsculpting lessons and contests, Nordic ski racing, the Mukluk Ball, snowshoe tours, snowmobile races, and musical concerts are all part of the fun during the 10-day event.

July: **Blueberry Art Festival** (218-365-6123 or 1-800-777-7281), Ely. Annual three-day arts fair held in late July.

September: **Harvest Moon Festival** (218-365-6123 or 1-800-777-7281), Ely. This annual Sept. festival includes three days of art and craft exhibits, children's activities, live musical performances, and food.

INTERNATIONAL FALLS/
VOYAGEURS NATIONAL PARK

The northern border of the state is an outdoorsman's paradise. Lake of the Woods and Rainy Lake are fine fishing lakes year-round, and there are ample opportunities for just about any other kind of outdoor activity you can imagine. Moreover, visitors can get a taste of what it must have been like for early pioneers as they navigated Chippewa National Forest or Voyageurs National Park, with acres of undeveloped lands to explore.

✳ To See and Do

✐ ♿ ✳ **Koochiching County Historical Museum/Bronko Nagurski Museum** (218-283-4316; www.bronkonagurski.com), 214 Sixth Avenue, International Falls. Open Mon. through Fri. 9–5. Adults $2, students $1; admission gains entrance to both museums. Two museums share one building, each focused on history specific to the region. Bronko Nagurski is a local legend, a farm boy who became one of the best professional football players in the sport's history. His side of the museum details not only his life and sports career, but also the impact of the times (the Depression, World War II) on his life and that of others. The Koochiching County Historical Museum has a well-rounded collection of artifacts reflecting the area's history with Native Americans and French voyageurs, as well as its relationship to Canada. Museum volunteers and staff are well versed in the collections and can answer questions and offer insightful tales.

Boise Cascade Paper Mill (218-285-5011), Second Street, International Falls. Open Mon. through Fri. 10–4, June through Aug. No admission fee. Children under 10 not allowed; cameras prohibited. Boise Cascade, one of the world's largest paper-making companies, offers both mill tours and woodland tours. Call ahead for reservations—these tours are very popular.

✳ Green Space and Outdoor Activities

Not surprisingly, this area is full of activities in the great outdoors, some more rustic than others.

FISHING Rainy Lake/Rainy River (www.rainylake.org). Rainy Lake, which stretches north into Canada, has some of the best fishing in the state, particularly for walleye, and there are many resorts and houseboats offering accommodations and fishing guides (see *Lodging*). Rainy River connects Rainy Lake with Lake of the Woods to the west; its 80 miles of river provide not only excellent fishing opportunities (walleye, smallmouth bass), but also great canoeing and kayaking.

GOLF Falls Country Club (218-283-4491; www.fallscc.com), 4402 County Route 152. Designed by Joel Goldstrand, the Falls Country Club golf course is challenging and beautiful, and it's open to the public.

RAINY RIVER

PARKS AND PARKWAYS
Waters of the Dancing Sky (www.watersofthedancingsky.org), MN 11. Named after the Northern Lights, this stretch of highway that travels more than 190 miles from the North Dakota border into Voyageurs National Park covers a full range of northern Minnesota scenery: rivers, lakes, prairies, farmland, and a host of small towns. Note: The western edge of the byway is completed when MN 11 connects with US 59, then MN 175.

Voyageurs National Park (218-283-6600; www.nps.gov/voya), 3131 US 53, International Falls. Centuries ago, French traders paddled these waters on their way to Canada, looking to trade animal pelts and goods with the natives. Today Voyageurs National Park is a haven for those who love to be on the water, whether by canoe, kayak, or houseboat. Hikers, snowshoers, and cross-country skiers travel the grounds year-round. A series of

LAKE KABETOGAMA

THE WOODENFROG REFECTORY WAS BUILT AS A CONCESSIONAIRE BY THE CCC.

connected lakes and bays, as well as miles of untouched forest, provide an intimate north woods experience. Wildlife is abundant.

There are three visitors centers. The **Rainy Lake Visitor Center** (218-286-5258) is the primary source and the only one open year-round. Located 10 miles east of International Falls, it is open daily 9–5 from late May through Sept., Wed. through Sun. 10–4 from Oct. through Memorial Day. The **Kabetogama Lake Visitor Center** (218-875-2111) is open daily 9–5 from late May through Late Sept., and the **Ash River Visitor Center** (218-374-3221) is open Thurs. through Sun. 9–5, late May through Sept.

Boat tours from the visitors centers are offered during the summer, as is a tour to **Ellsworth Rock Gardens,** a lush garden spot built over a period of 20 years by Jack Ellsworth and maintained today by the National Park Service.

There are campgrounds available on a first-come, first-served basis (groups can reserve ahead of time with one of the visitors centers), but note that the campgrounds within the park are only accessible by boat. A free permit is required for camping, which can be obtained at the visitors centers or at self-permit stations within the park. If you're interested in camping but would rather be able to drive up to your campsite, look into reserving a site at the **Woodenfrog State Campground** (218-365-7229), County Route 122, Ray. Located in Kabetogama State Forest, part of Voyageurs National Park, Woodenfrog has campsites available from mid-May to mid-Sept. that don't require boat access.

✳ Lodging

Within International Falls itself are several small motels or budget hotels, such as the Days Inn and Super 8 on US 53. Most accommodations that provide more of the "northern" experience are on the outskirts, or along MN 11 east to Voyageurs National Park.

CABINS

International Falls

⚲ 🐾 ✳ **Camp Idlewood** (218-286-5551; www.campidlewood.com), 3033 County Route 20, International Falls. Camp Idlewood has nine cabins with knotty pine interiors and full kitchens; the resort itself has a beach, and a canoe, paddleboat, inner tubes, and tow ropes available at no fee. Boats and motors can be rented, or you can bring your own; each cabin has one dock space included, and additional spaces can be rented. Expensive.

⚲ 🐾 ♈ ✳ **Island View Lodge and Cabins** (218-286-3511 or 1-800-777-7856; www.rainy-lake.com), 1817 MN 11 E., International Falls. Actually located 12 miles east of International Falls, Island View sits on the edge of Rainy Lake with gorgeous views and direct lake access. There are 15 cabins available, as well as several lodge rooms. An adjacent spa has a hot tub and sauna, and the lodge has a dining room and lounge. Expensive.

⚲ ♈ ✳ **Woody's Rainy Lake Resort** (218-286-5001 or 1-866-410-5001; http://fairlyreliable.com), 3481 Main Street, Ranier. Woody's offers seven cabins with full kitchens, all near or on Rainy Lake. The lodge has a pub with pizza and beer, and is the headquarters for Woody's Fairly Reliable Guide Service. The tongue-in-cheek name reflects the jovial nature of Woody's resort but is an understatement in terms of service: Woody's knows Rainy Lake, and they can help with summer and winter fishing needs. Expensive.

⚲ **Sha Sha Resort on Rainy Lake** (218-286-3241 or 1-800-685-2776; www.shashaonrainylake.com), 1664 MN 11 E., International Falls. Open May through Sept. Literally at road's end, Sha Sha Resort is the final destination for MN 11 east from International Falls. The resort offers 11 beautiful log cabins, plus a private island getaway cabin a mile away. Another of

THE BAR AND DECK AT SHA SHA RESORT

the resort's benefits is a sprawling, multilayered outdoor deck where diners and libation seekers can enjoy the view of Rainy Lake. Very expensive.

Lake Kabetogama

✐ ☗ **Voyageur Park Lodge** (218-875-2131 or 1-800-331-5694; www.voyageurparklodge.com), 10436 Waltz Road, Kabetogama. Open mid-May through Sept. Ten cottages along Lake Kabetogama, along with a lodge suite, offer guests peaceful privacy. Full kitchen, barbecue grill, and campfire site are included with each cabin (campfires only when conditions allow). Use of canoes, kayaks, and paddleboats is free; fishing boats, pontoons, and motors can be rented on-site. Expensive.

✐ ☗ ❄ **Herseth's Tomahawk Resort** (218-875-2352 or 1-888-834-7899; www.hersethstomahawk resort.com), 10078 Gappa Road, Ray. Herseth's offers eight cabins and one mobile home. The resort has a large sand beach with free canoes and paddleboats. Motorized boats available for rent. The proprietor is a certified scuba diver and is happy to arrange diving excursions into Lake Kabetogama. Expensive.

✐ ❄ **Moosehorn Resort** (218-875-3491 or 1-800-777-7968; www.moosehornresort.com), 10434 Waltz Road, Kabetogama. Moosehorn has nine cabins stretched along Lake Kabetogama with sandy beach. This is an especially family-friendly resort, located in a quiet bay that keeps the lake waters calmer than in other spots. Canoes, kid-sized kayaks, and a playground area are included for guests. Boats are available for rental. Expensive.

✐ ☗ ♈ ((ᵖ)) ❄ **Kec's Kove Resort** (218-875-2841 or 1-800-777-8405; www.kecskove.com), 10428 Gamma Road, Kabetogama. Kec's has eight cabins and a lodge with whirlpool and sauna; a massage therapist is available for guests. If you go fishing and need some help afterward, Kec's can provide fish cleaning and freezing services. Motorized boats are available for rent; paddleboats, canoes, and kayaks are complimentary. Expensive.

✐ ☗ **Northern Lights Resort, Outfitting, and Youth Quest** (218-875-2591 or 1-800-318-7023; www.nlro.com), 12723 Northern Lights Road, Kabetogama. Northern Lights offers 10 cabins along Lake Kabetogama, as well as a number of activities for all interest levels. Guides can be arranged for fishing or other expeditions; a ladies' pontoon cruise is held weekly, with coffee and muffins; an adults social cruise is offered weekly in the evening; and the Youth Quest program is available for kids ages 5 to 17, with planned activities including kayaking, canoeing, tomahawk-throwing training, and island cookouts. Younger kids are separated from the older kids, and activities are age appropriate. Expensive.

HOTELS

International Falls

✐ 🍸 ❄ (ᵞ) **AmericInn** (218-283-8000 or 1-800-331-4443; www.hiifalls.com), 1500 US 71, International Falls. A well-appointed hotel within International Falls, the AmericInn has an indoor pool, restaurant, and even a garden walk down to the river, where guests can fish. Expensive.

✐ ❄ **Bear Ridge Guest House** (218-286-5710; www.bearridgeguesthouse.net), 210 Fourth Avenue, International Falls. Offering one-, two-, and three-bedroom suites, the Bear Ridge Guest House is a great choice for visitors to Rainy Lake. It's located on a hill overlooking the lake, with private decks to enjoy the view. Some suites have full kitchens and fireplaces. Expensive.

✐ 🍸 ❄ **Rainy Lake Inn & Suites at Tara's Wharf** (218-286-5699 or 1-877-724-6955; www.taraswharf.com), 2065 Spruce Street Landing, Ranier. Near Woody's, the Rainy Lake Inn offers four suite accommodations in a charming "seaside" setting. The ice cream shop will keep everyone happy. Expensive.

HOUSEBOATS

An alternative to hotels and resorts is the houseboat experience. Rainy Lake has two companies that have several houseboats available for rental.

✐ **Northernaire Houseboats** (1-800-854-7958; www.northernairehouseboats.com), 2690 County Route 94, International Falls. Open May through Sept. Northernaire offers 10 houseboats of varying sizes and levels of amenities, including some with open decks and some with screened-in decks. Rentals include a tow-behind boat, free delivery on the lake twice weekly (for groceries, etc.), and a guide service for the first 4 miles to orient you to the maps and buoy systems. Order ahead, and your boat's kitchen will be stocked with foods and beverages of your choice. Expensive.

✐ **Rainy Lake Houseboats** (218-286-5391 or 1-800-554-9188; www.rainylakehouseboats.com), 2031 Town Road 488, International Falls. Open mid-May through mid-Oct. Rainy Lake's fully equipped houseboats have kitchens, a tow-behind boat, swim platforms and water slides, and deck table and chairs. Guide service is available with prearrangement, and groceries can be ordered ahead as well. Very expensive.

Voyageurs National Park

⚓ ☡ **Kettle Falls Hotel** (218-240-1724; www.kettlefallshotel.com), 10502 Gamma Road, Kabetogama. Open early May to early Oct. While I have not visited this hotel personally, it's enough of a legend that it can't be ignored. Located on an odd geographical twist that allows you to stand on the Minnesota side and look south to Canada, this hotel is the only lodging within Voyageurs National Park, and it's accessible only by plane or by boat. Nearly a century old, Kettle Falls Hotel has a rich history that includes bootleggers selling whiskey during Prohibition. Today the hotel has 12 rooms with shared baths, a full-service restaurant, and a saloon that still bears the marks of wilder early years. Moderate.

❋ Where to Eat

EATING OUT ⚓ ❋ **Giovanni's** (218-283-2600; www.giosifalls.com), 301 Third Avenue, International Falls. Open daily for lunch and dinner. A cheerful, family-friendly American-Italian restaurant with pizza, pasta, pierogies, and burgers. A buffet is available, as is an arcade area for kids. Moderate.

⚓ ❋ (ᵗᵖ) **Coffee Landing** (218-283-8316), 444 Third Street, International Falls. Open daily. A full-service coffee, espresso, and tea shop, along with a limited but tasty food menu including breakfast items, pastries, and quiche. Inexpensive.

⚓ ❋ **Rose Garden Restaurant** (218-283-4551), 311 Fourth Avenue, International Falls. Open

COFFEE LANDING, INTERNATIONAL FALLS

daily for lunch and dinner. Classic Chinese-American food, with large portions at reasonable prices. Moderate.

✒ ✳ **Chocolate Moose Restaurant Company** (218-283-8888; www.chocolatemooserestaurant.com), US 53 S., International Falls. Open daily for all three meals. The Chocolate Moose serves up platter-sized portions of pancakes, burgers, pasta, and dinner entrées including steak and shrimp. Moderate.

✒ ✳ **Grandma's Pantry** (218-286-5584), 2079 Spruce Street, Ranier. Open Mon. through Fr. for breakfast, lunch, and early dinner; Sat. for breakfast only. Breakfast is the specialty, and it's served all day in gigantic portions, but the homemade sandwiches, soups, and dinners are tasty, too. Inexpensive.

✳ Selective Shopping

✒ **Border Bob's** (218-283-4414; www.borderbobs.com), 200 Second Avenue, International Falls. Open daily Memorial Day through Labor Day. The quintessential souvenir shop, with local goods such as maple syrup, commemorative Minnesota/Canada items, T-shirts, and other tourist goods. Also a great place to stop for ice cream.

Pine Ridge Gift Shop (218-875-3313), 9903 Gamma Road, Lake Kabetogama. Open daily May through Sept. Pine Ridge is housed in a log cabin on Gamma Road, near CR 122; located near a cluster of resorts on Lake Kabetogama, the shop is easy to find. Its merchandise runs the gamut from touristy to collectible. Local arts, crafts, quilts, cabin amenities, Christmas decorations, candles, locally produced foods (including their own roasted coffee), and clothing make up the bulk of this shop, staffed by cheerful locals who know the area well.

✳ Special Events

February: **Icebox Days** (218-283-9400 or 1-800-325-5766; www.internationalfallsmn.us/iceboxdays.shtml), International Falls. This annual festival includes such winter fun as frozen turkey bowling, smoosh races (four people on two skis), a human sled dog race, snowshoe races, a talent contest, and the Freeze Yer Gizzard Blizzard Run. Occurs in late Feb.

June: **Birders Spring Rendezvous** (218-286-5258; www.nps.gov/voya), Voyageurs National Park. Held the first weekend in June, the Birders Spring Rendezvous is a series of events and activities designed to help beginning and expert birders discover what can be seen in Voyageurs National Park. Theme walks, canoeing, a cruise along Kettle Falls, expert speakers, and, of course, plenty of bird-watching is offered.

THE IRON RANGE

The Iron Range is the mini melting pot of Minnesota. Immigrants from more than 40 countries settled here in the 19th century, joining the population of Native Americans already in the region. Mining was a driving force here for many years. The Iron Range (or simply "the Range," as locals call it) is the birthplace of several notable people, not least of whom is Bob Dylan.

✴ To See and Do

✄ ♂ ♿ ✳ **Minnesota Discovery Center** (218-254-7959 or 1-800-372-6437; http://mndiscoverycenter.com), 105 Discovery Drive, Chisholm. Open Tues. through Sun. 10–5 (until 9 on Thurs.). Adults $5, children 7–17 $3, children 6 and under free. Admission is free for everyone on Thurs. after 5 PM. The Minnesota Discovery Center is a wonderful stop for visitors to the Iron Range. The grounds themselves are beautiful (and frequently used for weddings and receptions). An indoor museum details the Iron Range's extensive history and hosts traveling exhibits, while a trolley takes visitors to the Glen Location, a former mining town where people can explore the historical buildings. Heritage Park includes a series of re-created pioneer homes.

✄ ♿ **Greyhound Bus Museum** (218-263-5814; www.greyhoundbus museum.org), 1201 Greyhound Boulevard, Hibbing. Open Mon. through Sat. 9–5 and Sun. 1–5, mid-May through Sept.; open by request for groups in the off-season. Adults $5, senior citizens $4, students $2, children 6–12 $1, children under 6 free; $10 for families and $3 per person for tour groups. Documents the development of the U.S. bus industry from its days as a single vehicle in Hibbing to the current national route.

✄ ♿ ✳ **U.S. Hockey Hall of Fame** (1-800-443-7825; www.ushockeyhall .com), 801 Hat Trick Avenue, Eveleth. Open Mon. through Sat. 9–5 and Sun. 10–3, Memorial Day through Labor Day; Sat. and Sun. 9–5, Labor

Day through Memorial Day. Adults $8, senior citizens and students 13–17 $7, children 6–12 $6, children under 6 free. A must-see for hockey fans— and the Iron Range tends to have a lot of local hockey fans—the hall of fame includes memorabilia not just from local hockey teams, but also from national events, including the 1980 "Miracle on Ice" Olympic team and the 1998 women's gold-medal Olympic team.

✍ **Finnish Heritage Homestead Tours** (218-984-2084; www.embarrass .org), MN 135 and County Route 21, Embarrass. Open Thurs. through Sat. at 1 PM, Memorial Day through Labor Day. Adults $6 ($5 per person for large groups), senior citizens $4, children 12 and under free. This three-hour guided tour to the small town of Embarrass illustrates the Finnish part of Minnesota's history. Handcrafted log structures, antique farm and weaving machinery, and a gift shop are all part of the tour.

HISTORIC FIRE TOWER AT THE FOREST HISTORY CENTER

Bob Dylan's Childhood Home, 2425 Dylan Drive, Hibbing. While it's not open for tours, fans of Bob Dylan can drive by the childhood home on the renamed street.

✍ ♿ ❋ **Paulucci Space Theatre** (218-262-6720; www.spacetheatre .mnscu.edu), 1502 E. 23rd Street, Hibbing. Hours and admission vary. A 3D IMAX screen shows films about space and planets.

✍ ♿ ❋ **Forest History Center** (218-327-4482 or 1-888-727-8386; www.mnhs.org), 2609 County Route 76, Grand Rapids. Open Mon. through Sat. 10–5 and Sun. noon–5, Memorial Day through mid-Oct.; weekdays (except for holidays) 8–4:30, mid-Oct. through Memorial Day. Cross-country ski trails open daily. Adults $8, senior citizens $6, children 6–15 $5, children under 6 free. The Forest History Center has a visitors center and a re-created turn-of-the-20th-century logging camp with costumed characters for guides. Visitors can board a floating cook shack, climb a 100-foot fire tower,

TRAIL AT THE FOREST HISTORY CENTER

and crawl through a decayed log while learning about Minnesota's logging history. A trail system takes visitors through the forest and along the Mississippi River.

♂ & ※ **The Judy Garland Museum** (1-800-664-5839; www.judygarland museum.com), 2727 US 169 S., Grand Rapids. Open daily 10–5, Memorial Day through Sept. 30; Fri. and Sat. 10–5, Oct. through Mar.; Mon. through Sat. 10–5, Apr. through Memorial Day. Admission is $8 for those older than age one; under age one is free. Admission includes the Children's Discovery Museum. Judy Garland was born in Minnesota in 1922 and spent her first four years here. The home she lived in has been moved from its original street to a location on US 169, a busy highway across from Home Depot, which detracts slightly from the house's charm. The house has been lovingly restored with considerable attention to detail, and the curators have procured a wide variety of artifacts, including the carriage Dorothy rode in upon her arrival at Oz. The museum did have a pair of ruby slippers, but those were stolen in 2005, and it's clearly a theft that the community still grieves. The museum hosts an annual Judy Garland Festival (see *Special Events*), which draws visitors from all over the country.

THE JUDY GARLAND MUSEUM

♂ & ※ **Children's Discovery Museum** (218-326-1900 or 1-866-236-5437; www.cdmkids.org), 2727 US 169 S., Grand Rapids. Open daily 10–5, Memorial Day through Sept. 30; Fri. and Sat. 10–5, Oct. through Mar.; Mon. through Sat. 10–5, Apr. through Memorial Day. Admission is $8 for those older than age one; under age one is free. Admission includes the Judy Garland Museum. This hands-on children's museum includes a kid-sized town, a river forest with talking tree (but a friendlier tree than the ones encountered by Dorothy on her way to Oz), a "Dino Dig," and an art room.

✳ Green Space and Outdoor Activities

Wellstone Memorial and Historic Site (651-645-3939; www.wellstone.org), US 53 and Bodas Road, Eveleth. A wooded 5-acre site is the memorial to Minnesota senator Paul Wellstone and the other travelers who died when their plane crashed near this site in 2002. Trails are lined with boulders naming the victims and interpretive signs explaining Wellstone's work and legacy.

Hill Annex Mine State Park (218-247-7215; www.dnr.state.mn.us/state _parks/hill_annex_mine/index.html), US 169, Calumet. Open daily 9–5, year-round; tours given Wed. through Sun. and on holidays in summer. Tours are adults $10, children 5–12 $6, children under 5 free. This area was mined for 65 years, ending in 1978, and can now be explored during the summer months by taking one of three guided tours—a mine tour, a boat tour, and fossil hunt.

Mineview in the Sky (218-741-2717), US 53, Virginia. Open daily 9–6, May through Sept. No admission, but donations are welcome. An overlook of the Rouchleau Group of mines, with an observation deck originally used by site foremen to observe the mine's operation in an open pit almost 3 miles long and 450 feet deep.

✳ Lodging

BED & BREAKFASTS
✳ **Mitchell-Tappan House** (218-262-3862 or 1-888-662-3862; www .mitchell-tappanhouse.com), 2125 Fourth Avenue E., Hibbing. Built in 1897 for a mine superintendent, the Mitchell-Tappan House was moved, as many Hibbing houses were, in the early 1920s when it was discovered that ore ran right underneath it. Today this bed & breakfast has five rooms, four with shared bath, plus cozy common areas. Full breakfast is included. Moderate.

HOTELS ✐ ✚ ✳ ⟨⟨ᵞ⟩⟩ **AmericInn Lodge & Suites** (218-741-7839 or 1-888-741-7839; www.americinn .com), 5480 Mountain Iron Drive, Virginia. This member of the AmericInn chain provides a solid, reliable choice, with hotel rooms and suites (some with fireplaces),

an indoor pool, and daily continental breakfast. Expensive.

✐ ✳ **Chisholm Inn & Suites** (218-254-2000 or 1-877-255-3156; www.chisholminn.com), 501 Iron Drive, Chisholm. Similar to the AmericInn, the Chisholm Inn offers hotel rooms and suites, and breakfast is included for guests. Larger rooms offer whirlpool baths. The hotel also has an indoor pool and sauna. Moderate.

✐ ✚ ✟ ✳ ⟨⟨ᵞ⟩⟩ **Coates Plaza Hotel** (218-749-1000; www.coatesplaza hotel.com), 502 Chestnut Street, Virginia. Located in downtown Virginia, the Coates Plaza's rooms all overlook the indoor pool area, which includes a whirlpool and sauna. The hotel's restaurant, Brantz Roadhouse BBQ Grill (see *Where to Eat*), serves lunch and dinner, and the Coate Tails provides full bar service. Moderate.

🖉 & ❋ (ᵖ) **Hibbing Park Hotel** (218-262-3481 or 1-800-262-3481; www.hibbingparkhotel.com), 1402 E. Howard Street, Hibbing. One of Hibbing's nicest hotels, the Hibbing Park has 120 rooms and suites, as well as an indoor pool. The hotel was recently renovated, and the rooms have been updated. The hotel's restaurant, Grandma's in the Park (see *Where to Eat*), is similar to the Duluth-area Grandma's. Expensive.

❋ Where to Eat

EATING OUT 🖉 & ⏦ ❋ **Grandma's in the Park** (1-800-262-3481; www.hibbingparkhotel.com), 1402 E. Howard Street. Open daily for lunch and dinner. While not a direct branch of the Duluth Grandma's restaurants, this dining spot, in the Hibbing Park Hotel (see *Lodging*), is related and has a similar menu, complete with ribs, pasta, steak, and fish. Moderate.

& ⏦ ❋ **Brantz Roadhouse BBQ Grill** (218-749-0898; www.coates plazahotel.com/restaurant), 502 Chestnut Street, Virginia. Open daily for lunch and dinner. In the Coates Plaza Hotel (see *Lodging*), Brantz serves steak, ribs, chicken, and prime rib in generous portions. Moderate.

🖉 & **A&W Drive In** (218-229-2240), 103 Main Street S., Aurora. Open daily for lunch and dinner, mid-May through mid-Sept., weather permitting. An honest-to-goodness drive-in restaurant,

A&W serves you your burgers and fries in your car so you can eat it on the spot. Be sure to order a big frosty mug of root beer. Inexpensive.

🖉 & ❋ **K&B Drive In** (218-744-2772; www.kandbdrivein.com), US 53 and Cedar Island Drive, Eveleth. Open daily for lunch and dinner. K&B ups the ante by having a drive-in open year-round. Besides the typical drive-in fare of burgers and hot dogs, K&B also has gyros and pasties. Inexpensive.

🖉 & ⏦ ❋ **Zimmy's Bar & Restaurant** (218-262-6145 or 1-866-305-3849; www.zimmys.com), 531 E. Howard Street, Hibbing. Open daily for lunch and dinner. Located in a historic building that has seen many incarnations, Zimmy's other claim to fame is its extensive collection of Bob Dylan memorabilia. The lunch and dinner menus are peppered with Dylan references, while the food is hearty American style: burgers, ribs, sandwiches, steaks, and pasta. A gift shop sells Dylan-related clothing and items. Moderate.

🖉 & ⏦ ❋ **Adventures** (218-741-7151; www.adventuresrestaurants .com), 5475 Mountain Iron Drive, Virginia. Open daily for lunch and dinner. With a north woods exploration theme, Adventures breaks its menu into sections for "Tenderfoots," "Light Hiker," and "Less Adventurous." Typical entrées include burgers, sandwiches, salads, and pasta; walleye sandwiches and wild rice meat loaf are great choices. Moderate.

♪ ♿ 🍸 ❋ **Grandma's Saloon & Grill** (218-749-1960; www.grand masrestaurants.com), 1302 12th Avenue S., Virginia. Open daily for lunch and dinner. One of the Duluth Grandma's Restaurants family, this branch, like its Duluth siblings, provides reliable grill food and a sturdy drink menu. Moderate.

❋ Special Events

February: **Laskianen Finnish Sliding Festival** (218-638-2551; www.ironrange.org), Aurora. The first weekend of Feb. brings this annual celebration of ethnic— particularly Finnish—traditions. The three-day event includes a ball, sleigh and carriage ride, theater, special dinners, and, of course, sliding.

May: **Dylan Days** (218-262-6145 or 1-866-305-3849; www.dylan days.com), Hibbing. This Iron Range city celebrates its musical hero with the annual Dylan Days, taking place each year in May, around the time of Dylan's birth date (May 24). Special events include special dinners, a Dylan Days Bus Tour of historic Dylan sites, and live musical concerts (but don't expect Dylan himself).

June: ♪ **Land of the Loon Festival** (218-749-5555; www.landof theloonfestival.com), Virginia. Taking place annually the third

weekend of June, Land of the Loon bills itself as an ethnic arts and crafts festival. The two-day festival offers a parade, more than 300 vendors, live music, and a kid's area with a petting zoo and face painting. A variety of ethnic foods (German, Finnish, Mexican, Greek, and Cuban, among others) is available for sale.

Judy Garland Festival (1-800-664-5839; www.judygarland museum.com), Grand Rapids. The Judy Garland Museum (see *To See and Do*) sponsors this annual festival, which occurs in late June, after Garland's birth date (June 10). It's a popular event, attracting visitors from around the United States, so plan ahead if you'd like to attend. The festival includes speakers on Judy Garland, informal sing-alongs, screenings of *The Wizard of Oz*, a gala dinner and fund-raiser, a collector's exchange, a seminar on the dangers of drug use, and occasional visits from the actors who portrayed some of the Munchkins.

September: **Chisholm Fire Days** (218-254-7930; www.chisholm chamber.com), Chisholm. Ten days of festival fun beginning after Labor Day. Events include special dinners, sports and games tournaments, a parade, a Kid's Day, and a craft fair.

Northern Lakes/ Red River Valley

4

NORTHERN LAKES/
RED RIVER VALLEY

The northern lakes region and the Red River Valley provide visitors with a range of geological vistas. The lakes area is made up of rolling and heavily forested land, while the valley, contradictory to its name, is flat agricultural plains, where you can drive for miles and see nothing but sunflowers, corn, and soybean crops. This is a region shaped by former glacial lakes and settled by Chippewa Indians, followed by French traders and eventually Scandinavians, looking for fertile farmland.

The lakes that punctuate the region are known for excellent fishing and boating, and not just in the summer. The fishing season has been extended to the winter by increased technology; today many northern lakes are dotted by buildings ranging from little more than shacks to "sleepers"—larger, heated buildings with attached portable potties. No matter the level of grandeur, all are considered ice houses. Ice fishing, combined with other winter sports such as cross-country skiing, snow-mobiling, and snowshoeing, have made the northern region a year-round destination rather than a summer-only spot.

Rivers, as well as lakes, play an important role in this region. The Mississippi River has its starting point here in Itasca State Park, where the Headwaters, first accurately identified by explorer Henry Schoolcraft in 1832, can be crossed easily by foot, giving no sign of its becoming the Mighty Mississippi. The Red River on the northwestern side of the state is not the most scenic of rivers, but the flatlands surrounding it are an agricultural center for the state.

The plains give way to the lake-heavy region around Detroit Lakes, bodies of water carved by the glaciers that moved through centuries ago. Now the region is a popular tourist destination for lake lovers. Tourism plays a major role in this area's economy, and the annual WE Fest has become one of the country's largest country music festivals, attracting

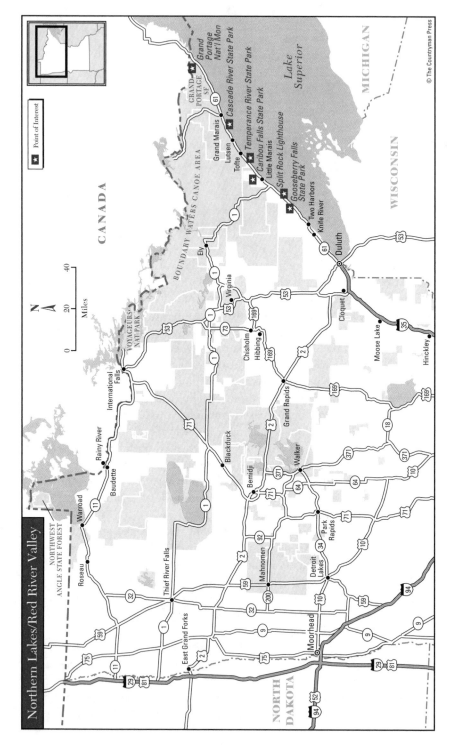

Northern Lakes/Red River Valley

★ Point of Interest

© The Countryman Press

50,000 people each year. (See the WE Fest sidebar in the "Thief River Falls/Red River Valley/Detroit Lakes" chapter.)

GUIDANCE **Leech Lake Chamber of Commerce** (218-547-1313 or 1-800-833-1118; www.leech-lake.com), 205 Minnesota Ave. W., Walker.

Park Rapids Chamber of Commerce (218-732-4111 or 1-800-247-0054; www.parkrapids.com), US 71 S., Park Rapids.

Visit Bemidji (218-759-0164 or 1-877-250-5959; http://visitbemidji.com). An online-and phone-based tourism affiliate for the Bemidji area.

Lake of the Woods Tourism Bureau (218-634-1174 or 1-800-382-3474; www.lakeofthewoodsmn.com), MN 11, Baudette. Open daily in the summer, Mon. through Fri. the rest of the year. Provides tourism information for the general Lake of the Woods area that runs along the Canadian border, including Baudette, Warroad, and the Northwest Angle.

Roseau Convention and Visitors Bureau (1-800-815-1824; www.city .roseau.mn.us). Provides information on lodging and events in the Roseau area.

Thief River Falls Convention and Visitors Bureau (218-686-9785; www.visittrf.org), 2042 MN 1 NE, Thief River Falls. A tourist board for all things Thief River Falls.

Moorhead Travel Information Center (218-299-5944), eastbound I-94, 1 mile east of US 75. Provides information for visitors to the twin city of Fargo, North Dakota.

Detroit Lakes Regional Chamber of Commerce (218-847-9202 or 1-800-542-3992; www.visit detroitlakes.com), 700 Summit Ave., Detroit Lakes. Serves as the central tourist information center for the greater Detroit Lakes area.

MISSISSIPPI HEADWATERS AT ITASCA STATE PARK

GETTING THERE *By air:* Regional commercial airlines, primarily Delta and Mesaba, serve the cities of Bemidji, Thief River Falls, and Fargo (across the river from Moorhead). Taxis and rental cars are available from the airports: **Bemidji Regional Airport** (218-444-2438; www.bemidjiairport.org/), 3824 Moberg Drive NW, Bemidji;
Thief River Falls Regional Airport (218-681-6688; www.citytrf.net /transportation.htm), 13722 Airport Drive, Thief River Falls; and **Hector International Airport** (701-241-1501; www.fargoairport.com/), 2801 32nd Avenue NW, Fargo, ND.

By car: Park Rapids is served by MN 34 and US 71. MN 34 ends at MN 200 in Walker; MN 200 and MN 371 are the primary routes through Walker. MN 371 ends at US 2, while MN 200 merges with US 71, both of which are the major highways through Bemidji. Follow US 71 north to MN 72 in order to head north to Baudette; from Baudette, MN 11 is the major road crossing west to Warroad and Roseau. The primary highway to East Grand Forks is US 2; to Moorhead (and Fargo, North Dakota), I-94 is the major freeway, while US 10 also serves Moorhead, as well as Detroit Lakes.

The Northwest Angle, a ridge of land bordering Canada, is the northernmost part of the contiguous United States, and it can be accessed by car through Canada (with U.S. passport), or by seaplane or boat. Lake of the Woods Passenger Service (218-634-1342, ext. 438; www.lakeofthewoods passengerservice.com) can arrange transportation across the water.

By rail: **AMTRAK's** (1-800-872-7245; www.amtrak.com) Empire Builder route offers rail service between Minneapolis/St. Paul and Fargo/Moorhead. Local stations include **Midway Station,** at 730 Transfer Road in St. Paul, and **Station Building,** 420 Fourth Street N., in Fargo, North Dakota.

GETTING AROUND Having a vehicle is a necessity when traveling around the northern lakes region.

WHEN TO COME The summer months see an influx of tourists who come to enjoy the multitude of lakes and beaches, but summer isn't the only popular time, especially for fishing enthusiasts who cast their poles in open water in summer and through holes in the ice in winter. Hunters and winter sports aficionados appreciate the fall and winter seasons as well.

MEDICAL EMERGENCY Call 911.

St. Joseph's Hospital (218-732-3311 or 1-800-556-3311; www.sjahs.org), 600 Pleasant Ave. S., Park Rapids.

Sanford Bemidji Medical Center (218-751-5430; www.nchs.com), 1300 Anne St. NW, Bemidji.

LifeCare Medical Center (218-463-2500; www.lifecaremedicalcenter .org), 715 Delmore Dr., Roseau.

Northwest Medical Center Hospital (218-681-4240; www.sanford health.org), 120 LaBree Ave., Thief River Falls.

MeritCare Hospital (701-234-2000; www.meritcare.com), 801 Broadway N., Fargo, ND.

Essentia Health St. Mary's (218-847-5611; http://www.trustedcarefor life.org/), 1027 Washington Ave., Detroit Lakes.

PARK RAPIDS/WALKER

The north-central part of the state has a number of worthy venues for visitors, including Walker and Leech Lake, a large lake popular for sailors and fishing enthusiasts (and also home to the annual Eelpout Festival; see *Special Events*), and Dorset, a food-minded village on the Heartland Trail. Dense forests and countless lakes make up the scenery here in a most Minnesotan way.

✳ To See and Do

✦ ⚲ ❄ **Northern Lights Casino and Hotel** (1-800-252-7529; www .northernlightscasino.com), 6800 Y Frontage Road NW, Walker. Open daily. Slots, poker, and blackjack are open 24/7. Two restaurants and a snack bar are in the casino, while the attached hotel has an indoor pool and sauna, and extensive arcade.

⚲ **Forestedge Winery** (218-224-3535; www.forestedgewinery.com), 35295 MN 64, LaPorte. Open Tues. through Sun. noon–5:30, Mother's Day through Dec. Northwest of Walker is this winery, which produces wines from hardy northern crops such as chokecherries, blueberries, raspberries, and plums. Forestedge's rhubarb wine has won several awards. Stop by for a sample, and enjoy the beautiful gardens. Tables are available if you'd like to enjoy a bottle right on the spot.

FORESTEDGE WINERY

✿ **Northland Bison Ranch** (218-652-3582 or 1-877-453-9499; www.northlandbison.com), 22376 Glacial Ridge Trail, Nevis. Open daily mid-June through Labor Day. Call for hours. Adults $7.50, kids $5. This working bison ranch offers guided tours (reservation required) during the summer. See the bison in their habitat and learn their history.

✳ Green Space and Outdoor Activities

✳ **Heartland Trail** (www.dnr.state.mn.us/state_trails/heartland/index .html), Park Rapids. This 49-mile trail uses old railroad grades to create a multiuse trail system. The trail is paved and can be used by hikers, bicyclists, and bladers (but be aware that the terrain is very steep in some areas and rough in others), and an adjacent grass trail can be used by horseback riders and mountain bikers. Snowmobile enthusiasts will find the trail is groomed all winter long.

✳ **Leech Lake** (www.leechlake.org). North of the popular Brainerd Lakes area is Leech Lake, a favored fishing lake surrounded by forests and opportunities for year-round outdoor activities. Hundreds of resorts flank the lake (see *Lodging* for some examples) and boaters, anglers (both summer and winter), skiers, snowmobilers, and hunters have all contributed to the growth of this area as a four-season destination.

✳ Lodging

BED & BREAKFASTS

✳ (ᵔᵧᵔ) **Heartland Trail Bed and Breakfast** (218-732-3252; www .heartlandbb.com), Dorset. The Restaurant Capital of the World (see the "Dorset—Restaurant Capital of the World" sidebar) is also home to this charming bed & breakfast, a renovated 1920s community school building. The inn has five spacious guest rooms, all with private baths and fireplaces; full breakfast is served daily. Located on the Heartland Trail (see *Green Space and Outdoor Activities*). Moderate.

✳ (ᵔᵧᵔ) ↝ **Embracing Pines Bed and Breakfast** (218-224-3519; www.embracingpines.com), 32287 County Route 38, Walker. This quiet inn has two rooms with a shared bath and a suite with private bath. The rooms are decorated with a north woods theme, and the common area evokes a log cabin. Embracing Pines is an active participant in the Minnesota Bed & Breakfast Association's Green Journeys Program, implementing ecologically friendly practices and products throughout the home. Expensive.

CABINS ✎ 🐾 ♿ ✳ **Breezy Point Resort** (218-573-3125 or 1-800-939-2630; www.breezypoint.com), 54852 MN 34, Osage. Breezy Point has nine log cabins with knotty pine interiors, spacious and comfortable. A mobile home farther away from the lake is the 10th accommodation. The resort offers boat and motor rental, and guided fishing trips can be arranged.

There's a sandy beach with a variety of beach toys—paddleboats, hydro bikes, and kayaks—included in the rates. Pets accepted in the off-season. Moderate.

✏ ♿ ⚲ **Crow Wing Crest Lodge** (218-652-3111 or 1-800-279-2754; www.crowwing.com), 31159 County Route 23, Akeley. Open mid-May through Oct. Crow Wing's 19 cabins, set on a pristine lake, vary from rustic to upscale. The resort prides itself on its environmental stance; the proprietors recycle lake water, use no pesticides or herbicides, and use only all-natural cleaning products. The owners also have a holistic approach to vacations, and reflexology, aromatherapy, massage, and yoga are offered. Kids' activities are offered daily during the summer; that is, if they aren't entertained enough on the sandy beach with the beach toys, paddleboats, kayaks, or the playground, or the fishing dock. Moderate.

✏ ((ᵠ)) **Bailey's Resort on Leech Lake** (218-547-1464 or 1-800-458-7540; www.baileysresort.com), 33216 CR 38, Walker. Open mid-May to early Oct. Bailey's has nine cabins situated on 24 acres, making it an uncrowded retreat that focuses on families. There are water toys galore, bikes for rent, and a boat launch from a narrow harbor onto Leech Lake. Expensive.

✏ ✳ **Brindley's Harbor Resort** (1-888-547-5477; www.brindleys harbor.com), 9530 Pine Point Road NW, Walker. This quiet resort on Leech Lake has 15 cottages, a lake home, and five luxury log cabins. A huge sandy beach has four piers for fishing as well as a boat slip and marina. The use of canoes, kayaks, sailboats, bikes, and hammocks are all included; boats and ice houses are available for guest rental. The staff will clean and freeze your catch of fish. Moderate.

✏ ♿ � ✳ **Chase on the Lake** (218-547-1464; www.chaseonthe lake.com), 502 Cleveland Boulevard, Walker. Chase on the Lake is a classic upscale resort with lovely hotel rooms and condos, the latter of which come equipped with full kitchens and laundry units. There's a full-service spa on-site, and golf packages at two nearby 18-hole courses are available. Chase has its own two-lane bowling alley, and a supervised kids program is offered during the summer. If you don't feel like cooking, fine dining is on-site, too (see *Where to Eat*). Expensive.

✳ Where to Eat

DINING OUT

♿ ☿ ✳ **The Boulders** (218-547-1006; www.thebouldersrestaurant .com), 8363 Lake Land Trail NW, Walker. Open daily for dinner. An upscale restaurant with a casual atmosphere, the Boulders offers steak, salmon, lamb chops, and even paella, which is beautifully prepared and served. A good special-occasion choice. Expensive.

✏ ♿ ☿ ✳ **Lucky Moose Bar and Grill** (218-547-0801; www.lucky moosebargrill.com), 441 Walker

Bay Boulevard, Walker. Open daily for lunch and dinner. A casual bar and grill housed in a log building. Expensive.

& Y **Ranch House Supper Club** (218-547-1540; www.ranchhouse supperclub.com), 9420 MN 371 NW, Walker. Open daily for dinner, Sun. for brunch. This old-fashioned supper club serves steaks and prime rib, plus there are all-you-can-eat specials each night. Expensive.

✄ & Y ❄ **The 502 at Chase on the Lake** (218-547-7777; www .chaseonthelake.com), 502 Cleveland Boulevard, Walker. Open daily for lunch and dinner, Sat. and Sun. for breakfast. The restaurant at the Chase on the Lake resort (see *Lodging*) is a special-occasion restaurant for locals and serves up sizable portions of chicken, steak, and seafood. There is prime rib on weekends and an all-you-can-eat

DORSET—RESTAURANT CAPITAL OF THE WORLD

This tiny town has, tongue firmly in cheek, billed itself as the Restaurant Capital of the World, and certainly it's hard to believe any other town has as many restaurants per capita as this one does. With just 22 residents, Dorset has four restaurants—that's one for every 5.5 villagers. (This is also a town that once elected a local five-year-old as its mayor.) What's more surprising is that while the restaurants may not be profiled in *Food & Wine* anytime soon, they are worthy of a visit if you're in the neighborhood (which is east of Park Rapids on County Route 18, north of MN 34). Just follow the boardwalk down the main street (or take a detour from the Heartland Trail if you're out hiking or biking), and you'll find a good meal somewhere.

✄ & Y **LaPasta Italian Eatery** (218-732-0275; www.dorset-lapasta.com /lapasta.htm), County Route 7. Open daily for all three meals, June through Aug.; Sat. and Sun. for all three meals, May and Sept. Breakfast features include the standard pancakes and omelets, along with stuffed French toast and potato pancakes; lunch offers a few pasta items, along with burgers and sandwiches; and dinner is a changing roster of Italian foods. Moderate.

✄ & Y ❄ **Dorset Café** (218-732-4072), CR 7. Open Mon. through Fri. for dinner and Sat. and Sun. for lunch and dinner, year-round. This café fish fry on Fri. "Boat up" service is available to the restaurant's expansive lakeside patio. Expensive.

EATING OUT ✎ **MinneSoda Fountain** (218-732-3240), 205 S. Main, Park Rapids. Open for more than 80 years in the heart of this small town, the MinneSoda falls under the category of "don't miss." When you visit this 17-stool confectionary, leave the calorie counter at home. Inexpensive.

✎ ♿ ♈ ❄ **Charlie's Up North/ Charlie's Boathouse** (218-547-0222; www.charliesupnorth.com), 6841 MN 371 NW, Walker. Charlie's Up North is open daily year-round for all three meals; the Boathouse is open for lunch and dinner during the summer. Charlie's is a casual, friendly dining spot serving three hearty meals a day, with a special Chinese menu on Tues. and Thurs., and prime rib on Sat. and Sun.

serves steaks and seafood and has a full bar. Moderate.

✎ ♿ ♈ **Dorset House Restaurant and Soda Fountain** (218-732-5556), CR 7. Open daily for lunch and dinner in the summer. Choose from the buffet or from a pizza and burger menu. For dessert there are homemade pies and, of course, ice cream. Inexpensive.

✎ ♿ ♈ **Companeros** (218-732-7624; www .companerosofdorset .com), CR 7. Open daily for lunch and dinner,

COMPANEROS RESTAURANT, DORSET

June through Aug.; Thurs. through Sun. for dinner and Sun. for brunch, May and Sept. Americanized Mexican food served in cheerful abundance. Moderate.

The Boathouse is a freestanding outdoor bar with an extensive patio wrapped around an old boat rehabbed into the bar; it's a good spot for enjoying a sunny day. Moderate.

✷ Entertainment

Long Lake Theater (218-732-0099; www.longlaketheater.net), County Route 6, Hubbard. Open Wed. through Sat. on selected dates, June through Sept. Summer stock theater offering four to five productions each year, along with holiday productions of *A Christmas Carol*.

Northern Light Opera Company (218-237-0400 or 1-866-766-7372; www.northernlightopera .org), 11700 Island Lake Drive, Park Rapids. Productions on occasion; check website for schedule. The name of this company is a play on words; the *light* refers to light opera more than northern lights. This grass-roots organization has diligently been putting together productions, primarily of Gilbert and Sullivan, since 2001. Their success is demonstrated by their growth and their branching out, including performances of *Oklahoma* and *Amahl and the Night Visitors*.

✐ **Jaspers Jubilee Theater** (218-237-4333; www.jasperstheater .com), MN 34, Park Rapids. Open Thurs. and Sat., June through Aug. Adults $19, senior citizens $18, children 4–16 $9, children under 4 free if sitting on an adult's lap. Discounts available for groups of 20 or more. A lively family-friendly live show incorporating music, magic, juggling, yodeling, dancing, and comedy skits.

✐ **Woodtick Musical Theater** (218-652-4200 or 1-800-644-6892; http://woodticktheater.net), MN 34, Akeley. Open Wed. through Sat., mid-June through mid-Sept. Adults $16.50, senior citizens $15.50, children 13–17 $9.50, children 6–12 $6.50, children under 6 free. Billing its show as similar to those in Branson, Missouri, the Woodtick theater offers a musical variety show each summer that's appropriate for all ages. The music encompasses country, folk, bluegrass, and gospel, and is accompanied by a comedy show.

✷ Special Events

February: **Eelpout Festival** (www.eelpoutfestival.com), Walker. Admission is $10. Held mid-Feb. each year, the Eelpout Festival, besides having one of the odder names for a state festival, is a good-natured celebration of winter and the joys of ice fishing. Events during the three-day event include, of course, ice fishing, as well as a 5K run, an ice-house decorating contest, on-ice auto and snowmobile races, rugby on ice, and the Polar Plunge, an opportunity to raise money for the local community center by collecting pledges and agreeing to jump in the lake—in Feb.

July: **Moondance Jam** (1-877-666-6526; www.moondancejam .com), Walker. Ticket prices for the four-day festival start at $95 for a one-day pass and $425 for a three-day VIP ticket. The latter includes special seating; a VIP tent with free beer, pop, and water; discounted cocktails; occasional meet-and-greets with some of the bands; dinner and hors d'oeuvres daily; and preferential parking. Tickets go on sale nearly a year in advance, and the closer to festival date, the more they cost. Campsites should be reserved ahead of time. The classic-rock version of WE Fest (see the WE Fest sidebar in the "Thief River Falls/Red River Valley/Detroit Lakes" chapter), this four-day event held in early July draws thousands of people from across the country to hear live concerts by the likes of Def Leppard, Kansas, Alice Cooper, and REO Speedwagon. Children are not prohibited, but organizers note this is an event intended for adults and may not be appropriate for kids. A country-music version of this event was launched in 2007; information can be found at www.jammincountry.com.

August: **Leech Lake Regatta** (218-547-1819; www.shoresof leechlake.com/regatta.htm), 6166 Moriss Point Road, Walker. Race participation is $75; additional fees apply for boat mooring. This early-Aug. event in a multiclass sailboat race for all skill levels. Many sailors opt to spend several days after the race on the water.

BEMIDJI AREA

B emidji (pronounced "buh-MIDJ-ee") is not far from Itasca State Park, home to the Mississippi Headwaters, and Bemidji itself is the first city geographically on the Mississippi River. There are nearly 40 lakes within a 25-mile radius of Bemidji, so water sports are a major draw. But winter is popular, too, with snowmobiling, skiing (cross-country and down-hill), ice fishing, and snowshoeing favored activities.

✳ To See and Do

FOR FAMILIES ✍ **Paul Bunyan Amusement Park** (no phone), 300 Bemidji Avenue, Bemidji. Open daily 10–dusk, weather permitting, Memorial Day through Labor Day. There is no general admission fee, but tickets are available for purchase for individual rides and mini golf. Rides for small children and old-fashioned miniature golf.

MUSEUMS AND COMMUNITY ARTWORK ✍ ⅙ ✳ **Bemidji Art Walk** (218-759-0164 or 1-800-458-2223, ext. 105). On the lakefront, Bemidji. Open daily. Stop at the tourist information center to begin your tour of sculptures and murals that appear lakeside and into downtown.

✍ ⅙ ✳ **Beltrami County History Center** (218-444-3376; www.beltrami history.org), 130 Minnesota Avenue SW, Bemidji. Open Mon. through Sat. 10–4. Adults $5, senior citizens and students $4, children 12 and under $1, historical society members free. The history center resides in the restored 1912 Great Northern Railway Depot, which was the last depot built by railroad baron James J. Hill. The building's architecture itself is worth a visit, but the collection within is entertaining and enlightening, from Native American artifacts to a restored telegraph office. A separate research area offers historians access to archival materials.

✍ ⅙ ✳ **Headwaters Science Center** (218-444-4472; www.hscbemidji .org), 413 Beltrami Avenue, Bemidji. Open Mon. through Sat. 9:30– 5:30, Sun. noon–5. Visitors 12 and older $5, children under 12 $4, HSC members free. Essentially a children's science museum, the HSC offers a variety of hands-on activities, as well as a collection of live animals (snakes, turtles, salamanders) for kids to learn about and handle.

⚓ ♿ ❋ **Bemidji Community Art Center** (218-444-7570; http://bcac .wordpress.com), 426 Bemidji Avenue, Bemidji. Open Tues. through Fri. noon–5, Sat. 10–2. The art center is located in the historic Carnegie Library building on the lakeshore, which is listed on the National Register of Historic Places. Inside there are three galleries that display national and regional artists, as well as host live music and poetry readings. New exhibits appear monthly from Feb. through Dec. The art center also sponsors a series of First Fridays, which showcase art and live performances both in the center and around Bemidji.

⚓ ♿ ❋ *Paul Bunyan* and *Babe the Blue Ox,* Bemidji lakefront, near the tourist information center. Open daily. A visit to Bemidji isn't quite complete without a photo opportunity near the legendary Paul Bunyan statues. Besides, it's a good starting point for visiting the Bemidji Art Walk.

OTHER ATTRACTIONS ⚓ ♿ ❋ **Concordia Language Villages** (218-586-8600 or 1-800-222-4750; http://clvweb.cord.edu/prweb), 8607 Thorsonveien NE, Bemidji. This renowned language school, headquartered in Moorhead, holds the majority of its classes and camps at an expansive site just outside Bemidji. The languages (including French, German, Spanish, Korean, Russian, Norwegian, and Swedish) are taught in villages created to resemble a town in the country of origin. Most of the villages in Bemidji are centered near Turtle Lake, but a few are about 10 miles north. Each village is separate from the other. Programs are offered for kids and adults, but even if you're not planning on learning a foreign language, the lovingly re-created international villages are worth a stop for the beautiful sightseeing alone.

❋ Green Space and Outdoor Activities

Not surprisingly, green space is abundant in the northern part of the state.

PARKS AND PARKWAYS Chippewa National Forest (218-335-8600; www.fs.fed.us/r9/forests/chippewa), 200 Ash Avenue NW, Cass Lake. With more than 666,000 acres, Chippewa National Forest has ample opportunity for outdoor adventures. The forest has 160 miles of hiking trails and cross-country ski trails, 330 miles of snowmobiling trails, 23 developed campgrounds and 380 camping sites, and a sandy swimming beach. Three visitors centers have programs and information: Norway Beach, Cut Foot Sioux, and Edge of the Wilderness Discovery Center. For water fans, the forest holds two of Minnesota's five biggest lakes, and there are nine

THE GENERAL STORE AT LAKE WINNIE, CHIPPEWA NATIONAL FOREST

canoe routes across various rivers and Leech Lake. (Note: Some of these routes are more treacherous than others; when planning a canoe trip, check with the Chippewa National Forest for recommendations based on your skill level.)

Edge of the Wilderness Scenic Byway. East of Bemidji is MN 38, which is the road for the Edge of the Wilderness Byway, a 47-mile roadway that runs from Grand Rapids to Effie. It showcases heavy forests and wetlands, with profusions of wildflowers in the warmer months followed by spectacular foliage colors in the fall. The route is open year-round, with the exception of the occasional snowstorm.

The byway goes through the **Black Spruce/Tamarack Bog Habitat.** Lining both sides of the road, this habitat was formed 16,000 years ago when the last of the glaciers still existed. Spruce and tamarack tower over the road, and if you were to wander into the bog, you'd find the ground to be wet and spongy.

For an adventurous detour—and a glimpse into a way of life long gone—turn right on County Route 60 and drive several miles to Blue Water Lake Road, where you'll find a parking lot for the Trout Lake–Joyce Estate Hiking Trail. From the trailhead, the hike to the **Joyce Estate** is about 6 miles round-trip. The Joyce Estate was built on the shores of Trout Lake between 1917 and 1935 by David Joyce, whose fortunes were made in the logging industry. He built a massive complex out of native stone and lumber, with 40 buildings, a seaplane hangar, nine-hole golf

NORTHERN LAKES/RED RIVER VALLEY

course, and clubhouse. The caretaker's complex itself had 17 buildings. It's a fascinating place to explore how the wealthy lived decades ago in the woods.

Another facet of the area's history is on display at the **Camp Rabideau National Historic Landmark,** one of the best preserved Civilian Conservation Corps projects in the country. You can take a guided tour, or you can go on your own; interpretive displays with detailed information are present throughout.

Itasca State Park/Mississippi Headwaters (218-266-2100; www.dnr .state.mn.us/state_parks/Itasca/index.html), 36750 Main Park Drive, Park Rapids. Open daily 8 AM–10 PM, year-round. This is Minnesota's oldest state park, and a large one (although not the largest) at 32,000 acres. It's also well known for being the starting point of the Mississippi River, and the point at which you easily walk across the river. But Itasca State Park has several other spots to visit, including a 500-year-old Indian cemetery and Wegmann's Cabin, a pioneer artifact. Pines inhabit the Wilderness Sanctuary, a 2,000-acre stand of white and red pines, some upward of 300 years old. There are 49 miles of hiking trails and 16 miles of paved biking trails (bike rental is available within the park, as are boat and canoe rentals). Plan ahead if you'd like to stay at Douglas Lodge (see *Lodging*), located right within the park.

INDIAN CEMETERY AT ITASCA STATE PARK

THE LOST 40 SCIENTIFIC AND NATURAL AREA

Near the junction of MN 1 and US 71 is this historical scientific and natural area (SNA). The Lost 40, which is actually 144 acres, is a tract of land that was accidentally misidentified as a lake by a surveyor during the logging boom time. Consequently, it remained untouched when forests around it were decimated. There are pine trees that are more than 300 years old in the Lost 40, and wildflowers are prolific in the late spring. A 1-mile hiking trail guides you through this special and beautiful untouched wilderness.

Lake Bemidji State Park (218-308-2300; www.dnr.state.mn.us/state _parks/lake_bemidji/index.html), 3401 State Park Road NE, Bemidji. Open daily 8 AM–10 PM, year-round. It may not have the Mississippi Headwaters, but Lake Bemidji State Park is a worthy stop, with acres of forest, access to Lake Bemidji for boating and fishing, a paved bike trail, and scores for birds to watch.

BIG BOG BOARDWALK

Big Bog State Recreation Area (218-647-8592; www.dnr.state .mn.us/state_parks/big_bog /index.html), 55716 MN 72 NE, Waskish. Open daily 8 AM–10 PM, year-round. Opened in 2005, this recreation area provides a way for visitors to explore the ecology of a bog without overly disturbing it. A mile-long boardwalk was installed through the bog, so visitors can go deep into the natural area without damaging the plant life. Signs posted frequently along the way explain the significance of the bog and point out different aspects of plants and wildlife that can be viewed from the walk.

SKIING AND WINTER SPORTS Buena Vista Ski Village (218-243-2231 or 1-800-777-7958; www.bvskiarea.com), 19276 Lake Julia Drive NW, Bemidji. Open for winter sports mid-Nov. through Mar., depending on weather. The mountains may not be the highest, but Buena Vista offers beautiful scenery to enjoy with its 16 runs. Cross-country skiing, tubing, snowboarding, and horse-drawn sleigh rides are all offered while there's snow. In the summer, the ski resort transforms into **Buena Vista Ranch,** a logging village and visitors center. Activities include covered wagon tours, horsemanship training clinics, and fall foliage rides. Reservations are recommended; call for information.

✳ Lodging

BED & BREAKFASTS

❋ ((ρ)) **Villa Calma Bed and Breakfast** (218-444-5554; www.villacalma.com), 915 Lake Boulevard NE, Bemidji. This bed & breakfast, located near Lake Bemidji, offers four rooms, two with private bath and two with shared bath. All rooms have upgraded bed coverings and bathrobes, and full breakfast is included, as is an early-evening glass of wine. A common great room serves as the breakfast point, with lovely views of the lake, and the backyard has a fire pit and double hammock for guest relaxation. Villa Calma is on the Paul Bunyan Trail, a 17-mile paved trail open for bikes and inline skates. Expensive. Packages are available.

HOTELS

✍ ᘯ Ⴑ ❋ ((ρ)) **Hampton Inn** (218-751-3600 or 1-800-426-7866; www.hamptoninn.com), 1019 Paul Bunyan Drive S., Bemidji. The Hampton Inn is right on Lake Bemidji, a short walk from the tourist information center and the beginning of the Bemidji Art Walk. Full breakfast is included in the rates, and all rooms have high-speed Internet access. The hotel also has a Green Mill pizza restaurant (see *Where to Eat*) for lunch and dinner. Expensive.

✍ ᘯ ❋ ((ρ)) **AmericInn Motel & Suites** (218-751-3000 or 1-800-634-3444; www.americinn.com), 1200 Paul Bunyan Drive NW, Bemidji. Near the Paul Bunyan Mall, the AmericInn offers 59 units, 26 of which are suites. The property has in indoor pool, whirlpool, and sauna, and the rates include continental breakfast. Moderate.

✍ ᘯ ❋ ((ρ)) **Holiday Inn Express** (218-751-2487; www.ichotelsgroup.com), 2422 Ridgeway Avenue NW, Bemidji. A basic but comfortable Holiday Inn, near the Paul Bunyan Mall. Most rooms have two queen beds, while a few upgraded rooms have king beds and Jacuzzi baths. Expensive.

LODGES AND RESORTS

✏ ☀ ♿ ⛾ ❄ **Ruttger's Birchmont Lodge** (218-444-3463 or 1-888-788-8437; www.ruttger.com), 7598 Bemidji Road NE, Bemidji. A family resort that's something of a tradition on Lake Bemidji, Ruttger's offers both lodge and cabin accommodations. The Cedar Lodge offers the most luxurious suites, with lakefront setting and fireplaces, while the Main Lodge offers the more economical rooms. Cedar Lodge is open year-round, while the Main Lodge is open only in the summer. In addition, there are 22 cottages (mostly open only mid-May to Labor Day) and seven villas (open year-round), which are larger than the cottages. The resort has a restaurant and bar open during the summer months. There is an indoor pool and hot tub, open all year, and boat and bike rental during the summer. A large sandy beach makes for a great summer resting spot, and during the summer Ruttger's offers a supervised kids' program for children ages 4–12. Moderate.

✏ ❄ ((•)) **Douglas Lodge** (1-866-857-2757; www.stayatmnparks.com), Itasca State Park. This gorgeous lodge was built in 1905 with timber from Itasca State Park and houses five guest rooms, a dining room, and a lounge. There is also a clubhouse with rooms available, as well as several cabins. Common areas center around a large stone fireplace, and rocking chairs rest on the spacious porch. It's an easy walk down to the fishing pier and hiking trails. Campgrounds can be reserved as well. Expensive.

✴ Where to Eat

As Bemidji has grown, thanks to the university, county government, and the local health-care system, the restaurant scene has not quite kept pace. There are plenty of chains to choose from—including Applebee's, Ground Round, Perkins, Country Kitchen, Bonanza, McDonald's, Burger King, Pizza Hut, Subway, and Quizno's—but there are also some restaurants without a major chain behind them that offer good dining.

EATING OUT ✏ ♿ ⛾ ❄ **Peppercorn's** (218-759-2794; www.peppercornrestaurant.com), 1813 Paul Bunyan Drive. Open daily for lunch and dinner. A steakhouse with a friendly staff and generous portions, Peppercorn's emphasis is on steak, ribs, and seafood. On Mon. through Thurs. nights there is a rotating all-you-can-eat selection, varying from crab legs to chicken and ribs. The food is good, and the service is quick. Moderate.

✏ ♿ ❄ **Raphael's Bakery Café** (218-759-2015; www.gr8buns.com), 319 Bemidji Avenue. Open Mon. through Sat. for breakfast and lunch. The quintessential small-town bakery and café, Raphael's serves delicious breakfasts and lunches, and sells baked goods to go. The menu may be limited (salads, sandwiches, soups), but the baked goods are pleasingly fresh, and the soups are homemade and worth buying extra for take-out. Inexpensive.

✿ ♿ ☿ ✳ **Brigid's Cross** (218-444-0567; www.brigidsirishpub.com), 317 Beltrami Avenue. Open daily for lunch and dinner. This cheerful Irish pub offers the usual suspects (fish-and-chips, ploughman's lunch, shepherd's pie) and some not-so-Irish variations (macaroni and cheese bites, mini burger basket). The food is hearty, a full bar is available, and a variety of events is offered, from open mike to trivia contests to live music. Moderate.

✿ ♿ ☿ ✳ **Keg & Cork** (218-444-7600), 310 Beltrami Avenue NW. Open daily for lunch and dinner. A friendly neighborhood bar and

grill. The locals love it, so you know it's good. Moderate.

✿ ☿ ✳ **Dave's Pizza** (218-751-3225; www.davespizza.biz), 422 W. 15th Street. It's not much to look at, but Dave's has been meeting pizza lovers' needs for decades. Moderate.

✿ ♿ ☿ ✳ **Green Mill Restaurant** (218-444-1875; www.greenmill.com), 1025 Paul Bunyan Drive S. Open daily for lunch and dinner. Yes, it's a chain, but it's also got a prime location at the Hampton Inn (see *Lodging*), with great views of Lake Bemidji. Plus the pizza is excellent. Moderate.

PAUL BUNYAN PLAYHOUSE, BEMIDJI

✳ Entertainment

Paul Bunyan Playhouse (218-751-7270; www.paulbunyanplay house.com), 314 Beltrami Avenue, Bemidji. With more than 55 years of productions, this is one of the country's longest continuously operating summer stock theaters. The Paul Bunyan Playhouse uses both national professional actors as well as locals for its summer season. Veterans of the playhouse have gone on to professional theater careers in the Twin Cities.

✳ Selective Shopping

✳ **Paul Bunyan Mall** (218-751-3195; www.paulbunyanmall.com), 1401 Paul Bunyan Drive NW, Bemidji. Open daily. The Paul Bunyan Mall is anchored by JCPenney, Herberger's, and Kmart; other stores include Footlocker, Claire's, Bath & Body Works, and General Nutrition Center.

✳ **Bemidji Woolen Mills** (1-888-751-5166; www.bemidjiwoolen mills.com), 391 Irvine Avenue NW, Bemidji. Open daily; closed Thanksgiving, Christmas, and Easter. Manufacturer and retailer of woolen apparel, Woolen Mills's products are high in quality; the store also carries Hudson's Bay, Woolrich, and Dale of Norway wool clothing.

✳ Special Events

The northern lakes region isn't short of festivals and events. Note: This list does not include an extensive, ongoing list of events that take place at Concordia Language Villages (see *To See and Do*). Check Concordia's website for detailed information on their festivals and weekend events.

January: **Bemidji Polar Daze** (218-444-3451 or 1-800-458-2223; www.visitbemidji.com), Bemidji. This festival, which often jokingly is called the "Brrrrmidji Polar Daze" ("Ber-midji" being a common mispronunciation of the city's name, which is correctly pronounced "buh-MIDJ-ee"), is held each year the third weekend in Jan. Events include the Taste of Northern Minnesota, a dining event featuring several local eateries; a poker tournament; a 5K run/walk; night skiing; snowshoeing; and stock car ice racing.

February: **Logging Days** (218-243-2231 or 1-800-777-7958; www.bvskiarea.com), Buena Vista Ski Area, 19276 Lake Julia Drive NW, Bemidji. Visitors 13 and older $6, children 6–12 $4, children 5 and under free; family rate (up to six people) $25. This annual festival, held the first Sat. in Feb., is a day packed with logging and winter activities. Stump and log pulling, chainsaw sculptures, rop-

ONE OF THE BIG BLACK DUCKS IN BLACKDUCK

ing contests, a treasure hunt, square dancing, all-you-can-eat flapjacks, live music, and craft displays are all part of the fun.

June: **Chippewa Triathlon** (1-800-356-8615; www.casslake.com), Cass Lake. The traditional triathlon elements of a run (7 miles) and bike ride (28 miles) are combined with a 14-mile canoe ride. Held annually in June.

July: **Art in the Park** (218-444-7570; http://bcac.wordpress.com), Lake Bemidji. This annual event, which has taken place for 40 years, showcases local and national artists, and offers food and live entertainment. Dates are scheduled for mid-July.

Woodcarver's Festival (218-835-4949; www.blackduckmn.com/), Blackduck. This annual festival has grown from its beginnings in 1983 to include woodcarvers from across the United States. and Canada. Held the last Sat. in July, the outdoor festival (rain or shine) brings visitors from all over the region. Carvers exhibit their wares for purchase, and food is available for sale. Look for the Uffda Taco.

BAUDETTE/ROSEAU/WARROAD

The northwestern border of Minnesota is all about the outdoors and year-round outdoor activities: fishing, hiking, snowmobiling, skating, cross-country skiing. There are some attractions and historical sites, but the emphasis here is outside, not inside.

✳ To See and Do

Attractions are open year-round unless otherwise noted.

MUSEUMS AND HISTORIC SITES 𝒮 ⅙ **Lake of the Woods County Museum** (218-634-1200; www.lakeofthewoodshistoricalsociety.com), 119 Eighth Avenue SE, Baudette. Open Tues. through Fri. 10–4 and Sat. 10–2, mid-May through Labor Day; off-season by appointment. No admission fee. This small but well-stocked museum has exhibits on various aspects of northern Minnesota's history and development, including a re-created homestead kitchen, school, country store, and tavern, as well as information on the geology of the area.

𝒮 ⅙ ✳ **The Polaris Experience Center** (218-463-4999; www.polaris industries.com), 205 Fifth Avenue SW, Suite 2, Roseau. Open Mon. through Fri. 11–1, Sat. 11–6. No admission fee. One of the leading manufacturers of snowmobiles, Polaris built this visitors center adjacent to its plant to showcase the company's history. The exhibits range from the earliest snowmobile prototypes to today's sleeker machines, as well as history and trivia from the age of snowmobiles. Free tours of the Polaris Plant itself are scheduled daily at 2 PM; call ahead or stop by the office to sign up.

𝒮 ⅙ **Pioneer Village** (218-463-3052; www.roseaupioneerfarm.com), MN 11, Roseau. Open Mon. through Fri. noon–5, May through Aug.; other times by appointment. Admission is free. This lovingly preserved village is a testament to the pioneer days of northwestern Minnesota's agricultural history. Most of the 16 buildings are restored artifacts, done primarily by volunteer labor (volunteer opportunities are available on Tues.; call the village for more information). Visitors are welcome to explore on their own or take a guided tour through the post office, parish hall, church, barn, blacksmith shop, and log cabin. Bathroom facilities are, fittingly, of an outhouse nature, in a vintage porta-potty.

✍ **Fort St. Charles** (218-223-4611), The Point, Lake Street NE, Warroad. Open daily 10–4, Memorial Day through Sept., weather permitting. Admission is free. In the early 1700s a French explorer and trader by the name of Pierre Gaultier de Varennes, Sieur de la Verendrye, established this fort as a base for trading and for launching expeditions. However, lack of food and hostility from local Sioux made the fort difficult to maintain, and it was abandoned after 1760. The buildings were discovered and reconstructed as a historical site in the mid-1900s.

PIONEER VILLAGE, ROSEAU

✍ ♿ ❋ **Wm. S. Marvin Training and Visitor Center** (218-386-4334; www.marvin.com), MN 11 and 313, Warroad. Open Mon. through Fri. 8–6, Sat. and Sun. 1–4. Admission is free. The Marvin Visitor Center is a historic and industrial exhibition featuring the growth and technology behind Marvin Windows and Doors. Theatrical highlights include a recounting of the fire that destroyed the Marvin plant in 1961 and how the Marvin company rebuilt and expanded. Tours of the Marvin plant itself are available by appointment Mon. through Fri. by calling 218-386-4333.

OTHER ATTRACTIONS

✍ ♿ ❋ *Willie Walleye,* Bayfront Park, Baudette. No visit to the northern lakes would be complete without a photo op at the walleye equivalent of the Paul Bunyan statues in Bemidji (see *To See and Do* in the "Bemidji Area" chapter). Forty feet long and weighing 2 tons, *Willie* represents Baudette's claim of being the Walleye Capital of the World.

BAUDETTE'S *WILLIE WALLEYE*

✷ Green Space and Outdoor Activities

The northwestern stretch of the state is geared primarily toward visitors who want to enjoy outdoor activities, including fishing (both summer and winter), boating, hiking, hunting, snowmobiling, snowshoeing, and cross-country skiing. Consequently, many resorts in this area are open year-round to cater to clients who favor activities in the different seasons. Note: Because winter can be unpredictable, don't head out to this part of the state in the middle of January without a snow emergency kit in your vehicle, as well as a charged-up cell phone. Pay close attention to the weather, as snowstorms (complete with dangerous winds and wind chills) can arise quickly.

CANOEING Lake of the Woods, north through the Northwest Angle, makes for excellent canoeing, as does the meandering Rainy River.

FISHING Lake of the Woods is one of the nation's largest lakes (after the Great Lakes and Salt Lake), and it's become a favored place of anglers from all over the country and Canada. The region is proud of its walleye population (although its claim as Walleye Capital of the World is disputed by other walleye lakes), but there are many kinds of fish for the catching: Lake sturgeon, northern pike, smallmouth and largemouth bass, perch, and muskie are just some of the plentiful fish. You can bring your own boat and manage your fishing yourself, or you can hire a guide through

LAKE OF THE WOODS AT ZIPPEL BAY STATE PARK

one of the many guide services (and through many of the dozens of resorts throughout the area) available to assist you.

There is a separate summer and winter fishing season. Winter's ice fishing has gained considerable ground as more resorts offer ice houses for rent, many of which are outfitted with propane heaters and cooktops. The popularity of "sleeper" fish houses, outfitted like rustic cabins, also continues to grow. Fish spearing is another activity that is increasing in interest.

Official seasons and regulations can be found through the **Minnesota Department of Natural Resources** (651-296-6157 or 1-888-646-6367; www.dnr.state.mn.us/regulations/fishing/index.html).

HUNTING Deer hunting in Minnesota begins in late October for bow hunters and early November for firearms. Besides deer, duck, grouse, and goose hunting are all popular activities. Because there is so much open land near Lake of the Woods, it's easy to mistake private property for public hunting grounds. Check with the local tourist offices or with your resort owners, who can provide necessary information to help you avoid trespassing. **Minnesota DNR** (651-296-6157 or 1-888-646-6367; www.dnr .state.mn.us/regulations/hunting/index.html) has specific licensing and regulation information.

PARKS Zippel Bay State Park (218-783-6252; www.dnr.state.mn.us /state_parks/zippel_bay/index.html), County Route 8, Williams. Fishing, swimming, camping, bird-watching—Zippel Bay State Park offers these and more in its 3,000-plus acres along Lake of the Woods. Six miles of hiking trails available during the summer are expanded to 11 miles in the winter for cross-country skiers.

SNOWMOBILING There are more than 400 miles of snowmobile trails in the Lake of the Woods area, most groomed and maintained by a local snowmobiling organization, the **Lake of the Woods Drifters Snowmobile Club** (218-634-3042; www.lowdrifters.org), in Baudette. The Drifters can provide maps and trail conditions during the winter season. If you're going to be using the trails extensively, it's worth considering a Drifters membership (annual individual fee is $25, family rate is $35) in order to participate in one of the many events they sponsor during the snowmobiling season.

GOLF

Golf's charm is felt this far north, and there are several courses available to the public across the region.

Oak Harbor Golf Course (218-634-9939; www.oakharborgolfcourse .com), 2805 24th Street NW, Baudette. Open May 1 through Oct. 15, weather permitting. Nine-hole course.

Oakcrest Golf Club (218-463-3016; www.oakcrestgolfcourse.com), Fifth Street S., Roseau. Open mid-May to mid-Oct., weather permitting. An 18-hole championship course that winds along the river and through the woods.

Warroad Estates Golf Course (218-386-2025; www.warroadestates .com), 37293 Elm Drive, Warroad. Open Apr. 15 through Oct. 15, weather permitting. An 18-hole course that straddles the U.S.-Canadian border.

Northwest Angle Country Club (218-223-8001; www.pasturegolf.com), Angle Inlet. Open May through Sept., weather permitting. When a golf course's location is described as "north of northern Minnesota," you know you're truly going "up north." This nine-hole course may not be the most pristinely groomed course you've ever played, but you may never be able to see quite so much wildlife while golfing, either.

✳ Lodging

HOTELS ✎ ⅘ ✳ ((ᵠ)) **AmericInn Baudette** (218-634-3200 or 1-800-634-3444; www.americinn .com), MN 11 W., Baudette. The nicest hotel in Baudette is the AmericInn, which offers rooms and suites, an indoor pool, cold-weather hookups, a fish-cleaning area, and free high-speed Internet access. Upgraded rooms include a fireplace. Moderate.

✎ ⅘ ✳ ((ᵠ)) **AmericInn Roseau** (218-463-1045 or 1-800-634-3444; www.americinn.com), MN 11 W., Roseau. Like the Americ-Inn in Baudette, this is one of the nicest hotels in Roseau, offering rooms and suites, an indoor pool, and cold-weather hookups. Moderate.

✎ ⅘ ✳ **North Country Inn and Suites** (1-888-300-2196; www.north countryinnandsuites.com), 902 Third Street NW, Roseau. This motel offers 49 rooms and suites, all with refrigerators and micro-waves, and daily continental breakfast. There is an indoor pool and hot tub as well. Moderate.

✳ **St. Mary's Motel Room** (218-386-2474), 202 Roberts Avenue NE, Warroad. The most distinc-tive lodging in this part of the state is a room in a local historical church, in the former balcony area, with 22-foot-high ceilings and a kitchenette. Moderate.

RESORTS ✎ ⅄ ✳ ((ᵠ)) **Border View Lodge** (1-800-776-3474; www.borderviewlodge.com), 3409 MN 172 NW, Baudette. This year-round resort north of Baudette, located where the Rainy River meets Lake of the Woods, has sev-eral cabins, all of which are fully equipped and have the option of full daily maid service (i.e., bed making, dish washing). Border View also offers ice houses, both for daily use and for accommoda-tion for that all-night ice fishing getaway. There's a bar and restau-rant in the lodge. Expensive. Packages are available.

✎ 🐾 ⅘ ⅄ ✳ **Wigwam Resort** (218-634-2168 or 1-800-448-9260; www.wigwamresortlow.com), 3502 Four Mile Bay Drive NW, Baudette. The Wigwam offers both hotel rooms in the lodge and cabins for rental. Guests can book accommodations only, or they can reserve packages that include meals at the resort's restaurant and charter fishing with a guide. Moderate.

✎ ✳ **Zippel Bay Resort** (1-800-222-2537; www.zippelbay.com), 6080 39th Street NW, Williams. Zippel Bay has both budget cabins and deluxe log cabins complete with fireplace and Jacuzzi; the log cabins are attractive and spacious, located on the water's edge. The resort has an outdoor pool for the summer months and a restaurant. Packages are available with or without meals; during the winter, sleeper ice houses can be rented. (Not to mention the Zippel Igloo, an on-ice "igloo" offering catered food and drinks, and even a satel-lite TV.) Expensive.

THE BEACH AT ZIPPEL BAY RESORT

✳ Where to Eat

Because so many of the fishing and outdoor-activity resorts are located well out of city limits, many of the resorts offer restaurants or cafés themselves. Within the cities of Baudette, Roseau, and Warroad, there are several fast-food options, plus these selections.

DINING OUT ✐ ᴕ ❦ ❄ **Lake-view Restaurant** (218-386-1225), 1205 E. Lake Street, Warroad. Open daily for lunch and dinner. A more upscale restaurant located at the Seven Clans Casino. Steak, shrimp, and burgers are served while diners enjoy a stellar view of the lake. Expensive.

EATING OUT ✐ ᴕ ❦ ❄ **Ranch House** (218-634-2420), 203 W.

Main Street, Baudette. Open daily for all three meals, all of them hearty. Burgers and ribs are the specialty. Moderate.

✐ ᴕ ❄ **Williams Café** (218-783-3474), 2335 94th Avenue NW, Williams. Open Tues. through Sun. for breakfast and lunch. Williams Café has plates full of home-cooked breakfasts and juicy burgers. Inexpensive.

✐ ᴕ ❦ ❄ **Reed River Restaurant and Bar** (218-463-0993), 205 Fifth Avenue SE, Roseau. Open daily for lunch and dinner. A full restaurant and bar located near the Polaris Experience Center (see *To See and Do*), Reed River has burgers, sandwiches, steaks, and ribs. Moderate.

✐ ᴕ ❦ ❄ **Izzy's Lounge and Grill** (218-386-2723; www.patch motel.com/izzys.htm), 801 State

Avenue N., Warroad. Open daily for lunch and dinner. At this local bar and grill, the bar is fully stocked, and the grill provides enormous meals in the form of burgers and chicken. Service is friendly, and the casual environment, with a large stone fireplace, is downright cozy. Moderate.

✳ Special Events

June: **Willie Walleye Day,** Baudette. Held in early June, Willie Walleye Day celebrates Baudette's claim that it's the Walleye Capital of the World with a day of fun and frolic, including a 5K run/walk, lumberjack show, chainsaw carving, and, of course, food.

Scandinavian Festival, Roseau. Held each year in mid-June, the two-day Scandinavian Festival celebrates the region's roots with events in the town of Roseau and at the Pioneer Village (see *To See and Do*).

August: **Pioneer Village Festival** (218-463-3052; www.roseaupioneer farm.com), MN 11, Roseau. This event, held each year the last weekend of Aug. before Labor Day weekend, re-creates pioneer entertainment by having a pancake breakfast, children's games and activities, demonstrations of pioneer skills, and a parade.

Blueberry Festival and Chili Cook-Off (1-866-692-6453), Northwest Angle. An annual Aug. event celebrating the fruit of the season in a variety of cooked forms, as well as a chili cook-off among several resorts.

THIEF RIVER FALLS/ RED RIVER VALLEY/ DETROIT LAKES

In this region, the topography of Minnesota changes dramatically within a short distance, from flat agricultural areas to rolling wooded countryside dotted with lakes. Along the state's edge, you'll see miles of sunflowers, soybeans, and beets; veer east, and the views are pastoral. There's history and nature in abundance.

✳ To See and Do

GAMING ✔ ⓰ ⓨ ✳ **Shooting Star Casino** (218-935-2711 or 1-800-453-7827; www.starcasino.com), 777 Casino Road, Mahnomen. Open 24/7. North of Detroit Lakes is this casino, run by the White Earth Band of Ojibwe Indians. Large and well run, the casino has slots, blackjack, bingo, and poker, as well as child care and a kids' arcade. Live concerts are offered regularly in the casino's main stage, and there is dining in four venues. A hotel is attached to the casino (see *Lodging*).

MUSEUMS AND HISTORIC SITES ✔ ⓰ **Peter Engelstad Pioneer Village** (218-681-5767; www.pvillage.org), 825 Oakland Park Road, Thief River Falls. Open daily 1–5, Memorial Day through Labor Day. Adults $5, children under 12 with paid adult free. Like the Pioneer Village in Roseau (see *To See and Do* in the "Baudette/Roseau/Warroad" chapter), this is a collection of 19 historical buildings, each housing several artifacts from the early settler days of northwestern Minnesota. Buildings include a church, a school, log cabins, and a two-story Victorian house.

✔ ⓰ **Heritage Village** (218-791-6764; www.egfheritage.com), MN 220 N. and 20th Street NE, East Grand Forks. Open by appointment. Festivals and events open to the public are held frequently; call or check the website for details. A preserved historic village re-creating life in pioneer days, including a variety of farm implements.

✎ & ❄ **Rourke Art Museum** (218-236-8861; www.wix.com/therourke /rourke), 521 Main Avenue, Moorhead. Open Fri. through Sun. 1–5. Adults $5, students $2. A small but thoughtful collection of permanent and traveling exhibits focused on contemporary American, Hispanic, African, and Native American art.

✎ **Comstock House** (218-291-4211; www.mnhs.org/places/sites/ch), 506 Eighth Street S., Moorhead. Open Thurs. 5–8 and Sat. and Sun. 1–4:30, Memorial Day through Labor Day. Adults $6, senior citizens $5, children 6–12 $4, children under 6 and Minnesota Historical Society members free. The 1882 home of Solomon Comstock, who founded Moorhead State University. The home has been restored and includes original furnishings.

TOURS ✎ & ❄ **Arctic Cat** (218-681-8558; www.arcticcat.com), 601 Brooks Avenue S., Thief River Falls. Open Mon. through Fri. A large manufacturer of snowmobiles and ATVs, Arctic Cat offers tours of its plant at 1 PM. Call ahead for reservations.

✎ ❄ **Digi-Key** (218-681-5703; www.digikey.com), 701 Brooks Avenue S., Thief River Falls. Open Mon. through Fri. This manufacturer of electrical components offers tours by appointment.

WINERIES ⵯ **Two Fools Vineyard** (218-465-4655; www.twofoolsvine yard.com), 12501 240th Avenue SE, Plummer. Open Sat. and Sun. noon–3, June through Oct. Thumbing their noses at those who say grapes can't be grown in northern climates, Carol and LeRoy Stumpf grow grapes (among other fruits) and make wines such as pinot noir, chardonnay, and orange muscat.

❄ Green Space and Outdoor Activities

Historical Riverwalk (1-800-827-1629), Thief River Falls. More than 7 miles of trails wind through Thief River Falls along the Thief and Red Lake rivers. The trail is open for walking, biking, and cross-country skiing, and it passes through several city parks, some historical sites, and near the dam.

Agassiz National Wildlife Refuge (218-449-4115; www.fws.gov/midwest /agassiz), 22996 220th Street NE, Middle River. Open daily during day-light hours, May through Oct. The headquarters is open for questions and visitor assistance Mon. through Fri. 7:30–4, excluding federal holidays. Admission is free. This refuge has more than 60,000 acres encompassing a wide variety of environments—wetland, forest, and prairie—and is home to a diverse assortment of wildlife; bald eagles, ducks, geese, wolves, herons, moose, and deer are just a few of the animals residing here. There

A MAN, A DREAM, AND A BOAT

The Hjemkmost Center is named after the replica Viking ship built by a local man who wanted to sail it to Norway. He completed the ship and took it on Lake Superior, but before he could journey farther, he died; family and friends rallied and sailed the ship to Norway in 1982. The ship is on display as a permanent exhibit, along with a Norwegian stave church replica and a historical Red River Valley exhibit. Don't miss the center's introductory film; although a bit on the sappy side, the actual footage taken during the ship's voyage to Norway is amazing. Temporary exhibits are brought in on rotation, and the center sponsors several special events each year. Call or check the website for specific events.

PROW OF REPLICA VIKING SHIP, HJEMKMOST CENTER

✎ ♿ ❄ **Hjemkmost Center** (218-299-5511; www .hjemkomstcenter.com), 202 First Avenue N., Moorhead. Open Mon. through Sat. 9–5 (Tues. until 9), Sun. noon–5. Adults $7, senior citizens and college students $6, children 5–17 $5, children under 5 free. Admission is free every third Tues. 5–8.

is a 4-mile self-guided habitat drive as well as a 0.5-mile hiking trail; a 100-foot observation tower with a 14-foot observation deck is available during nonsnow times. Check in at headquarters to obtain the key for the tower.

❄ **Red River State Recreation Area** (218-773-4950; www.dnr.state.mn .us/state_parks/red_river/index.html), 515 Second Street NW, East Grand Forks. Open daily 8 AM–10 PM. A state park permit is required for admission; a day pass is $5 per vehicle. One of the state's newer recreation areas was created after the disastrous 1997 floods, which destroyed homes and farms along the river. More than 500 homes and buildings were removed from the area after the floodplain was reconfigured, and a 1,200-acre recreation area was created instead. Hiking and biking trails, fishing and boating access, and campsites are now available within easy access of both East Grand Forks and Grand Forks, North Dakota.

❊ **Tamarac National Wildlife Refuge** (218-847-2641; www.fws.gov /midwest/tamarac), 35704 County Route 36, Rochert. Open daily 5 AM– 10 PM. No admission fee. Tamarac has 43,000 acres set aside for wildlife preservation. The visitors center, open weekdays 7:30–4 and weekends 10–5, has exhibits and a video presentation explaining what the refuge contains. Self-guided driving and hiking tours can lend views of bald eagle, deer, porcupine, and even the occasional black bear. In the winter, ice fishing, cross-country skiing, and snowshoeing are all available.

❊ Lodging

✎ ♿ ❊ (ꜱ) **AmericInn Lodge and Suites Thief River Falls** (218-681-4411 or 1-800-634-3444; www .americinn.com), 1920 US 59 SE, Thief River Falls. This property has rooms and suites, some of the latter with fireplaces and whirlpools. There's an indoor pool and a complimentary daily breakfast; for winter enthusiasts, the hotel offers cold-weather vehicle hookups. Moderate.

✎ ♿ ❊ **C'mon Inn** (218-681-3000 or 1-800-950-8111; www.cmoninn .com), 1586 US 59 S., Thief River Falls. A small but comfortable hotel with 44 rooms, an indoor pool and hot tub, and daily continental breakfast. Expensive.

✎ ♣ ♿ ♟ ❊ (ꜱ) **AmericInn Lodge and Suites Moorhead** (218-287-7100 or 1-800-634-3444; www .americinnofmoorhead.com), 600 30th Avenue S., Moorhead. This is one of the larger AmericInns in the state, and as such it has more amenities than most. Like most AmericInns, it has an indoor pool, but this hotel also has a kiddy pool and mini golf course, both indoors. There is a hot tub for all hotel guests, and four of the suites have private hot tubs. Continental breakfast is included in the rates, but unlike most AmericInns, this one also has a restaurant, lounge, and comedy club on-site. Moderate.

✎ ♿ ♟ ❊ (ꜱ) **Courtyard Moorhead** (218-284-1000 or 1-800-321-2211; www.marriott.com), 1080 28th Avenue S., Moorhead. The Courtyard, a Marriott property, was designed primarily for business travelers, so the rooms are well equipped with two phone lines, free high-speed Internet access, and higher-end desks and desk chairs. The hotel also has an indoor pool, and a restaurant on-site that is open for breakfast and dinner. Expensive.

🗲 ♿ ❄ ((ᵞ)) **AmericInn Lodge and Suites Detroit Lakes** (218-847-8795 or 1-800-634-3444; www.americinn.com), 777 US 10 E., Detroit Lakes. This AmericInn is in the process of redecorating its rooms and suites (the latter having fireplaces and Jacuzzis), and eventually all rooms will have HDTVs. The hotel has an indoor pool and includes a full breakfast daily. Cold-weather hookups are available, and there is access from the hotel to local snowmobile trails. Moderate.

🗲 ♿ ❖ ❄ ((ᵞ)) **The Lodge on Lake Detroit** (218-847-8439 or 1-800-761-8439; www.thelodgeon lakedetroit.com), 1200 E. Shore Drive, Detroit Lakes. This lakefront hotel, opened in 2006, boasts rooms that all face the lake; first-floor rooms have walkout patios, and most second- and third-floor rooms have private balconies. The rooms are nicely appointed, all coming with HDTV and free Internet access, and are the most luxurious in the area. Suites have additional features, such as gas fireplaces or full kitchens. There's a sandy beach outside for the summer, and an indoor pool and hot tub for inclement weather. A full-service spa is on-site. Full breakfast is served daily, and the lounge offers drinks and appetizers in the evening, but other meals are not provided. Expensive. Packages are available.

🗲 ♿ ❖ ❄ ((ᵞ)) **Holiday Inn Lakeside** (218-847-2121 or 1-877-251-9348; www.holidayinndl.com), US 10 E., Detroit Lakes. A lakeside property, the Holiday Inn has a sandy beach, as well as an indoor pool, whirlpool, and sauna. The rooms are standard Holiday Inn issue, but there is a full-service restaurant on-site (the Ice House Bar and Grill) serving three meals daily. Moderate.

🗲 ♿ ❖ ❄ ((ᵞ)) **Shooting Star Casino Hotel and RV Park** (218-935-2711 or 1-800-453-7827; www.starcasino.com), 777 Casino Road, Mahnomen. Attached to the casino (see *To See and Do*) is a hotel with a range of accommodation options, from standard rooms to deluxe suites. There's an indoor pool and hot tub, and room service from the casino's restaurants is available. Behind the hotel is an RV park with water, sewer, and electricity hookups. Moderate.

❖ **Where to Eat**

DINING OUT

🗲 ♿ ❖ ❄ **The Blue Moose Bar and Grill** (218-773-6516; www.thebluemoose.net), 507 Second Street NW, East Grand Forks. Open daily for lunch and dinner, Sun. for breakfast. Perhaps one of the few restaurants in history to have crossed a river, the Blue Moose did so following the Red River flooding in 1999. Now housed on the river in a comfortable lodge setting, this restaurant serves hearty steaks and sandwiches in huge portions. Expensive.

♿ ❖ ❄ **Sarello's** (218-287-0238; www.sarellos.com), 28 Center

Mall Avenue, Moorhead. Open daily for dinner. If you're looking for a quiet adult night out, this is the place. The best restaurant in the area, Sarello's serves upscale Italian cuisine in an elegant environment. The wine list is extensive. Reservations are strongly recommended. Expensive.

& Y ❋ **The Fireside** (218-847-8192; www.firesidedl.com), 1462 East Shore Drive, Detroit Lakes. Open daily for dinner, Memorial Day through Sept.; Mon. through Sat. for dinner, Oct. through May. Call for details. One of the best choices for an upscale dining experience, the Fireside serves old-fashioned supper-club foods with a contemporary flair. Steaks are available in all sizes, and walleye comes either as a pan-fried fillet or stuffed with seafood. The meat loaf with Asiago cheese is a good bet if you're not in a steak or seafood mood. Expensive.

EATING OUT ✐ & Y ❋ **Evergreen Eating Emporium** (218-681-3138), 700 MN 32 S., Thief River Falls. Open daily for lunch and dinner. Housed in a large Tudor-style building, the Evergreen has two dining areas situated around a large stone fireplace, as well as private dining rooms on the second floor. The cozy ambience comes with good food served in enormous portions: sandwiches and salads at lunch, heavier fare such as ribs and steaks at dinner. But the dinner menu also includes a limited selection of smaller-portion entrées for a lower price

with no age restrictions, something other restaurants could emulate. Moderate.

✐ ❋ **Johnnie's Café** (218-681-8102), 304 Main Avenue N., Thief River Falls. Open Mon. through Sat. for breakfast and lunch. A classic small-town café popular with the locals, Johnnie's breakfasts are primarily eggs and pancakes, but they're plentiful and good (be sure to get the hash browns). Lunch is classic sandwiches (Reuben, grilled cheese) and burgers. Nothing fancy, but done well. Inexpensive.

✐ & Y ❋ **Black Cat Sports Bar and Grill** (218-681-8910; www.blackcattrf.com), 1080 MN 32 S., Thief River Falls. Open daily for lunch and dinner. This is a sports bar with a snowmobiling theme, thanks to the memorabilia on display from local manufacturer Arctic Cat. The food is about what you'd expect from a sports bar: heavy on burgers and appetizers. Basic and reliable. Moderate.

✐ & Y ❋ **The Speakeasy** (218-844-1326; www.speakeasydl.com), 1100 N. Shore Drive, Detroit Lakes. Open daily for lunch and dinner, Sun. for brunch. A kitschy throwback to the 1920s, the Speakeasy's servers dress as flappers, and the lounge comes complete with a Ford Model A. Pasta is the house specialty, either in a signature style or in a "design your own." Oddly for an Italian restaurant with a 1920s theme, the Speakeasy has a Cinco de Mayo celebration each year, when their menu changes to Mexican. Moderate.

✿ ☗ ❄ **Zorbaz on the Lake** (218-847-5305; www.zorbaz.com), 402 W. Lake Drive, Detroit Lakes. Open daily for lunch and dinner. A beach bar with Mexican food, pizza, pasta, and plenty of beer. Take the kids for the arcades. A dock is provided for diners arriving by boat. Moderate.

✿ ☖ ☗ ❄ **Shooting Star Casino** (218-935-2711 or 1-800-453-7827; www.starcasino.com), 777 Casino Road, Mahnomen. This casino, north of Detroit Lakes, offers four restaurants from sit-down to casual quick food, including a buffet that's plentiful. Moderate.

❋ Entertainment

✿ ☖ **Log Cabin Folk Art Center** (218-299-5252), 315 Fourth Street S., Moorhead. Open Tues. evenings, June through Aug. A cabin built in 1859 now serves as an artists' space, with Tues. nights open to the public. On those nights, a working folk artist is on-site, along with live music, and carriage rides to the Red River are offered.

❋ Special Events

May: **Festival of Birds** (218-847-9202 or 1-800-542-3992; www .visitdetroitlakes.com), Detroit Lakes. A basic event fee of $10 for the full festival or $5 per day is required, plus fees ranging from $7 to $75 for the individual events. This annual event, held in

May, is for serious birders. The Detroit Lakes area is home to more than 200 kinds of birds, and the festival provides birdwatchers with three days of guided tours, presentations by experts, early-morning and evening field trips, workshops, and a dinner in the forest.

June: **Scandinavian Hjemkomst Festival** (218-299-5452; www .hjemkomstcenter.com), Hjem-komst Center, 202 First Avenue N., Moorhead. Adult pass is $10, youth 18 and under free. Held each year in late June, the festival is all things Scandinavian—children's story hours, a midsummer's fest picnic, a Swedish *smorbrod* (smorgasbord), a banquet, dance and music performances and lessons, art exhibits, and food and craft sales.

August: **Barnesville Potato Days** (1-800-525-4901; www.potato days.com), Barnesville. As you might expect, Barnesville is a major potato producer, and this annual festival, held the last weekend in Aug., reflects that heritage. This festival draws more than 14,000 people each year due to its good-natured view of potato activities, including mashed potato wrestling, mashed potato sculpting, potato peeling and mashed potato eating contests, and potato car races. There's also a Miss Tater Tot Pageant, a 5K/10K race, softball, and a demolition derby. Mashed potatoes, lefse (a Scandinavian potato-based pastry), and french fries are readily available, as is—oddly—chocolate.

Heritage Days Festival (218-791-6764; www.egfheritage.com), MN 220 N. and 20th Street NE, East Grand Forks. An annual festival held in late Aug. at the Heritage Village, Heritage Days takes visitors back in time to the beginning of the last century with blacksmith demonstrations, threshing, broom making, and a tractor pull. A parade and bountiful food round out the celebration.

September: **Rollag Western Minnesota Steam Threshers Reunion** (218-238-5407; www.rollag.com), MN 32, Rawley. Labor Day weekend. Daily tickets are $14 for ages 15 and older, 14 and under free. Season pass available for $20. This popular event is spread out over 200 acres and includes demonstrations of various generations of farm power, including horse-, gas-, and steam-powered equipment. Food and craft demonstrations are held daily, as are train (full-sized and miniature) rides, merry-go-round rides, and a parade.

Greater Moorhead Days (218-299-5296; www.ci.moorhead.mn.us), Moorhead. A 10-day celebration held in early Sept., Greater Moorhead Days includes a medallion treasure hunt, the Power Bowl Parade and Power Bowl college football game, boccie ball tournament and golf scramble, and the Wings & Wheels Fly-In and Car Show, a custom car show with pancake breakfast and pig roast.

December: **First Night** (218-230-4231), East Grand Forks/Grand Forks, North Dakota. Admission $8 in advance, $10 at the door

WE Fest (1-800-493-3378; www.wefest.com), 25526 County Route 22, Detroit Lakes. A three-day celebration of country music held annually since 1983, the festival is held outdoors, rain or shine, in early Aug. and attracts more than 50,000 people from around the country. The festival is sited at the Soo Pass Ranch on US 59, southeast of Detroit Lakes. Tickets are sold at varying levels, from general admission and reserved lawn seats to reserved box seats, with prices for the three days ranging from $100 to $300. Many attendees return year after year, and an entire culture has built up at this festival, with some visitors setting up stores or "cafés" where they sell grilled foods and beverages off-limits to drinkers under 21. Campsites are available, but reserve well in advance—this is a very popular option for WE Fest attendees. Note: While children are not prohibited, WE Fest tends to be an adult event; campers frequently bring in large quantities of alcohol to enjoy, and not all of the entertainment is family friendly.

(buttons required for admission). A New Year's Eve event with a wide variety of entertainment (musicians, dancers, jugglers, singers) at numerous venues across the greater Grand Forks area. An ice sculpture garden is on display, and the evening ends with a fireworks display. No alcohol is served, and shuttle buses run throughout the evening for participants.

Central Lake District

5

ST. CLOUD AND ENVIRONS

MILLE LACS

WILLMAR

ALEXANDRIA LAKES

BRAINERD

THE CENTRAL LAKE DISTRICT

I f lakes are what people think of when they think about Minnesota, it's likely that they're thinking about the Central Lake District, particularly the Brainerd area. Slightly more than two hours north of the Twin Cities, this area has long been a popular weekend getaway spot in the summer, where a community of mom-and-pop resorts and upscale enclaves serve all types of interests. Brainerd and its twin city of Baxter are the most prominent communities, but they are not the only cities to consider when looking at a lake vacation; many of the small towns surrounding Brainerd, including Nisswa, Pequot Lakes, and Crosslake, are all good bets. These are towns that grew up during the railroad and logging boom, and when that died back, they turned to the abundant lakes to develop tourism.

But even beyond the Brainerd region are good options for water enthusiasts. Going west to the area around Willmar, visitors can find beautiful rolling countryside and lakes created by glaciers 10,000 years ago, although those seeking higher-end accommodations may be disappointed. Northwest of Brainerd is the Alexandria Lakes area, a growing and highly scenic multiple-lake community. Minnesota's second-largest lake, Lake Mille Lacs, rests east of Brainerd and is also an idyllic area for visitors, especially avid fishermen, summer and winter.. Along the way, whether en route to Brainerd/Mille Lacs or Willmar, are a number of historical and cultural sites of interest, particularly through the St. Cloud area.

Because these popular lake regions are relatively close to the Twin Cities, traffic can be heavy, especially on weekends. The route to Brainerd has been improved by the addition of traffic lanes on MN 371, but Brainerd and Baxter are not towns designed for heavy traffic flow; be prepared for slow going at times.

GUIDANCE The St. Cloud Convention and Visitors Bureau (320-251-4170; www.granitecountry.com), 525 US 10 S., Suite 1, St. Cloud. Provides information for St. Cloud lodging and tourism.

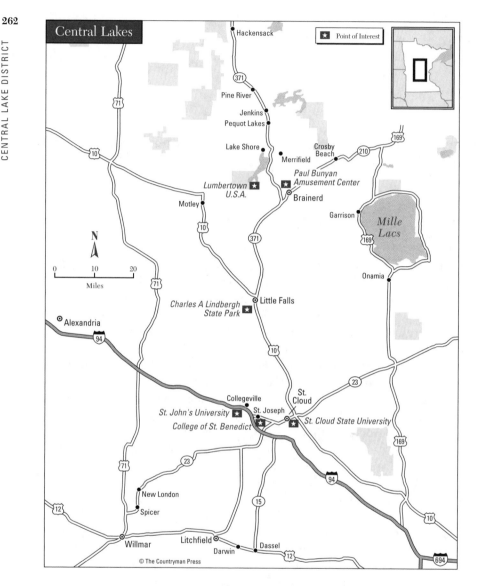

Mille Lacs Lake Area Tourism (320-676-9972 or 1-888-350-2692; www.millelacs.com), 630 W. Main St., Isle.

Willmar Lakes Area Chamber of Commerce (320-235-0300; www .willmarareachamber.com), 2104 E. US 12, Willmar.

Brainerd Lakes Chamber and Convention and Visitors Bureau (218-829-2838 or 1-800-450-2838; www.explorebrainerdlakes.com), 7393 MN 371 S., Brainerd. The Brainerd Lakes Chamber offers extensive lodging and activity information for the Brainerd/Baxter region and surrounding areas. The visitors center on MN 371 is large and well equipped with information and brochures about the Brainerd Lakes area.

Alexandria Lakes Area Chamber of Commerce (320-763-3161 or 1-800-235-9441; www.alexandriamn.org), 206 Broadway, Alexandria.

GETTING THERE *By air:* Delta Air Lines and its Mesaba subsidiary serve the cities of Brainerd and St. Cloud. Willmar has a municipal airport that can handle small corporate planes. Taxis and rental cars are available from the airports: **Brainerd Lakes Regional Airport** (218-825-2166; www.brainerdairport.com/), 16384 Airport Road, in Brainerd, and **St. Cloud Regional Airport** (320-255-7292; www.stcloudairport.com/), 1550 45th Avenue SE, in St. Cloud.

By car: I-94 and US 10 both traverse St. Cloud. From St. Cloud, US 10 meets MN 371, which continues north to Brainerd. Willmar is served from the east and west by US 12, and from the north and south by US 71. The Mille Lacs area is ringed by US 169 and MN 18, MN 27, and MN 47.

GETTING AROUND Having a vehicle is a necessity when traveling around the Central Lakes region, unless you plan to stay solely at your resort.

WHEN TO COME The summer months see an influx of tourists who come to enjoy the multitude of lakes and beaches, but summer isn't the only popular time, especially for fishing enthusiasts who cast their poles in open water in summer and through holes in the ice in winter. Hunters and winter-sports aficionados appreciate the fall and winter seasons as well.

MEDICAL EMERGENCY Call 911.

St. Cloud Hospital (320-251-2700 or 1-800-835-6652; www.centracare .com), 1406 Sixth Ave. N., St. Cloud.

Mille Lacs Health System (320-532-3154; www.millelacshealth.com), 200 N. Elm St., Onamia.

Long Prairie Memorial Hospital (320-732-2414 or 1-877-836-0014; www.centracare.com), 20 SE Ninth St., Long Prairie.

Melrose Area Hospital (320-256-4231; www.centracare.com), 11 N. Fifth Ave. W., Melrose.

Rice Memorial Hospital (320-235-4543; www.ricehospital.com), 301 SW Becker Ave., Willmar.

St. Joseph's Medical Center (218-829-2861 or 1-888-829-8261; www .brainerdlakeshealth.org), 523 Third St. N., Brainerd.

Douglas County Hospital (320-762-1511; www.dchospital.com), 111 17th Ave. E., Alexandria.

ST. CLOUD AND ENVIRONS

St. Cloud is home to four colleges and universities, giving it a youthful population and a wide variety of activities, both historical and cultural. Its history is reflected in its nickname, Granite City, and granite is still produced and carved in the area. It's somewhat of a gateway to the north, as most travelers heading to the Brainerd area or Lake of the Woods will pass through here. Consequently, traffic through the city can be quite congested, especially on summer weekends.

✳ To See and Do

Attractions are open year-round unless otherwise noted.

MUSEUMS AND HISTORIC SITES ✐ ᵹ ✳ **Stearns History Museum** (320-253-8424 or 1-866-253-8424; www.stearns-museum.org), 235 33rd Avenue S., St. Cloud. Open Mon. through Sat. 10–5, Sun noon–5; closed holidays. Adults $5, children $2, museum members free. This county historical museum walks the fine line between education and entertainment, and succeeds on both counts. A clothing exhibit reflects the changing attitudes toward clothes and employment over the years; the area's agricultural history is documented, and there is a life-sized replica of a granite quarry. Documents from pioneers traveling to and settling in this region are displayed, and there is a young children's learn-and-play area.

✐ **Charles A. Lindbergh Historic Site** (320-616-5421; www.mnhs.org), 1620 Lindbergh Drive S., Little Falls. Open Thurs. through Sat. 10–5 and Sun. noon–5, Memorial Day through Labor Day; Sat. and Sun. noon–4, Sept. and Oct. Open some Mon. holidays; call for information. Adults $7, senior citizens $6, children 6–17 $5, children under 6 and Minnesota Historical Society members free. Charles Lindbergh's childhood home, complete with original furnishings and belongings, is on display. Next door is a visitors center with exhibits and films about Lindbergh's life and time, and a gift shop. An interpretive trail leads visitors along the river.

✐ ❋ **Grasshopper Chapel** (320-685-3653), MN 23 and Chapel Hill Road, Cold Spring. Open daily. No admission fee, although donations are welcome. A few miles west of St. Cloud is this little chapel, built originally in 1877 in response to a grasshopper plague that was decimating crops. The governor declared a day of prayer, and local townsfolk promised to build a chapel if the grasshoppers were removed. The grasshoppers disappeared the next day due to an unusual sleet storm, and the chapel was built as promised. The original wood building was destroyed by a tornado in 1894, but it was rebuilt in the 1950s with donated granite. Today the tiny chapel is in a wooded, peaceful area, a beautiful spot to visit.

♿ ❋ **Saint Benedict's Monastery Haehn Museum** (320-363-7115; www.sbm.osb.org), 104 Chapel Lane, St. Joseph. Open Tues. through Fri. 10–4, Sat. and Sun. 1–3:30. The 150-year history of the Sisters of Saint Benedict in on display, with items dating back to the monastery's founding. Rotating exhibitions have included explorations of sustainability, liturgical vestments and needlework, Native American cultures where the sisters lived and worked, and the important role of music.

MUNSINGER AND CLEMENS GARDENS

♿ ❋ **St. Cloud State University** (320-308-0121; www.stcloudstate .edu), 720 Fourth Avenue S., St. Cloud. The university has two art exhibits that are of note. The first is the Atwood Collection, in the Atwood Memorial Center (hours vary by season; no admission fee), which is an ever-growing collection of contemporary American art. The second is the Kiehle Gallery (hours vary by season; no admission fee), a frequently changing collection bringing in guest artists on a national level as well as promoting local and student artists.

WINERIES ❋ **Millner Heritage Vineyard & Winery** (320-398-2081; www.millnerheritage.com), 32025 MN 15, Kimball. Open Thurs. 11–7, Fri. and Sat. 11–8, and Sun. 11–6, Apr. through Dec.; Sat. 11–7, Jan. through Mar. Millner

CHARLES LINDBERGH HOME

gives trolley tours of its vineyard, which grows eight weather-hardy varietals. Wine tastings are offered as well, and catered dinners are available.

✳ Green Space and Outdoor Activities

HIKING AND BIKING Lake Wobegon Trail (320-255-6172; www.lake wobegontrails.com). A 46-mile paved hiking and biking trail that stretches from St. Joseph to Sauk Centre. Snowmobilers have access to it in the winter. The trail is highly scenic, winding through woods, near lakes, and through several small towns. Near Osakis, it intersects with the Central Lakes Trail (see *Green Space and Outdoor Activities* in "Alexandria Lakes").

PARKS AND GARDENS Munsinger and Clemens Gardens (320-255-7216; www .munsingerclemens.com), Killian Boulevard SE. Open daily 7 AM– 10 PM, spring through fall. No admission fee, although donations are requested. Two beautiful gardens

MUNSINGER AND CLEMENS GARDENS

THE SAINT JOHN'S BIBLE AND SAINT JOHN'S UNIVERSITY

Visiting the campus of Saint John's University in Collegeville is worth-while for several reasons, including the beauty of the lakeside campus itself, the 2,700-acre arboretum, and Saint John's Pottery, a working studio that not only examines the artistry, but the ethics, behind the potter's work. Tour the abbey, an impressive piece of unique religious architecture with the world's largest stained-glass window. The campus's spiritual center offers accommodations (see *Lodging*).

In addition to these other highlights, the Saint John's Bible project should be included in any visit to the campus. A deeply felt homage to the days when monasteries kept literature alive by hand-transcribing texts in elaborate calligraphy, the Saint John's Bible is a newly written bible complete with extravagant illustrations and exquisite handwritten text. The project was completed in September 2011 after 15 years in the making. Parts will remain on display at Saint John's, with other sections to be loaned out to other museums.

✐ ⑤ **Saint John's Bible** (320-363-3351; www.saintjohnsbible.org), Hill Museum and Manuscript Library, Saint John's University, Collegeville. Open Mon. through Fri. 8–4:30 and Sat. noon–4, May through Christmas. No admission fee.

along the banks of the Mississippi, the Munsinger and Clemens Gardens offer both historic and contemporary gardening highlights. Munsinger Gardens was developed in the 1930s and named after the superintendent of parks; it's an informal garden space, with winding paths lined with wild-flowers and pine trees. Clemens Gardens was constructed in the 1990s and is a more formal set of gardens, complete with rose gardens and the tallest fountain in Minnesota, the 24-foot Renaissance Fountain.

❋ **Quarry Park and Nature Preserve** (320-255-6172; www.co.stearns.mn.us), County Route 137, Waite Park. Open daily 8 AM to one half hour after sunset. A park permit is required for entrance; a one-day permit is $4, an annual permit is $14. Quarry Park is comprised of land that has gradually grown back to a natural state after years of granite quarrying. More than 600 acres of parkland provide a wide array of experiences for visitors: open prairie, wetlands, wooded areas, a 116-foot-deep swimming hole, granite reflecting pools, and 30 granite quarries. Certified scuba divers traveling with scuba buddies can dive in one of four swimming holes, and with the proper permit, visitors can tackle some rock climbing. Mountain bikers can ride across terrain made up of billion-year-old bedrock, while hikers can explore woodlands and open prairie. Winter brings ample cross-country skiing or snowshoeing opportunities.

✳ Lodging

All accommodations are open year-round unless otherwise noted.

BED & BREAKFASTS

✳ **Heritage House Bed and Breakfast** (320-656-5818 or 1-888-547-4422; www.heritagehouse-bbmn.com), 402 Sixth Avenue S., St. Cloud. This inn, built in 1904 and listed on the National Register of Historic Places, offers four rooms, all with private bath and full breakfast by request. The rooms are themed by nationality (French, Swedish, German, and English, with the last being the most luxurious), and decor varies from wooden floors to canopy beds. Two of the rooms have separate sitting areas as well. The public area includes a pool table and game table. Expensive.

✳ **Riverside Guest Haus** (320-252-2134 or 1-888-252-2134; www.riversideguesthaus.com), 912 Riverside Drive SE, St. Cloud. This charmer was built in 1937 and is within walking distance of Munsinger and Clemens Gardens (see *Green Space and Outdoor Activities*). The inn has just two guest rooms, each with private bath and beautifully appointed with European lace, Oriental rugs, and handmade quilts. The Garden Room has access to a private second-floor patio garden balcony, while the River Room has river views, an electric fireplace, and separate sitting area. Full breakfast is included. Expensive.

✳ (ʂ) **Victorian Oaks Bed and Breakfast** (320-202-1404 or 1-866-842-6257; www.vicoaks.com), 404 Ninth Avenue S., St. Cloud. *Victorian* is the perfect description for this inn, located walking distance from St. Cloud State University and the civic center. Listed on the National Register of Historic Places, Victorian Oaks was built in 1894 and now has two guest rooms and a suite. Decorated lavishly with antiques befitting the period, the rooms are on the second floor, while the first floor has a charming sitting area, dining room, and elaborate main staircase. Expensive.

HOTELS ✎ ⅄ ✳ (ʂ) **Le St-Germain Suite Hotel** (320-654-1661 or 1-888-201-1718; www.lestgermainsuitehotel.com), 404 W. St. Germain, St. Cloud. The prime choice in St. Cloud, the former Radisson is now a sister hotel to Minneapolis's Graves 601 hotel (see *Lodging* in "Minneapolis"). Le St-Germain, connected by skyway to the St. Cloud Civic Center along the shores of the Mississippi River, is an all-suite property with larger accommodations including sitting areas and river views. The hotel has an indoor pool, whirlpool, and sauna, as well as a fine-dining restaurant, De La Pointe (see *Where to Eat*). Expensive. Packages are available.

✍ 🐾 ♿ 𝐘 ❉ ((ᵠ)) **Holiday Inn and Suites** (320-253-9000 or 1-888-465-4329; www.holidayinn.com/st cloudmn), Division Street and 37th Avenue, St. Cloud. The Holiday Inn was fully renovated in 2007 and offers an indoor pool, whirlpool, basketball court, sauna, and fitness center. Two restaurants are on-site, one a family-oriented café (kids eat free with paying adults) and one a bar and grill. Moderate.

UNIQUE LODGINGS ♿ ❉ **St. Benedict's Monastery** (320-363-7115; www.sbm.osb.org), 104 Chapel Lane, St. Joseph. This 150-year-old monastery has a spiritual center that welcomes guests for day-, week-, or month-long visits. Private retreats can be customized with spiritual counseling, or visitors can simply relax in the quiet grounds and facilities, complete with a garden labyrinth, and visit the Haehn Museum (see *To See and Do*). Moderate.

❉ Where to Eat

DINING OUT ✍ ♿ 𝐘 ❉ **De La Pointe** (320-654-1661; www .radisson.com/stcloudmn), 404 W. St. Germain, St. Cloud. Open Mon. through Sat. for lunch and dinner. De La Pointe, in the chic Le St.-Germain Suite Hotel (see *Lodging*), rises well above average hotel fare and is possibly the best

fine-dining restaurant in St. Cloud. It offers French bistro food prepared by a creative and ambitious chef. Expensive.

✍ ♿ 𝐘 ❉ **Anton's** (320-253-3611; www.antonsrestaurant.com), 2001 Frontage Road N., Waite Park. Open Mon. through Sat. for lunch, daily for dinner. Originally a speakeasy during the Prohibition years, Anton's is now a laid-back log cabin restaurant specializing in grilled meats and sandwiches. If that's not enough to make someone happy, the bar's impressive Scotch list should take care of it. Expensive.

EATING OUT ✍ ♿ 𝐘 ❉ **Ace Bar & Grill** (320-251-0232), 423 E. St. Germain, St. Cloud. Open daily for all three meals. This cheerful bar and grill has been open for 75 years and is particularly—and justifiably—proud of its barbecued ribs. But the menu has much more than ribs, with choices varying from sandwiches to burgers to casseroles (or "hot dishes" in the Minnesota vernacular). Moderate.

✍ ♿ 𝐘 ❉ **Mexican Village** (320-252-7134; www.mexicanvillagest cloud.com), 509 W. St. Germain, St. Cloud. Open daily for lunch and dinner. Don't go looking for authentic Mexican; instead, plan on enjoying reasonably priced Americanized Mexican served in a cheerfully (and unrepentantly) kitschy atmosphere. Inexpensive.

✍ 🍴 ❉ **Val's Rapid Serv** (320-251-5775), 626 E. St. Germain Street, St. Cloud. This local landmark, in

VAL'S RAPID SERV

business for decades, has changed very little; from its A-frame building on the corner to its inexpensive but tasty burgers and heaping orders of fries, it's still the same. The only nod to modern times is several touchscreen order devices. There's no sitting area—this is grab-and-go food. Inexpensive.

✴ Entertainment

Probably because it's a college town, St. Cloud has a large number of live-performance venues for a city its size.

🗢 ♿ ✴ **Paramount Theatre and Visual Arts Center** (320-259-5463; www.paramountarts.org), 913 W. St. Germain. A vintage 1920s movie theater, the Paramount has gone through its era of neglect and has emerged as a classy setting for a variety of live performances. The St. Cloud Symphony Orchestra, Chamber Music Society, St. Cloud Civic Theater, and Great River Educational Theatre all perform here regularly, and traveling performers include jazz and Broadway productions.

♿ ✴ **Fine Arts Series** (320-363-5777; www.csbsju.edu/finearts/), Benedicta Arts Center, College of Saint Benedict/Saint John's University, St. Joseph. The College of Saint Benedict opened a new performing arts center in 2006, and an active schedule of fine arts performers keeps the center open and busy. Recent performers include Nachito Herrera, readings by Seamus Heaney and Sarah Vowell, Prudence Johnson, and the Minnesota Orchestra.

Y ❋ **DB Searle's** (320-253-0655; www.dbsearles.com), 18 Fifth Avenue S. Open Mon. through Sat 4 PM–2 AM. DB Searle's is housed in a historic building first used as the African Saloon and Barbershop. Then the site was bought by lawyer and Civil War veteran Dolson Bush Searle, who built a sturdy brick building that has been, through the years, everything from a bank to a funeral home. Today it's a restaurant and nightclub with live music several nights a week and karaoke on Tues.

❋ **Bo Diddley's Pub & Deli** (320-255-9811), 216 Sixth Avenue. Open Mon. through Fri. 10–9:30, Sat. and Sun. 10–8:30. A mellower-than-expected venue with live music on Wed. and most weekends.

❋ Selective Shopping

DOWNTOWN SHOPS Unlike some small towns, St. Cloud has managed to keep an active downtown area in spite of the growth of shopping centers and strip malls. Here are a few of the independent retailers worth visiting.

✍ ❋ **Books Revisited** (320-259-7959; www.booksrevisited.com), 607 W. St. Germain. Open Mon. through Sat. While there's also a location at Crossroads Center, the downtown branch is the original store, and it's packed floor-to-ceiling with new and used books, including some rare items.

❋ **Electric Fetus** (320-251-2569; www.electricfetus.com), 28 S.

Fifth Avenue. Open daily. Electric Fetus has one of the largest music inventories in the state (along with its sister locations in the Twin Cities and Duluth), as well as gifts and jewelry. Check the website for in-store performances.

❋ **Arts Co-Op** (320-252-3242; www.risingsundesigns.com), 619 St. Germain. Open Mon. through Sat. Represents local and national artists in varying media.

❋ **Loft Fine Art Gallery** (320-251-8180), 819 W. St. Germain. Open Mon. through Fri. Presents works of local artists, both fine art and literary.

❋ **Antiques Gallery** (320-202-9068; www.antiquesgallerysc.com), 619 St. Germain. Open Mon. through Sat. Fine antiques store specializing in china, glassware, pottery, and figurines.

MALLS ✍ ♿ ❋ **Crossroads Center** (320-252-2856; www.crossroads center.com), 4101 W. Division Street. Open daily. This large mall has many of the classic national retailers, including Gap, J.Jill, Macy's, and Footlocker. The mall itself is surrounded by smaller strip malls. Note: The retail area here is very popular, and the roads that surround and run through it (primarily County Route 15) struggle with the traffic loads during busy times. Be prepared to spend a considerable amount of time inching along through stoplights en route to your shopping.

✴ Special Events

Weekend after Memorial Day:
Minnesota Homegrown Kickoff
(1-800-635-3037; www.minnesota
bluegrass.org), El Rancho Mañana,
Richmond. Rates vary $14–50,
including camping. Old-time bluegrass, swimming, horseback riding, and camping, all in one
three-day festival.

June: **The Caramel Roll** (320-
356-7191; www.lakewobegon
trails.com/caramelroll.htm), St.
Joseph. Advance registration
prices: adults $25, children 7–15
$20, children 6 and under free.
Rates are $5 more for day-of-
event registration. An annual bike-
and-eat event with your choice of
8-, 15-, or 25-mile routes, with pit
stops for caramel rolls. As the
Lake Wobegon Trails Association
people say, "A sweet roll on a
sweet trail."

Granite City Days (320-255-
7295; www.granitecitydays.com),
St. Cloud. This four-day festival in
June includes a golf tournament,
historic homes and downtown St.
Cloud tours, a parade, a block
party, and a fly-in pancake breakfast, among other events.

July: **Tour of Saints** (320-363-
1311 or 1-800-651-8687; www.tour
ofsaints.com), College of Saint
Benedict, St. Joseph. Adults $28,
children 5–16 $22. This is not a
religious event, but one for serious
bikers. The tour starts and ends at
the college, and riders choose
either a 35- or 50-mile route
through the rolling countryside
and small towns in the St. Cloud
area.

Halfway Jam (1-877-425-3526;
www.halfwayjam.com), Rice. Tickets start at $39. Named for its
location halfway between the Twin
Cities and northern Minnesota,
the Halfway Jam brings in several
oldies rock bands for three days of
concerts. Camping can be purchased for the entire festival only.
Festival organizers discourage parents from bringing children.

MILLE LACS

The state's second-largest lake is Lake Mille Lacs, and as such, it draws thousands of fishing and water-sports lovers each year. Located on the Mille Lacs Reservation, Mille Lacs is just about as popular in winter as it is in summer, thanks to continued growing interest in ice fishing. The region has responded by adding more options for ice house rental, including some very deluxe buildings with electricity and heat.

✳ To See and Do

GAMING ✎ ৬ ♟ ✳ **Grand Casino Mille Lacs** (1-800-626-5825; www .grandcasinomn.com), 777 Grand Avenue, Onamia. Open 24/7. A full-scale gambling complex with slots, blackjack, and bingo, it also has several restaurants (see *Where to Eat*), a hotel, a theater with frequent live performances, a Kids Quest child-care area, and an extensive video arcade.

MUSEUMS AND HISTORIC SITES ✎ ৬ **Mille Lacs Indian Museum** (320-532-3632; www.mnhs.org/places/sites/mlim/), 43411 Oodena Drive, Onamia. Open Tues. through Sat. 11–4, Memorial Day through Labor Day; Sat. 11–4, Apr., May, Sept., and Oct.; off-season by appointment. Adults $7, senior citizens $6, children 6–17 $5, children under 6 and Minnesota Historical Society members free. This museum is a joint venture between the Mille Lacs Indians and the Minnesota Historical Society, and it's a thoughtful, detailed collection of exhibits showing how Native Americans of the region lived and worked centuries ago. The crafts room has an especially lovely collection of beadwork and birch bark basketry. An adjacent trading post, a re-creation of a 1930s-era trading post, sells Native American gift items (open weekends year-round).

✳ Green Space and Outdoor Activities

The Lake Mille Lacs area is all about the outdoor activities, many of which are centered around the massive lake (the second largest lake in Minnesota). Fishing, hunting, boating, biking, hiking, cross-country skiing, snowshoeing, snowmobiling—it's all here.

LAKE MILLE LACS

Kathio State Park (320-532-3523; www.dnr.state.mn.us/state_parks /mille_lacs_kathio/index.html), 15066 Kathio State Park Road, Onamia. Open daily. Near the Mille Lacs Indian Museum (see *To See and Do*) is the entrance to this park, which has year-round opportunities for recreation. The Rum River flows through the park from its source in Lake Mille Lacs, and visitors can use canoes or rowboats to explore. A swimming beach is open during the summer, as is a 100-foot observation tower and a wide variety of campsites and cabins (some of which are available year-round). Winter enthusiasts can cross-country ski, snowshoe, or snow-mobile on groomed trails.

LAKE MILLE LACS

Mille Lacs Wildlife Management Area (320-532-3537; www .dnr.state.mn.us/wmas/index.html), 29172 100th Avenue, Onamia. Open daily. This small wildlife management area (61 acres) is a carefully preserved area of forests and wetlands. During hunting season, camping is allowed, and hunters with permits can hunt deer, bear, and small game.

✴ Lodging

✐ ᵫ ⴾ ❋ **Izatys Resort** (1-800-533-1728; www.izatys.com), 40005 85th Avenue, Onamia. On the shores of Lake Mille Lacs, this luxury complex includes townhomes and villas (ranging from two to four bedrooms), as well as a lodge offering hotel rooms. Boat rental, two 18-hole golf courses, fishing and hunting guides, tennis courts, seasonal kids program, and indoor and outdoor pools are all available on-site. There is also a fine-dining restaurant (see *Where to Eat*). Moderate to very expensive.

✐ ᵫ ⴾ ❋ **Grand Casino Mille Lacs** (1-800-468-3517; www.grand casinomn.com), 777 Grand Avenue, Onamia. This huge hotel has several room types, including a number of luxurious suites with four-person Jacuzzis and separate living areas. The large indoor swimming pool and whirlpool are in a nicely decorated wing. Moderate.

✐ ❋ **Mille Lacs Lodge** (320-532-3384; www.millelacslodge.com), 8673 340th Street, Onamia. This rustic, cozy lodge has just six rooms, which can be rented individually, or a group can rent the entire lodge at a discount from the individual room rate. All rooms have private baths. The lodge grounds have a covered picnic area and a fire pit; hunting and fishing guides can be arranged, as can home-cooked meals. Expensive.

✐ 🐾 ᵫ ⴾ ❋ **Twin Pines Resort** (320-692-4413; www.twinpines millelacs.com), 7827 US 169, Garrison. A family-friendly resort with cabins and motel rooms on Lake Mille Lacs, the property is a good value, with summer and winter fishing guides available (as well as ice house rental in the winter). A restaurant/bar is on-site. Moderate.

✴ Where to Eat

DINING OUT ✐ ᵫ ⴾ ❋ **Izatys** (1-800-533-1728; www.izatys.com), 40005 85th Avenue, Onamia. Open daily for dinner year-round, seasonally for lunch (check their website). One of the few fine-dining restaurants in the area, Izatys has an upscale dinner menu that includes traditional steakhouse foods as well as some inventive Latin American and Southwestern dishes. Expensive.

EATING OUT ✐ ᵫ ⴾ ❋ **Grand Casino Mille Lacs** (1-800-626-5825; www.grandcasinomn.com), 777 Grand Avenue, Onamia. The casino has four restaurants on-site, one of which (Plums, a quick-service burger-and-pizza café) is open 24 hours Wed. through Sun. There's also a buffet restaurant, a casual grill restaurant, and a steakhouse open for dinner only. Inexpensive.

✂ ☂ ❋ **Svoboda's Spotlite** (320-692-4692), 111 Madison Street, Garrison. Open daily for all three meals. Breakfast is served all day at this friendly café, a local institution. The home-cooked foods are simple but delicious, and prices are reasonable. Kids' and senior citizens' menus available. Inexpensive.

WILLMAR

The Willmar area has not seen the same kind of tourism growth experienced by the Brainerd area, which is not necessarily a bad thing; the rolling, forested countryside and quiet lakes can provide the utmost in tranquility. The downside is that there is less to do for visitors who don't want to spend their entire vacation on the lake. But for those who appreciate a restful, beautiful retreat, the Willmar area has plenty to offer.

✳ To See and Do

FOR FAMILIES ✍ **Big Kahuna Fun Park** (320-796-2445; www.spicer fun.com), 190 Progress Way, Spicer. Open daily 11–9, Memorial Day through Labor Day. Rates for individual activities vary from $3 to $5. This outdoor amusement park has mini golf, bumper boats, two go-cart tracks, and a kids' Power Wheels course.

MUSEUMS AND HISTORIC SITES ✍ ♿ ✳ **The Mikkelson Collection** (320-231-0384; www.fallsflyer.com), 418 Benson Avenue SE, Willmar. Call for appointment. An astonishing collection of vintage toy and full-sized boats and outboard motors, some of which are the only ones still in existence.

✍ ♿ **Schwanke's Museum** (320-235-7045; www.schwanketractor.com /museum.html), 3310 US 71 S., Willmar. Open Mon. through Sat. 1–4 in the summer. Adults $5, children under 12 $2. The vehicular counterpart to the Mikkelson Collection, this museum has more than 300 antique tractors, cars, and trucks.

✍ ♿ ✳ **Cokato Museum** (320-286-2427; www.cokato.mn.us/cmhs), 175 W. Fourth Street, Cokato. Open Tues. through Fri. 8:30–4, Sat. 8:30–3. Admission is free. The region's Finnish and Swedish heritage is celebrated and documented in this museum, which includes a log home and sauna, as well as a rather intimidating early dentist's office.

OTHER ATTRACTIONS ⌀ ♿ ❊ **World's Largest Ball of Twine,** US 12, Darwin. Open daily. Memorialized in song by Weird Al Yankovic, the centerpiece of the little town of Darwin (east of Willmar) is the giant ball of twine, the largest to be rolled by one person. It took Francis Johnson (son of U.S. senator Magnus Johnson) nearly 30 years to roll this ball, which now stands 11 feet tall.

❊ Green Space and Outdoor Activities

The Willmar lakes area is really about the outdoor activities. There are more than 100 lakes scattered throughout the rolling land, punctuated by farmland and forest, and ringed with small resorts. Fishing, boating, biking, hiking, snowmobiling, cross-country skiing—it's a playground for the outdoors lover.

HIKING AND BIKING **Glacial Lakes Trail** (www.dnr.state.mn.us /state_trails/glacial_lakes/index.html). A great way to get a feel for the glacier-created topography of the area is to explore the Glacial Lakes Trail, a 22-mile paved trail that travels from Stearns County on the east into Willmar, Spicer, New London, and Hawick. There are large segments of the trail that have horseback trails adjacent, and the trail (a former Burlington

---

GOLF

While lake-related activities are extremely popular, golf is also a big draw in this area.

Eagle Creek Golf Course (320-235-1166; www.willmargolf.com), 1000 26th Avenue NE, Willmar. An 80-year-old course situated right between two lakes, Eagle Creek offers 18 holes and the only full driving range in the area.

Little Crow Country Club (320-354-2296 or 1-877-659-5023; www.www .littlecrowgolf.com), 15980 MN 23, Spicer. Little Crow has three nine-hole courses.

Island Pine Golf Club (320-974-8600), 1601 Wyoming Avenue W., Atwater. Island Pine has an 18-hole championship course and some of the largest greens in the area.

Hawk Creek Country Club (320-967-4653; www.hawkcreekcc.com), 100 Spicer Avenue NE, Raymond. Hawk Creek offers a nine-hole course, driving range, and putting green.

Northern Railroad grade) has become very popular with hikers, bikers, and inline skaters. Parts of the trail are groomed for winter activities, but studded tracks are prohibited.

PARKS Sibley State Park (320-354-2055; www.dnr.state.mn.us/state _parks/sibley/index.html), 800 Sibley Park Road NE, New London. Open daily 8 AM–10 PM. A state park permit is required; a day pass is $5 per vehicle. Sibley State Park has a wide variety of activities, including hiking to the top of Mount Tom, the tallest hill for miles, and swimming, fishing, boating, and canoeing on one of the many lakes. Camping is allowed, including one camping area specifically for horse riding campers.

✳ Lodging

BED & BREAKFASTS

❄ (ꞵ) **Spicer Castle Bed and Breakfast** (320-795-5870 or 1-800-821-6675; http://spicercastle .com), 11600 Indian Beach Road, Spicer. Home to the Murder Mystery Dinner (see *Entertainment*), the large property has eight rooms in the main house, two in the Garden House, two in the Honey House, four in the Carriage House, and two separate cottages. The main house was built in 1895 by John Spicer, and the rooms are named after his descendants. Each room has a private bath and is lovingly decorated, including artwork done by Spicer family members. Daily rates include full breakfast and an afternoon tea. Expensive. Packages, including Murder Mystery Dinners, are available.

CABINS ✎ (ꞵ) **Willow Bay Resort** (320-796-5517 or 1-877-796-5517; www.willowbayresort .com), 5280 132nd Avenue NE, Spicer. Open May through Oct. Nine cabins, all either lakefront or lakeview. Cabins come with a boat;

outboard motor rental is extra. A small swimming beach has plenty of plastic kayaks and paddleboats for a good playtime. Expensive.

✎ ♿ ❄ **Sunset Shores Resort** (1-877-813-7317; www.sunset shoresresort-mn.com), 18986 County Route 5 NW, New London. This resort on Norway Lake has 10 cabins, including one with six bedrooms. The beach area has a wide number of toys for kids of all ages, including a water raft, paddleboats, and kayaks, and activities include fishing, tubing, and waterskiing. Winter visitors can prearrange ice house rental. Expensive.

✎ 🐾 ♿ **Island View Resort** (1-800-421-9708; www.islandview resort-nestlake.com), 5910 132nd Avenue NE, Spicer. Open Apr. through Sept. Island View is located on quiet Nest Lake, and the resort has a decent sandy beach. The resort offers several small but comfortable cabins, all with private fire rings. There are plenty of beach toys, and boat and motor rental are available. Be sure to stop by the resort's store to meet the parrot that can whistle the *Andy Griffith Show* theme song. Expensive.

✳ Where to Eat

EATING OUT ✍ ✳ ((ᵖ)) **LuLu Beans** (320-214-9633; www.lulu beans.net), 1020 First Street S., Willmar. Open Mon. through Fri 6:30 AM–10 PM, Sat. 7 AM–10 PM, and Sun. 7–6. This cozy coffee shop and café is popular with locals and visitors alike, no doubt due in no small part to the scrumptious pastries. Inexpensive.

& ㅜ ✳ **Blue Sky** (320-796-0203; www.blueskyinspicer.com), 194 Progress Way, Spicer. Open Tues. through Sat. for dinner, Sun. for breakfast and dinner. The menu changes seasonally at this newer establishment, where you're likely to find versions of supper-club staples, like chicken and steak, done with a twist. Moderate.

✍ & ✳ **Westwood Café** (320-796-5355; http://westwoodcafe.com), 142 Lake Avenue N., Spicer. Open daily for breakfast and lunch, Wed. through Sat. for dinner. Solid diner food, hearty and flavorful. Moderate.

✳ Entertainment

& ㅜ ✳ **Spicer Castle Murder Mystery Dinners** (320-795-5870 or 1-800-821-6675; http://spicer castle.com/mystery.html), 11600

Indian Beach Road, Spicer. Fri. and Sat. evenings. Tickets start at $55. If you like a little mystery with your dinner, make reservations at the Spicer Castle (see *Lodging*) for an evening of food and sleuthing. It includes a five-course dinner themed to match the locale of the murder. The dinner can be purchased separately or as part of a lodging package at the castle.

✳ Special Events

June: **Lakes Area Studio Hop** (320-231-8560; www.studiohop .org), Willmar. Taking place in late June, the Hop allows guests to visit nearly 40 artists in and around the Willmar area, either in their private studios or in local art galleries.

July: **Sonshine Festival** (1-800-965-9324; www.sonshinefestival .com), Willmar. Tickets start at $65 and include space for camping. A massive three-day Christian music festival spread over five stages, complete with kids' activities, camping, and a skateboard park.

September: 🐾 **Prairie Pothole Day** (www.prairiepotholeday .com). In early Sept., thousands of people descend on Stoney Ridge Farm near Spicer to play games, climb rock walls, and learn about the environment. Dogs are not only welcome, but are actively encouraged to attend.

ALEXANDRIA LAKES

E asy to get to, hard to leave" is the Alexandria Lakes–area motto, and it's an apt one. Alexandria itself has been around for more than 150 years and was named after the town's first postmaster. The abundance of lakes makes it a valued tourist attraction. One of Alexandria's claims to fame is the story of its being the birthplace of windsurfing back in 1960, when Al Seltz and Lewis Whinnery experimented with the then-new technology of fiberboard to see how it would work with pleasure boats and surfboards. Another claim to fame, although one hotly disputed, is that it's the home of the infamous Kensington Runestone (see the Runestone Museum in *To See and Do*).

ALEXANDRIA

Alexandria Hotel & Hospitality, CVB

CENTRAL LAKE DISTRICT

✴ To See and Do

MUSEUMS AND HISTORIC SITES ✐ ♿ ✳ **Runestone Museum**

(320-763-3160; www.runestonemuseum.org), 206 Broadway, Alexandria. Open Mon. through Fri. 9–5, Sat. 9–4, and Sun. 11–4 in summer; Mon. through Sat. 10–4 in winter. Adults $6, seniors $5, students 5–17 $3, and children under 5 free. A family rate is capped at $15. The highlight of this museum is the highly controversial Kensington Runestone, discovered in 1898 but thought to date back to 1362. The 200-pound stone is carved with runes and, if authentic, would indicate that Scandinavian explorers had arrived in the Midwest far earlier than previously supposed. However, that point is hotly disputed by a variety of experts. Nevertheless, the Runestone Museum is an interesting place to visit, not just for the Runestone itself, but also for an extensive collection of other historical artifacts and a pioneer village.

✐ ♿ **Minnesota Lakes Maritime Museum** (320-759-1114; www.mn lakesmaritime.org), 205 Third Avenue W., Alexandria. Open Mon. through Sat. 10–5 and Sun. noon–4, May 15 through Oct. 15. Closed holidays. Adults $6, seniors $5, students 5–17 $3, and children under 5 free. A family rate is capped at $15. You don't need an ocean to have a maritime museum. This set of exhibits includes numerous rare wooden boats, vintage yachts, and toy boats, and fishing and fishing club memorabilia. There's also an exhibit focused on the history of Chris-Craft, as well as one about the extensive resort history of the area.

BIG OLE, A 28-FOOT-TALL VIKING WARRIOR, IS NEAR THE RUNESTONE MUSEUM.

Alexandria Hotel & Hospitality, CVB

✐ ✳ **Douglas County Historical Society** (320-762-0382; www .dchsmn.org), 1219 Nokomis Street, Alexandria. Open Mon. through Fri. 9–3 for guided tours. Admission is $2. Housed in the former home of statesman Knute Nelson, the DCHS has extensive holdings of photos and slide shows about the communities in the Alexandria Lakes area.

✐ **Sinclair Lewis Boyhood Home** (320-352-5359), 820 Sinclair Lewis Avenue, Sauk Centre. Open Tues. through Sat. 9:30–5 and Sun. 10:30–5, Memorial Day to Labor Day; by appointment Labor Day to Memorial Day. Adults $5, high school and college students with ID $3.50, children 6–12 $2, children under 6 free. Talk about making lemonade out of lemons. Sinclair Lewis, the Nobel Prize–winning American novelist who skewered Sauk Centre in his novel *Main Street,* spent his formative years in the home that is now a museum. In spite of—or perhaps because of—the attention, Sauk Centre has guarded Lewis's legacy in this carefully preserved home (a National Historic Landmark), as well as in the Sinclair Lewis Interpretive Center on I-94 coming into town. To cap things off is the annual Sinclair Lewis Days (see *Special Events*). Today Lewis's boyhood home is a beautiful piece of nostalgia, whether or not you're a fan of his work. Kids who haven't read his works will enjoy the old-time ambience of the home, including some dangerous (by today's standards) heating methods.

WINERIES ⅁ ❋ ⟨⟨ᵞ⟩⟩ **Carlos Creek Winery** (320-846-5443; www.carloscreekwinery.com), 6693 County Route 34 NW, Alexandria. Open Mon. through Sat. 11–6 and Sun. noon–6, Apr. through Dec.; Sun. through Thurs. noon–5 and Fri. and Sat. 11–6, Jan. through Mar. Winery tours, tastings, and, during the summer, plenty of special events. Carlos Creek is Minnesota's first federally designated Viticulture Area.

❋ Green Space and Outdoor Activities

GOLF Geneva Golf Club (320-762-7089; www.genevagolfclub .com), 4181 Geneva Golf Club Drive, Alexandria. Geneva Golf Club has a 27-hole championship course designed by Joel Goldstrand, as well as a well-regarded dining room (see *Where to Eat*).

HIKING AND BIKING Central Lakes Trail (www.centrallakes trail.com). This 55-mile paved trail winds from Fergus Falls to Osakis

MILL LAKE

and is open to nonmotorized vehicles in the summer, although snowmobiles are allowed in the winter. There are few road crossings, making this a particularly safe trail for families. The Central Lakes Trail connects in Osakis to the Lake Wobegone Trail (see *Green Space and Outdoor Activities* in "St. Cloud and Environs").

PARKS Runestone Park, County Route 103, Kensington. In conjunction with the Runestone Museum (see *To See and Do*) is this park, the former farm of Olaf Ohman, the man who discovered the Kensington Runestone. A memorial marks the spot where he discovered the controversial slab, and other historical buildings have been moved onto the farm for visitors as well.

✳ Lodging

The Alexandria Lakes area has a nice mix of bed & breakfasts and resorts of all sizes and amenities.

BED & BREAKFASTS ✳ **Cedar Rose Inn** (320-762-8430 or 1-888-203-5333; www.cedarroseinn.com), 422 Seventh Avenue W., Alexandria. This 1903 beauty resides in what was known as the Silk Stocking District and offers four spacious rooms with private baths. Located near shops and antiquing opportunities. Expensive. Packages are available.

✳ **Lake Le Homme Dieu Bed and Breakfast** (320-846-5875 or 1-800-943-5875; www.llbedandbreakfast.com), 441 S. Le Homme Dieu Drive NW, Alexandria. On the shores of Lake Le Homme Dieu, this newer construction offers easy access to the Central Lakes Trail. There are four rooms with private bath; amenities include an outdoor hot tub. Expensive.

✳ **Country Gardens on Lake Mina** (320-762-8502; wwww

.countrygardensonlakemina.com), 360 Karen's Way NW, Alexandria. Located on Lake Mina, Country Gardens has great views. There are two rooms with private baths and hot tub areas. Expensive.

🐾 **Just Ridin' Inn** (320-239-2444 or 520-625-6621; www.justridininn.com), 24569 310th Avenue, Starbuck. Open Mar. to mid-Oct. This bed & breakfast, which has three rooms with shared bath and a new bunkhouse with three bedrooms and two baths, is unique in that it welcomes families and horse boarding. Moderate.

CABINS 🐾 **Shady Lawn Resort** (320-763-3559; www.shadylawnresort.net), 1321 S. Darling Drive NW, Alexandria. Open Memorial Day through Labor Day. Eight cabins along Lake Darling, with plenty of children's amenities and fishing options. Expensive.

Canary Beach Resort (320-554-2471; www.canarybeachresort.com), 17405 County Route 28, Villard. Open Memorial Day

Alexandria Hotel & Hospitality, CVB

HISTORIC DOWNTOWN ALEXANDRIA

through Labor Day. Canary Beach has been welcoming visitors since 1920 and offers eight cabins and two larger "dens" along an 800-foot groomed sandy beach. Three-night minimum. Expensive.

♦ ❄ (ᵗᵖ) **Brophy Lake Resort** (320-762-8386; www.brophylake resort.com), 1532 Brophy Park Road NW, Alexandria. There are 13 cabins here, and they are far more deluxe than usually expected from a small resort. Most of the cabins are on Lake Brophy, but a few are on Mina Creek, which connects to the lake. Expensive.

❄ **Westridge Shores Resort** (320-886-5434; www.westridge shores.com), 6907 MN 114 SW, Alexandria. Eleven cabins on Lake Mary, and ice fishing houses avail-

able for rental during the winter. Guests can make appointments (kids, too) to try their hand in the on-site pottery studio. Two-night minimum stay. Very expensive.

✸ Where to Eat

DINING OUT ♦ ❡ **Geneva Grill** (320-762-7092; www.genevagolf club.com), 4181 Geneva Golf Club Drive, Alexandria. Open daily for lunch and dinner during golf season. Located at the Geneva Golf Club (see *Green Space and Outdoor Activities*), the grill has a wide variety of sandwiches, pastas, and chicken/pork/steak /seafood items. Expensive.

❡ ❄ **Sixth Avenue Wine and Ale** (320-759-2277; www.sixthavenue wineandale.com), 115 Sixth

Avenue E., Alexandria. Open Tues. through Sat. for dinner. This cozy bar and bistro has 70 wines by the glass and 40 beers by the bottle, plus a menu of foods easy to pair with either, including a Beer Lover's Plate and a Wine Lover's Plate. Expensive.

EATING OUT ✍ ❈ **Jan's Place** (320-763-3877), 612 Third Avenue W., Alexandria. Open daily for breakfast and lunch. Hearty plated breakfasts; soups and sandwiches at lunchtime. Inexpensive.

✍ ♿ ❈ **Bistro to Go** (320-846-0777; www.bistrotogo.net), 613 Broadway, Alexandria. Open daily for lunch. This cute deli and caterer in Alexandria prepares hearty sandwiches and salads for dine-in or take-out. Inexpensive.

❋ **Entertainment**

✍ ♿ **Theatre L'Homme Dieu** (320-846-3150; www.www.tlhd .org), 1875 County Route 120 NE, Alexandria. Open summers only. Tickets start at $17. A local theater that also hosts touring shows,

Theatre L'Homme Dieu has been keeping summer visitors and residents alike entertained for 50 years. A mix of comedies, dramas, and musicals make up each season, including such productions as *Grease, Of Mice and Men, Proof,* and *Dirty Rotten Scoundrels.*

❋ **Special Events**

July: **Sinclair Lewis Days** (320-352-5201), Sauk Centre. This annual celebration of the life of Sauk Centre's most famous and possibly most contentious former resident occurs in late July. A week of events includes a 5K run, horseshoe and softball tournaments, street dance, live music, and the crowning of Miss Sauk Centre.

August: **Boats, Blues & BBQ** (320-759-1114), Alexandria. Held each year in early Aug. at the Minnesota Lakes Maritime Museum (see *To See and Do*). Visitors can eat, listen to great music, and see an awe-inspiring variety of boats.

BRAINERD

Arguably one of the most popular lake areas in the state, the Brainerd lakes area has undergone a shift over the last several years. The small-town community with a few large resorts and dozens of small mom-and-pop resorts is evolving into a larger-scale resort community, complete with more lodging, restaurant, and off-the-lake entertainment activities. The increased efforts to bring in more traffic year-round have succeeded, and that means the area is perhaps not as restful as some of the other resort areas, particularly around Willmar and Spicer. That said, for visitors wanting a wider variety of options for their vacations, the Brainerd area is hard to beat.

✳ To See and Do

FOR FAMILIES 🛈 **Pirate's Cove Mini-Golf and Billy Bones Raceway** (218-828-9002; www.pirates cove.net), 17992 MN 371 N., Brainerd. Open daily 10 AM–11 PM, Memorial Day through Labor Day; weekends (call for hours) from the last weekend in Apr. through third weekend of Oct. Rates start at $7.95 for adults and $7.50 for children. At this very fun pirate-themed mini golf course, you can play one of the two 18-hole courses, or play both at a discount. Next door is the Billy Bones Raceway, which has three go-cart tracks.

🛈 ♿ **Paul Bunyan Land and This Old Farm** (218-764-2524;

PIRATE'S COVE MINI-GOLF

www.paulbunyanland.com), 17553 MN 18, Brainerd. Open daily 10–6, Memorial Day through Labor Day; selected weekends in Oct. and Dec. (for Halloween and Christmas). Adults 18 and older $12.95, senior citizens $11.95, children 2–17 $14.95, children under 2 free. Part history village, part amusement park, Paul Bunyan Land's attractions include a 26-foot-tall talking Paul Bunyan, amusement rides, and the Pioneer Village, which includes an original log cabin, dentist's office, schoolhouse, and post office.

MUSEUMS AND HISTORIC SITES ✍ ♿ ❄ **Crow Wing County Historical Museum** (218-829-3268; www.crowwinghistory.org), 320 Laurel Street, Brainerd. Open Tues. through Sat. 10–3. Adults $3, children under 12 free. This lively museum used to be the sheriff's office and county jail. Now it houses a wide-ranging collection of historical items detailing the region's lumber, railroad, and mining history, as well as Native American artifacts.

✍ ♿ **Nisswa Pioneer Village** (218-963-0801), Nisswa. Open Wed. through Sat. 10–4, mid-June through Aug.; weekends 10–4, May through mid-June. Admission is $1. Nisswa Pioneer Village is comprised of nine buildings, including log homes and a schoolhouse, while the old caboose and train depot hold railroad relics. An annual Scandinavian festival attracts large crowds (see *Special Events*).

NISSWA PIONEER VILLAGE

OTHER ATTRACTIONS
✍ ♿ **Brainerd International Raceway** (218-824-7223 or 1-866-444-4455; www.brainerdraceway.com), 5523 Birchdale Road, Brainerd. Races usually start in early May and run until early Oct. Drag racing and road racing at its finest. Paul Newman was among the racing participants.

Nisswa Turtle Races, Nisswa Trailside Information Center, Main Street, Nisswa. No worries about breakneck speeds in these races, held every Wed. at 2 PM, rain or shine, in the summer months.

NISSWA'S SIDEWALKS ARE DECORATED WITH TURTLES.

They're immensely popular with kids, and participation can rise into the hundreds. If you don't have your own turtle, it's possible to rent one.

✳ Green Space and Outdoor Activities

HIKING AND BIKING Pequot Lakes Fire Tower, County Route 11, Pequot Lakes. Admission is free. It's definitely not for the faint of heart or weak of knees, but if you'd like a spectacular view of the surrounding forestland, climb this 100-foot tower. The tower itself is not the only climb; the walk from the parking lot is straight uphill as well.

Paul Bunyan State Trail (www.paulbunyantrail.com). Starting at Paul Bunyan Land (see *To See and Do*), this is the longest bike trail in Minnesota, with 110 paved miles. The Paul Bunyan Trail connects several other state trails and currently ends at Lake Bemidji State Park (see *Green Space and Outdoor Activities* in the "Bemidji Area" chapter). Long-term plans aim to extend it to Crow Wing State Park. The trail isn't just for bikes, but also for hiking and inline skating. The trail runs parallel to several swimmable lakes, and bike-in campsites are available.

PARKS ✳ **Northland Arboretum** (218-829-8770), 14250 Conservation Drive, Brainerd. Open year-round. Rather incongruously located behind the Westgate Mall in Brainerd, this nature preserve covers 500 acres of forest and prairie that has evolved on the site of a former landfill. The Nature Conservancy owns about 40 percent of the arboretum. There are several miles of hiking and cross-country ski trails.

✳ **Crow Wing State Park** (218-829-8022; www.dnr.state.mn.us/state _parks/crow_wing/index.html), 3124 State Park Road, Brainerd. Not only a pristine state forest, Crow Wing State Park is also a remnant of the area's past as a fur trading hotbed. The town of Crow Wing flourished during the heyday, but when the railroad decided to pass through Brainerd rather than Crow Wing, the town's fate was sealed. Today the nearly 2,100-acre park has several miles of hiking trails (some of which are groomed for cross-country skiing in the winter) and excellent canoeing opportunities, including a canoe-in campsite. Within the park is the Beaulieu House, the last remaining building from the fur trading days.

✳ Lodging

BED & BREAKFASTS

🌀 🐾 ♿ 🍴 ❄ **Nordic Inn Medieval Brew and Bed** (218-546-8299; www.vikinginn.com), 210 First Avenue NW, Crosby. Get truly into the spirit of ancient Minnesota history with a stay at this bed & breakfast. Housed in a former Methodist church, the Nordic Inn has five rooms with disparate themes, including Odin's Loft, decorated with armor and weapons, and the Locker Room, decorated with Minnesota Vikings football fans in mind. Breakfast is included in the room rates. On nights when enough rooms are occupied, guests can participate in an interactive Viking dinner theater performance, complete with Viking feast. Moderate. Packages are available.

RESORTS 🌀 ♿ 🍴 ❄ ((ᵠ)) **Cragun's Resort** (1-800-272-4867; www.craguns.com), 11000 Craguns Drive, Brainerd. This is one of Minnesota's biggest resorts, and it's also one of the nicest. Besides the well-appointed rooms, cabins, and reunion houses, the resort has a 22,000-square-foot indoor sports complex with tennis and basketball courts, a running track, and fitness center. The hotel itself has an indoor pool. A full-service spa is on-site. There are three restaurants that are open year-round, plus two more open in the summer. Fifty-four holes of golf will keep golfers happy, while boaters and anglers have direct access to Gull Lake. (Note: Cragun's does not allow personal watercraft, or Jet Skis, to be stored or launched from their property.) Bikes can be rented, and snowmobiles can be hired during the winter. Expensive. Packages and off-season discounts are available.

🌀 ♿ 🍴 ❄ ((ᵠ)) **Grand View Lodge** (218-963-2234 or 1-866-801-2951; www.grandviewlodge.com), 23521

GRAND VIEW LODGE

A TRADITIONAL FAMILY ESCAPE

Madden's, one of the state's largest and nicest resorts, comes with a nice bit of history. The resort's roots rest in the need of early-20th-century residents of St. Louis and Kansas City to seek refuge from terribly hot summers (there being no air-conditioning then) by escaping north. The early days were a bit rough-and-tumble, with the resort's then-remote location offering perfect hideaways from 1920s gangsters and Prohibition scofflaws. But Madden's survived to become a highly respected resort of the *Dirty Dancing* variety, with families spending weeks of their summers there. Today, the sophisticated complex has everything from rustic hotel rooms to cabins, deluxe golf villas, and reunion houses. Three 18-hole golf courses are on the property, along with one nine-hole social course. Fishing, boating, hiking, swimming, croquet, and tennis are all offered, as are trapshooting (with one week's notice) and sea plane certification. A full-service spa is on-site, and a kids' program is offered from July through mid-Aug. for kids 4–12. There are seven restaurants, three fine dining and four casual. The amenities are attractive enough to keep some of those Kansas City and St. Louis guests, some of which are fourth generation, returning year after year.

✂ ♿ 🍸 (((•))) **Madden's** (218-829-2811 or 1-800-642-5363; www.maddens .com), 11266 Pine Beach Peninsula, Brainerd. Open late Apr. through late Oct. Expensive. Packages are available.

BEACHSIDE AT MADDEN'S

Nokomis Avenue, Nisswa. Grand View hearkens back to the grand old days of lake resorts. Built in 1919, this venerable resort has maintained its historic elegance while modernizing with the amenities today's resort travelers want. The resort offers lodge rooms, cabins, and suites, and villas on the property's golf course. An indoor pool and water slide share a building with a fitness center, but in good weather swimming is done at the sandy beach. Boats can be rented, as can bikes and horses for riding. There are three 18-hole golf courses and one nine-hole course. The full-service spa is open year-round, as are the resort's six restaurants. Two separate kids' clubs, one for ages 3–6 and the other for ages 7–12, give parents a break. Expensive. Packages and off-season discounts are available.

✿ 👌 🍸 ❄ (🛜) **Breezy Point Resort** (1-800-432-3777; www .breezypointresort.com), 9252 Breezy Point Drive, Breezy Point. Located on Pelican Lake, this resort has a huge variety of accommodations to choose from—lodge rooms, one- and two-bedroom apartments, and a series of lodgings called Unique Retreats (log cabins, A-frame cabins, and full houses). The largest has 10 bedrooms and can accommodate 18 people. For recreation, there are two 18-hole golf courses, an indoor pool, and an extensive sandy beach with boat rentals. The summer months bring live musical

performances. Winter brings a new round of activity, including a nine-hole golf course set up directly on the frozen lake, skating rinks, cross-country skiing (equipment available for rental), and a snow tubing hill adjacent to the resort. The resort has two full-service dining areas, the most attractive of which is the Antlers Dining Room, which was built with post-and-beam construction and features two large antler chandeliers. Expensive. Packages are available.

✿ 👌 🍸 **Lost Lake Lodge** (218-963-2681 or 1-800-450-2681; www.lostlake.com), 7965 Lost Lake Road, Lakeshore. Open mid-May to early Oct. This small but lovely resort has beautifully outfitted cabins in a quiet, tucked-away location on Lost Lake. Rates are all-inclusive, meaning daily full breakfast and four-course dinner are included in the rates, and the food is well worth it. (Dinner is available to the public; see *Where to Eat.*) The use of canoes, fishing boats, and bikes are also included in the rates, and fishing guides as well as massage therapists can be hired at an additional fee. Expensive. Packages are available.

✿ 👌 ❄ **Train Bell Resort** (1-800-252-2102; www.trainbellresort .com), 21489 Train Bell Road, Merrifield. North of Brainerd on North Long Lake, Train Bell Resort is owned and operated by Mike and Connie Bruesch, who left corporate life to run this family-friendly resort. There are several

LOST LAKE LODGE

well-maintained lakeside cabins as well as a condo complex, but the resort still keeps its cozy feeling, assisted by weekly activities such as a pancake breakfasts, minnow races, and Fri. night dances. Fishing boats are available for rental, and use of the kayaks and paddleboats at the sandy beach are included in the rates. Expensive. Packages are available.

🌊 ❄ ((ɪ)) **Campfire Bay Resort** (1-800-677-7263; www.campfire bayresort.com), 31504 Azure Road, Cushing. Located on beautiful Fish Trap Lake, Campfire Bay Resort has 16 one- to four-bedroom cabins, all fully equipped with household items. During summer weekends there are special family activities such as Nature Day, woodworking, and ice

cream socials. Expensive. Packages are available.

🌊 ((ɪ)) **Pine Terrace Resort** (1-800-953-1986; www.pine terrace.com), 35101 Pine Terrace Road, Crosslake. Open May through Oct. Pine Terrace is the only resort on Star Lake, and it offers 13 cabins with lake views and 34 acres of grounds, including nature trails. Most of the cabins have one or two bedrooms, with one larger building housing seven bedrooms. Expensive. Packages are available.

🌊 ❄ **Black Pine Beach Resort** (218-543-4714 or 1-877-575-1455; www.blackpinebeach.com), 10732 County Route 16, Pequot Lakes. The resort, with 13 lake cottages, all with kitchens and fireplaces, also has its very own Secret

Garden, complete with an elfin mailbox young visitors can deliver letters to. Expensive.

✳ Where to Eat

DINING OUT ✎ ⚘ ⚲ **Brauhaus German Restaurant and Lounge** (218-652-2478; www .brauhaus-german.com), 28234 MN 34, Akeley. Open Wed. through Sun. for dinner and Sun. for lunch, May through Oct. A cheerful, casual German restaurant with an extensive menu of German foods, as well as American items for the finicky eaters. Expensive.

✎ ⚘ ⚲ ✳ **Prairie Bay Grill** (218-824-6444; www.prairiebay.com), 15115 Edgewood Drive, Baxter. Open daily for lunch and dinner. Pizza, pasta, sandwiches, and meat-and-potato dishes, served in a casual yet upscale environment. Kids are welcome, as are vegetari-ans, who have several options on the menu. Expensive.

✎ ⚘ ⚲ ✳ **Black Bear Lodge and Saloon** (218-828-8400; www.black bearlodgemn.com), 14819 Edge-wood Drive, Baxter. Open daily for lunch and dinner, Sun. for brunch. Standard bar and grill fare, including sandwiches and burgers, steaks, and seafood. Expensive.

⚲ ✳ **The Classic Grill** (1-800-642-5363; www.maddens.com), 11266 Pine Beach Peninsula, Brainerd. Even though Madden's Resort (see the "A Traditional Family Escape" sidebar) is only open part of the year, this stand-alone restaurant is open daily year-round for lunch and dinner. The dining room overlooks one of the resort's golf courses, and large stone patios with patio heaters stretch the outdoor season as long as possible. The food is upscale

THE CLASSIC GRILL OVERLOOKS ONE OF THE GOLF COURSES AT MADDEN'S.

THE DECK AT ZORBAZ ON GULL LAKE

and gourmet, with seafood, steak, veal, and a risotto of the day all great choices. Expensive.

🕯 ♿ 🍸 **Lost Lake Lodge** (218-963-2681 or 1-800-450-2681; www.lostlake.com), 7965 Lost Lake Road, Lakeshore. Open daily for dinner, Memorial Day through Labor Day; weekends for dinner the rest of the year. One of the best fine-dining options in the Brainerd lakes area, Lost Lake Lodge takes food staples such as walleye and chicken and turns them into unexpected and delicious offerings. Expensive.

EATING OUT 🕯 ♿ ❄ **371 Diner** (218-829-3356), 14901 Edgewood Drive, Brainerd. Open daily for all three meals. Located on US 371 through Brainerd, the 371 is a replica of a 1950s diner and has a respectable (if high-calorie) menu of burgers, sandwiches, and ice cream treats. Kids get their meals served in a cardboard race car. Inexpensive.

🕯 ♿ ❄ **Sawmill Inn** (218-829-5444), 601 Washington Street, Brainerd. Open daily for all three meals. It doesn't look like much on the outside, but the Sawmill is the classic small-town café, complete with huge breakfasts and hearty sandwiches. Inexpensive.

🕯 🍸 ❄ **Zorbaz on the Lake** (218-963-4790: www.zorbaz.com), 8105 Lost Lake Road, Nisswa. Open daily for lunch and dinner in the summer; daily for dinner, weekends for lunch the rest of the year. This is a beach bar with Mexican food, pizza, pasta, and plenty of beer, not to mention a groaningly silly menu. Take the kids for the arcade. A dock is provided for diners arriving by boat. Moderate.

✳ Selective Shopping

ANTIQUES Just north of Brainerd on MN 371, Pequot Lakes has some browse-worthy antiques shops. If you'd like to explore a little more in the antiques realm, you might want to detour slightly here and go a few miles north on MN 371 to Jenkins, a very small town, but with a crowded antiques store right on the highway.

❋ **Beautiful Antiques** (218-568-5166; http://beautifulantiques .com), 30960 Government Drive. Hours change seasonally, so call to confirm.

❋ **The Flour Sack Antiques Shop** (218-568-5658), 29119 MN 371. Hours change seasonally, so call to confirm.

NISSWA SHOPPING

The little town of Nisswa, just north of Brainerd on MN 371, has become a central shopping spot with several small but fun shops.

✎ ❋ **Rainy Days** (218-963-4891; http://rainydaysnisswa.com), 25491 Main Street. Open daily. This is a bookseller for book lovers, with a wide range of reading material for grown-ups and for kids.

❋ **Sculpture Gardens** (218-963-1313 or 1-888-326-0063; www.sculpture gardens.com), 24428 Smiley Road. Open Tues. through Sat. Unique home decorating items and accessories, from vases and wall hangings to iron sculptures and birdbaths.

✎ **Rebecca's Dolls and Miniatures** (218-963-0165; www.rebeccasdolls .com), 541 Main Street. Open daily May through Oct. Dolls and dollhouses and accessories, movie memorabilia, miniatures, and shadow boxes.

❋ **Totem Pole** (1-866-506-5244; www.totempolemn.com), 25485 Main Street. Open daily. All Minnetonka moccasins, all the time.

❋ **Blue Canoe Boutique** (218-963-7330), 25497 Main Street. Open daily. Casual and elegant clothing and jewelry.

Simpler Thymes of Nisswa (218-963-9463; www.simplerthymesofnisswa .com), 25410 Main Street. Open daily Memorial Day through Labor Day;

❋ **Castoffs** (218-568-6155; www .facebook.com/pages/Castoffs -Secondhand), 4242 Jokela Drive. Open daily.

❋ **Mercantile Cooperative** (218-568-8626), 30924 Government Drive. Open daily.

BOOKS ✄ ❋ **Cat Tale's Books and Gifts** (218-825-8611), 609 Laurel Street, Brainerd. Open Mon. through Sat. A browser-friendly shop full of new and used books as well as cards, jewelry, and other gifts.

GIFTS ❋ **Rough Around the Edges** (218-692-1880), 14307 Gould Street, Crosslake. Open Tues. through Sat. Country-themed gifts and home decor.

WOMEN'S CLOTHING ❋ **Among the Pines** (218-828-6364; www.amongthepines.com), 15670 Edgewood Drive, Baxter.

THE CHOCOLATE OX, NISSWA

limited hours Apr., May, Sept., and Oct. Gift shop focused on personal luxuries, including lotions and soaps, candles, gourmet foods (many locally produced), robes, and women's accessories.

✄ **The Chocolate Ox** (218-963-4443; www.chocolateox.com), Main Street. Open daily Apr. through Jan. Gourmet truffles, an extensive collection of licorice and saltwater taffies, and a huge variety of vintage candies—it's a place kids and adults can enjoy together.

Gifts, women's clothing, and yarn supplies.

✳ Special Events

January: **Brainerd Jaycees Ice Fishing Extravaganza** (http://icefishing.org), Brainerd. This annual fishing tournament takes place in late Jan. Significant prizes, including ATVs and underwater cameras, are offered; competitors must purchase tickets, with the proceeds going to charity.

June: **Granite City Days** (www.granitecitydays.com). Each year in late June, St. Cloud celebrates its quarrying history with a multiday festival featuring an art fair, 5K, talent show, canoe rides, fishing derby, and plenty of live music and food.

Nisswa-Stämman Festival (www.nisswastamman.org), Nisswa. This popular annual festival takes place in early June and features Scandinavian folk music, including traditional Scandinavian musical instruments. There are several live performances, dances, kids' activities, and classes and workshops.

Tour of Lakes Bicycle Ride (218-833-8122; www.paulbunyancyclists.com), Brainerd. This annual ride, held in early June, is not a race, but a way to use a bicycle to take in the spectacular scenery around the Central Lakes area. There are two routes each year, although the routes change every year to maximize scenery possibilities. Preregistration is recommended.

July: **Bean Hole Days** (218-568-8911), Trailside Park, Pequot Lakes. This two-day event draws on the traditional cooking of baked beans by burying them in large kettles for 24 hours, then raising them back up for the impatient consumers. A craft fair and Bean Hole Days coronation ceremony help make the waiting easier.

November: **Fish House Parade,** Aitkin. The day after Thanksgiving marks not only the official start of the holiday retail season, but to this annual rite of passage into winter. Participants parade their fish houses, usually decorated to the hilt in what appears to be a one-upmanship show of hilarity.

St. Croix Valley 6

UPPER ST. CROIX

LOWER ST. CROIX

ST. CROIX VALLEY

This small but highly scenic region derives its beauty from the St. Croix River and the surrounding landscapes, as well as the wealthy New England families who settled here more than a century ago, re-creating their home villages along the riverside, small towns that remain intact and as charming and historic as they were when they were first built. Along with the New Englanders came the Scandinavians, building tight agricultural and cultural enclaves, and today there is still a close-knit community known informally as Little Sweden. Going up the river can provide insight into some of Minnesota's Scandinavian heritage. Logging and the fur trade drove the growth of the area during the 19th century, and today's visitors can still find remnants of those trades, primarily in place-names, but also in the quaint, wonderful small towns. Artists have not been immune to the area's beauty, and there is a strong and growing arts community throughout the valley.

GUIDANCE Falls Chamber of Commerce (715-483-3580; http://taylors fallschamber.org), 106 N. Washington, St. Croix Falls, WI. Open Mon. through Thurs. Provides visitor info for Taylors Falls in Minnesota and St. Croix Falls in Wisconsin.

Stillwater Chamber of Commerce (651-439-4001; www.ilovestillwater .com), 1950 Northwestern Ave., Suite 101, Stillwater.

Afton Area Business Association (651-436-8883; www.aftonmnarea .com), Afton.

GETTING THERE *By air:* Air service is through the **Minneapolis–St. Paul International Airport** (612-726-5555; www.mspairport.com).

By car: From the Twin Cities, take I-35W north to US 8 east to Chisago City. Follow US 8 east through Lindstrom, Center City, and Taylors Falls. Take US 8 south to MN 95 (St. Croix Trail) to reach Franconia. Continue

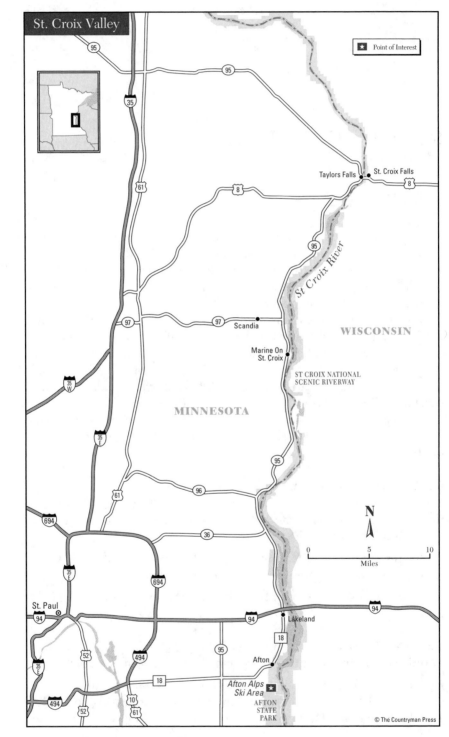

St. Croix Valley

★ Point of Interest

95

95

35

61

Taylors Falls • St. Croix Falls

8

8

95

St Croix River

97 97 Scandia

WISCONSIN

Marine On
St. Croix

35
W

ST CROIX NATIONAL
SCENIC RIVERWAY

MINNESOTA

95

61

96

N

694

36

0   5   10
Miles

35
E

694

St. Paul

94

94 • Lakeland

35
E

52

494

18

95

Afton

18

Afton Alps
Ski Area ★

494

52

10

61

AFTON
STATE
PARK

© The Countryman Press

on MN 95 to MN 97, turning right to arrive in Scandia. Return to MN 95 and travel south to County Route 4 (Maple Street) to stop in Marine on St. Croix. Follow MN 95 south to Stillwater. From Stillwater, you can take MN 96 or MN 36 back to the Twin Cities.

GETTING AROUND Having a vehicle is a necessity when traveling around the St. Croix Valley region.

WHEN TO COME Summer is the most popular time to visit, and Stillwater in particular can be quite busy and congested as shoppers and boaters converge upon the quaint little town. Fall is busy with leaf-peepers, but the area quiets down in the winter as traffic involves mostly shoppers.

MEDICAL EMERGENCY Call 911.

Lakeview Hospital (651-439-5330 or 1-800-423-7212; www.lakeview .org), 927 Churchill St. W., Stillwater.

UPPER ST. CROIX

The upper St. Croix Valley, from Marine on St. Croix up toward Hinckley (see the chapter of that name in part 3, "North Shore and the Arrowhead"), is full of natural beauty, from rivers to woodlands to prairies to glacial trails, and is a park lover's dream region. Some of Minnesota's most beautiful state parks are in this area, running along the river and offering nearly every kind of recreational opportunity, including swimming, canoeing, hiking, camping, horseback riding, cross-country skiing, and snowshoeing. The little village of Marine on St. Croix is peaceful and picturesque, and the river town of Taylors Falls has an area (the Angel Hill District) that could have been lifted right out of a New England portrait. Scandinavian culture is alive and well in Scandia and in the series of little towns known as Little Sweden, and the region's popularity with artists is demonstrated in Franconia.

✳ To See and Do

Inland from the river, in an area heavily populated with lakes and farmland, is a part of the state known as America's Little Sweden. A series of small towns—including Chisago City, Lindstrom, and Center City—settled by Swedish (and other Scandinavian) immigrants, Little Sweden is a place you can still hear faint traces of Swedish accents in the residents and are likely to see store and street signs in both English and Swedish. Most of these communities have active

PAINTED FLOWERBOX IN LINDSTROM

ST. CROIX RIVER AT INTERSTATE STATE PARK

relationships with sister cities in Sweden, and the food and culture still strongly reflect that ancestry.

MUSEUMS AND HISTORIC SITES Chisago County History Center (651-257-5310; www.chisagocountyhistory.org), 13112 Third Avenue N., Lindstrom. This county historical society is caretaker to several historical properties, and visits can be arranged by contacting the center. The Moody Round Barn, Gustaf Anderson House, and the Delmore-Fransen Log House are part of the collection, as well as the Polish Shtetl House, a replica built and used during the filming of the Coen brothers' film *A Serious Man.*

VILHELM MOBERG

Vilhelm Moberg, a Swedish author and historian, was best known for The Emigrant novels, fictional accounts of a Swedish family's journey to Chisago County to build a new life against harsh odds. Moberg spent time in this true-life Swedish American community in 1948 to research his series, and they have not forgotten him. Chisago City has Vilhelm Moberg Park, which includes a statue of Moberg and his bicycle, which he was famous for riding about the town. Lindstrom has a statue of Karl Oskar and Kristina, a fictional couple featured in The Emigrant series (in fact, they're also represented on Lindstrom's city logo), and south of Lindstrom is Kichi-Saga Park, the site of Nya Duvemåla, the house Moberg used as a model for Karl Oskar and Kristina's fictional home. A boulder in front of the house was donated by Volvo from Åseda, Sweden. Today, Karl Oskar Days are celebrated every summer (see *Special Events*).

VILHELM MOBERG STATUE IN CHISAGO CITY

❋ **Chisago Lake Evangelical Lutheran Church** (651-257-6300; www
.chisagolakelutheranchurch.org), Center City. This is the oldest continuously operating church in the area. It opened in 1854 and has been in its
current building since 1889.

❋ **Center City Historic District,** Summit Avenue, Center City. Original
homes of the Swedish pioneers can be seen along Summit Avenue, which
has numerous homes of first- and second-generation families, built in
period style.

✄ **Folsom House** (651-465-3125; www.mnhs.org/places/sites/fh), 272 W.
Government Street, Taylors Falls. Open Wed. through Mon. 1–4:30,
Memorial Day weekend through Oct. 15; also open the two weekends following Thanksgiving. Adults $5, children 6–12 $1, children under 6 and
Minnesota Historical Society members free. This charming home looks
like it was plucked out of a New England landscape, along with several of
its neighbors, and replanted in the Angel Hill District of Taylors Falls.
Home of a lumber baron and state senator, the Folsom House gives a view
of Minnesota's early days—and of the St. Croix River.

✄ ❋ **Angel Hill District,** Taylors Falls. Just up the hill from the Folsom
House is a historic residential district known as Angel Hill. Many of Taylors Falls's early wealthy settlers built here, and the homes have been
beautifully maintained. A stroll before or after a Folsom House tour will
give visitors a strong sense of the historical roots of the area.

Stone House Museum (651-433-2061), 241 Fifth Street, Marine on St.
Croix. Open Sat. and Sun. 2–5, Memorial Day through Labor Day. Admission is free, but donations are requested. This historic Scandinavian site is

THE FOLSOM HOUSE, TAYLORS FALLS

TAYLORS FALLS'S ANGEL HILL DISTRICT HAS MANY BEAUTIFUL HISTORIC HOMES.

tucked into the small, picturesque town of Marine on St. Croix. The Stone House, aptly named for its Scandinavian stone architecture, was originally the town meetinghouse. Today it's a repository for artifacts and photographs documenting the Scandinavian settlers who arrived in the early 19th century.

✿ & **Gammelgården** (651-433-5053; www.gammelgarden museum.org), 20880 Olinda Trail, Scandia. Buildings are open Fri. through Sun. 1–3 (the grounds are open longer), May 1 through mid-Oct.; special events are offered throughout the year. Adults $5, children under 12 free. Gammel-gården is a living-history museum paying tribute to the Scandinavian roots of the region. Several original immigrant homes and other buildings, including a church, have been restored on 11 acres of farm-land. The site is open for public tours during the summer, but year-round the museum offers a vast array of special events and classes

ANTIQUE SCANDINAVIAN CUPBOARD AT GAMMELGÅRDEN

GAMMELGÅRDEN GUEST HOUSE

(see website for details), including music festivals, sausage-making classes, and an annual Midsommar Dag (Midsummer Day) celebration (see *Special Events*). On a sunny summer day, it's worth a visit just to stroll the beautiful grounds.

HAY LAKE SCHOOL MUSEUM, SCANDIA

✦ **Hay Lake School Museum** (651-433-4014; http://wchsmn.org /museums/scandia), Olinda Trail N. and Old Marine Trail, Scandia. Open Fri. through Sun. 1–4, June through Aug.; Sat. and Sun. 1–4, May, Sept., and Oct. Adults $5, children 16 and under $1, Washington County Historical Society members free. If Gammelgården isn't enough history for you, check out the nearby Hay Lake School Museum. Listed on the National Register of Historic Places, this museum is made up of a former schoolhouse and a log home built in the late 1800s.

WINEHAVEN VINEYARD, CHISAGO CITY

WINERIES ❅ **WineHaven Winery and Vineyard** (651-257-1017; www.winehaven.com), 9757 292nd Street, Chisago City. Open Mon. and Thurs. through Sat. 10–5, Sun. 11–5. At this award-winning vineyard that's been owned and operated by the same family for four generations, take a tour, learn about viticulture, and sample the specialty: Stinger Honeywine (mead).

OTHER ATTRACTIONS
❅ **Lindstrom Water Tower,** 12849 N. First Avenue, Lindstrom. It's not just a water tower—it's a coffeepot-shaped water tower with rosemaling designs welcoming visitors.

✳ Green Space and Outdoor Activities

There are lakes in this area, but the primary source of outdoor recreation in the St. Croix Valley rests along the riverbanks.

LINDSTROM'S FAMOUS WATER TOWER

CANOEING St. Croix National Scenic Riverway (715-483-3284; www
.nps.gov/sacn/). This is what the region is all about—252 miles of lush
river scenery, starting in Wisconsin and including both the St. Croix River
and the Namekagon River. The headquarters for information is the St.
Croix Visitor Center in St. Croix Falls, Wisconsin, which is just across the
river from Taylors Falls. Where the St. Croix ambles south along the Minnesota border, canoeing and camping are popular activities, but check
with the visitors center before making plans—there are restrictions
regarding use of campsites and boats to protect the river itself and the
land on either side of it. In times of low rainfall, fire restrictions are strictly
enforced.

PARKS Franconia Sculpture Park (651-257-6668; www.franconia.org),
US 8 and MN 95, Franconia. Open daily. Admission is free. The Franconia Sculpture Park is, intentionally, a work in progress. There are more
than 75 exhibits in this rural exhibition area, and each year somewhere
between 15 and 25 artists are invited to work and contribute art on a
rotating basis. There are concerts in the summer, as well as hands-on
classes for kids. The artworks are spread across a field with flat
mowed paths; self-guided tours and guided tours are offered.

ONE OF THE WORKS OF ART ON DISPLAY
AT FRANCONIA SCULPTURE PARK

Wild River State Park (651-583-
2125; www.dnr.state.mn.us/state
_parks/wild_river/index.html),
39797 Park Trail, Center City.
Open daily. Thirty-five miles of
hiking and cross-country ski trails,
guesthouse and camping within the
park, and 18 miles of riverside
beauty make this park a gem.
There are also campsites for visitors with horses. Spring provides
some of the most beautiful wildflower displays in the state. For
those with GPS units and an itch to
explore, the aforementioned Minnesota DNR site provides coordi-
nates for historical searches within
the park.

William O'Brien State Park
(651-433-0500; www.dnr.state
.mn.us/state_parks/william_obrien
/index.html), 16821 O'Brien Trail

WILD RIVER STATE PARK

WILLIAM O'BRIEN STATE PARK

N., Marine on St. Croix. Open daily. This small but lovely park is just north of Marine on St. Croix. Named after a lumber baron who had originally cleared the land of trees, the park is now (more than a century later)

St. Croix State Park (320-384-6591; www.dnr.state.mn.us/state_parks /st_croix/index.html), 30065 St. Croix Park Road, Hinckley. Open daily. The state's largest state park was built as a Civilian Conservation Corps (CCC) project during the Depression years. More than 34,000 acres of former farmland has been redeveloped into open parkland, and the buildings built by the CCC helped lead to the park's designation as a National Historic Landmark.

But besides the history, recreational opportunities abound. In addition to the St. Croix River, the park also has the Kettle River, the first State Wild and Scenic River. There are 100 miles of trails for hiking, some of which are open to horseback riders and mountain bikers, and during the summer visitors can rent bikes at the Adventure St. Croix Store by the campground. A swimming beach is available, and canoers and kayakers can launch on the river of their choice. Splendid views are available by climbing the park's 100-foot fire tower, or spend some time in the company of your fishing pole. A six-bedroom guesthouse, cabins, and rustic campsites can be reserved in advance (the guesthouse is open year-round). During the winter, trails are groomed for cross-country skiers and snowmobilers.

GLACIAL POTHOLES?

Interstate State Park is located on US 8 just at the entrance of Taylors Falls. The park's name reflects its cross-river location, with the park stretching from Minnesota to Wisconsin. River access makes kayaking and canoeing popular, and interesting geological formations, including exposed lava flows and glacial deposits, make this an intriguing area for exploration. Of particular interest are the glacial potholes, immense holes (the deepest one is 60 feet) made in the bedrock when the Glacial St. Croix River forced its way through. Interstate State Park has more of these glacial potholes in one area than any other place in the world. Rock climbing is popular, and during the fall, the autumn colors provide a major draw.

HIKING AT INTERSTATE STATE PARK

Interstate State Park (651-465-5711; www.dnr.state .mn.us/state_parks/inter state/index.html), US 8, Taylors Falls. Open daily.

reforested and full of wildlife and river access. It's open year-round and offers trails for cross-country skiing and snowshoeing, as well as campsites with electricity for winter camping. There's a swimming beach in the summer with a large picnic area adjacent, and canoeing on the river is made possible by rentals in the park. Canoe shuttle service is offered during summer. Birdwatchers can spot hundreds of different birds. The visitors center has a seasonal checklist of what might be seen, from the more commonly found Canada goose and northern flicker to the uncommon (but still possible!) great blue heron, ruffed grouse, and scarlet tanager.

SKIING Wild Mountain & Taylors Falls Recreation (651-465-6315 or 1-800-447-4958; www.wildmountain.com), 37200 Wild Mountain Road, Taylors Falls. Wild Mountain takes advantage of the rolling terrain in the river area to run 25 ski and boarding runs during the winter, along with a snow-tubing course. During the summer, the "recreation" part of the company offers a water park with alpine slide and go-cart tracks, as well as public and private charter river cruises, canoe and kayak rental, and an RV park and campground.

✳ Lodging

The upper St. Croix Valley has been compared to quaint New England villages, so it's fitting that there are several charming bed & breakfasts in the area.

✳ **The Old Jail** (651-465-3112; www.oldjail.com), 349 Government Street, Taylors Falls. Three suites and a cottage are offered in two buildings, one a former jail, the other having housed a wide variety of businesses: saloon, chicken-plucking factory, and mortuary. Despite its gruesome history, the suites are lovely, all including private bath, some including old-fashioned record players, one including a bathroom in a cave, and one not recommended for people over 6 feet tall. Rates include breakfast served to the room. Expensive.

✳ **The Cottage** (651-465-3595; www.the-cottage.com), 950 Fox Glen Drive, Taylors Falls. Open Feb. through Dec. There's only one unit, but it's a suite with private dining area overlooking the St. Croix River, decorated in a cozy French country style. Expensive.

Asa Parker House (651-433-5248; www.asaparkerbb.com), 17500 St. Croix Trail N., Marine on St. Croix. This lovely Greek Revival home, built in 1856, overlooks the village of Marine on St. Croix. There are four guest rooms,

ASA PARKER HOUSE BED AND BREAKFAST, MARINE ON ST. CROIX

all with private bath; the Alice O'Brien suite (named after the O'Brien lumber family's daughter who donated land for the William O'Brien State Park; see *Green Space and Outdoor Activities*) has a private porch. The property is close enough to Stillwater for easy access to restaurants and shops, but just far enough to provide an idyllic, peaceful retreat. Expensive. Packages and extras are available.

Women's Environmental Institute at Amador Hill (651-583-0705; www.w-e-i.org), 15715 River Road, North Branch. Located in an organic apple orchard on the edge of Wild River State Park, the WEI offers four rooms for guests or groups. Two of the rooms share a bath, and the largest room has a fireplace. The rooms are simple but attractive; it's the location that makes this a worthwhile getaway. Moderate.

✳ Where to Eat

DINING OUT

✎ ♿ ☗ ❋ **Meredee's Bistro** (651-257-9144;www.meredeesbistro.com), 11347 North Avenue, Chisago City. Open daily for lunch and dinner, Sat. and Sun. for breakfast. Serves hearty supper-club food, including shrimp and steak, and has a sizable salad bar. Expensive.

✎ ♿ ☗ ❋ **Tangled Up in Blue** (651-465-1000), 425 Bench Street, Taylors Falls. Open Wed. through Sun. for dinner. A French fusion restaurant with upscale fare and a good wine list. Expensive.

EATING OUT ✎ ❋ **George's Smokin' BBQ** (651-257-3227), 29346 Old Towne Road, Chisago City. Open daily for lunch and dinner. Exactly what it says—a smokin' barbecue with generous portions. Moderate.

GEORGE'S SMOKIN' BBQ, CHISAGO CITY

✎ ✳ **Swedish Inn** (651-257-4072), 12678 Lake Boulevard, Lindstrom. Open daily for breakfast and lunch. Get your Swedish on here, especially with the breakfast foods—Swedish pancakes, anyone? Inexpensive.

✳ **Lindstrom Bakery** (651-257-1374), 12830 Lake Boulevard, Lindstrom. Open Mon. through Sat. All the baked goods are worthwhile (and some are organic), but what you really want is a Scandinavian doughnut, crunchy

THE DRIVE IN, TAYLORS FALLS

on the outside, soft on the inside. Inexpensive.

✎ ♈ ✳ **Dinnerbel** (651-257-9524; www.dinnerbel.com), 12565 Lake Boulevard, Lindstrom. Open daily for lunch and dinner. This restaurant operates in a historical site that's served as a restaurant on and off for more than 120 years. Basic comfort food is what you'll find, with burgers, sandwiches, pasta, and daily specials that sometimes include George's Smokin' BBQ (see previous listing). Moderate.

✎ ✳ **Eichten's Bistro & Market** (651-257-1566; www.theeichtens bistro.com), 16440 Lake Boulevard, Center City. Open Sun. through Thurs. for lunch; Fri. for lunch and dinner; Sat. for all three meals. Eichten's, a purveyor of locally farmed meats and locally produced cheese, also has this casual bistro, serving salads, sandwiches, and home-baked pies. Inexpensive.

✎ ♿ **The Drive In** (651-465-7831), 572 Bench Street, Taylors Falls. Open daily for lunch and dinner, mid-Apr. through mid-Oct. It's retro, it's got a giant rotating root-beer cup on a stick, and its burgers and malts are served to your vehicle by carhops. Inexpensive.

✎ ♿ ✳ **Scandia Café** (651-433-4054; www.scandiamn.com /scandiacafe/index.htm), 21079 Olinda Trail N., Scandia. Open daily for breakfast and lunch. This classic small-town café is often

THE GROUNDS AT GAMMELGÅRDEN

busy with locals who come in for the daily soup specials and turkey luncheon. Inexpensive.

✳ Special Events

June: **Midsommar Dag** (651-433-5053; www.gammelgardenmuseum .org/midsommar.shtm), Scandia. Held each year in late June at the Gammelgården Museum (see *To See and Do*), Midsommar Dag is a celebration of the community's Scandinavian heritage. The traditional raising of the maypole is accompanied by food, music, and dancing in traditional costumes.

July: **Karl Oskar Days** (651-257-1177; www.facebook.com/pages /Karl-Oskar-Days), Lindstrom. The annual celebration of Vilhelm Moberg's fictional Swedish immigrant couple is the county's largest festival and includes a Taste of Sweden, arts and crafts, a parade, live entertainment, and a street dance.

August: **Spelmansstamma Music Festival** (651-433-5053; www .gammelgardenmuseum.org /spelmansstamma.shtm), Scandia. Held each year at the Gammelgården Museum (see *To See and Do*), the Spelmansstamma Music Festival provides a variety of traditional Scandinavian folk music, with a Swedish smorgasbord, craft fair, and children's activities.

LOWER ST. CROIX

Stillwater is the central attraction on the lower part of the St. Croix Valley. Calling itself the Birthplace of Minnesota, it's one of the oldest cities in the state, built by lumber barons and transplanted New Englanders. Like any town that suffers the loss of its primary industry, Stillwater went through its slump in the early 20th century. But the natural beauty surrounding the area combined with the charm of the downtown streets and buildings drove a renaissance that has created thriving shops and galleries and a busy tourist trade, particularly on summer weekends, when driving down Main Street can require patience and time.

But the payoff is in the ability to stop, shop, wander along the river and watch the Stillwater Lift Bridge operate, see the sailboats and yachts dotting the water, and have almost more choices of places to dine than seems reasonable. Whether wandering on your own for a private retreat, as part of a couple's romantic getaway, or with a family, Stillwater is a lovely place to spend a day or two. Add in the recreation and dining options south of Stillwater, and the stay could be longer.

✴ To See and Do

❧ **Warden's House Museum** (651-439-5956; http://wchsmn.org/museums /wardens_house), 602 N. Main Street, Stillwater. Open Thurs. through Sun. 1–5, May through Oct. Adults $5, children 16 and younger $1, Washington County Historical Society members free. The Warden's House was built in 1853 and used as a residence for prison wardens and superintendents until 1941, when the building was sold to the Washington County Historical Society. Several of the rooms are furnished as they would have been in the late 19th century, while a few rooms are reserved for displays relevant to the region's overall history, including the lumber industry and children's items.

❧ ✴ **Joseph Wolf Brewery Caves** (651-430-0560; www.lunarossawine bar.com/cavetour.html), 402 S. Main Street, Stillwater. Tours offered daily

DOWNTOWN STILLWATER

noon–5, Memorial Day through Labor Day; weekends and by appointment the rest of the year. Adults $7, children 5–12 $5, children 4 and under free. These caves were once used for breweries, and today tours illuminate both the caves and the history behind the brewing. Private wine tastings can be arranged through the adjacent Luna Rossa Wine Bar (see *Where to Eat*).

✳ Green Space and Outdoor Activities

PARKS Afton State Park (651-436-5391; www.dnr.state.mn.us/state _parks/afton/index.html), Afton. A beautiful nature preserve that provides a strenuous workout for visitors. There are 20 miles of hiking trails, most of which have some sharply steep inclines. However, the views of the St. Croix River make it worth the effort. One area allows horseback riders, and several miles of trail are open for cross-country skiers in the winter. Year-round camping is available.

SKIING Afton Alps (651-436-5245 or 1-800-328-1328; www.aftonalps .com), Afton. This is one of the biggest Minnesota ski resorts, with 40 trails and 18 lifts, a snowboard park, and a tubing hill. During the summer, the resort is open for mountain bikers, and an 18-hole course is available for golfers.

TOURS St. Croix Boat & Packet Company (651-430-1234; www .andiamo-ent.com), 525 S. Main Street, Stillwater. Open May through mid-Oct. Cruise the St. Croix River on your choice of a lunch, dinner, brunch, or live-music cruise. Boats are also available for private charter. Reservations are recommended.

Gondola Romantica (651-439-1783; www.gondolaromantica.com), 425 E. Nelson Street, Stillwater. Open daily May through Oct., weather permitting. Who needs Venice? This entrepreneurial effort brings romantic gondola rides to the St. Croix River. Options include everything from 20-minute sight-seeing cruises to a five-course dinner cruise. The company offers customized cruises as well. Gondolas hold six people, but if you'd like a private excursion, reserve ahead.

HOT-AIR BALLOONING

Given the beautiful scenery and the charming small towns, it's only logical that hot-air balloon rides would be a popular pastime in the lower St. Croix Valley. The following companies all offer hot-air balloon service daily May through October, weather permitting. Contact the individual companies for off-season possibilities.

Stillwater Balloons (651-439-1800; www.stillwaterballoons.com), 14791 N. 60th Street, Stillwater. Morning or late-afternoon departures are offered during the summer, but balloon rides (dependent on weather) can be done all year long, and all flights conclude with a champagne celebration. Rides start at $245 per person.

Wiederkehr Balloons (651-436-8172; www.angelfire.com/nm/flyballoons /main.html), Lakeland. Morning and afternoon departures are available, with a maximum of eight passengers at a time. Champagne is served at the conclusion of the ride. Rates start at $250 for the first person and $200 for subsequent guests in the same party. If a couple wishes to reserve a private balloon, rates start at $795.

Aamodt's Hot Air Balloon Rides (651-351-0101 or 1-866-546-8247; www .aamodtsballoons.com), Stillwater. Aamodt's offers hot-air balloon rides with departures from their apple orchard in Stillwater. Rides are reserved for two people only and include a champagne toast. Most rides are scheduled late in the day to take advantage of the views over the St. Croix, but sunrise departures can be accommodated. Rates start at $750 per couple.

Stillwater Trolley (651-430-0352; www.stillwatertrolley.com), 400 E. Nelson Street, Stillwater. Open daily May through Oct., weekends Apr. and Nov. Stillwater Trolley operates enclosed, climate-controlled trolleys that take visitors on a 45-minute guided tour of the Stillwater area.

WINERIES ❋ Northern Vineyards (651-430-1032; www.northernvine yards.com), 223 Main Street N., Stillwater. Open daily. This award-winning winery, which uses Minnesota and Wisconsin grapes, is open for tastings and tours. In the summer, enjoy a glass of wine on their back patio, overlooking the lift bridge across the river.

OTHER ACTIVITIES Lumberjack Sports Camp (651-439-5626), 12360 75th Street, Stillwater. Takes place each year in July during Lumberjack Days (see *Special Events*). Got a hankering to find out what life in the lumber industry was really like? Sign up for this camp, which will put you to work learning about log rolling and cross-cut sawing.

❋ Lodging

Stillwater is blessed with a number of historic—and romantic—inns for visitors, as well as bed & breakfasts.

BED & BREAKFASTS ❋ The Elephant Walk (651-430-0559 or 1-888-430-0359; www.elephant walkbb.com), 801 W. Pine Street, Stillwater. This detailed Victorian home is the residence of globe-trotting owners who have filled the interior with finds from their travels in Europe and Asia. Each of the four sumptuously decorated rooms has a theme: The Rangoon, Chiang Mai, Cadiz, and Raffles rooms are all decorated according to their geographic designation. All rooms have fireplaces and refrigerators with complimentary nonalcoholic beverages; a bottle of wine and appetizers, as well as a four-course breakfast, are included in the rates. Expensive.

❋ (ᵖ) **The Ann Bean Mansion** (651-430-0355 or 1-877-837-4400; www.annbeanmansion.com), 319 W. Pine Street, Stillwater. This whimsical home has a colorful history, complete with riches and scandal, and today it has five lovely rooms, all with fireplaces and private baths. The Tower Room is a particularly cozy choice. Rooms come with plush robes, and rates include an afternoon glass of wine and full breakfast daily. Expensive.

❋ **Rivertown Inn** (651-430-2955; www.rivertowninn.com), 306 W. Olive Street, Stillwater. Sitting on a hillside above Stillwater, the Rivertown provides beautiful views along with four rooms and five suites, all elaborately decorated and named after literary heavyweights (Lord Byron, Longfellow). The inn is open year-round, but summer visitors will enjoy the use of the private gardens and screened gazebo. All accommodations have luxurious bedding, plush robes, turndown service with handmade chocolates, full breakfast, and evening social hour. Very expensive.

✳ **Lady Goodwood** (651-439-3771 or 1-866-688-5239; www.ladygoodwood.com), 704 First Street S., Stillwater. This lovingly restored 1895 Queen Anne home has several original details, including a parlor fireplace. The three guest rooms are all lavishly decorated in Victorian style and have private baths; the St. Croix Suite comes with a round king-sized bed. Expensive. Packages are available.

INNS ⚹ ⅄ ✳ **Lowell Inn** (651-439-1100; www.lowellinn.com), 102 N. Second Street, Stillwater. The Lowell Inn is the granddaddy of historic hotels in Stillwater. Built in 1927 on the site of a former lumberjack hotel, this stately building has 23 impeccably decorated rooms, some with stained-glass windows, antique furnishings, and fireplaces, but all with modern conveniences. Several rooms have Jacuzzis. The romance factor here is high. The hotel also has two highly regarded restaurants on-site (see *Where to Eat*). Moderate. Packages are available.

⚹ ⅄ ✳ **Water Street Inn** (651-439-6000; www.waterstreetinn.us), 101 Water Street S., Stillwater. A small luxury inn with rooms and suites, most with gas fireplaces. The rooms are decorated as befit-

ting the upscale visitors of the lumber boom days. A well-regarded restaurant and pub round out the amenities. Expensive. Packages involving meals, flowers, and massages are available.

✎ ⚹ ⅄ **Afton House Inn** (651-436-8883; www.aftonhouseinn.com), 3291 S. St. Croix Trail, Afton. Afton House has 46 rooms, most with canopy or four-poster beds, and deluxe rooms have balconies overlooking the St. Croix River. The location near Afton Alps (see *Green Space and Outdoor Activities*) makes this a good choice for a ski weekend, with a warm, romantic hideaway to return to at the end of the day. The inn has a restaurant and bar on-site. Expensive. Packages are available.

✷ Where to Eat

The lower St. Croix Valley enjoys an affluent resident population and close proximity to the Twin Cities, giving it an abundance of notable dining options, even off-season.

DINING OUT ✎ ⚹ ⅄ ✳ **Luna Rossa** (651-430-0560; www.lunarossawinebar.com), 402 S. Main Street, Stillwater. Open daily for lunch and dinner. Luna Rossa bills itself as an Italian steakhouse, but that's somewhat of a misnomer; there are plenty of steak and grilled meat options, but the restaurant also has a respectable list of Italian pasta and pizza dishes that are equally worthy of attention. You

LUNA ROSSA IS JUST ONE OF SEVERAL DINING AND SHOPPING OPTIONS IN HISTORIC DOWNTOWN STILLWATER.

can add some sight-seeing to your meal by booking a Joseph Wolf Brewery Cave Tour (see *To See and Do*). Expensive.

DOCK CAFÉ

✐ ♿ ⛾ ❄ **Savories** (651-430-0702; www.savoriesbistro.com), 108 N. Main Street, Stillwater. Open Tues. through Sun. for lunch and dinner, Thurs. through Sun. for all three meals. The menu changes seasonally at this European bistro-themed restaurant, and there is always something innovative offered. Entrées combine Italian and Latin foods, and vegetarians are not ignored. Don't skip dessert. Expensive.

⛾ ❄ **Dock Café** (651-430-3770; www.dockcafe.com), 425 S. Nelson Street, Stillwater. Open daily for lunch and dinner. It's open year-round, but this is the place to be during the warm weather months. Situated right on the banks of the St. Croix, the Dock

Café has outdoor seating that gives diners full views of river life. Not surprisingly, the outdoor patio is popular—plan to arrive early, or wait. However, the indoor ambience is attractive as well, with a fireplace and wide windows. Menu items run heavily to meats and seafood. Expensive.

 ⛟ ♈ ❄ **Lowell Inn** (651-439-1100; www.lowellinn.com), 102 N. Second Street, Stillwater. Open daily for lunch and dinner. Within the historic Lowell Inn (see *Lodging*) are two restaurants worth noting. The formal restaurant, in the elegant George Washington Room, serves classic dinner entrées such as duck à l'orange and beef Wellington, while the Matterhorn Room serves a four-course Swiss dinner fondue each evening. Expensive.

🖊 ⛟ ♈ ❄ **Lake Elmo Inn** (651-777-8495; www.lakeelmoinn.com), 3442 Lake Elmo Avenue N., Lake Elmo. Open daily for lunch and dinner. Housed in a former stagecoach stop, the Lake Elmo Inn serves upscale fare in a "come as you are" ambience. Seafood (local and saltwater), pork, and pasta are the specialties, but be sure to save room for the Sin of the Inn dessert (if it's still on the periodically changing menu). Kids are welcome to check out the "young adult" menu, and there are vegetarian and gluten-free menus as well. Expensive.

🖊 ♈ ❄ **Smalley's Caribbean Barbeque and Pirate Bar** (651-439-5375; www.smalleyspiratebbq.com), 423 Main Street S., Stillwater. Open daily for lunch and

SMALLEY'S CARIBBEAN BARBEQUE, STILLWATER

dinner. Wonder chef Tim McKee teamed up with Shawn Smalley to create this casual barbecue spot on the southern end of downtown Stillwater. You can't go wrong with any of the barbecued entrées, including sugar-cane-skewered shrimp and jerk-grilled ahi tuna along with more traditional grilled meats, but this is also a restaurant that pays attention to its side dishes. The mac 'n' cheddar, chiles and bacon optional, is outstanding, as are the curried vegetables and roasted sweet potatoes with sausage and pork. Smalley's has an attractive outdoor patio and frequently offers live music. The bar has more than 150 kinds of rum available, including the high-octane Kill Devil. Expensive.

✔ ⵏ ❄ **Patriot's Tavern** (651-342-1472; www.patriotstav.com), 145 New England Place, Stillwater. Open daily for lunch and dinner. An American-themed tavern right down to its architecture, Patriot's offers up a solid menu of pizzas, sandwiches, and entrées like Dingle Fish Pie and Ale Potted Beef Skillet. Expensive.

ⵏ ❄ **Phil's Tara Hideaway** (651-439-9850; www.tarahideaway.com), 15021 60th Street N., Stillwater. Open daily for lunch and dinner. This highly regarded new entry into Stillwater's restaurant scene offers a combination of Mediterranean and American cuisine in a log-cabin-themed building. The food tastes high-end, but prices are reasonable given the quality. Expensive.

EATING OUT ✔ ♿ ❄ **Aprille's Showers Tea Room** (651-430-2004; www.aprilleshowers.com), 120 N. Main Street, Stillwater. Open Tues. through Sun. for tea and luncheon. Walk-ins welcome, but call ahead for special theme teas, including American Girl doll tea parties. Aprille's Showers offers 35 kinds of tea, as well as the traditional tea foods such as scones and finger sandwiches. Moderate.

✔ ❄ **The Bikery** (651-439-3834; www.thebikeryshop.com), 904 Fourth Street S., Stillwater. Open daily. A combination coffee shop, bakery, and bike shop, the Bikery offers gourmet pastries and high-quality coffee, along with bicycle sales and service. Inexpensive.

❄ Selective Shopping

Stillwater's main city center, along the riverfront, has developed into a visitor's shopping haven full of small, charming shops, with hardly any chain stores to be seen. Antiques enthusiasts flock to this community for its large concentration of antiques stores and dealers, but there are plenty of other kinds of retail as well.

ANTIQUES ❄ **Staples Mill Antiques** (651-430-1816 or 1-888-489-6682; www.staplesmill antiques.com), 410 N. Main Street, Stillwater. Open daily. Located in a historic mill, Staples Mill Antiques is comprised of nearly 80 antiques and collectibles dealers spread over 10,000 square feet and three floors. A great spot for serious antiquing or window shopping.

❋ **Midtown Antique Mall** (651-430-0808; www.midtownantiques.com), 301 S. Main Street, Stillwater. Open daily. A good source for antiques enthusiasts, the Midtown Antique Mall has more than 100 dealers, including several furniture dealers.

ARTS AND CRAFTS ❋ **North Main Studio** (651-351-1379; www.northmainstudio.com), 402 N. Main Street, Stillwater. Open only by appointment. Local resident and artist Carl Erickson displays and sells the pottery he creates here. Visitors are welcome to watch him at work.

❋ **Tamarack House Gallery** (651-439-9393; www.tamarackgallery.com), 112 S. Main Street, Stillwater. Open daily. Local and national artists are represented in various mediums, including painting, etching, sculpture, and photography.

❋ **Art 'n' Soul/Stillwater Beads** (651-275-0255), 202 S. Main Street, Stillwater. Open daily. There are upscale and humorous gifts at Art 'n' Soul, while Stillwater Beads sells a wide variety of beads, including some unusual and hard-to-find items.

✄ ❋ **Darn Knit Anyway** (651-342-1386; www.darnknitanyway.com), 423 Main Street, Stillwater. Located near Smalley's Caribbean Barbeque (see *Where to Eat*),

Darn Knit Anyway offers a vast and wide-ranging selection of knitting and crochet items, as well as fabric for the sewing enthusiast.

BOOKS ❋ **Loome Antiquarian Booksellers** (651-430-1092; www.loomebooks.com), 201 S. Main Street, Stillwater. Open Mon. through Sat. A bookseller for serious book collectors, Loome has hundreds of thousands of books available. There are also framed engravings for sale, as well as medieval manuscript leaves. A short walk away is the store's sister, Loome Theological Booksellers, specializing in secondhand books on theology and religion.

GIFTS ✄ ❋ **The Chef's Gallery** (651-351-1144; www.thechefsgallery.com), 324 S. Main Street, Stillwater. Open daily. The store for all things cookery, Chef's Gallery has a wide selection of cooking tools and gadgets. The shop also offers an extensive list of cooking classes.

TREATS ✄ ❋ **St. Croix Chocolate Company** (651-433-1400; www.stcroixchocolateco.com), 261 Parker Street, Marine on St. Croix. Open Thurs. through Sun. Handcrafted, beautiful, decadent chocolates, made with chocolate from Belgium, Switzerland, and Venezuela, in combination with locally sourced cream and honey from the store owner's own honeybees.

✳ Special Events

May: **Rivertown Art Festival** (651-439-4001; www.rivertownart festival.com), Stillwater. Held each year in late May, the Rivertown Art Festival takes place on the banks of the St. Croix River and brings dozens of artists in various mediums, some local and some national, to display their work. Food and kids' activities are available.

Afton May Fair (651-263-5159; www.aftonmnarea.com), Afton. Complete with maypole and ribbons, the Afton May Fair takes place in late May each year, with three days of music, art shows, wine tasting from local vineyards, Native American storytelling, and Scandinavian folk dancing.

July: **Lumberjack Days** (651-430-2306; www.lumberjackdays .com), Stillwater. A summer tradition, Lumberjack Days is held in Lowell Park on the St. Croix in mid-July and offers three days of historically themed fun and frolic. Among the events is the Lumberjack Sports Camp (see *Green Space and Outdoor Activities*), a chess tournament, massive parade, an 1860 vintage "base ball" exhibition, treasure hunt, 5K and 10K races, and lumberjack skills championships.

October: **Fall Colors Fine Art & Jazz Festival** (651-439-4001; www.ilovestillwater.com), Stillwater. An early-Oct. celebration of vivid fall colors, the festival showcases the talents of 100 artists, as well as live jazz daily, a Main Street Art Crawl, and a variety of kids' activities.

Mississippi River Bluff Country

7

HASTINGS

RED WING

WABASHA

WINONA

LANESBORO

AUSTIN

ROCHESTER

NORTHFIELD

INTRODUCTION TO THE MISSISSIPPI RIVER BLUFF COUNTRY

The southeastern corner of the state, bordered by the mighty Mississippi to the east, has some of the loveliest terrain in Minnesota: river valleys, rolling hills, woods, and wildflowers in season, and one charming small town after the other, including some of the oldest towns in the state, most with many intact historic buildings and landmarks. Unlike more northern reaches, which were leveled and redesigned during the last ice age, the bluff country mostly escaped the glacial ravages and kept instead a variable terrain that includes 500-foot limestone bluffs and deep valleys. The climate here is slightly different, too, warmer and with more rainfall, leading to vegetation not seen elsewhere in the state, including black walnut trees. The region is also home to Minnesota's only poisonous snakes, the timber rattlesnake and the massasauga, which reside mostly in the bluffs themselves or in the swampy areas close to the river. But these snakes are as timid of humans as we are of them and are slow to strike.

Bike trails abound, many of which are paved and can be used for cross-country skiing in the winter months. As you travel westward from the river, clusters of tight-knit Amish communities stand in contrast to the sophistication of cities like Rochester and the tasteful attraction of SPAM in Austin.

GUIDANCE Hastings Area Chamber of Commerce (651-437-6775 or 1-888-612-6122; www.hastingsmn.org), 111 E. Third St., Hastings.

Red Wing Convention and Visitors Bureau (651-385-5934 or 1-800-498-3444; www.redwing.org), 420 Levee St., Red Wing.

Wabasha/Kellogg Chamber of Commerce and Convention and Visitors Bureau (651-565-4158 or 1-800-565-4158; www.wabashamn.org), 137 Main St., Wabasha.

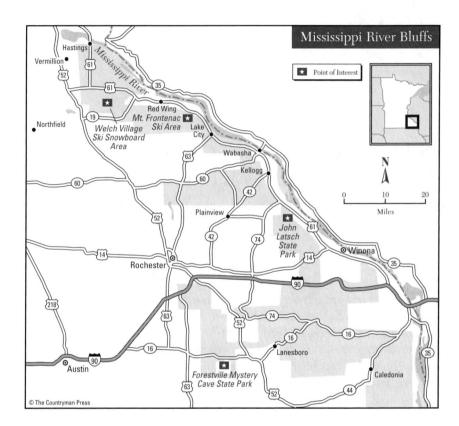

Visit Winona (507-452-0735 or 1-800-657-4972; www.visitwinona.com), 924 Huff St., Winona. Offers extensive lodging and activity information for the Winona area.

Rochester Convention and Visitors Bureau (507-288-4331 or 1-800-634-8277; www.rochestercvb.org), 30 Civic Center Dr. SE, Suite 200, Rochester.

Northfield Convention and Visitors Bureau (507-645-5604 or 1-800-658-2548; www.visitingnorthfield.com), 205 Third St. W., Suite A, Northfield.

Lanesboro Chamber of Commerce (507-467-2696 or 1-800-944-2670; www.lanesboro.com), 100 Milwaukee Rd., Lanesboro.

GETTING THERE *By air:* Regional commercial airlines, primarily Delta Air Lines and its Mesaba branch, serve the city of Rochester. Taxis and rental cars are available from **Rochester International Airport** (507-

By car: US 52 leads south from the Twin Cities into Rochester and connects south of Rochester with I-90, which heads west to Austin or east to Wisconsin. Visitors to Northfield can use MN 19 from US 52. To visit the towns closest to the Mississippi River area, US 61 travels south along the river until it merges with I-90.

By rail: **AMTRAK** (1-800-872-7245; www.amtrak.com) has stops in Red Wing and Winona, crossing through from either Minneapolis/St. Paul or Chicago. Local stations include the **Red Wing Station,** 420 Levee Street, Red Wing, and the **Winona Station,** 65 E. Mark Street, Winona.

GETTING AROUND Having a vehicle is a necessity when traveling around the Mississippi River bluffs region.

WHEN TO COME The summer months are the most popular time to visit the river bluffs area, although fall foliage continues to draw larger numbers as well. Rochester benefits from the Mayo Clinic's presence to bring in people year-round.

MEDICAL EMERGENCY Call 911.

Regina Medical Center (651-480-4100; www.reginamedical.org), 1175 Nininger Rd., Hastings.

Fairview Red Wing Medical Center (651-267-5000 or 1-866-297-9215; www.redwing.fairview.org), 701 Fairview Blvd., Red Wing.

St. Elizabeth's Hospital (651-565-4531; www.ministryhealth.org), 1200 Grant Blvd. W., Wabasha.

Community Memorial Hospital (507-454-3650 or 1-800-944-3960; www.winonahealth.org), 855 Mankato Ave., Winona.

Northfield Hospital (507-646-1000; www.northfieldhospital.org), 2000 North Ave., Northfield.

Rochester Methodist Hospital (507-266-7890; www.mayoclinic.org /methodisthospital/), 201 W. Center St., Rochester. Part of the Mayo Clinic's broad range of medical services.

Saint Marys Hospital (507-255-5123; www.mayoclinic.org/saintmarys hospital/), 1216 Second St. SW, Rochester. The second of two Mayo Clinic hospitals.

HASTINGS

Hastings is truly a river town, with the Mississippi, St. Croix, and Vermilion rivers all part of the city. It was initially created in 1820 by a military detachment sent to guard blocked shipments of supplies to Fort Snelling. Later it was expected to be a major Midwestern city, given its river access, but the financial downturn of 1857 stalled its growth. Today, it's a charming city with plenty of reminders of its historic river past for visitors to enjoy.

✳ To See and Do

GAMING ᕃ 🍸 ✳ **Treasure Island Resort and Casino** (1-800-222-7077; www.treasureislandcasino.com), 5734 Sturgeon Lake Road, Welch. Open 24/7. Slots, blackjack, poker, and bingo are all available in this massive complex southeast of Hastings. Four restaurants and several cocktail bars provide sustenance, and an attached hotel (see *Lodging*) and marina provide options besides gambling.

MUSEUMS AND HISTORIC SITES ✑ **The LeDuc House** (651-437-7055; www.dakotahistory.org/LeDuc/home.asp), 1629 Vermillion Street, Hastings. Open Wed. through Sat. 10–5 and Sun. 1–5, Memorial Day through Oct.; also for special holiday events (see website). Adults $6, seniors and military personnel $5, children 6–17 $3, children 5 and under and Dakota County Historical Society members free. This beautiful piece of history and architecture, built in 1866, was designed by Andrew Jackson Downing and is rare in that it is virtually untouched. The former home of William LeDuc, a commissioner of agriculture under President Rutherford Hayes, the building itself is a delight to visit, but the 4.5-acre grounds are lovely as well, encompassing an apple orchard and forests.

WINERIES ᕃ 🍸 **Alexis Bailly Vineyard** (651-437-1413; www.abvwines.com), 18200 Kirby Avenue, Hastings. Open Fri. through Sun.

11–5:30, May through Thanksgiving; Fri. and Sat. 11–5:30, Apr. and Thanksgiving through Christmas. Closed Christmas through Mar. Minnesota's first and arguably foremost vineyard, Alexis Bailly first produced a vintage in 1978. The winery works with classic and new-breed grapes that have been found to withstand extreme cold.

✳ Green Space and Outdoor Activities

BIKING Hastings Trail System (651-480-6175), Hastings. The 15-mile paved bike trail winds through Hastings and along the Mississippi River.

PARKS ♿ Carpenter St. Croix Valley Nature Center (651-437-4359; www.carpenternaturecenter .org), 12805 St. Croix Trail, Hastings. Open daily. Admission is free. This small (425 acres) but lavish nature preserve was once a private estate and apple orchard. Today it is a well-maintained natural area, the release site for the University of Minnesota's Raptor Rehabilitation Program, and offers 10 miles of trails, some of which have been adapted for visitors with limited mobility.

Vermillion Falls Park, 215 21st Street E., Hastings. This park, right in the heart of Hastings, has both beautiful waterfalls and trails for hiking and biking. An oasis in the city.

Kim Hoffbeck, Hoffbeck Photography

HASTINGS

✳ Lodging

BED & BREAKFASTS ❋ **Classic Rosewood Inn** (651-437-3297; www.thorwoodinn.com), 620 Ramsey Street, Hastings. This beautiful 1880 Queen Anne home has been updated to include modern amenities in a classic B&B venue. Eight rooms and suites, all with private bath and most with fireplaces and whirlpools, are richly decorated and large enough to allow massage therapists to set up tables for private sessions (reserve in advance). A full breakfast is included each day, either in the dining room or privately. Expensive. Packages are available.

HOTELS ✈ ♿ ♟ ❋ **Treasure Island Resort and Casino** (1-888-867-7829; www.treasure islandcasino.com), 5734 Sturgeon Lake Road, Welch. With more than 200 rooms and suites, an elaborate indoor pool and whirl-pool, a fitness center, and child-care center, Treasure Island caters to the gambling crowd but offers additional amenities to bring in nongambling spouses and family members. Moderate. Packages are available.

❋ Where to Eat

DINING OUT ✈ ♿ ♟ ❋ **The Busted Nut** (651-438-6887; www .thebustednut.com), 118 Second Street E., Hastings. Open Tues. through Sun. for lunch and din-ner. Solid tavern menu in a charming building in historic downtown Hastings. Expensive.

EATING OUT ✈ ♿ ♟ ❋ **RJ's Tav-ern** (651-437-8772; http://rjstavern .com), 106 Second Street E., Hastings. Open daily for lunch and dinner. Near the Busted Nut, RJ's is a cozy, historic tavern with hearty sandwiches and soups. Moderate.

✈ ♿ ❋ **Karl's Red Rock Café** (651-437-5002; http://karlsredrock cafe.com), 119 Second Street E., Hastings. Open daily for breakfast and lunch. Great diner food, right

down to the occasional hot plate special. Inexpensive.

❋ Selective Shopping

ANTIQUES ✈ ♿ ❋ **The Empo-rium** (651-438-5444; www.the emporiumofhastings.com), 213 E. Second Street, Hastings. Open daily. A two-story antiques and consignment gallery specializing in vintage furniture, dolls, jewelry, and primitive tools and pottery.

❋ **Antiques on Main** (651-480-8129), 205 Second Street E., Hastings. Open daily. Twenty dealers, many of whom buy entire estates.

❋ **The Briar Patch** (651-437-4400), 103 E. Second Street, Hastings. Open Tues. through Sat. Vintage clothing, jewelry, and accessories.

ARTS AND CRAFTS
♿ ❋ **Mississippi Clayworks** (651-437-5901; www.mississippi clayworks.com), 214 Second Street E., Hastings. Open Mon. through Sat. Locally made pottery, including custom orders.

❋ Special Events

Memorial Day Weekend through September: ✈ **Hastings Down-town Saturday Night Cruise-In** (651-437-4400; www.hastings downtown-mn.com/cruise-in /index.html), Hastings. Summer Sat. nights in Hastings draw thou-sands of visitors for this annual tradition. Cars that are at least 30

Kim Hoffbeck, Hoffbeck Photography

HISTORIC DOWNTOWN HASTINGS

years old are given cruising rights down the main drag, with prizes and special weekly events.

July: ⚓ ♿ **Little Log House Pioneer Village and Antique Power Show** (651-437-2693; www.littleloghouseshow.com/), 13746 220th Street E., Hastings. Held the last weekend in July. This pioneer village is larger than most, with 45 buildings, a replica bridge, extensive gardens, and even a dirt racetrack for vintage-auto races. The only downside to the village is that it's not open to the general public except during this annual event, which displays antique vehicles and machines, and offers demonstrations, live music, Old West reenactments, tractor and truck pulls, and a parade. Campsites and RV sites available for rental.

RED WING

P roximity to the Mississippi River and lush farmlands gave Red Wing its start in the wheat and milling business, until the railroads gave Minneapolis access to southern Minnesota crops. But Red Wing became a favorite place to visit, especially for day-trippers from the Twin Cities, due to its spectacular surrounding river-bluff views and the shopping available from local manufacturers of Red Wing Shoes and Red Wing Pottery.

✳ To See and Do

✂ ♿ ✳ **Goodhue County Historical Society** (651-388-6024; www.good huehistory.mus.mn.us), 1166 Oak Street, Red Wing. Open Tues. through Fri. 10–5, Sat. and Sun. 1–5. Adults $5, seniors $3, unaccompanied

RED WING

343

children over 10 $0.25, accompanied children under 16 and historical society members free. This sizable regional museum has extensive collections on numerous aspects of the area's history, including archaeology, business, geology, immigration, and agriculture. A clothing exhibit has samples for kids to try out, and there's a tepee to play in. Note: The historical society is in the process of placing signage throughout the county, noting the prior existence of what are now known as ghost towns.

♂ ♿ ❋ **Red Wing Shoe Museum** (651-385-1811), 315 Main Street, Red Wing. Open Mon. through Fri. 9–8, Sat. 9–6, and Sun. 11–5. Admission is free. Red Wing Shoes are indeed manufactured in Red Wing, and this small but lively museum in the Riverfront Centre has hands-on and historical exhibits showing how the shoes are made and sold, including the opportunity to try to build your own shoe.

♂ ♿ ❋ **Red Wing Pottery Museum** (www.rwcsfoundation.org/museum .htm), Historic Pottery Place Mall, 2000 Old W. Main Street, Red Wing. Open Mon. through Sat. 10–6, Sun. 11–5. Admission is free. Just like Red Wing Shoes, Red Wing Pottery is made in Red Wing, and it has a museum. Located within a former pottery factory (see *Selective Shopping*), this museum has displays illustrating the pottery process and history, and has an impressive collection of finished objects and historical pieces.

❋ Green Space and Outdoor Activities

BIKING Cannon Valley Trail (507-263-0508; www.cannonvalleytrail .com). A 20-mile paved trail that runs on an old railroad track from Red Wing to Cannon Falls along the Cannon River. A Wheel Pass (adults $4

RED WING CITY PARK

FRONTENAC STATE PARK

per day, or $25 for the season) is required. **Cannon Falls Canoe and Bike** (507-263-4657 or 1-877-882-2663; www.cannonfallscanoeandbike .com) in Cannon Falls offers kayak, canoe, and bike rentals as well as shuttle services. Bike offerings include tandem and recumbent bikes, as well as baby carts.

PARKS AND PARKWAYS Great River Road (1-800-657-3700), US 61. This section of the scenic byway that runs from Canada to the Gulf of Mexico departs Red Wing and travels to La Crescent, running along the Mississippi River. The 107-mile byway encompasses river views, forests, small and historic river towns and villages, and countless opportunities for natural and wildlife exploration.

Frontenac State Park (651-345-3401; www.dnr.state.mn.us/state_parks /frontenac/index.html), 29223 County Route 28 Boulevard, Frontenac. This state park is especially valuable for birdwatchers, with more than 250 species of birds recorded here. Camping, hiking, and a winter sliding hill are among the amenities spread across the park's prairie, forest, and river bluff settings.

SKIING Welch Village (651-258-4567; www.welchvillage.com), 26685 County Route 7 Boulevard, Welch. Fifty runs of varying difficulty for skiers and snowboarders, as well as a terrain park. The village also offers slopeside bunkhouses for rental, which are rustic with shared baths but offer the utmost in convenient access for devoted skiers and boarders.

✳ Lodging

Red Wing is a community full of historic inns and bed & breakfasts. As many of these inns are small and Red Wing is a popular destination, be sure to book ahead.

✐ ♿ ☿ ❄ (((•))) **St. James Hotel** (1-800-252-1875; www.st-james -hotel.com), 406 Main Street, Red Wing. Built in 1875, the St. James is *the* hotel in Red Wing. All rooms are decorated in handsome Victorian style; larger rooms have whirlpools, and two deluxe rooms include spacious seating areas.

THE ST. JAMES HOTEL

Two full-service restaurants stand on their own (the Port being a popular restaurant that draws many Twin Cities diners; see *Where to Eat*), and there's a pub and coffee shop as well. Expensive. Packages are available.

✐ 🐾 ❄ (((•))) **Moondance Inn** (651-388-8145 or 1-866-388-8145; www.moondanceinn.com), 1105 W. Fourth Street, Red Wing. This beautiful stone inn has five spacious guest rooms, all with private bath and fireplace, and featuring antique furniture and sumptuous decor. Rates include daily breakfast as well as wine and cheese on weekends. Next to the Moondance is the Guesthouse Next Door, a 1904 Victorian home that is rented as a whole unit. It holds 10 people, and children and pets are welcome. Expensive to very expensive. Packages are available.

❄ **Round Barn Farm** (651-385-9250 or 1-866-763-2276; www .roundbarnfarm.com), 28650 Wildwood Lane, Red Wing. Round Barn Farm, built in 1861 just 4 miles outside of Red Wing, offers five spacious rooms beautifully decorated in vintage country style, complete with antique furniture, private baths, and fireplaces or Franklin stoves. Breakfast is provided daily in the dining room, which features a massive limestone fireplace. The property is located on 35 acres complete with walking trails and a gazebo. Expensive. Packages are available.

❄ (((•))) **Candlelight Inn** (651-388-8034 or 1-800-254-9194; www

.candlelightinn-redwing.com), 818 W. Third Street, Red Wing. A striking Victorian home offering five rooms and suites, all with private baths and fireplaces. While all the rooms are beautifully decorated, the Butternut Suite in particular is a lesson in opulence and luxury. Full breakfast and afternoon appetizers, wine, and lemonade provided for guests daily. Expensive. Packages are available.

❈ **Golden Lantern Inn** (651-388-3315 or 1-888-288-3315; www.goldenlantern.com), 721 East Avenue, Red Wing. Built in 1923 by the former president of the Red Wing Shoe Company, this English tudor has five lush rooms and suites, and several public rooms available to guests. Bedrooms all have private baths, and some have fireplaces, sitting rooms, and private balconies. Full breakfast is included daily and is available in the dining room, bedroom, or (during warmer months) on the stone patio. During the summer months, guests have access to the lavish gardens behind the inn. Expensive. Packages are available.

❈ **Hungry Point Inn** (651-437-3660; www.hungrypointinn.com), 1 Olde Deerfield Road, Welch. Four rooms with private baths, as well as a separate log cottage, in a New England–esque setting. Accommodations are meticulously appointed with antiques and decorations befitting the early American ambience, although the building itself dates from 1967

(meaning modern amenities are firmly in place). One of the rooms has a fireplace, while two others have vintage soaking tubs. Full breakfast is included. Expensive.

✳ Where to Eat

DINING OUT ♿ ⍵ ✳ **The Port Restaurant** (651-388-2846 or 1-800-252-1875; www.port -restaurant.com), 406 Main Street, Red Wing. Open Tues. through Sat. for dinner. Located in the St. James Hotel (see *Lodging*), this warmly elegant, romantic restaurant offers steakhouse foods (steaks, seafood, pasta) with unconventional twists. The food is excellent, and reservations are strongly recommended. Expensive.

EATING OUT ✐ ♿ ✳ **The Veranda** (651-388-2846 or 1-800-252-1875; www.port-restaurant .com), 406 Main Street, Red Wing. Open daily for breakfast and lunch. A more casual full-service restaurant in the St. James Hotel (see *Lodging*), the Veranda overlooks the Mississippi and has outdoor dining in season. Traditional breakfast and lunch fare is served. Moderate.

✐ ♿ ⍵ ✳ **Liberty's** (651-388-8877; www.libertysonline.com), 303 W. Third Street, Red Wing. Open daily for all three meals. There can be no complaints about access to this restaurant—not only do they deliver throughout Red Wing, they also provide free shuttle service to and from boats and hotels. The menu aims to please with Italian, Mexican, burgers, and steaks; breakfast includes all-you-can-eat pancakes. Moderate.

✦ ♿ ❋ Lily's Coffee House (651-388-8797; www.lilyscoffee house.com), 419 W. Third Street, Red Wing. Open Tues. through Sun. for breakfast and lunch. A quintessential charming small-town coffee shop and café, Lily's surprisingly sizable menu includes sandwiches, salads, and soups, plus a wide variety of coffee drinks. Inexpensive.

✦ ♿ ♟ ❋ Blue Moon (651-385-5799; www.bluemoonrw.net), 427 W. Third Street, Red Wing. Open daily for all three meals. The Blue Moon started life as a bagel shop, then grew into a coffee shop, restaurant, and live-entertainment venue. Sandwiches, soups, and quesadillas are offered all day, and wine and beer are available. Live music is scheduled every weekend. Inexpensive.

❋ Entertainment

✦ ♿ ❋ Sheldon Theatre (651-388-8700 or 1-800-899-5759; www.sheldontheatre.org), 443 W. Third Street, Red Wing. This lovely turn-of-the-20th-century gem is a venue for a wide range of performances, including all genres of music, silent films, and stage productions.

❋ Selective Shopping

♿ ❋ **Historic Pottery Place Mall** (651-388-1428; www.rw potteryplace.com), 2000 W. Main Street, Red Wing. Open daily. Not all shopping malls are bland boxes. The Pottery Place Mall, in a renovated pottery factory and houses, has the Red Wing Pottery Mu-

THE SHELDON THEATRE

ANTIQUES

Red Wing has several good antiques stores that draw visitors from great distances. It helps that the antiques are sold in such a charming, historic locale.

& ❈ **3rd Floor Antiques** (651-388-3087; www.rwpotteryplace.com), Historic Pottery Place Mall, 2000 W. Main Street. Open daily.

& ❈ **Pottery Place Antiques** (651-388-7765; www.potteryplaceantiques .com), Historic Pottery Place Mall, 2000 W. Main Street. Open daily.

❈ **Memory Maker Antiques** (651-385-5914), 415 Main Street. Open daily.

❈ **Al's Antique Mall** (651-388-0572), 512 Plum Street. Open daily.

❈ **Teahouse Antiques** (651-388-3669), 703 W. Fourth Street. Generally open daily, but call ahead.

seum (see *To See and Do*), antiques shops, art galleries, home furnishings stores, gift shops, and purveyors of fine chocolates.

✿ & ❈ **Red Wing Pottery** (651-388-3562 or 1-800-228-0174; www .redwingpottery.com), 1920 W. Main Street, Red Wing. Open daily. In addition to a huge retail selection of Red Wing Pottery items (as well as Fiestaware), the Red Wing Pottery facility has several smaller but no less charming shops, including a Minnesota gift store, a candy shop, and a home and garden gift shop.

✿ & ❈ **Red Wing Shoe Store** (651-388-6233; www.redwingshoe .com), Riverfront Centre, 315 Main Street, Red Wing. Open daily. Not surprisingly, the flagship store of the Red Wing Shoe company sells a wide variety of their high-quality work and athletic shoes.

✿ & ❈ **Uffda Shop** (651-388-8436 or 1-800-488-3332; www .uffdashoponline.com), Bush and Main streets, Red Wing. Open daily. *Uffda,* which is a Norwegian exclamation, is the tongue-in-cheek name for this deeply Scandinavian store, filled with specialty baking needs (krumkake irons, lefse grills), fine porcelain tableware, and other gift items.

✳ Special Events

October: **Red Wing Fall Festival of Arts** (651-388-7569; www.red wingartsassociation.org), Red Wing. This event, taking place annually for more than 40 years, offers two days of art exhibitions, sales, and related activities.

WABASHA

Wabasha is the oldest continuously occupied city on the Mississippi River, having been founded in 1830 (but with residents documented in 1826). Besides its lovely riverside location, Wabasha is also known for being the site of the movies *Grumpy Old Men* and *Grumpier Old Men*. A large population of nesting eagles gave rise to the National Eagle Center, a popular attraction that houses live bald eagles and a golden eagle.

✳ To See and Do

✎ ♿ ✳ **National Eagle Center** (651-565-4989 or 1-877-332-4537; www.nationaleaglecenter.org), 50 Pembroke Avenue, Wabasha. Open Sun. through Thurs. 10–5, Fri. and Sat. 9–6. Adults $8, senior citizens $6, children 4–17 $3, children 3 and under free. Group discounts are available; call ahead for reservation. Located on the Mississippi River banks, the NEC has a 14,000-square-foot interpretive center with resident eagles, a viewing deck, housing for injured or sick eagles, exhibits with preserved animals and other artifacts, and demonstration and classroom areas. Every autumn the NEC holds a special "deck opening" event to mark the arrival of bald eagles for the winter; this area of the Mississippi has one of the

HISTORIC DOWNTOWN WABASHA

largest concentrations of bald eagles in the contiguous United States.

✔ **Wabasha County Historical Museum** (651-753-2893; www.wabashacountyhistory.org), US 61, Reads Landing. Open Sat. and Sun. 1–4, mid-May through mid-Oct., or by appointment. Admission is free. This small museum on the second floor of a former schoolhouse is not necessarily the most comprehensive historical museum in the state, but it does have some items of interest to fans of Laura Ingalls Wilder.

NATIONAL EAGLE CENTER

✔ ♿ ❄ **Arrowhead Bluffs Museum** (651-565-3829), 17505 667th Street, Wabasha. Open daily 10–5, May through Dec. Adults $6, students 12–18 $4, children 11 and under $3. A museum for hunting enthusiasts, the Arrowhead Bluffs has a large assortment of mounted wildlife specimens, pioneer and Native American artifacts, and a complete collection of Winchester guns manufactured from 1866 to 1982.

CITY PARK IN WABASHA

✳ Green Space and Outdoor Activities

❧ ⚓ ♀ **Lake Pepin Paddleboat** (651-345-5188; www.pearlofthelake .com), 100 Central Point Road, Lake City. Public cruises offered Wed. through Sun., mid-May through Oct. Private charters available. A replica of the grand old paddleboats that once dotted the local lakes and rivers, *Pearl of the Lake* offers public tours and dinner cruises, with snacks and full bar available on all sailings.

✳ Lodging

BED & BREAKFASTS

✳ **American Eagle Bluff Bed and Breakfast** (651-564-0372; www.americaneaglebluffbedand-breakfast.com), 70519 MN 61, Reads Landing. This lovely spot just outside Wabasha offers rooms in an 1870 redbrick farmhouse overlooking both the Mississippi River Valley and the Chippewa River Valley. The property has two suites, each with private baths. Expensive.

✳ ((ɲ)) ⌁ **The River Nest Bed and Breakfast** (651-560-4077; www .therivernest.com), 20073 County Route 77, Reads Landing. A newer-construction building right on the Mississippi, River Nest's two private suites each have a Jacuzzi tub and fireplace. The proprietors use geothermal heating and cooling. Expensive.

UNIQUE LODGINGS ❧ **Great River Houseboats** (651-789-4411; www.greatriverhouseboats .com), 1009 E. Main Street, Wabasha. Open May through Oct., weather permitting. Three houseboats for rent, two of which hold up to 10 people, one that holds a

maximum of four. The smaller boat rents for a two-night minimum, while the larger ones require a week. Very expensive.

❧ ✳ **America's Lofts of Wabasha/Eagles on the River** (651-565-3509 or 1-800-482-8188; www.eaglesontheriver.com), 152 W. Main Street, Wabasha. A historic building on the river now features suites and lofts, some of which are family friendly. Expensive.

✳ Where to Eat

DINING OUT ⚓ ♀ ✳ **Nosh** (651-345-2425; www.noshrestaurant .com), 310 S. Washington Street, Lake City. Open Wed. through Sun. for dinner. The arrival of Nosh in the small town of Lake City, midway between Red Wing and Wabasha, brought an upscale, trendy cuisine to the area that's been lacking. The food is Mediter-ranean based, but whenever possi-ble the chefs source locally for their foods, bringing in a Midwest theme as well. The main courses are spectacular, but an excellent meal can be had off the eatery's small plates menu. Save room for dessert. Expensive.

EATING OUT

✐ ♿ ♈ ❊ **The Olde Triangle Pub** (651-565-0256; www.theolde trianglepub.com), 219 Main Street, Wabasha. Open daily for lunch and dinner. A casual, friendly neighborhood spot with good pub grub, including bangers and mash, and Irish stew. Moderate.

✐ ♿ ♈ ❊ **Slippery's** (1-866-504-4036; www.slipperysumr.com), 10 Church Avenue, Wabasha. Open daily for lunch and dinner. Slippery's claim to fame was being mentioned in the *Grumpy Old Men* movies, which were filmed in the Wabasha area. The restaurant also has a boat-in feature and great views of the river. Burgers, steaks, and Mexican items are served in hearty portions. Moderate.

❋ Selective Shopping

✐ ❊ **LARK Toys** (507-767-3387; www.larktoys.com), US 61, Kellogg. Open daily Mar. through Dec., Fri. through Sun. Jan. and Feb. This massive toy complex (more than 30,000 square feet) is more than just a store, it's a playground. A working carousel offers rides, and a mini golf course is available during the warmer months. LARK stands for Lost Art Revival by Kreofsky, and vintage toys, many made out of wood, are produced and sold here, along with children's books. A café is on-site.

WINONA

The town of Winona was founded by a steamboat captain who saw the potential of having a river town set on an island in the Mississippi. During the lumber boom years, Winona was a thriving shipping town. Today it's a destination for tourists who enjoy the historical sites and the gorgeous bluffs—not to mention the quirky houseboats along the river.

✳ To See and Do

✿ ♿ ✳ **Historic Downtown Winona.** Winona has more than 100 buildings listed on the National Register of Historic Places, most built between 1857 and 1916 in Italianate or Queen Anne style. The best way to take in this large collection of Victorian commercial buildings (the largest concentration in Minnesota) is by foot. Free walking-tour brochures of the district are available from the convention and visitors bureau (507-452-0735 or 1-800-657-4972; 160 Johnson Street), the visitors center (924 Huff Street), or the Winona County Historical Society (507-454-2723; 160 Johnson Street).

✿ ♿ ✳ **Winona County Historical Museum** (507-454-2723; www .winonahistory.org), 160 Johnson Street, Winona. Open Mon. through Fri. 9–5 and Sat. and Sun. noon–4, Mar. through Dec., Mon. through Fri. 9–5, Jan. and Feb. Adults $5, students $3, children under 7 and Winona County Historical Society members free. The museum showcases a large and fascinating collection of local and regional historic exhibits, covering the

HISTORIC DOWNTOWN WINONA

usual (geologic history, river trade) as well as the less so (Cold War parking plans in the event of nuclear war). It's kid friendly, with lots of hands-on activities, including a climb-through cave and river steamboat.

BUNNELL HOUSE

🖋 **Bunnell House** (507-452-7575; www.winonahistory.org), MN 61 and County Route 14, Homer. Open Wed. through Sat. 10–5 and Sun. 1–5, June through Aug.; or by appointment. Adults $5, students $3, children under 7 and Winona County Historical Society members free. Built in the mid-1800s by a fur trader named Willard Bunnell, the wood-framed Bunnell House was built in the Rural Gothic style. Tours take visitors through all three floors, which are furnished with many pieces original to the time period.

🖋 ⅃ **Arches Museum of Pioneer Life** (507-523-2111; www.winona history.org), US 14, Winona. Open Wed. through Sun. 1–5, June through Aug.; or by appointment. Adults $5, students $3, children under 7 and Winona County Historical Society members free. A tribute to the long-lost days of roadside museums, the Arches has the collection of Walter Rahn, who apparently was fascinated with pioneer life and either collected or built items himself to illustrate their uses. The grounds also have a log cabin and a one-room schoolhouse.

MINNESOTA MARINE ART MUSEUM

🖋 ⅃ ❋ **Minnesota Marine Art Museum** (507-474-6626 or 1-866-940-6626; www.minnesotamarine art.org), 800 Riverview Drive, Winona. Open Tues. through Sun. 10–5. Adults $6, students $3, immediate families $20, children 4 and under free. This attractive new museum, located along the Mississippi, has an extensive collection of marine art, folk art, photography, maps, and historical displays. The lively and varied artworks include pieces by Monet, O'Keeffe, Van Gogh, and Picasso.

✂ & ❋ **Polish Cultural Institute** (507-454-3431; www.polish museumwinona.org), 102 Liberty Street, Winona. Open Mon. through Sat. 10–3, May through Oct.; Thurs. through Sat. 10–3, Nov. through Apr. Admission $2. Group discounts are available. At one time, Winona had the largest concentration of Polish immigrants in the United States, and this museum reflects that heritage with antiques, folk art, religious items, and displays detailing the immigrant experience.

POLISH CULTURAL INSTITUTE, WINONA

WATER MILL AT THE PICKWICK MILL

✂ **Pickwick Mill** (507-457-0499; www.pickwick mill.org), 26421 County Route 7, Pickwick. Open Tues. through Sat. 10–5 and Sun. 11–5, June through Aug.; weekends 11–5, May, Sept., and Oct.; by appoint-ment Nov. through Apr. Adults $3, teens $2, children 12 and younger $1. A Civil War–era water-powered gristmill, the Pickwick operat-ed continuously until 1978, and many of its original components and machines are on display today. The views from the upper floors of the mill are lovely.

✳ Green Space and Outdoor Activities

CITY PARKS Winona has several city parks, three of which are of special interest.

Windom Park, Huff and W. Broadway Street. Small, only a city block in size, it's surrounded by several Victorian homes (some of which are listed on the National Register of Historic Places), and it has a gazebo and a fountain with a sculpture of Princess Wenonah.

PICKWICK MILL

Lake Park, 900 Huff Street. On the shores of Lake Winona, Lake is a popular city park with an attractive rose garden (C.A. Rohrer Rose Garden), fishing piers, and a bandshell with weekly live concerts during the summer.

Gavin Heights City Park, Gavin Heights Road. Nearly 600 feet above the city, this overlook is spectacular, especially on a clear day.

LAKE WINONA

THE VIEW FROM THE TOP OF JOHN A. LATSCH STATE PARK

STATE PARKS John A. Latsch State Park (507-643-6849; www.dnr
.state.mn.us/state_parks/john_latsch/index.html), 43605 Kipp Drive,
Winona. One of the lesser-visited state parks, this is worth a trip if you're
ready for some exercise; there's a 0.5-mile stairway hike up to the top of
bluffs, which leads to outstanding views of the Mississippi and surrounding bluffs.

✳ Lodging

BED & BREAKFASTS

❉ **Alexander Mansion Bed and Breakfast** (507-474-4224; www.alexandermansionbb.com), 274 E. Broadway, Winona. Four elaborately detailed Victorian rooms, all with private bath; five-course breakfast and evening hors d'ouevres are included. The 1886 mansion also has an extensive screened porch for guests to enjoy. Expensive.

❉ **Carriage House Bed and Breakfast** (507-452-8256; www.chbb.com), 420 Main Street, Winona. Built by lumber baron Conrad Bohn, the Carriage House was literally that—it originally housed six carriages and several horses. Today the renovated house has four bedrooms, all with private baths, decorated in a cozy Victorian style. Breakfast is included daily, as is the use of single and tandem bicycles and, by prearrangement, a Model A Ford for local touring. Expensive.

❉ **Windom Park Bed and Breakfast** (507-457-9515 or 1-866-737-1719; www.windompark.com), 369 W. Broadway, Winona. Located near Windom Park, this Colonial Revival home was built in 1900 and has four beautiful rooms in the main house, all with private bath, and two lofts in the nearby carriage house. The lofts have fireplaces and two-person Jacuzzis. Breakfast is included each day, and guests are encouraged to use the other public rooms, which are also impeccably appointed. Innkeepers Craig and Karen Groth can assist with restaurant and theater recommendations and reservations. Expensive.

HOTELS ✎ 🐾 ♿ ♟ ❄ ((ᵞ)) **Holiday Inn Express** (507-474-1700 or

ALEXANDER MANSION BED AND BREAKFAST, WINONA

1-888-465-4329; www.ichotels
group.com), 1128 Homer Road,
Winona. Of the more conventional
hotels in Winona, the Holiday Inn
is the nicest, with an indoor pool,
sauna, and a daily hot breakfast
bar. Expensive.

♂ & ❋ (ᵂ) **AmericInn** (1-877-946-
6622; www.americinnmn.net), 60
Riverview Drive, Winona. The
AmericInn, located on the Mississippi River, has an indoor pool and
whirlpool, and includes continental breakfast daily. Less typical of
the usual AmericInn, this one has
a two-story Lighthouse Suite,
which has a private hot tub and
second-floor deck overlooking the
river. Moderate.

✳ Where to Eat

DINING OUT & Υ ❋ **Signatures**
(507-454-3767; www.signatures
winona.com), 22852 County Route
17, Winona. Open daily for lunch
and dinner. Don't let the somewhat blah interior fool you; the
food here is excellent, and you can
feast on the outdoor views
through the generous windows.
Signatures works closely with local
food producers, and this has
resulted in some of the region's
best and most innovative foods.
Expensive.

EATING OUT ♂ & Υ ❋ **Betty Jo
Byoloski's** (507-454-2687; www
.bettyjos.com), 66 Center Street,
Winona. Open daily for lunch and
dinner. Burgers, steak, shrimp,
sandwiches, salads—that's Betty
Jo's. This casual neighborhood

institution serves up the food in
hearty portions at reasonable
prices. Moderate.

♂ & ❋ (ᵂ) **Blue Heron Coffee
House** (507-452-7020; www.blue
heroncoffeehouse.com), 162 W.
Second Street, Winona. Open
Mon. through Sat. 7–6 and Sun.
9–4. Great home-cooked food
with an emphasis on local, seasonal, and organic when possible.
The menu of soups and sandwiches offers plenty of choices
for vegetarians and vegans. Check
out the list of local microbrews.
Inexpensive.

♂ & Υ ❋ **Green Mill** (507-452-
5400; www.greenmill.com), 1025
US 61, Winona. Open daily for
lunch and dinner. Pizza, pasta,
sandwiches, and salads. The deep-
dish pizza is the chain's specialty.
Moderate.

✳ Special Events

June–July: **Great River Shakespeare Festival** (507-474-7900;
http://grsf.org), Winona. Held late
June through late July. When
Great River opened its premier
season in 2003, there were plenty
of skeptics: Who would drive to
Winona to watch professional
Shakespearian theater? Turns out
plenty of people are happy to do
just that, especially when it takes
them into the heart of the river
bluff country. Great River performs two plays each year, a
tragedy and a comedy, and the
festival has quickly gained national
stature.

LANESBORO

The little town of Lanesboro is worth seeing in and of itself; the entire business district is on the National Register of Historic Places. This is arguably one of the most beautiful towns in the state. Take some time to wander at your leisure.

✳ To See and Do

Along the Minnesota-Iowa border is a small but thriving Amish community, and there are tour companies that offer rides through the beautiful area as well as stops at selected farms and shops. (For other more active tours, see *Green Space and Outdoor Activities*.)

✧ ♿ **Amish Tours of Harmony** (507-886-2303 or 1-800-752-6474; www.amish-tours.com), Harmony. Tours are given Mon. through Sat., Apr. through Nov. Adults $25, teens $20, children 4–12 $8, children 3 and under free. Discounts given if you use your own vehicle.

✧ ♿ **Flaby's Amish Tours** (507-467-2577 or 1-800-944-0099; http://flaby .tripod.com), Lanesboro. Tours are given Mon. through Sat., May through Oct. Adults $25, children $8, children 3 and under free.

✳ Green Space and Outdoor Activities

BIKING AND BOATING Root River and Harmony-Preston Valley Trails (www.rootrivertrail.org). This 60-mile paved trail system wanders along the Root River and through Lanesboro, offering both level trails (along a former railroad grade) and more challenging inclines that lead to gorgeous vistas. Those adventurous enough to bike the entire trail will be rewarded with changing scenery that includes wooded areas, rivers and bluffs, and an attractive array of wildlife. The trails are open for cross-country skiers in the winter (seasonal fees apply).

If the riverways are what you want, local outfitters will rent canoes, kayaks, and inner tubes. Contact **Root River Outfitters** (507-467-3663;

HISTORIC DOWNTOWN LANESBORO

www.rootriveroutfitters.com), which offers shuttle service for one-way journeys, or **Little River General Store** (507-467-2943; www.LRGeneral Store.net), which rents boating equipment. Both outfitters also rent bikes and offer shuttle service with them.

PARKS Forestville/Mystery Cave State Park (507-352-5111 or 507-935-3251; www.dnr.state.mn.us/state_parks/forestville_mystery_cave/index.html), 21071 County Route 118, Preston. Park is open daily. Cave tours offered daily Memorial Day through Labor Day, weekends mid-Apr. through Memorial Day and Labor Day through Oct. Forestville tours offered Tues. through Sat. Memorial Day through Labor Day, weekends Sept. and Oct. Cave tours: adults $10, children 5–12 $6, children under 5 free. Forestville tours: adults $6, senior citizens $5, children 6–17 $4, children under 6 and Minnesota Historical Society members free. This state park has something for everyone. Mystery

ROOT RIVER OUTFITTERS

Cave takes visitors to underground pools and geological cave formations; aboveground, hikers and horse riders have 15 miles of trails that wind through the bluff areas and through wildflowers (in the spring), and skiers and snowmobilers are welcome in winter. Forestville is a trip back in time to a once-functioning town that declined after the railroad bypassed it. Today visitors cross the Carnegie Steel Bridge to visit the general store, where costumed guides lead tours and demonstrate activities from the store's late-1800s roots, and give tourists the chance to work with the farm laborers in the garden.

✐ ♂ **Eagle Bluff Environmental Learning Center** (507-467-2437; www.eagle-bluff.org), 28097 Goodview Drive, Lanesboro. This environmental learning center, with 80 acres nestled into 1,000 acres of state forest, welcomes thousands of schoolchildren each year for environmental education. However, Eagle Bluff also welcomes families, retreats, and even weddings. Of special interest is the ropes course, in which participants (using safety gear, of course) cross a wire 30 feet high in the sky, along the treetops.

TOURS ✐ ♿ **Bluff Country Jeep Tours** (507-467-2415), Deep River Road, Lanesboro. Tours offered daily Apr. through Oct. (weather permitting). $60 per jeep load (three people maximum) per ride. For an adventurous ride, try this tour, which goes over rough terrain and up into the hills and bluffs overlooking the river. Tours last one hour; think hard if you get carsick easily.

LODGING AT EAGLE BLUFF ENVIRONMENTAL LEARNING CENTER

OLD GRIBBEN MILL

OTHER ATTRACTIONS Old Gribben Mill, County Route 23, Whalan. Just off a dirt road in the Richard J. Dorer Memorial Hardwood State Forest is the remnants of an old mill, now a stone shell of itself, but beautiful to look at. Hiking back behind the mill will bring you to a seeping waterfall.

✴ Lodging

Not surprisingly, this historic area has more than its fair share of historic bed & breakfasts.

✳ **Wenneson Historic Inn** (507-875-2587), 425 Prospect Street, Peterson. Nine rooms, all with private bath, are offered between the main house and the carriage house. Rooms are named for their color schemes, and all have period furniture and decor. The inn is a short walk from the Root River Trail. Continental breakfast served on weekends. Expensive.

✳ **The 1898 Inn** (507-467-3539; www.1898inn.com), 706 Parkway

LANESBORO HAS MANY HISTORIC BED & BREAKFASTS.

THE 1898 INN, LANESBORO

building began its history as a county jail in 1870 and now has 12 rooms and suites, all with private baths, some with dainty names like the Sun Room and other with more pointed titles like Drunk Tank and Court Room. The Cell Block room gives visitors the chance to sleep behind bars. The rooms are beautifully decorated in Victorian style. Breakfast is included. Moderate (but note that their rate sheet stipulates this price range is for "friendly people").

❋ **Mrs. B's Historic Lanesboro Inn** (507-467-2154; www.mrsbsinn .com), 101 Parkway Avenue, Lanesboro. A large and lovely limestone building on the Root River and right in downtown Lanesboro, Mrs. B's has 10 rooms with private baths (with rubber ducky) and are warmly decorated

Avenue S., Lanesboro. Two rooms with private bath are available in this charming renovated Queen Anne home. Breakfast is a special event, with home-baked breads and local, organic eggs and produce. Expensive.

❋ **Historic Scanlan House B&B** (507-467-2158 or 1-800-944-2158; www.scanlanhouse.com), 708 Parkway Avenue S., Lanesboro This 1889 Queen Anne mansion is a striking piece of architecture, and the seven rooms and suites, all with private baths, are elaborately finished and very romantic. The home itself is packed with antiques, and beds and windows are dressed in linens and lace. Full breakfast is included (and if you've reserved the Safari Suite, you can have it served in your room). Expensive. Packages are available.

❋ **Jailhouse Inn** (507-765-2181; www.jailhouseinn.com), 109 Houston Street NW, Preston. This

JAILHOUSE INN, PRESTON

with color and quilts. Full breakfast is included. Expensive.

✎ ❋ **Stone Mill Suites** (507-467-8663 or 1-866-897-8663; www
.stonemillsuites.com), 100 Beacon Street E., Lanesboro. This limestone mill has served as both an egg and poultry processing plant and as a grain company since it was built in 1885. In 1999, the current owners bought it and created a B&B. Each of the 10 rooms and suites is named and decorated after an aspect of the region, including the Amish Room, Grain Room, and the Egg Jacuzzi Suite. All rooms have private baths. Continental breakfast is served daily. Kids are welcome. Moderate. Packages are available.

✎ ❋ **Art Lofts** (507-467-2446; www.artlofts.org), 103 Parkway Avenue N., Lanesboro. Located above the Lanesboro Arts Center (see *Selective Shopping*) are two simple but attractive loft rooms

BERWOOD HILL INN

designed for guests who wish to enjoy artistic endeavors of their own; the rooms both have good access to daylight. Exposed brick walls and original artwork highlight the space's arts-center neighbor. Expensive. Discounts for weeklong stays are offered.

♂ ❋ **Berwood Hill Inn** (1-800-803-6748; www.berwood.com), 22139 Hickory Road, Lanesboro. Just outside town is this gorgeous inn, located on a hill overlooking the valley. The historic home has been beautifully renovated and is surrounded by lush gardens. Adirondack chairs perch atop the hill, giving guests the option of winding down while enjoying the view of the valley below. Expensive.

LOBBY AT THE STONE MILL SUITES

✻ Where to Eat

DINING OUT ✄ ♿ 🍷 **Riverside at the Root** (507-467-3663; www.rootriveroutfitters.com), 109 Parkway Avenue S., Lanesboro. Open daily for dinner, Fri. through Mon. for lunch. This casual but choice restaurant is located on the Root River, with a patio and deck that take advantage of the location. Some standard steakhouse items are offered, such as steak, pork, and walleye, along with pizza and pasta, and occasionally game items (elk). Riverside also offers special events, such as wine dinners. Expensive.

♿ 🍷 ✳ **Old Village Hall Restaurant & Pub** (507-467-2962; www.oldvillagehall.com), 111 Coffee Street, Lanesboro. Open daily for dinner and Fri. through Sat. for lunch, May through Nov.; Wed. through Sun. for dinner the rest of the year. The former village hall and jail, on the National Register of Historic Places, houses Lanesboro's nicest restaurant. The stone building has been beautifully renovated, and the outdoor patio is a delight in summer. Changing seasonally and taking advantage of local foods, including herbs from the restaurant's own herb garden, the creative menu might include items like lamb chops with couscous or salmon in curry sauce. Expensive.

EATING OUT ✄ ♿ **Das Wurst Haus German Village & Deli** (507-467-2902), 117 Parkway Avenue N., Lanesboro. Open daily

for lunch, Apr. through Nov. Das Wurst Haus may sound kitschy, but make no mistake—it's the real thing. Generations-old family recipes are used to prepare the restaurant's meats, breads, desserts, and even the root beer. You can enjoy your hearty sandwich or soup while listening to live polka music. An adjacent shop sells meats, mustard, and cheese. Moderate.

✄ ♿ ✳ **Chat 'n' Chew** (507-467-3444), 701 Parkway Avenue S., Lanesboro. Open daily for breakfast and lunch. This small diner is

OLD VILLAGE HALL RESTAURANT & PUB, LANESBORO

a good place to grab a quick sandwich or burger. Inexpensive.

♂ & ⊻ ✳ **Pedal Pushers Café**
(507-467-1050; www.pedalpushers
cafe.com), 121 Parkway Avenue
N., Lanesboro. Open daily for
lunch and dinner. A 1950s-style
restaurant with sandwiches and
burgers for lunch, and comfort
food like chicken potpie and
homemade meat loaf for dinner.
Fountain treats and homemade
pie round out the menu, which
also has daily blue plate specials.
Moderate.

♂ & **Aroma Pie Shop** (507-467-
2623), 618 Main Street, Whalan.
Open limited hours May through
Oct.; call for specifics. This little
diner, close to the Root River
Trail, serves up lunch staples like
sandwiches and soups, ice cream
and frozen yogurt, and—best of
all—homemade pie. Inexpensive.

✳ Entertainment

♂ & **Commonweal Theatre**
(1-800-657-7025; www.common
wealtheatre.org), 208 Parkway
Avenue N., Lanesboro. The Commonweal is a national expert on
the works of Henrik Ibsen, and his
work is included in each season's
repertoire. The theater also has a
major hand in the annual Ibsen
Festival (see *Special Events*).
Besides Ibsen, Commonweal produces at least four other plays
each year, sponsors readings of
new works, and produces a live
radio show every summer. The
theater has an unusual employee
arrangement that has the resident
artists not only perform onstage,
but also handle the behind-the-
scenes marketing and administrative work. The building is a recent
renovation and includes an art
gallery on the first floor made up

AROMA PIE SHOP, WHALAN

of whimsical local antiques and artifacts.

✳ Selective Shopping

✍ ♿ **Lanesboro Art Center** (507-467-2446; www.lanesboro arts.org), 103 Parkway Avenue N., Lanesboro. Open Tues. through Sun. Apr. through Oct., Mon. by appointment. An art gallery exhibiting and selling artwork by local and national artists, it also has lofts for rent (see *Lodging*).

✳ Special Events

April: **Bluff Country Studio Art Tour** (1-800-428-2030; www.bluff country.com), Lanesboro. Held in late Apr., this art tour spans several communities in the bluff country region, opening private studios and artist work spaces to visitors and potential art buyers.

Varied dates: **Ibsen Festival** (1-800-657-7025; www.common wealtheatre.org/), Lanesboro. Dates vary; check the website or call for specifics each year. A three-day festival celebrating the life and work of Norwegian playwright Henrik Ibsen. Typical events include discussions and films about Ibsen's work, staged performances of Ibsen's plays, Scandinavian arts and crafts exhibits and classes, Scandinavian music performances, and Scandinavian meals.

AUSTIN

Home of Hormel Foods, Austin proudly refers to itself as SPAM Town, USA.

☀ To See and Do

🖊 ♿ ❋ **SPAM Museum** (1-800-444-5713; www.spam.com), I-90, Austin. Open Mon. through Sat. 10–5 and Sun. noon–5, May 1 through Labor Day; Tues. through Sat. 10–5 and Sun. noon–5, Labor Day through Apr. 30. Admission is free. Sure beats an art museum—at least, that's what the SPAM Museum's website says. This homage to canned meat manages to be both informative and irreverent. (You can't fault the museum for including showings of the Monty Python SPAM skit.) But besides the kitsch and humor, the museum has lively exhibits detailing the history of the Hormel Foods company, as well as films such as *SPAM: A Love Story*, that give insight into SPAM's role in history, especially during World War II.

SPAM MUSEUM, AUSTIN

🖊 ♿ ❋ **Hormel Historic Home** (507-433-4243; www.hormel historichome.org), 208 Fourth Avenue NW, Austin. Open Mon. through Fri. 10–4:30. A $2 donation is requested but not required. The Greek Revival home was built in 1871 for then-mayor John Cook, but it was the residence of the Hormel family in the early 1900s. Self-guided tours showcase this impressive building, and during

AUSTIN—SPAM TOWN, USA

the warmer months a visit to the Peace Gardens is included.

✳ Where to Eat

EATING OUT ✐ ⅊ ✳ **Johnny's SPAMarama Restaurant** (507-433-8875), 1130 N. Main Street, Austin. Open daily for all three meals. If the trip to the SPAM Museum made you hungry, all you have to do is walk across the street. SPAM and cheese omelet, SPAM Reuben, Superman SPAM burger—the possibilities are nearly endless. Moderate.

✐ ✳ **Tender Maid Sandwich Shop** (507-437-7907), 217 Fourth Avenue NE, Austin. This speedy diner serves up classic loose-meat burgers with a variety of seasonings, and generously portioned malts. Inexpensive.

ROCHESTER

Historic Rochester, home to the internationally renowned Mayo Clinic, also has a wide variety of dining options, driven by the diversity of foreign visitors.

✳ To See and Do

MUSEUMS AND HISTORIC SITES ✐ **Historic Mayowood Mansion** (507-282-9447; www.olmstedhistory.com), 3720 Mayowood Road SW, Rochester. Open Tues. through Sat. 11–2, May through Oct.; call for additional days during the year. Adults $12, children $5. The 38-room mansion was home to Mayo Clinic founders and family members, and much of the architecture was designed by Dr. Charles H. Mayo himself. The home is filled with antiques from all over Europe and remains decorated as it was when occupied by the Mayos. The surrounding gardens are breathtaking, overlooking the Zumbro River with a complex plan of paths, ponds, sculptures, a pergola, teahouse, and limestone walls.

✐ ♿ ✳ **Olmsted County History Center** (507-282-9447; www.olmsted history.com), 1195 W. Circle Drive SW, Rochester. Open Tues. through Sat. 9–5. Adults $5, children $2. More information about the Mayo family and the Mayo Clinic can be found at this small historical site, as well as information about another prominent Rochester community member, IBM. A hands-on pioneer cabin exhibit for kids and a display of artifacts from the 1883 tornado that ravaged the city are the must-sees here.

✐ ✳ **Plummer House of the Arts** (507-281-6160; www.ci.rochester .mn.us/departments/park/facilities/plummerhouse/index.asp), 1091 Plummer Lane SW, Rochester. Tours offered on Wed., June through Aug. Private group tours can be arranged. Admission is $3. Henry Plummer, a Mayo physician and engineer, poured his design talents and money into this 49-room Tudor mansion surrounded by 11 acres of gardens and forests. House tours focus on the history and spotlight the all-original furniture. The grounds are open daily and can be visited for free if no special events are in progress.

✍ **Heritage House** (507-282-2682), 225 First Avenue NW, Rochester. Open Tues., Thurs., and Sun. 1–3:30, June through Aug. Admission is free. Built in 1875, this home is one of the few that survived the devastating 1883 tornado, and today it provides insight into what life was like for residents who were not blessed with the wealth of the Mayos and the Plummers. Much of the furniture and decorations on display is original.

TOURS ✍ ♿ ❄ **Mayo Clinic** (507-538-0440; ww.mayoclinic.org /becomingpat-rst/tours.html), 200 First Street SW, Rochester. Tours

MAYO CLINIC, ROCHESTER

are free. Mayo Clinic is Rochester's biggest claim to fame, with medical experts in nearly every category drawing patients from all over the world. Several different tours are offered for visitors, some self-guided: The

THE HERITAGE HOUSE WAS BUILT IN 1875.

General Tour (Mon. through Fri. at 10 AM) presents a short film about the history of the clinic, which is followed by a 90-minute guided tour of the campus. **Art and Architecture** (Mon. through Fri. at 1:30 PM) is a 60-minute guided tour examining the priceless art owned by the Mayo. **Heritage Hall** (open Mon. through Fri.) is a self-guided tour of displays that detail the Mayo Clinic's history and future. The **Patients and Guests Self-Guided Tour** is an audio-enabled tour that visits the artwork, St. Mary's Hospital, or the Mayo Historical Suites (used by the Mayo family). Finally, the **High School/College Career Tour** (by request by calling 507-284-1496) is for students; it is designed to give them more insight into a career in medicine.

✳ Green Space and Outdoor Activities

Quarry Hill Park and Nature Center (507-281-6114; www.qhnc .org), 701 Silver Creek Road NE, Rochester. Open daily. An urban park with extensive grounds and an active nature center offering year-round programs. Fishing ponds, paved biking trails, sandstone caves, and classes at the nature center are among the many amenities.

Silver Lake Park (507-281-6160; www.ci.rochester.mn.us/departments /park/), Seventh Street and Second Avenue NE, Rochester. A haven for Canada geese, this lake and park just outside of downtown has ample recreational opportunities in the form of bike trails, and canoeing, kayaking, and paddleboating on the lake. Silver Lake Rentals (507-261-9049; www.silverlakefun.com) rents bikes and boats during the warmer months.

✳ Lodging

✒ ♿ ⅄ ❄ ((•)) **Kahler Grand Hotel** (507-280-6200 or 1-800-533-1655; www.kahler.com), 20 Second Avenue SW, Rochester. Across the street from the Mayo Clinic, to which it's connected by skyway, the grand dame of Rochester hotels has nearly 700 rooms and suites ranging from basic economy rooms to lavishly appointed suites. The hotel's recreation center, with pool and whirlpool, is domed to allow sky views. On-site there are several sit-down dining options, room service, a martini bar, and Starbucks coffee shop. Expensive to very expensive. Packages are available.

✒ ♿ ❄ ((•)) **Kahler Inn and Suites** (507-285-9200 or 1-800-533-1655; www.kahlerinnsuites.com), 9 Third Avenue NW, Rochester. The Kahler Grand's sister hotel is just down the street. It's smaller and less opulent, but still a good choice. The inn is connected to the Mayo Clinic via a pedestrian subway. An indoor pool and whirlpool are available for guests. Lodging includes free parking and daily continental breakfast. On-site dining includes a casual café, a Jimmy Johns sandwich shop, and a Caribou Coffee shop. Expensive. Packages are available.

🖉 🐾 ♿ 🍸 ❄ (ᵞ) **Marriott Rochester** (507-280-6000 or 1-877-623-7775; www.marriott .com), 101 First Avenue SW, Rochester. Also connected to the Mayo Clinic via skyway, the Marriott was renovated in 2006, creating brighter, more up-to-date

ETHNIC CUISINE

Due to the influence of international visitors, Rochester is developing a strong ethnic food scene, with the standby Asian and Mexican restaurants being joined by newcomers offering African and Middle Eastern cuisines.

🖉 ♿ 🍸 ❄ **Jenpachi Japanese Steak House** (507-292-1688), 3160 Wellner Drive NE. Open daily for dinner, Sun. for lunch. Sushi or the drama of tabletop hibachi cooking. Expensive.

🖉 ♿ 🍸 ❄ **Asian Kitchen** (507-252-8888; www.asiankitchenrochmn.com), 1117 Civic Center Drive NW. Open daily for lunch and dinner. Chinese and Japanese dishes, and diners can request adjustments in the level of spiciness to suit their palates. Inexpensive.

🖉 ♿ 🍸 ❄ **Zorba's Greek Restaurant** (507-281-1540), 924 Seventh Street NW. Open daily for lunch and dinner. Hearty Greek food from a surprisingly large menu. Expensive.

🖉 ♿ 🍸 ❄ **Victoria's** (507-280-6232; www.victoriasmn.com), 7 First Avenue SW. Open daily for lunch and dinner. Victoria's prides itself, rightfully so, on making quality Italian foods from fresh ingredients (local when possible). The menu is extensive and reasonably priced, and there a number of gluten-free offerings. Moderate.

🖉 ♿ 🍸 ❄ **Pazzo** (507-281-2978; www.cccrmg.com/redwoodroom.htm), 300 First Avenue NW. Open daily for dinner. An Italian restaurant housed in an old warehouse, Pazza has a small menu that changes frequently, featuring homemade pastas, steaks, and pizza. Traditional Ital-

rooms with upgraded technology. There's an indoor pool and whirlpool, and a restaurant and bar. Very expensive. Packages are available.

✂ ও Ⴟ ❄❄ ((ᵠ)) **Hilton Garden Inn** (507-285-1234 or 1-877-782-9444; www.hilton.com), 225 S.

Broadway, Rochester. The Hilton has an indoor pool and on-site restaurant, and all rooms have either one king or two double beds. Expensive. Packages are available.

✂ 🐾 ও ❄ ((ᵠ)) **Fiksdal Hotel & Suites** (507-288-2671 or 1-800-

VICTORIA'S

ian foods are tweaked, such as the spaghetti with meatballs made of lobster. Expensive.

✂ ও Ⴟ ❄ **Fiesta Café Bar** (507-288-1116), 1645 Broadway Avenue N. Open daily for lunch and dinner. Mexican food in both Americanized and authentic incarnations. Staff is very friendly. Moderate.

ও Ⴟ ❄ **Chardonnay** (507-252-1310), 723 Second Street SW. Open Mon. through Sat. for dinner. French cuisine, heavy on seafood and steak, and an extensive wine list. Very expensive.

366-3451; www.fiksdalhotel
.com), 1215 Second Street SW,
Rochester. This modest hotel has
spacious rooms, recently renovated,
and offers complimentary continental breakfast daily and cookies
each night. Moderate.

⚓ & ❋ (ᵠ) **Hampton Inn** (507-
287-9050 or 1-800-426-7866;
www.hamptoninn.com), 1755 S.
Broadway, Rochester. This attractive chain hotel offers comfortable, spacious rooms and suites, as
well as full breakfast daily in its
"cyber café," which has high-
speed Internet outlets. Week-
nights, a soup social mixer is
offered. There is an indoor swimming pool and whirlpool, and
complimentary shuttle service to
Mayo Clinic. Moderate. Packages
are available.

❋ Where to Eat

DINING OUT & ⅂ ❋ **Broadstreet Café & Bar** (507-281-
2451; www.cccrmg.com/broad
street.htm), 300 First Avenue NW,
Rochester. Open daily for dinner.
Possibly the best restaurant in
Rochester, Broadstreet is in a cozy
renovated warehouse and has an
ambitious, inventive menu, including orange-crusted fresh scallops
or wild mushroom and brandy
ostrich, along with variations on
steak and seafood. Expensive.

EATING OUT

⚓ & ⅂ ❋ **Michael's Restaurant
and Lounge** (507-288-2020;
www.michaelsfinedining.com), 15
Broadway Avenue S., Rochester.

Open Mon. through Sat. for lunch
and dinner. This local staple has
been around for more than 50
years and continues to serve a
wide array of Greek-influenced
American foods, with several specials each evening. Comfort foods
show up, too; try the Salisbury
steak if it's offered. Moderate.

& ⅂ ❋ **Sönte's** (507-292-1628;
www.sontes.com), 4 Third Street,
Rochester. Open Mon. through
Sat. for dinner. Upscale tapas-style
restaurant with an extensive wine
list (including 40 varietals offered
by the glass). Small plates, entrées
including steaks and sea bass
(served as shared plates), and
unique pizzas are offered, with
ingredients changing seasonally.
The cheese courses are nicely chosen. Moderate.

⚓ & ⅂ ❋ **Roscoe's Root Beer &
Ribs** (507-285-0501, 603 Fourth
Street SE, Rochester; 507-281-
4622, 4180 18th Avenue NW,
Rochester; www.roscoesbbq.com).
Open Tues. through Sun. for
lunch and dinner. This locally
owned, award-winning barbecue
joint features ribs, pork, chicken,
beef, and ham in generous portions, with traditional barbecue
sides (cole slaw, potatoes, baked
beans). Friendly staff, quick service, mouthwatering barbecue
sauce. Moderate.

⚓ & ⅂ ❋ **Bilotti's Italian Village**
(507-282-8668; www.bilottispizza
.com), 304 First Avenue SW,
Rochester. Open daily for dinner,
Mon. through Sat. for lunch. It's
not much to look at, but the huge

ANTIQUES

Rochester is an antiques shopper's paradise, with numerous shops and dealers.

Old Rooster Antique Mall (507-287-6228; www.oldroosterantiques.com), 106 Broadway Avenue. N. Open daily.

Antique Mall on Third Street (507-287-0684), 18 Third Street SW. Call for hours.

Blondell Antiques (507-282-1872; www.blondell.com/antiques), 1406 Second Street SW. Open daily.

Mayowood Galleries (507-288-2695; www.kahler.com), 20 Second Avenue SW. Open Mon. through Fri.

John Kruesel's General Merchandise (507-289-8049; www.kruesel.com), 22 Third Street SW. Open Tues. through Sat.

menu is full of Italian starchy goodness, especially the pizzas. Moderate.

✳ Entertainment

Jon Hassler Theater (507-534-2900 or 1-866-548-7469; www .jonhasslertheater.org), 412 W. Broadway, Plainview. Named after Minnesota novelist Jon Hassler, who spent part of his youth in the small town of Plainview, this professional regional theater produces at least four shows per season. Offerings include Hassler adaptations, productions of works by Edward Albee and Lanford Wilson, and a tribute to Frank Sinatra.

✳ Selective Shopping

✄ ♿ ✳ **Grand Shops** (www .kahler.com), 20 Second Avenue SW, Rochester. Adjacent to the Kahler Grand Hotel (see *Lodging*) is this retail complex with 60 shops, including art galleries (Callaway Galleries, Kay Hoecker Gallery), Hanny's clothiers, Clever Kids Toy Shop, Chocolate Oasis, and Mayo Clinic retailers.

✄ ♿ ✳ **Apache Mall** (507-288-8056; www.apachemall.com), 333 Apache Mall, Rochester. The area's largest shopping mall has 100 shops, including most of the usual chain stores: J.Jill, Abercrombie & Fitch, Champs Sports,

Victoria's Secret, Gap/Gap Kids, and Coldwater Creek.

✳ Special Events

June: **Rochesterfest** (507-285-8769; www.rochesterfest.com), Rochester. Rochesterfest, held for a week in late June, is devoted to celebrating Rochester past and present. The festival packs a lot into a week: lumberjack championships, a guided walk through Oakwood Cemetery, live theater and music, soccer tournaments, disc dog Frisbee championships, street dance, waterskiing show, hot-air balloon race, fiddle contest, even a plane pull (in which teams of 20 humans compete to be the fastest to pull a 727 jet 12 feet).

A CHAIN STORE RISES ABOVE

Much has been made of chain stores and big-box retailers creating soulless retail environments, but there is a spectacular exception to that in downtown Rochester. Barnes & Noble, the national bookseller, renovated the old Chateau Theatre, carefully retaining its charming architecture and making for an unusual and fun book-shopping experience. It's at 15 First Street SW (507-288-3848; www.bn.com).

NORTHFIELD

Not far from the Twin Cities is this quintessential 19th-century European village, home to Carleton and St. Olaf colleges, the mill that produces Malt-O-Meal cereal, and a history involving the infamous Jesse James bank robbery.

✳ To See and Do

MUSEUMS AND HISTORIC SITES ✐ ✳ **Northfield Historical Society Museum** (507-645-9268; www.northfieldhistory.org), 408 Division Street, Northfield. Open Mon. through Sat. 9:30–6, Sun. 1–6. Adults $4, seniors and students with ID $3, children 6–12 $1.50, children under 6 free. The First National Bank, famous for its Jesse James connection, is part of this museum. Many of the bank's fixtures are original, and other exhibits highlight the infamous bank robbery as well as non–Jesse James parts of Northfield's history. The museum's gift shop hearkens back to the general store days of the late 1800s while carrying a wide variety of local books.

♿ ✳ **Northfield Arts Guild Gallery** (507-645-8877; www.northfieldarts guild.org), 304 Division Street, Northfield. Open Mon. through Fri. 10–5, Sat. 10–3. Free admission. The Northfield Arts Guild is part visual arts and part theater, with art classes and exhibits in the gallery. Local and national artists are displayed in a wide variety of mediums.

♿ ✳ **Flaten Art Museum** (507-786-3248; www.stolaf.edu/), Dittmann Center, St. Olaf Avenue, St. Olaf College, Northfield. Open Mon. through Fri. 10–5 (Thurs. until 8), Sat. and Sun. 2–5. Free admission. St. Olaf's art collection encompasses both U.S. and European artists, with an emphasis on textiles, ceramics, and sculpture.

TOURS ✐ ♿ ✳ **Outlaw Trail Tour** (507-645-5604 or 1-800-658-2548; www.northfieldchamber.com). Take a self-guided tour of the route the James-Younger gang took on that fateful day in 1876. Brochures and maps

are available from the Northfield
Chamber of Commerce. Large
groups and tour buses can request
a tour guide from the chamber.

✄ ♿ ✴ **Historic Sites and Points
of Interest Tour** (507-645-5604
or 1-800-658-2548; www.north
fieldchamber.com). It's not the
most exciting name for a tour, but
this self-guided venture takes visitors through the beauty and charm
of Northfield, with its century-old
buildings and architecture.
Brochures and maps are available
from the Northfield Chamber of
Commerce. Large groups and tour
buses can request a tour guide
from the chamber.

OTHER ATTRACTIONS
✄ ♿ ✴ **Goodsell Observatory**
(507-646-4000; www.carleton.edu),
Carleton College, Northfield.
Open the first Fri. evening of each

NORTHFIELD ARTS GUILD

month (hours vary by season), weather permitting. Free admission. The
sky through the telescope is almost as beautiful as the stately architecture
of the observatory building itself. Hope for clear skies—on cloudy nights
the observatory is closed.

NORTHFIELD WELCOMES YOU.

✳ Green Space and Outdoor Activities

Cowling Arboretum (507-646-5413; http://apps.carleton.edu/campus /arb/), Carleton College, Northfield. Open daily. Carleton's Cowling Arboretum has 800 acres of wooded trails along the Cannon River valley. The trails are open to hikers and bikers, and in the winter to cross-country skiers, but be sure to stay on the trails; protected flora and fauna that are being studied by Carleton students are off-limits to visitors.

✳ Lodging

❄ ((ᵖ)) **Archer House River Inn** (507-645-5661 or 1-800-247-2235; www.archerhouse.com), 212 Division Street, Northfield. This is the place to stay when in Northfield. This grand old inn has 36 impeccably decorated and maintained rooms filled with antique furniture, many with river views. Two restaurants are on-site (Chapati and Tavern of Northfield; see *Where to Eat*), although breakfast is not included in the surprisingly reasonable rates. Moderate.

❄ ((ᵖ)) **Magic Door Bed & Breakfast** (507-581-0445; www.magicdoorbb.com), 818 Division Street S., Northfield. This B&B's location, just out of the hubbub of downtown, gives it a quiet ambience, while its romantic decor makes it a wonderful getaway. The three guest rooms all have private baths and are beautifully decorated with vibrant but tasteful colors. The Summer Suite has a gas fireplace and whirlpool tub. Not only is a full breakfast included, but so is a glass of wine or beer in the afternoon; a "bottomless" cookie jar is left out for guests. Expensive.

✳ Where to Eat

DINING OUT と ♈ ✳ **Fermentations** (507-645-8345; www .fermentations-bistro.com), 236 Railway Street N., Dundas. Open Tues. through Sat. for dinner. A meticulously planned seasonal menu incorporates locally grown products, using them to great effect. Seasonal highlights include roasted butternut squash ravioli and pan-seared pork tenderloin, served with sweet potatoes (with marshmallows!). Very expensive.

と ♈ ✳ **Chapati** (507-645-2462; www.chapati.us), 214 Division Street, Northfield. Open Tues.

THE ARCHER HOUSE

through Sat. for lunch and dinner. In the Archer House River Inn (see *Lodging*), this restaurant's huge menu has choices for both novice and experienced Indian-food enthusiasts. Servers will consult with you as to your preferred level of spiciness. Expensive.

EATING OUT ✎ ᶑ ❋ **Kurry Kabab** (507-645-9399; www .kurrykabab.com), 2018 Jefferson Road, Northfield. Open daily for lunch and dinner. Don't let the silly spelling or the strip-mall environment scare you away from this very respectable Indian restaurant. Its menu rivals Chapati's. Moderate.

✎ ᶑ ♈ ❋ **El Tequila** (507-664-9139), 1010 MN 3, Northfield. Open daily for lunch and dinner. Offering plentiful, quality Mexican food, this place is popular, so plan ahead. Moderate.

✎ ᶑ ♈ ❋ **Tavern of Northfield** (507-663-0342), 212 Division Street, Northfield. Open daily for all three meals. Located at the Archer House River Inn (see *Lodging*), the tavern has a wide-ranging menu including pasta, steaks, burritos, and pita sandwiches. Moderate.

❋ **Entertainment**

ᶑ ❋ **Northfield Arts Guild Theater** (507-645-8877; www.north fieldartsguild.org), 304 S. Division Street, Northfield. The theatrical arm of the Northfield Arts Guild (see *To See and Do*), this group

produces several plays each year, staged in a former church down the street from the guild's art gallery. The company also auditions new plays and conducts staged readings.

❋ **Special Events**

September: **Defeat of Jesse James Days** (www.djjd.org), Northfield. Held annually the first weekend after Labor Day. When your town has something as exciting as this in its history, it's best to have a festival, complete with dramatic reenactments. This popular event is built around the Jesse James shootout, and there's also a parade, golf tournament, antique tractor pull, vintage "base ball," a rodeo, square dance, steak fry, 5K and 10K races, and a bike tour. Plan ahead and reserve hotel rooms early if you'd like to stay in the area.

November–December: **St. Olaf Christmas Festival** (507-786-3811; www.stolaf.edu/christmas fest/), St. Olaf College, Northfield. Held in late Nov. or early Dec., this annual tradition began in 1912 and has become a premier event for the state. Several college choral ensembles and the college orchestra put together a magnificent program of Christmas carols and hymns, which are performed live (as well as broadcast on public radio and TV). Purchase tickets well in advance, as they usually sell out quickly.

Southern Minnesota

MINNESOTA RIVER VALLEY

SOUTH THROUGH THE PRAIRIE

THE I-35 CORRIDOR

INTRODUCTION
TO SOUTHERN MINNESOTA

The southwest quadrant of the state is primarily agricultural, with miles of prairie land dotted with small towns and intriguing and even occasionally mysterious historic sites. The Minnesota River, which has its source in Ortonville on the South Dakota border, ambles southeast, until Mankato provides the literal turning point for a northerly twist to the Twin Cities. It's an area of pioneers, Native Americans, wildlife, and history, including the Dakota Conflict of 1862, a time of great losses that is still remembered and memorialized today.

The attractions may be spread farther apart than they are in other parts of the state, but stops like Pipestone National Monument and the Jeffers Petroglyphs, state parks like Blue Mounds, towns entrenched in European heritage like New Ulm, and, of course, the pioneer appeal of Walnut Grove and the Laura Ingalls Wilder Historic Highway have much to offer. As visitors come to the southwest corner of the state, they'll discover more wide open spaces than in other parts of Minnesota, as well as a geological feature known as the Coteau des Prairie, a ridge that runs from western Iowa to the northeast corner of South Dakota that is made up from the debris of glaciers that retreated centuries ago. The wide-open land is a stark contrast to the forests on the other end of the state and is home to what little native prairie remains in Minnesota. However, local communities in the southwest quadrant are starting to try to rebuild the prairie grasses and flowers that were once so dominant.

GUIDANCE Albert Lea Convention and Visitors Bureau (1-800-345-8414; www.albertleatourism.org), 102 W. Clark St., Albert Lea.

Le Sueur Area Chamber of Commerce (507-665-2501; www.lesueur chamber.org), 500 N. Main St., Le Sueur.

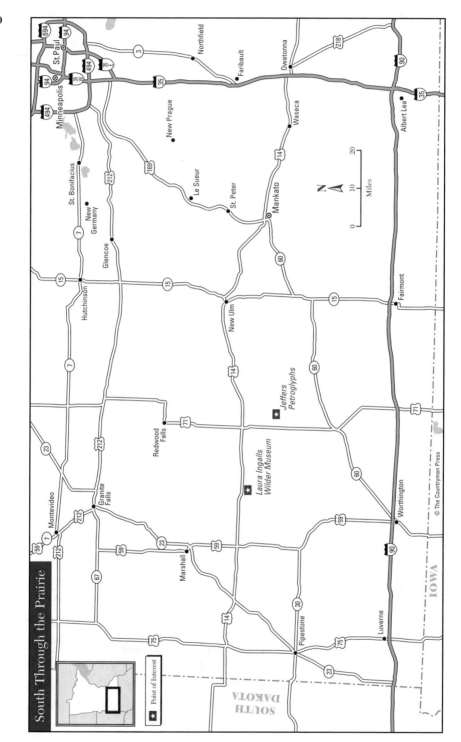

South Through the Prairie

★ Point of Interest

© The Countryman Press

New Ulm Convention and Visitors Bureau (1-888-463-9856; www .newulm.com), 1 N. Minnesota St., New Ulm. Offers extensive lodging and activity information for New Ulm and the Minnesota River Valley.

Worthington Area Chamber of Commerce (507-372-2919 or 1-800-279-2919; www.worthingtonmnchamber.com), 1121 Third Ave., Worthington.

Marshall Chamber of Commerce (507-532-4484; www.marshall-mn .org), 317 W. Main St., Marshall.

Faribault Chamber of Commerce (507-334-4481 or 1-800-658-2354; www.visitfaribault.com), 530 Wilson Ave., Faribault.

Greater Mankato Chamber of Commerce (507-385-6660 or 1-800-657-4733; www.greatermankato.com), 112 Riverfront Dr., Mankato.

Western Minnesota Prairie Waters Regional Tourism (1-866-866-5432; www.prairiewaters.com), 323 Schlieman Ave., Appleton. A good source for information in the Madison and Montevideo areas.

Pipestone Chamber of Commerce (507-825-3316 or 1-800-336-6125; www.pipestoneminnesota.com), 117 Eighth Ave. SE, Pipestone.

City of Luverne (507-449-2388; www.cityofluverne.org), 305 E. Luverne St., Luverne.

Lake Benton Convention and Visitors Bureau (507-368-9577; www .itctel.com/lbenton), 110 S. Center, Lake Benton.

GETTING THERE *By air:* Commercial air service is available into **Minneapolis–St. Paul International Airport** (612-726-5555; www.mspair port.com); there are regional airports, such as the one in Mankato, that offer private or corporate service.

By car: The primary routes in the southwestern part of the state, connecting Montevideo, Marshall, Pipestone, and Luverne, are MN 7 and MN 29 into Montevideo, US 212 from Montevideo to Granite Falls, and MN 23 from Granite Falls through Marshall to Pipestone, where US 75 travels south to Luverne.

From Luverne, I-90 travels directly east through Worthington, Fairmont, Blue Earth, and into Albert Lea, where it connects with I-35 heading north to Owatonna and Faribault.

West of Owatonna is Mankato, which is accessed by US 14 and US 169, as well as MN 22, MN 68, and MN 66. MN 68 travels west to New Ulm, while US 169 and MN 22 travel north to St. Peter. US 169 continues north to Belle Plaine. Before it reaches Belle Plaine, MN 19 travels east to New Prague. MN 13 travels south from New Prague to Montgomery.

GETTING AROUND Having a vehicle is a necessity when traveling around the southern prairie region.

WHEN TO COME The summer months see an influx of tourists who come to enjoy not only the wide-open prairies and vast state parks, but also the multitude of lakes and beaches. Summer isn't the only popular time, however, especially for fishing enthusiasts who cast their poles in open water in summer and through holes in the ice in winter. Hunters and winter sports aficionados appreciate the fall and winter seasons as well.

MEDICAL EMERGENCY Call 911.

Chippewa County–Montevideo Hospital (320-269-8877; www.monte videomedical.com), 824 N. 11th St., Montevideo.

Pipestone County Medical Center (507-825-5811; www1.avera.org), 916 Fourth Ave. SW, Pipestone.

Albert Lea Medical Center (507-373-2384 or 1-888-999-2386; www .mayohealthsystem.org), 404 W. Fountain St., Albert Lea.

New Ulm Medical Center (507-233-1000; www.allina.com/ahs/newulm .nsf), 1324 Fifth St. N., New Ulm.

Immanuel St. Joseph's Hospital (507-625-4031 or 1-800-327-3721; www.mayohealthsystem.org), 1025 Marsh St., Mankato.

River's Edge Hospital (507-931-2200; www.riversedgehealth.org), 1900 N. Sunrise Dr., St. Peter.

MINNESOTA RIVER VALLEY

Leaving the Twin Cities to explore the Minnesota River Valley is a lovely way to spend an afternoon. The Minnesota River was formed by glaciers during the last North American ice age, roughly 10,000 years ago. Today it flows southeast from Big Stone Lake in the western edge of the state, near the North and South Dakota borders, until it reaches Mankato, when it redirects northeast until it meets the Mississippi near the Twin Cities. It's an area full of changes, from closely wooded stretches along rolling riverbanks to wide-open prairie spaces.

It's also full of history, perhaps most notably the Dakota Conflict of 1862 (see sidebar of the same name). New Ulm served as a refuge for those trying to escape the conflict, and in the 1920s the town developed another type of infamy, as resident Whoopee John Wilfahrt and his musical magic gave New Ulm the moniker of the Polka Capital of the Nation. In addition to New Ulm's German heritage—apparent today in the architecture, landmarks, shops, restaurants, and festivals and celebrations that take place each year—the area is known for its numerous Native American sites, an unexpected partnership between a central Minnesota town and its counterpart in Uruguay, and the homes and hometowns of some iconic Minnesota people and companies, including the founder of the Mayo Clinic and the Jolly Green Giant.

✴ To See and Do

MUSEUMS AND HISTORIC SITES

Belle Plaine

Hooper-Bowler-Hillstrom House (952-873-6109; www.belleplainemn .com/about/HooperHouse.php), 410 N. Cedar Street. Open Sun. 1–4, Memorial Day through Labor Day; other days by appointment. Admission is $5. The former home of State Bank founder Samuel Bowler, this house was built in 1871, but its primary claim to fame, besides being an attractive

HOOPER-BOWLER-HILLSTROM HOUSE

version of a 19th-century home, is the addition Mr. Bowler added to accommodate his rather large family: a two-story outhouse. A skyway connects the second floor of the "five-holer" to the house; the upstairs facilities are situated farther back, so the waste landed behind the wall of the first floor. Souvenirs are available for sale. (Note: As of press time, the house was temporarily closed for repair and restoration. Call before visiting.)

THE DAKOTA CONFLICT OF 1862

The year 1862 was a dark time in Minnesota history. The state was young, and immigrants and pioneers shared land with the Native American population, a situation that made both sides uneasy. In the years leading up to the conflict, the U.S. government and its agents repeatedly broke promises and violated treaties previously agreed to with the Dakota, who were becoming perilously hungry and angry. Tensions broke out in August 1862 when a small Dakota hunting party killed five settlers who were also out hunting. A Dakota council decided at that point to attack white settlers throughout the region to drive them away permanently. It's not clear how many settlers died during the conflict, but the number is thought to be in the hundreds. By December, the U.S. Army stepped in and captured more than a thousand Dakota, who were jailed. The day after Christmas, 38 Dakota were hanged, the largest single-day execution in U.S. history. The remaining Dakota were sent to North and South Dakota, and their Minnesota reservations were abolished.

✒ ♿ ❀ **Le Sueur City Museum** (507-655-2050), 709 N. Second Street. Open Tues. through Thurs. 1–5, year-round; Fri. and Sat. 1–5, Memorial Day through Labor Day; or by appointment. No admission fee, but donations are welcome. A small museum in a former schoolhouse, the City Museum has most of what remains of the Green Giant legacy after Pillsbury bought Green Giant and moved its headquarters out of town. The Green Giant history room has a wide variety of memorabilia and antiques. Other displays include an old-time drugstore and an antique doll collection.

✒ **W.W. Mayo House** (507-665-3250; www.mayohouse.org), 118 N. Main Street. Open Thurs. through Sat. 10–4:30 and Sun. noon–4:30, July through Aug.; Fri. through Sun. noon–4, Apr. through June and Sept. through Nov. Adults $4, senior citizens $3, children 6–16 $2, children under 6 free. This little Gothic-style home was hand built in 1859 by Dr. Mayo himself, who then set up shop on the second floor. The Civil War interrupted his practice; he traveled to New Ulm to help with wounded veterans while his wife, Louise, remained in the house to shelter 11 refugee families. By 1864 the Mayo family was reunited and moved to Rochester, where they founded the Mayo Clinic. The home's story doesn't end there; in the 1870s, the Carson Nesbit Cosgrove family moved into the home. Cosgrove founded the Minnesota Valley Canning Company, which later became Green Giant.

MINNESOTA RIVER VALLEY

Mankato

∂ **The Betsy-Tacy Society** (507-345-8103; www.betsy-tacysociety.org), 332 Center Street. Open Sat. noon–3, Mar. through Dec.; or by appointment. Adults $3, children 6–16 $1, children under 6 free. Fans of the children's classic Betsy-Tacy series by Maud Hart Lovelace can visit the sites of the fictional Deep Valley in Lovelace's home city of Mankato. Tacy's home is open for tours; Betsy's house is around the corner. The society also has a brochure detailing 55 important stops in Mankato for Betsy-Tacy fans; the map was created in part by Lovelace herself. Check the society's website for the detailed walking map.

∂ & **R.D. Hubbard House** (507-345-5566; www.bechshistory.com /hubbard_house), 606 S. Broad Street. Open Sat. and Sun. 1–4, May and Sept.; Fri. and Sat. 10–4 and Sun. 1–4, June through Aug. Adults $5, children 5–17 $2, children under 5 free. This Victorian gem was occupied only by the Hubbard family before the Blue Earth County Historical Society acquired it, and the lack of turnover allowed the building to retain its turn-of-the-20th-century charm. Elaborate woodwork, stained glass, fabric wall coverings, and an adjacent carriage house with a collection of antique vehicles give visitors a true glimpse of the era.

∂ & ✿ **Blue Earth Heritage Center** (507-345-5566; www.bechshistory .com), 415 E. Cherry Street. Open Tues. through Sat. (hours vary by season) year-round. Adults $5, children 5–17 $2, children under 5 free. The museum of the Blue Earth County Historical Society has wide-ranging exhibits covering local historic events, including a Maud Hart Lovelace exhibit, displays featuring Native American artifacts, remnants from the region's early days of farming and milling, and a diorama of old Mankato.

Montevideo to Ortonville

∂ & ✿ **José Artigas Statue,** Artigas Plaza, Montevideo. This statue of the national hero of Uruguay might seem out of place in a central Minnesota town, until you realize that this town has been a sister city to its namesake in Uruguay for more than a century. The statue was a gift from the South American country in 1949, cementing the two communities' relationship, and every year visitors from South America travel to Minnesota to see their gift. The Minnesota Montevideo has an annual event to commemorate the friendship (see *Special Events*).

∂ **Olof Swensson Farm** (320-269-7636), County Route 6, Granite Falls. Open Sun. 1–5, Memorial Day through Labor Day. Adults $4, students $2, children 5 and under free. Olof Swensson was a Norwegian immigrant who settled in this area in 1872. He was a highly active resident, a builder who worked on his 22-room farmhouse and timber-framed barn, a Lutheran minister, and a political activist. The farm has been restored, including a

gristmill with hand-cut granite grist stones. The buildings were used during the filming of the movie *The Sweet Land.*

✒ ⅋ **Historic Chippewa City** (320-269-7636; www.chippewacohistory .org), 151 Arne Anderson Drive, Montevideo. Open daily 9–5 (1–5 on holidays), Memorial Day through Labor Day; Mon. through Fri. 9–5 the rest of Sept. Adults $4, children 6–18 $2, children under 6 free. Chippewa City was originally the county seat, but as a town it declined after Montevideo took over the governmental role. Today 24 restored buildings have been preserved as a living-history museum, including a buggy shop (containing a horse-drawn hearse), the village hall, and a log cabin. Parts of the movie *The Sweet Land* were filmed in the town.

✒ **Lac Qui Parle Mission** (320-269-7636; www.chippewacohistory.org), 151 Arne Anderson Drive, Montevideo. Open daily 8–8, May through Labor Day. Free admission. The mission, dating back to before Minnesota actually became a state, holds some "firsts" within the state, including the first church bell to toll and the first organized Dakota church, complete with the first Dakota Bible.

New Ulm

✒ ⅋ ❋ **Glockenspiel,** Minnesota Street and Fourth Street N. New Ulm is home to one of the world's few freestanding carillons. The 45-foot glockenspiel puts on its show three times a day (at noon, 3, and 5), more often during festivals; when the bells chime, 3-foot-tall polka figures dance out, except at Christmas, when a nativity scene appears instead.

NEW ULM'S GLOCKENSPIEL

✒ ⅋ ❋ **August Schell Brewery** (507-354-5528 or 1-800-770-5020; www.schellsbrewery.com). 1860 Schell Road. Museum open daily noon–5, Memorial Day through Labor Day. Afternoon tours are offered daily Memorial Day through Labor Day, Fri. through Sun. the rest of the year. Tour admission: visitors 13 and older $3, children 12 and under free. The museum does not charge an admission fee. The surrounding gardens and deer park are open

daily, no admission. Schell's is the second-oldest family brewing company in the United States, having opened in 1860. As the brewery offered hospitality to visiting Dakota, it was largely left alone during the Dakota Conflict. It also remained operational by producing "near beer" and root beer during Prohibition (it still produces root beer, called 1919 after the year the 18th Amendment was passed). Today the brewery is open for tours (kids are welcome—while the adults enjoy a beer tasting at the end, minors and nondrinkers can sample the 1919 Root Beer), and there's a small museum and gift shop. What's also very much worth a visit are the brewery grounds and gardens. Stop in the spring for the arrival of the bulbs, or midsummer to see the rest of the garden in full bloom. You might even see some wildlife in the adjacent deer park.

✇ **Hermann Monument** (www.hermannmonument.com), Center Street and Monument Street. Open daily 10–7, Memorial Day through Labor Day; weekends 10–7, day after Labor Day through Oct. Visitors six and older $2, children five and under free. This towering monument was built in 1897 in honor of Hermann of Cherusci, who is recognized for freeing Germany from Rome in A.D. 9 and is considered the liberator of the German people. The memorial stands 102 feet tall and, for those willing to climb the stairs, provides an excellent view of greater New Ulm. Bring a picnic lunch to enjoy in the park grounds.

✇ **Wanda Gág House** (507-359-2632; www.wandagaghouse.org), 226 N. Washington Street. Open Sat. 10–4 and Sun. 11–2, June through Aug., Dec., and festival weekends; by appointment year-round. Admission $2. Children's author Wanda Gág, author and illustrator of such classics as *Millions of Cats*, was born and raised in this home in New Ulm. The compact house with turrets and skylights makes for an interesting afternoon's exploration.

✇ ₺ ❋ **Brown County Historical Museum** (507-233-2616; www.brown countyhistorymnusa.org), 2 N. Broadway Street. Open Mon. through Sat. 9–5, May through Sept.; Tues. through Fri. and Sun. 9–5, Oct. through Apr. Adults $3, students and children free. Housed in a 1910 post office, the museum is a surprisingly diverse and comprehensive repository of historic and cultural artifacts and displays. German heritage, Native American presence, and the economic mainstays of the area (known as "beer, brats, and bricks") are all detailed in various exhibits. The Dakota Conflict is especially well covered.

✇ **John Lind House** (507-354-8802; www.thelindhouse.com), 622 Center Street. Open daily 1–4, June through Aug.; Fri. through Sun. 1–4, Apr., May, Sept., and Oct.; by appointment the rest of the year. Admission $3. Built in 1887, this Victorian beauty served as the home of Governor John Lind, as well as the site of state functions he hosted. The house had fallen into serious disrepair before being listed on the National Register of Historic Places and purchased by the newly formed Lind House Association, which restored it and operates it today. While tours are available, this is still a working building, home to the local United Way.

✐ **Harkin Store** (507-354-8666; www.mnhs.org/places/sites/hs/), County Route 21. Open Tues. through Sun. 10–5, Memorial Day through Labor Day; weekends 10–5, May and Sept. to mid-Oct. Adults $4, children 6–17 and seniors $2, children under 6 free. Eight miles northwest of New Ulm is this classic store, a piece of history still vibrant today. The Harkin Store was a community general store until the day the railroad decided to bypass it, and it was forced to close. Today, much of the merchandise seen on the shelves has been there since the closing. Costumed guides provide historical background and explain what some of the products, common in their day but unknown today, were for.

St. Peter

✐ ❋ **E. St. Julien Cox House** (507-934-4309; www.nchsmn.org), 500 N. Washington Avenue. Open hours vary by season. Adults $4, children 6–17 $3, children under 6 free; $7 for a combined pass with the Treaty Site History Center (see following listing). E. St. Julien Cox was a Civil War officer, attorney, and eventually state senator, and he built this Gothic/Italianate home in 1871. Filled with furnishings from the 1880s, the home is open for display; during the summer costumed guides explain the significance of both the home and the family. (Note: As of press time, the house was closed for repair and restoration. Call before visiting.)

✐ ⑆ ❋ **Treaty Site History Center** (507-934-2160; www.nchsmn.org), 1851 N. Minnesota Avenue. Open Mon. through Sat. 10–4, Sun. 1–4.

THE E. ST. JULIAN COX HOUSE

Adults $5, seniors $4, children 6–17 $3, children under 6 free; $7 for a combined pass with the E. St. Julien Cox House (see previous listing). The history center has permanent and seasonal exhibitions detailing the creation of what is now southern Minnesota, along with Iowa and South Dakota, in the signing of the Traverse des Sioux Treaty in 1851. History aficionados will note that the terms of the treaty were not upheld, leading to the Dakota Conflict several years later. The center doesn't shy away from the uglier side of the history, but if you need something more peaceful and soothing, take some time to explore the restored prairie that surrounds the center.

✧ ❋ **St. Peter Regional Treatment Center** (507-931-7250), 100 Freeman Drive. Open only by appointment. Free admission. This is worth calling ahead for. The treatment center is the first psychiatric hospital opened in the state, and the museum has a motley but fascinating array of artifacts from its original incarnation, including straitjackets.

WINERIES ⅋ **Morgan Creek Vineyards** (507-947-3547; www.morgan creekvineyards.com), 23707 478th Avenue, New Ulm. Open Fri. and Sat. 11–9 and Sun. noon–5, May through Oct.; Fri. and Sat. 11–6 and Sun. noon–5, Nov. and Dec. Morgan Creek is still the only Minnesota vineyard with an underground winery. Stop by during their regular business hours for tours and tastings, or check their website for one of the numerous special events.

❋ Green Space and Outdoor Activities

HIKING AND BIKING **Sakatah Singing Hills State Trail** (www.dnr .state.mn.us/state_trails/sakatah/index.html), Lime Valley Road, Mankato. A 39-mile paved trail utilizing a former railroad bed, the Sakatah winds from Mankato to Faribault through farmland and woods. The trail is multiuse, open to all forms of recreation (with the exception of snowmobiles with studded tracks—regular snowmobiles are welcome). A secondary trail is available for horseback riders only.

PARKS

Mankato
Minneopa State Park (507-389-5464; www.dnr.state.mn.us/state_parks /minneopa/index.html), 54497 Gadwall Road. Open daily. In the Dakota language, *minneopa* means "water falling twice," a perfect name for this park, home to Minnesota's largest waterfall. A winding trail leads to and around the falls, with a limestone stairway descending into the valley. Seppmann Mill, a wind-driven gristmill made of stone and wood, is no longer functional but continues to draw admirers. At one time there was a

MINNEOPA FALLS IS THE LARGEST WATERFALL IN MINNESOTA.

town here as well, but three consecutive years of grasshopper plagues in the 1870s drove the residents away. Tourists, however, continue to flock to this popular park, for the waterfalls and for the hiking/cross-country skiing trails and bird-watching. Campsites and one cabin are available for rental.

Montevideo to Ortonville
Big Stone National Wildlife Refuge (320-273-2191; www.fws .gov/midwest/bigstone/), 44843 County Route 19, Odessa. Open daily. An 11,500-acre wildlife refuge southeast of Ortonville, Big Stone counts more than 260 bird species, including bald eagles, and bison can be seen wandering in the 1,700 acres of prairie grasses. A 9-mile paved auto trail is open in summer, and hiking trails and canoe routes provide more intimate access.

MINNEOPA STATE PARK

Big Stone Lake State Park (320-839-3663; www.dnr.state.mn.us/state_parks/big_stone_lake/index.html), 35889 Meadowbrook State Park Road, Ortonville. Open daily. Big Stone Lake is the source of the Minnesota River. The southern part of the park is known as the Meadowbrook Area, which is the most user friendly in terms of amenities: campground, beach, canoe rental, good fishing, and hiking trails (noted for views of wildflowers in spring). The northern area is the Bonanza Area, designated as a Scientific & Natural Area for its 80 acres of native oak savanna and glacial till prairie habitat. There is a hiking trail here also, but be sure not to disturb the protected habitat.

New Ulm
Flandrau State Park (507-233-9800; www.dnr.state.mn.us/state_parks /flandrau/index.html), 1300 Summit Avenue. Open daily. At only 800 acres, this is a smaller park, but popular nonetheless due in no small part to the fact that it's within walking distance from downtown New Ulm. The sand-bottomed swimming pond and extensive campgrounds are a big draw here, as are the hiking trails. The trails are groomed for cross-country skiing in the winter, and ski and snowshoe rentals are available.

Lac Qui Parle State Park (320-734-4450; www.dnr.state.mn.us/state
_parks/lac_qui_parle/index.html), 14047 20th Street NW, Watson. Open
daily. *Lac Qui Parle,* which translates into "lake that speaks," was also
the name of the band of Wahpeton Dakota who built a small village
here centuries ago. In 1826, a trading post was built by explorer Joseph
Renville, and a mission soon followed, which saw the translation of the
bible into Dakota. Today all that remains of the trading post is an interpretive sign, but the mission is marked by a chapel that was rebuilt by
the WPA in the 1940s.

Besides Native American and trade history, Lac Qui Parle has 6
miles of trails for hiking and horseback riding, and the trails are
groomed in winter for cross-country skiing. Canoers can watch for
wildlife while canoeing on the Lack Qui Parle and Minnesota rivers.
There are several campsites and a small sandy beach. The park is adjacent to the 27,000-acre Lac Qui Parle Wildlife Management Area, which
is home to geese, deer, and bald eagles. The lake itself is a migratory
stopping point for thousands of Canada geese each spring and fall.

✳ Lodging
BED & BREAKFASTS
Henderson
❅ **Henderson House Bed &
Breakfast** (507-248-3356; www
.hendersonhousemnbb.com), 104
N. Eighth Street. A beautiful brick
home on a hill overlooking the
river valley, Henderson House was
built in 1875. The B&B offers four
rooms, two with private bath, and
all decorated with period antiques.
Full breakfast is provided daily,
sometimes including eggs from
the hens kept in the backyard.
Open year-round. Expensive.

Mankato
❅ **Butler House Bed & Breakfast** (507-387-5055; www.butler
house.com), 704 S. Broad Street.

This luxurious B&B offers five lavishly decorated suites, all with private baths, some with elaborate
wood or wrought-iron four-poster
beds and hand-painted murals.
Full breakfast is included, and
mystery theme dinners can be

HENDERSON HOUSE BED & BREAKFAST

arranged in advance for groups. Expensive.

New Ulm

❄ (ᵞ) ↝ **Deutsche Strasse Bed & Breakfast** (507-354-2005 or 1-866-226-9856; www.deutsche strasse.com), 404 S. German Street. Built in 1884, this congenial home has five rooms, all with private baths and most with fireplaces. Full breakfast is served in the cheerful sunroom. Expensive. Packages are available.

❄ (ᵞ) **Bingham Hall Bed & Breakfast** (507-354-6766 or 1-800-486-3514; www.bingham -hall.com), 500 S. German Street. This luxurious B&B has four rooms, all with private baths and queen-sized beds with down comforters. Most of the rooms have fireplaces or whirlpool baths, and one room (Elijah) has an air massage chair. Expensive.

HOTELS

Mankato

✎ ♿ ❄ (ᵞ) **AmericInn** (507-345-8011; www.americinnmankato .com), 240 Stadium Road. With 95 rooms and suites, some of which have fireplaces and whirlpools, the hotel also has an indoor pool and whirlpool. Daily continental breakfast is provided. Moderate.

✎ ♿ ♟ ❄ (ᵞ) **Country Inn and Suites** (507-388-8555 or 1-800-830-5222; www.countryinns.com /mankatomn), 1900 Premier Drive. All rooms include complimentary Wi-Fi, microwaves, refrigerators, and full daily breakfast. Suites have whirlpools and wet bars. An indoor pool is available for guests, and a T.G.I. Friday's is attached to the hotel for lunch and dinner. Moderate.

✎ ♿ ♟ ❄ (ᵞ) **Hilton Garden Inn** (507-344-1111; www.hiltongarden inn.hilton.com), 20 Civic Center Plaza. One of the nicest hotels in Mankato. Rooms and suites include complimentary high-speed Internet access and flat panel HDTV. There's an indoor pool and a full-service restaurant on-site as well. Expensive. Packages are available.

Montevideo to Ortonville

✎ 🐾 ♿ ❄ (ᵞ) **Crossings by Grandstay Inns and Suites** (320-269-8000 or 1-866-668-7439; www.crossingsmontevideo.com), 1805 E. County Route 7, Montevideo. Rooms and suites, as well as an indoor pool and whirlpool. Full breakfast included. Moderate.

New Ulm

✎ 🍴 ♿ ♟ ❄ (ᵞ) **Holiday Inn** (507-359-2941 or 1-888-465-4329; www.ichotelsgroup.com), 2101 S. Broadway. Even the Holiday Inn gets into the spirit of things with its old-world Germany exterior. Otherwise it's a standard Holiday Inn, with an indoor pool and an on-site restaurant (Otto's Bierstube). Moderate.

UNIQUE LODGINGS

❄ (ᵞ) ↝ **The Broodio at Moonstone Farm** (320-269-8971; www

.prairiefare.com/moonstone /farmstay.html), 9060 40th Street SW, Montevideo. A one-room cottage that used to be a chicken brooding house, the Broodio is a charming and idyllic getaway for the visitor looking for peace and quiet. Moonstone Farm is an organic, sustainable agriculture farm, and guests have access to a canoe, beach, and sauna. The owners are committed to permaculture design, solar technology, and organic, local foods when possible. Continental breakfast is delivered to the cottage. Moderate.

❋ Where to Eat

DINING OUT

Mankato

✐ ♿ ⅄ ❋ **The Neighbor's Italian Bistro** (507-625-6776; www.neighborsitalianbistro.com), 1812 S. Riverfront Drive. Open daily for lunch and dinner. This excellent Italian bistro serves homemade pastas and has a thoughtful menu. When available, try the butternut squash ravioli with maple sage butter and bacon. Expensive.

✐ ♿ ⅄ ❋ **Number 4 American Bar & Kitchen** (507-344-1444; www.number4mankato.com), 124 E. Walnut Street. Open daily for lunch and dinner. A gastropub, Number 4 offers both traditional pub foods and updated versions, including fish-and-chips and the Blue Penne, a blue-cheese fondue with penne pasta and spinach. Expensive.

✐ ♿ ⅄ ❋ **The Crossings at Montevideo** (320-269-8600; www .montegolf.com), 4490 W. MN 212, Montevideo. Open Tues. through Sun. for lunch and dinner, Mon. for dinner. The clubhouse at the Crossings Golf Course, also known as Johnny's on the Tee, offers plenty of steak, pork chop, and chicken dishes, as well as a long list of sandwiches and wraps. Expensive.

New Ulm

✐ ♿ ⅄ ❋ **George's Fine Steaks and Spirits** (507-354-7440; www .georgessteaks.biz), 301 N. Minnesota Street. Open Mon. through

GEORGE'S, NEW ULM

Sat. for dinner. A congenial steakhouse in a pretty bistro building, George's has steaks, ribs, walleye, lamb, duck, chicken, and some pasta options. The respectable beer and wine list includes items from New Ulm's Morgan Creek Vineyards and Schell's Brewery. Expensive.

EATING OUT

Mankato

♦ ⅙ ♈ ❄ **Wine Café** (507-345-1516; www.winecafebar.com), 301 N. Riverfront. Open daily for lunch and dinner. A charming bistro and wine shop with more than just wine. A limited bar menu is available for lunch and dinner, but there's a full bar, including 70 wines by the glass and a comparable number of beers. Live music on weekends, when the bar remains open until 2 AM. Moderate.

♦ ⅙ ♈ ❄ (ᵖ) **Whiskey River** (507-934-5600; www.riversp.com), 34166 MN 99. Open daily for all three meals. This congenial supper club offers traditional supperclub foods, including ribs, steak, and walleye; it also serves breakfast. Moderate.

♦ ⅙ ♈ ❄ **Tav on the Ave** (507-345-3308; www.thetavontheave), 1120 E. Madison Avenue. Open daily for lunch and dinner. Tav has solid bar food, especially the buffalo wings and burgers. Moderate.

♦ ⅙ ♈ ❄ **Dino's Pizzeria** (507-385-3466; www.dinospizzeria .com), 239 Belgrade Avenue.

Open daily for lunch and dinner. This New York–style pizzeria uses fresh ingredients for its pizzas, pastas, and sandwiches. Moderate.

Montevideo to Ortonville

♦ ⅙ ❄ **Valentino's** (320-269-5106), 110 S. First Street, Montevideo. Open Mon. through Thurs. for all three meals, Fri. and Sat. for breakfast and lunch. A surprisingly elegant yet casual restaurant, Valentino's has tasteful wood decor and artwork, and a simple but delectable menu of soups, sandwiches, and daily specials. Moderate.

♦ ⅙ ❄ (ᵖ) **Java River Café** (320-269-7106), 210 S. First Street, Montevideo. Open Mon. through Sat. for breakfast and lunch. Although its coffee is top-notch, Java offers much more than just coffee drinks: well-made sandwiches, soups, and pastries, frequently incorporating locally grown and raised food sources. Live music and book discussions are regularly scheduled. Moderate.

New Ulm

♦ ⅙ ♈ ❄ **Veigel's Kaiserhoff** (507-359-2071), 221 N. Minnesota Street. Open daily for lunch and dinner. New Ulm's oldest German restaurant, this place is a local institution, serving up heaping portions of German and American foods. The ribs are their specialty, but make sure to try the sauerkraut balls. Moderate.

✐ ♿ ✳ **Ulmer Café** (507-354-8122), 115 N. Minnesota Street. Open daily for breakfast and lunch. The local diner with plentiful breakfasts and lunches. Inexpensive.

✐ ♿ ✳ **Backerei and Coffee Shop** (507-354-6011), 27 S. Minnesota Street. Open Mon. through Sat. for breakfast and lunch. This longtime local bakery still knows how to produce the pastries, and the prices are very reasonable. Inexpensive.

✐ ♿ ✳ **Lola's Larkspur Market** (507-359-2500; www.lolaslarks purmarket.com), 16 N. Minnesota Street. Open Mon. through Sat. for breakfast and lunch, Thurs. through Sat. for all three meals. Offering sumptuous baked goods and a changing daily menu of lunch specials, the café is located within a gift shop full of kitchen and gourmet food products as well as bath and body gifts. Meals include a nice mix of Italian and home cooking. Moderate.

✳ **Entertainment**

LIVE PERFORMANCES **Highland Summer Theatre** (507-389-6661; www.MSUTheatre.com), 210 Performing Arts Center, Minnesota State University, Mankato. A professional summer stock theater for more than 45 years, Highland presents four productions each season (June and July), two of which are musicals.

SPORTING EVENTS ✐ ♿ **Minnesota Vikings Training Camp** (507-389-3000; www.vikings.com), Blakeslee Field, Minnesota State University, Mankato. Late July to mid-Aug. When the Vikings gear up for the season, they start out in Mankato. Practices are free, while scrimmages and games cost $10 for ages three and up. Get tickets in advance from the Vikings ticket office or from the Mankato Chamber of Commerce.

✳ **Selective Shopping**

✳ **Domeier's German Store** (507-354-4231), 1020 S. Minnesota Street, New Ulm. Open Mon. through Sat. Domeier's is packed full of German imports, from kitschy to classic to collector's items.

✳ **Guten Tag Haus** (507-233-4287; www.gutentaghaus.com), 127 N. Minnesota Street, New Ulm. Open Mon. through Sat. Importer of German gifts, including a large array of Christmas items.

✳ **Sausage Shop** (507-354-3300; www.newulmtel.net/~lendon/), 301 N. Broadway Street, New Ulm. Open Mon. through Sat. All kinds of meats—especially sausage—and baked goods, too.

✳ **Weeds & Reeds** (507-359-1147), 500 N. Broadway Street, New Ulm. Open Mon. through Sat. Fun home-and-garden gift store built into a renovated 1926 gas station.

WEEDS & REEDS

✳ Special Events

June: ✎ ♿ **Fiesta Days** (320-269-5527; www.montevideomn.org), Montevideo. An annual event for more than 60 years, Fiesta Days is celebrated Father's Day weekend and pays homage to the town's century-long partnership with Montevideo, Uruguay, complete with a parade, fireworks, and, of course, plenty of food.

Sauerkraut Days (www.hendersonmn.com), Henderson. Held in late June. Parades, tournaments, food, music, and a kraut-eating contest.

July: **Kolacky Days Czech Festival** (www.montgomerymn.org/events.html), Montgomery. Held in late July, this three-day festival has occurred every year since 1929, focusing on the town's Czech heritage. Kolacky is a Czech fruit-filled bun, and that's just one of the many ethnic foods that can be found during the festival. Events include softball, volleyball, and horseshoe tournaments; the Bun Run footrace; Tour de Bun bike race; contemporary and classic Czech music; and dancing.

September: **Mahkato Traditional Pow Wow** (www.greatermankato.com), Mankato. Held in Sept. The Land of Memories Park in Mankato is home to this annual event, where thousands of Native Americans of many different tribes gather to reenact ceremonial dance in traditional garb. Displays of Native American costumes, traditional foods, and crafts are offered.

ANTIQUING IN MANKATO

As befits a historic region, Mankato has a thriving antiques community.

Old Town Antiques (507-388-0600), 521 N. Riverfront Drive. Open Mon. through Sat.

Antique Mart (507-345-3393), 529 S. Front Street. Open Mon. through Sat.

Riverfront Antiques (507-388-5152), 1027 N. Riverfront Drive. Open Mon. through Sat.

Generations Antiques (507-345-7551), 615 S. Front Street. Open Mon. through Sat.

Playing Possum Antiques & Whimsy (507-934-5636), 218 S. Minnesota Avenue. Open Mon. through Sat.

The Downtowner Antiques & Espresso (507-386-7553), 239 Belgrade Avenue, North Mankato. Open Mon. through Sat.

October: **Oktoberfest** (www .newulm.com), New Ulm. Held the first two weekends in Oct. German food and beer, live music, trolley tours, and children's games.

River Crossings: an Art Fair in Motion (www.rivercrossingsart .org), St. Peter, Mankato. Held in early Oct. Juried art show, along with live music and spoken-word performances.

SOUTH THROUGH THE PRAIRIE

Along the border between Minnesota and South Dakota, from the Iowa border north, is an area known as the Coteau des Prairie. It's the remnant of many glacial movements and retreats. The highest part of the coteau in Minnesota is known as Buffalo Ridge, an area around Lake Benton and Pipestone with a bedrock of shale, sandstone, and clay that has settled over Sioux quartzite before being covered by layers of glacial drift. As opposed to other parts of Minnesota, which have dramatic hills and valleys covered with trees, the Coteau des Prairie has long, sloping hills that were once covered with tallgrass prairie. Today most of that natural prairie growth has given way to agricultural endeavors, with long stretches of soybean and cornfields. However, in the farthest southwest, there are still some natural prairie areas remaining or are in the process of being cultivated again. It's a unique kind of beauty. As Minnesota poet and essayist Bill Holm said in his essay "Horizontal Grandeur": "A woods man looks at twenty miles of prairie and sees nothing but grass, but a prairie man looks at a square foot and sees a universe; ten or twenty flowers and grasses, heights, heads, colors, shades, configurations, bearded, rough, smooth, simple, elegant. When a cloud passes over the sun, colors shift, like a child's kaleidoscope." Taking the time to explore this part of the state, less traveled than other areas, is a richly rewarding experience full of natural beauty, wide-open skies, wildlife, rivers, Native American sites, and the slowly returning prairie.

There are also several worthwhile communities to visit. **Luverne,** a town of about 4,600 people, is the county seat for Rock County. From a tourist's perspective, though, it's representative of what most people dream of when they envision small-town America: a walkable downtown with historic buildings, quiet residential streets with charming Victorian homes and cottages, and a pride of place and history. Perhaps its biggest claim to fame is being one of the four towns profiled in Ken Burns's landmark documentary, *The War.* The documentary interviewed several residents of Luverne, all World War II veterans, including fighter pilot Quentin Aanenson, for whom the local airport is named.

Pipestone, a town rich in Native American and quarrying history, is named after the red stone named pipestone, or catlinite after the artist and writer George Catlin, who visited the area first in 1836, sketching it and recording the local legends. The community was further memorialized by poet Henry Wadsworth Longfellow's "Song of Hiawatha," although Longfellow never actually traveled to Pipestone. The pipestone was, and still is, central to Native American ceremonial rites. They quarried it to create pipes and have been recorded doing so by Lewis and Clark in the early 1800s. (See the Pipestone National Monument sidebar for more details.)

A few miles north on US 75 is **Lake Benton,** located on the shores of Lake Benton (appropriately enough) and in the valley of the Buffalo Ridge. Around Lake Benton you'll see a number of wind turbines. These turbines take advantage of the rolling prairie land, relatively unobstructed by forest, to collect wind power. There are more than 70 of these turbines in operation, generating enough power to provide electricity to 125 homes.

One of the biggest draws in southwestern Minnesota is the **Laura Ingalls Wilder Historic Highway** and the connection to Laura Ingalls Wilder and her pioneer family and friends. A trip along this road (which primarily remains on US 14 in Minnesota but occasionally traverses county routes) and through Walnut Grove, Tracy, and Sanborn will take you back in time to the days of the Ingalls and the life they made here in the 1870s.

THE TOWN OF PIPESTONE WAS NAMED AFTER THE RED STONE OF THE SAME NAME.

✷ To See and Do

MUSEUMS AND HISTORIC SITES

Lake Benton
♂ ♿ ✷ **Heritage and Wind Power Learning Center** (507-368-9577), 110 S. Center Street. Open Mon. through Fri. 10–5 and

Sat. 10–3, Memorial Day through Labor Day; Mon. through Fri. 10–5, Labor Day through Memorial Day. No admission fee. The center, opened in 2001, offers changing exhibits that illustrate how the wind power is collected and how it's used.

Laura Ingalls Wilder Historic Highway

✍ ♿ **Laura Ingalls Wilder Museum** (507-859-2358 or 1-800-528-7280; www.walnutgrove.org), US 14, Walnut Grove. Open daily at 10 AM, Apr. through Oct.; closing hours vary by month. Adults $6, children 6–12 $6, children 5 and under free. The museum covers two different eras: that of Wilder's family's stay in the region back in the 1800s, and that of the popular 1970s TV series based on her life. The displays are fun and informative for visitors who are either general history buffs or fans of the Little House books. There are some items (including photos and a quilt sewn by Laura and her daughter, Rose) that either belonged to Laura herself or to friends and family (although serious Wilder buffs will note that most of the displays are replicas or photos from the Missouri museum), several exhibits related to the time period itself, and artifacts from the TV series.

✍ **Ingalls Dugout Site** (507-859-2358 or 1-800-528-7280; www.walnut grove.org), US 14, Walnut Grove. Open daily during daylight hours, May through Oct., weather permitting. Admission $5 per car or $30 per tour bus. Along the banks of Plum Creek is this dugout home, where the Ingalls family lived from 1874 to 1876 before selling it after several crop failures and moving to Iowa. The Ingalls's ownership was discovered by the books' illustrator, Garth Williams, who informed the current owners of the historic nature of their property. There's not much to see anymore; the original sod house disappeared long ago, leaving behind a depression in the ground, yet it's as worthy a visit as the museum (see previous listing). The site is scenic, and picnic tables are available.

✍ **Sod House on the Prairie** (507-723-5138; www.sodhouse.org), 12598 Magnolia Avenue, Sanborn. Open daily sunrise–sunset, Apr. through Oct. Admission $4; children six and under free. Laura Ingalls Wilder may not have lived here, but this is a nice accompaniment to the dugout site (see previous listing). This replica homesite includes a sod home, dugout, and log cabin; the "soddie" was built in the style of Laura's day, with 2-foot-thick walls and lumber roof and floor, as opposed to the dugout, which is dirt floor and roof.

✍ ♿ **Wheels Across the Prairie Museum** (507-629-3661; www.wheels acrosstheprairie.org), 3297 US 14, Tracy. Open daily 1–5, mid-May to Labor Day. Adults $3–5, children 11 and under free. Essentially a pioneer museum, Wheels Across the Prairie includes several vintage buildings, such as a one-room schoolhouse, Episcopal church, log cabin, and train depot. Tracy is the small town Laura Ingalls Wilder visited on her first train trip, so the railway exhibit is of particular interest.

Luverne

✎ ♿ ✳ **Rock County Courthouse/Veterans Memorial** (507-283-5065), 204 E. Brown Street. Veterans memorial open daily; courthouse open Mon. through Fri. 9–5. The community's respect for its veterans is evident in the Rock County Veterans Memorial, on the grounds of the beautiful Rock County Courthouse. The courthouse, built in 1888 of Sioux quartzite, is on the National Register of Historic Places.

✎ **Rock County Historical Society** (507-283-2122), 123 N. Freeman. Open Tues., Thurs., and Sat. 2–4, June through Aug. No admission fee. The building itself, a former Unitarian church built in 1899, is worth a stop. Inside are decades' worth of artifacts from rural schools in the area, law enforcement, and photos and documents.

✎ **Hinkly House** (507-283-9476), 217 N. Freeman. Open Tues., Thurs., and Sat. 2–4, June through Aug. Admission is free. Originally built by the town's mayor, the Hinkly House is a lovely Sioux quartzite building from 1892 and is on the National Register of Historic Places.

✎ ♿ ✳ **Brandenburg Gallery/Rock County Veterans Memorial Building** (507-283-1884 or 1-888-283-4061; www.jimbrandenburg.com), 213 E. Luverne Street. Open Mon. through Sat. 9–5. Internationally renowned nature photographer Jim Brandenburg, a Luverne native and *National Geographic* photographer, has a gallery of his works for viewing and for sale here, with a focus on the prairie lands around Luverne. He is also one of the founders of the Brandenburg Prairie Foundation and the Touch the Sky Prairie project (see *Green Space and Outdoor Activities*).

Pipestone

✎ ♿ ✳ **Pipestone Commercial Historic District** (www.pipestone minnesota.com). This stretch in the downtown area of Pipestone contains 30 buildings and is listed on the National Register of Historic Places. An easy walk of about 12 blocks, mostly along Main Street and N. Hiawatha Avenue, will take you past the towering stone buildings, each with its year of construction at the top, and sometimes the name of the original owner. The buildings are striking not just for their "days gone by" architecture, but also because of the distinctive red stone used to build them. Most of the building took place in the 1890s after railroad service was established. Of particular note is the use of Sioux quartzite in 17 of the buildings.

✎ ♿ **Pipestone County Museum** (507-825-2563; www.pipestone minnesota.com), 113 S. Hiawatha Avenue. Open daily Memorial Day through Labor Day, Mon. through Sat. the rest of the year. Call for hours. Admission $4; children under 12 free. This lovely, elaborate building was once the imposing city hall and now houses the historical museum. Check with the museum for its special events.

PIPESTONE'S HISTORIC MAIN STREET

✐ ✧ ❋ **Syndicate Block** (www.pipestoneminnesota.com), 201–205 W. Main Street. This block comprises the oldest and largest of the Sioux quartzite buildings. Originally containing a post office and meat market, the block is now mostly comprised of retail and offices.

✐ ✧ ❋ **Moore Block** (www.pipestoneminnesota.com), 102 E. Main Street. This smaller Sioux quartzite building is distinguished by the work of Leon Moore, an amateur sculptor who created the gargoyles and biblical scenes on the building's exterior.

Worthington

✐ ✧ **Pioneer Village** (507-376-3125; www.noblespioneervillage.com), Stower Drive. Open Mon. through Sat. 10–5 and Sun. 1–5, Memorial Day through Labor Day. Visitors 16–89 $6, children 6–15 $1, visitors 90 and up or 5 and younger free. Located on the county fairgrounds, this village is one of the largest collections of pioneer buildings in the state and a fascinating place to visit. There are nearly 50 items of interest, including an early hospital, millinery shop, gas station, farmhouse, and sod house (the latter constructed in the 1970s as a replica). Guided tours can be arranged, but brochures allow easy self-guiding. Picnic tables are available.

PIPESTONE NATIONAL MONUMENT

Pipestone National Monument is a significant historic and cultural site. The red pipestone, so called because its primary use is to be carved into ceremonial pipe bowls, has been quarried by Native Americans since at least the 17th century, and the quarry is viewed as a sacred site. The pipes from this quarry were highly acclaimed across the United States, and the land that produced it was, for the most part, neutral territory for different tribes because of the symbolic power of the site. Today, the only quarrying allowed is by Native Americans, a right they retained when they sold the land to the U.S. government in 1937. A comprehensive visitors center details the significance and history of the area, and there are locally made pipestone products in the gift shop. During the summer months, visitors can watch as quarrying takes place. Hiking the Circle Trail, a 0.75-mile walk from the visitors center, provides beautiful views of quartzite, as well as native prairie grasses. Other points of interest include Winnewissa Falls and the Oracle, a naturally occurring stone "face" that Native Americans believed to be a sentient being.

✐ ♿ ❄ **Pipestone National Monument** (507-825-5464; www.nps.gov /pipe), US 75, Pipestone. Open daily 8–5; closed holidays. Adults $3, children 15 and under free.

❋ Green Space and Outdoor Activities

Touch the Sky Prairie (507-283-4061; www.jimbrandenburg.com), County Route 20, Luverne. Nature photographer Jim Brandenburg (see Brandenburg Gallery in *To See and Do*) started the Brandenburg Prairie Foundation in 1999 to purchase, along with the U.S. Fish and Wildlife Service, more than 800 acres of land northwest of Luverne and developed a 15-year plan to return the prairie lands to their original state. Visitors to the site will get a glimpse of what real prairies looked like when the pioneers arrived so many years ago, experiencing just how beautiful a native prairie can be.

Blue Mounds State Park (507-283-1307; www.dnr.state.mn.us/state _parks/blue_mounds/index.html), 1410 161st Street, Luverne. This 1,800-acre park sits above surrounding farmland by virtue of a natural pedestal of Sioux quartzite. The Blue Mounds, named after its blue appearance to westward-moving settlers, is a 1,250-foot-long stretch of rock that runs in an east–west direction and is thought to have been placed by early Dakota. Interesting fact about the rock: Each year on the spring and autumn equinoxes, the sunrise happens right on the east end and the sunset on the west end. Deer, coyote, numerous birds, and even bison live here and can be seen by visitors.

The park is an excellent place to immerse yourself in the loveliness of the prairie, especially midsummer, when the wildflowers are in full bloom. The 13 miles of hiking trails wander deep into the prairie, and in some of the lower stretches hikers will find themselves threading a narrow path surrounded by wildflowers nearly 6 feet tall on either side. Bikers have access to 2 miles of paved trails as well. Rock climbing is available, as are swimming and camping. Don't miss the bison viewing stand—the park is home to a herd of bison that peacefully roams a large, fenced space.

✳ Lodging

BED & BREAKFASTS

Lake Benton
✳ **Benton House Bed & Breakfast** (507-368-9484; www.itctel .com/bentonhs), 211 W. Benton Street. If you're looking for a cozy, romantic escape, this Italianate Victorian charmer on the edge of town has three rooms, each with private bath. A full breakfast is included. Moderate.

✳ **Wooden Diamond Bed & Breakfast** (507-368-4305; www .woodendiamond.com), 1593 Shady Shore Drive. Just outside the city is the Wooden Diamond, which doesn't have any Victorian charm—but its location on the shores of Lake Benton more than makes up for it. There's just one suite, with private entrance. Full breakfast included. Moderate.

Laura Ingalls Wilder Historic Highway
♪ ✳ **Valentine Inn** (507-629-3827), 385 Emory Street, Tracy.

This Victorian home began its life as a hospital, but now it's a B&B with four rooms, all with private bath. Two rooms have walk-out porches. Expensive.

Worthington
✳ (ᵞ) **Historic Dayton House Bed & Breakfast** (507-727-1311; www.daytonhouse.org), 1311 Fourth Avenue. This grand home in Worthington was owned by three prominent families in succession, including the Dayton family, eventually of department store fame (the chain eventually was sold to Marshall Fields, then to Macy's). A local historic group took over the restoration of the building with excellent results, and there are now two plush suites available. Both have private baths, sitting areas, antique furnishings, high-speed Internet, and flat-screen TVs. A better-than-average continental breakfast is served daily. Expensive.

JEFFERS PETROGLYPHS

The petroglyphs are southwest of the Laura Ingalls Highway, but they're well worth the slight detour. Thought to date from 3000 B.C. to possibly as recently as the mid-1700s, there are more than 2,000 Native American carvings found across the islands of rock that appear throughout the prairie grasses. Two separate trails visit the glyphs, both starting at the visitors center, one only 0.5 mile round-trip, the other slightly over a mile. Interpreters are available to explain the significance of the glyphs, which have a wide range of subject matter and meaning; humans, arrows, elk, buffalo, deer, and turtles are just some of the identifiable figures. The glyphs detail the history of the region and the people, identifying significant events and sacred ceremonies. Native Americans still come today for religious visits. Note: For best viewing, visit early or late in the day—the midday sunlight can make it harder to see the glyphs.

It's not just the historic or spiritual aspects that make this a worthy visit. The landscape is striking: pink quartzite, prairie grasses, prickly pear cactus, and dozens of wildflowers. In the northern reaches, areas of buffalo rubs can be seen, where migrating bison would stop to rub their coats against the rocks, eventually leaving a glossy surface. Take some time after visiting the glyphs to admire the rest of the scenery.

HOTELS

Laura Ingalls Wilder Historic Highway
🌢 🏠 ♿ ❄ **Wilder Inn** (507-629-3350 or 1-866-211-7877), 1000 Craig Avenue, Tracy. A small motel a few miles from Walnut Grove. Each room has a microwave and mini fridge, and daily continental breakfast is included. Moderate.

INNS

Pipestone
🌢 ♿ 🍸 ❄ **Calumet Inn** (507-825-5871 or 1-800-535-7610; www.calumetinn.com), 104 W. Main Street. Built in direct response to the needs of travelers arriving with the new railroad, the Calumet has suffered its share of tragedies (fire on more than one occasion) over the

JEFFERS PETROGLYPHS

✐ **Jeffers Petroglyphs** (507-628-5591; www.mnhs.org/places/sites/jp/ or http://jefferspetroglyphs.com/), US 71, Comfrey. Open Mon. and Thurs. through Sat. 10–5 and Sun. noon–5, Memorial Day through Labor Day, by appointment Oct. through Apr. Adults $6, seniors $5, children 6–17 $4, children 5 and under and Minnesota Historical Society members free.

decades. At one point, the hotel was in such disrepair that it was closed, but in 1979 it was purchased and renovated. Today it offers 38 guest rooms furnished with period antiques, as well as a lounge and pub (see *Where to Eat*). Moderate.

✳ Where to Eat

DINING OUT

Lake Benton

✐ & ♟ ✳ **Knotty Pine Supper Club** (507-548-3781), 1014 County Route 10, Elkton, SD. Open Mon. through Sat. for lunch and dinner. Serves American cuisine. Expensive.

✍ ♿ ❋ **The Country House**
(507-368-4223), 405 E. Benton
Street, Lake Benton. Open Wed.
through Sun. for dinner. Serves
American cuisine. Expensive.

EATING OUT

*Laura Ingalls Wilder Historic
Highway*
✍ ♿ ❋ **Nellie's Café** (507-859-
2384), US 14, Walnut Grove.
Open daily for breakfast and
lunch, Mon. through Fri. for dinner. A basic but good small-town
café with breakfast specials and
sandwiches. Inexpensive.

Pipestone
✍ ♿ ☖ ❋ **Calumet Inn** (507-825-
5871 or 1-800-535-7610; www
.calumetinn.com), 104 W. Main
Street. Open daily for all three
meals. The historic Calumet Inn
(see *Lodging*) has a full-service
restaurant and bar with an extensive menu focused on hearty
American foods (steaks, ribs, walleye). Moderate.

✍ ♿ ❋ **Lange's Café and Bakery**
(507-825-4488), 110 Eighth Avenue
SE. Open 24/7. Serves home-
cooked meals, including the usual
sandwiches and soups, as well as
some more inventive pastas and
meat dishes. Be sure to have the
pie for dessert; Jane and Michael
Stern of *Roadfood* raved about the
sour cream/raisin. Moderate.

✍ ♿ ☖ ❋ **Glass House Restaurant** (507-348-7651), 711 MN 23.
Open Wed. through Sun. for
lunch and dinner. Steakhouse

menu, including seafood and
chicken, and a Sun. smorgasbord.
Moderate.

❋ Entertainment

CINEMA AND LIVE PERFORMANCES

Lake Benton
✍ ♿ ❋ **Lake Benton Opera
House** (507-368-4620; www.lake
bentonoperahouse.org), 110 E.
Benton Street. The Lake Benton
Opera House was first opened in
1896 but fell into disuse and disrepair in the late 1950s. In 1970, a
group of local residents launched
a campaign to save and restore the
building, a process that took nearly
30 years because of the efforts to
restore rather than replace. Now it
offers several Broadway musical
and family-friendly performances
each year.

Luverne
✍ ❋ **Historic Palace Theater**
(507-283-4339; www.palace
theater.us), Main Street. The
downtown area of Luverne along
Main Street is dotted with century-
old buildings, many constructed of
Sioux quartzite. Of particular note
is the Historic Palace Theater,
which has been showing movies
since 1915. Recent renovations
have modernized its operations,
but with its large pipe organ still
intact, it's as far from a modern
multiplex as you can get. It hosts
both movies and live theater, and
was also the site of the premiere
of Ken Burns's *The War*.

Pipestone

⚘ ♿ ✳ **Pipestone Performing Arts Center** (507-825-2020 or 1-877-722-2787; www.pipestone minnesota.com/artscenter), 113 S. Hiawatha. Housed in a Sioux quartzite building in the historic part of Pipestone, the performing arts center offers live performances year-round, with a variety of family-friendly shows and concerts.

✳ Special Events

June: **Worthington Windsurfing Regatta and Unvarnished Music Festival** (www.worthington windsurfing.com), Worthington. Held in June. Windsurfing championships and an indie music festival make for a great combination of interests. Beachfront waveboarding, an art fair, and possibly even fire eaters round up the entertainment.

July: **Laura Ingalls Wilder Pageant** (1-888-859-3102; www .walnutgrove.org), Walnut Grove. Held last three weekends in July. This annual homage to Laura Ingalls Wilder is held on the banks of Plum Creek and covers some of the significant points of the Little House books. Note: This is a very popular event, and tickets sell out well in advance. Local lodging options are limited, so book ahead (see *Laura Ingalls Wilder Historic Highway* under *Lodging*).

August: **Pipestone Civil War Days** (www.pipestoneminnesota .com), Pipestone. Held in mid-Aug. in even-numbered years (e.g., 2008, 2010). Life during the Civil War is brought back to life in various ways: battle reenactments, church services, children's games, etiquette and dancing lessons, a grand ball, and camp tours.

September: **King Turkey Day** (507-372-2919; www.kingturkey day.com), Worthington. Held the second Sat. after Labor Day. At this tongue-in-cheek festival, held annually since 1939, people have raced turkeys in an attempt to win the coveted title of King Turkey. Other highlights include pancake breakfasts, volleyball tournaments, and a parade. But the crowning event is the Great Gobbler Gallop, in which teams of wild racing turkeys take to the streets.

THE I-35 CORRIDOR

T he I-35 corridor, leading to Iowa, includes the communities of Albert Lea, Owatonna, and Faribault, areas that were once the domain of Native Americans. They have seen considerable agricultural growth and, in the case of Faribault, experienced a happier story than that of the Dakota Conflict (see "The Dakota Conflict of 1862" sidebar in the "Minnesota River Valley" chapter); founder Alexander Faribault learned the Dakota language and helped the tribe resettle in an effort to protect the trading fort Faribault established in the area.

✳ To See and Do

MUSEUMS AND HISTORIC SITES

Albert Lea

✐ ♿ ✳ **Story Lady Doll & Toy Museum** (507-377-1820; www.storylady museum.com), 131 N. Broadway. Open Tues. through Fri. 10–4, Oct. through Mar.; Tues. through Fri. 10–5, Apr. through Sept. Adults $2, children 12 and under $1. More than 1,500 dolls are in this amazing collection, from antique to current day. The adjacent gift shop has plenty of doll-adoption opportunities.

✐ ♿ ✳ **Freeborn County Historical Museum** (507-373-8003; www .smig.net/fchm/), 1031 Bridge Street. Open Tues. through Fri. 10–4, Oct. through Mar.; Tues. through Fri. 10–5, Apr. through Sept. Adults $5, youth 12–18 $1, children under 12 free. An extensive and eclectic collection of memorabilia and historical exhibits make this a worthwhile visit. Pop culture icons Eddie Cochran (early rock 'n' roll singer) and Marion Ross (of TV's *Happy Days*) both spent part of their childhoods here, and accordingly earned exhibits. But beyond celebrities, the museum has artifacts and displays from the Civil War, World War I, and World War II; stagecoaches and railroads; farm implements; formal clothing; and antique appliances, to name just a few. The adjacent village has several buildings, including a furnished parsonage, barber shop, and general store.

THE ALEXANDER FARIBAULT HOUSE

Faribault

🎨 **Alexander Faribault House** (507-334-7913; www.rchistory.org/content/alexander-faribault-house), 12 First Avenue NE. Open Mon. through Fri. 9–4, May through Sept.; other times by appointment. Adults $2, children 4 and under free. Built in 1853 by town founding father Alexander Faribault, this Greek Revival home is one of Minnesota's oldest surviving buildings. The Rice County Historical Society took over the daunting task of restoration in 1945, with the end result a beautifully preserved piece of Minnesota history. Furnishings aren't original, but they accurately reflect the period.

Owatonna

🎨 ♿ **Village of Yesteryear** (507-451-1420; www.steelecohistoricalsociety.org/village.php), 1448 Austin Road. Tours available Tues. through Sun. at 1:30, May through Oct.; other times by appointment. Adults $5, children 7–16 $3; free for children 6 and under with an adult. A collection of 15 pioneer buildings, many with original or period-appropriate furnishings.

🎨 ♿ ❋ **State School Orphanage Museum** (507-444-4315 or 1-800-423-6466; www.orphanagemuseum.com), 540 W. Hills Circle. Open Mon. through Fri. 8–5, Sat. and Sun. 1–5. No admission fee, though donations are welcome. The former home of more than 10,000 Minnesota orphans between 1886 and 1945, State School's large main building is impressive, but it must have been imposing for the children being sent here. There's video footage of the orphans from the 1930s, and visitors are welcome to explore the building and grounds, right down to the underground root cellar. Most poignant is the Children's Cemetery. The former dining room now houses the **Owatonna Arts Center** (507-451-0533; www.owatonnaartscenter.org/), which features local artists.

❋ Green Space and Outdoor Activities

Myre–Big Island State Park (507-379-3403; www.dnr.state.mn.us/state_parks/myre_big_island/index.html), 19499 780th Avenue, Albert Lea. Migrating waterfowl, evidence of possibly permanent Native American settlements that date back 9,000 years, 16 miles of hiking trails through oak savan-

STATE SCHOOL ORPHANAGE MUSEUM

na and prairie (several of which are groomed for winter sports), and camp-sites make this park a favorite of locals and visitors alike.

✳ Lodging

✑ ✳ **1858 Log Cabin Bed & Breakfast** (507-448-0089; www .1858-logcabin.com), 11859 755th Avenue, Glenville. South of Albert Lea, this pre–Civil War log cabin has been retrofitted for today's travelers (electricity and indoor plumbing, anyone?) but still offers a glimpse into living quarters of days past. Kids are welcome. Antique furniture with hand-painted Norwegian rosemaling and patchwork quilts strengthen the pioneer experience. Daily break-fast included. Moderate.

✳ Selective Shopping

✑ ♿ ✳ **Cabela's** (507-451-4545; www.cabelas.com), 3900 Cabela Drive, Owatonna. Open daily. The 150,000-square-foot hunting and fishing giant has been elevated to a major tourist attraction, including the arrival of tour buses. Hundreds of animal mounts are posted around the store, and not just of the Min-nesota variety; African animals, including elephant and baboon, are represented. A 60,000-gallon fresh-water aquarium has examples of Minnesota fish. You can shop, or you can sightsee, or you can do both. There's also a restaurant.

CABELA'S

✳ Special Events

June: **Heritage Days** (www
.faribaultheritagedays.com), Faribault. Held in June. Food, music,
carnival rides, dances, and a
parade celebrating Faribault's rich
ethnic history.

September: **Faribault Airfest
and Balloon Rally and Tree
Frog Music Festival** (www
.faribaultairfest.com), Faribault.
Held in Sept. It may seem like an
odd combination, but this way
there's something for everyone.

Hot-air balloon races, aircraft display, and helicopter rides take
place, along with performances by
several live bands, an art exhibit,
children's activities, and food (and
a beer garden) for everyone.

October: **South Central Minnesota Studio Art Tour** (www
.southcentralarttour.com), Faribault, Northfield, and Owatonna.
Held in late Oct. These three
communities join forces to sponsor this art tour, in which local
artists open their galleries and studios to the public.

INDEX